D1643477

Learning and
Libr
U

This

THE CROSSLINGUISTIC STUDY OF LANGUAGE ACQUISITION

Volume 5: Expanding the Contexts

THE CROSSLINGUISTIC STUDY OF LANGUAGE ACQUISITION

Volume 5: Expanding the Contexts

Edited by

DAN ISAAC SLOBIN
University of California at Berkeley

LEA LAWRENCE ERLBAUM ASSOCIATES, PUBLISHERS
1997 Mahwah, New Jersey   London

Lawrence Erlbaum Associates, Inc., Publishers
10 Industrial Avenue
Mahwah, New Jersey 07430

Library of Congress Cataloging in Publication Data
(Revised for vol. 5)

The crosslinguistic study of language acquisition.

Includes bibliographies and indexes.
Contents: v. 1. The data—v. 2. Theoretical
issues—v. 3. [without special title]—v. 4. [without special title]
—v. 5. Expanding the contexts.
1. Language acquisition. I. Slobin, Dan Isaac,
1939– .
P118.C69 1985   401′.93   85-27411
ISBN 0-8058-2421-9 (Vol. 5)
ISBN 0-8058-2311-5 (Set of Volumes 1, 2, 3, 4, and 5)

Printed in the United States of America
10 9 8 7 6 5 4 3 2 1

Contents

Format and Abbreviations for Glosses[1]

All foreign language examples are given in Italics. (Small caps are used for emphasis and other usual functions of Italics.) In running text, English glosses and grammatical codes are given in single quotes, and optional free translations follow in parentheses, indicated by an equal sign. Grammatical codes are always given in capital letters (see list, below). For example:

gel-me-di-n 'come-NEG-PAST-2SG' (= you didn't come).

In interlinear format, translation equivalents appear below the foreign language example and the free translation is placed below in single quotes:

gel-me-di-n
come-NEG-PAST-2SG
'you didn't come'

Hyphens in a morphological gloss always correspond to hyphens in the foreign example. If part of a foreign example corresponds to more than one grammatical code, the collection of codes is joined by colons; e.g., *gel-medin* 'come-NEG:PAST:2SG', or even *gelmedin* 'come:NEG:PAST:2SG'. If it is relevant to indicate the possibility of segmentation, plus signs can be used in place of colons. The preceding example consists of segmentable morphemes, and could also be glossed, for example, as *gel-medin* 'come-NEG+PAST+2SG'. Use of colons is neutral with regard to the possibility of segmentation, and in most instances either colons or hyphens are used. (The degree of precision of segmentation and glossing of an example, of course, depends on the role it plays in the exposition.)

---

[1]The abbreviations are adapted from a list used by Bernard Comrie (*The languages of the Soviet Union*, Cambridge University Press, 1981, p. xv). The format is based on useful suggestions offered by Christian Lehmann in "Guidelines for interlinear morphemic translations: A proposal for a standardization" (Institut für Sprachwissenschaft, Universität Köln, Arbeitspapier Nr. 37, 1980). The system presented here is offered as a proposal for standardization in child language studies.

If a single lexical item in the original is expressed by several lexical items in a gloss, those items are separated by a period; e.g., *hipil* 'made.fall', *kalk* 'get.up'. A period is also used when the name of a grammatical element consists of more than one item; e.g., DEF.ART = definite article. Combining the principles for use of colons and periods in grammatical codes, consider the gloss for the German definite article in its masculine singular accusative form: *den* 'DEF.ART:MASC:SG:ACC'.

LIST OF GRAMMATICAL CODES

1 First Person
2 Second Person
3 Third Person
ABESS Abessive ('without X')
ABL Ablative ('from X')
ABS Absolutive
ACC Accusative
ACT Active
ADESS Adessive ('towards X')
ADJ Adjective, Adjectival
ADMON Admonitive
ADV Adverb(ial)
AFFIRM Affirmative
AGR Agreement
AGENT Agent
ALLAT Allative ('to(wards) X')
AN Animate
ANTI Antipassive
AORIST Aorist
APL Applicative
ART Article
ASP Aspect
AUG Augmentative
AUX Auxiliary
BEN Benefactive
BT Baby Talk
C Consonant
CAUS Causative
CL Clitic
CLASS Classifier
CMPLR Complementizer
CNTR Contrastive
COMIT Comitative ('(together) with X')
COMM Common
COMPAR Comparative

COMPL Completive
CONC Concessive
COND Conditional
CONJ Conjunction
CONN Connective
CONSEC Consecutive
CONT Continuous, Continuative
CONTEMP Contemporative
COP Copula
DAT Dative
DECL Declarative
DEF Definite
DEICT Deictic
DEM Demonstrative
DER Derived, Derivation
DESID Desiderative
DIM Diminutive
DIREC Directional
DO Direct Object
DU Dual
DYN Dynamic (Nonstative)
ELAT Elative ('out of X')
EMPH Emphatic
EQU Equative
ERG Ergative
ESS Essive ('as X')
EVID Evidential
EXCL Exclusive
EXCLAM Exclamatory
EXIS Existential
EXP Experiential
EXT Extension
FACT Factive
FEM Feminine
FIN Finite

FOC Focus
FUT Future
GEN Genitive
HAB Habitual
HABITA Habitative
HON Honorific
HUM Human
ILL Illative ('into X')
IMP Imperative
INAN Inanimate
INCH Inchoative
INCL Inclusive
INCOMPL Incompletive
INDEF Indefinite
INDIC Indicative
INESS Inessive ('in X')
INF Infinitive
INFER Inferential
INSTR Instrumental
INT Interrogative
INTENT Intentive
INTERJ Interjection
INTRANS Intransitive
IO Indirect Object
IPFV Imperfective
IRR Irrealis
ITER Iterative
LOC Locative
MASC Masculine
MKR Marker
MOD Modal
N Noun
NEG Negative
NEUT Neuter
NEUTRAL Neutral
NOM Nominative
NOML Nominal
NONPAST Non-past
NONVIR Non-virile
NUM Numeral, Numeric
OBJ Object
OBL Oblique
OBLIG Obligatory
OPT Optative
PART Participle
PARTIT Partitive
PASS Passive

PAST Past
PAT Patient
PERF Perfect
PERS Personal
PFV Perfective
PL Plural
POL Polite
POSS Possessive
POST Postposition
POT Potential
PP Past Participle
PRE Prefix
PREP Preposition
PRES Present
PRESUM Presumptive
PRET Preterite
PRO Pronoun
PROG Progressive
PROL Prolative ('along X')
PROLOC Prolocative
PTL Particle
PURP Purposive
PVB Preverb
Q Question
QUANT Quantifier
QUOT Quotative
RC Relative Clause
RECENT Recent
RECIP Reciprocal
REFL Reflexive
REL Relative
REM Remote
REPET Repetition
REPORT Reportative
RES Resultative
SG Singular
SIMUL Simultaneous
STAT Stative
SUBJ Subject
SUBJV Subjunctive
SUBL Sublative ('onto X')
SUFF Suffix
SUPER Superessive ('on X')
SUPERL Superlative
TAGQ Tag Question
TAX Taxis
TEMP Temporal

TNS Tense

TOP Topic

TRANS Transitive

TRANSL Translative ('becoming X')

V Verb

VBLR Verbalizer

VIR Virile

VN Verbal Noun

VOC Vocative

VOL Volitional

Preface

In this fifth volume, we attempt to "expand the contexts" in which child language has been examined crosslinguistically. The chapters open themes that have been touched on, anticipated, and promised in earlier volumes of this series. The study of child language has been situated in the disciplines of psychology and linguistics and has been most responsive to dominant issues in those fields, such as nativism and learning, comprehension and production, errors, input, and universals of morphology and syntax. The context has been, primarily, that of the individual child, interacting with a parent, deciphering the linguistic code. In these volumes, the code has been generally treated as a system of morphology and syntax, with little attention to phonology and prosody. Attention has been paid, occasionally, to the facts that the child is acquiring language in a sociocultural setting and that language is used in contexts of semantic and pragmatic communication. And there has been a degree of attention paid to the interactions between language and cognition in the processes of development. As for individual differences between children, they have been discussed in those studies where they could not be avoided, but such variation has rarely been the focus of systematic attention. Differences between individual languages have been of great interest, of course, but these differences have not often been placed in a framework of systematic typological variation. And although languages, and their grammars, change over time, the focus of attention on the individual child learner has generally led to neglect of explanatory principles that are best found on the level of linguistic diachrony, rather than the level of innate ideas or patterns of learning and cognition in the individual child. Here we seek to explore some of these neglected contexts in more depth.

In my introductory chapter, "The Universal, the Typological, and the Particular in Acquisition," I propose that languages—and the processes by which they are acquired and used—fall into typological patterns. That is, each language is not totally different from every other, and the tasks of acquisition do not vary without limit. I suggest a mission for the crosslinguistic study of child language: "THE CHARTING OF CROSSLINGUISTIC DIVERSITY IN LANGUAGE ACQUISITION AND THE

EMPIRICAL DETERMINATION OF ITS PRINCIPLED LIMITATIONS." The expanded context in that chapter is typological analysis: "One cannot make claims about the acquisition or use of a grammatical form without situating it typologically, in a network of interactive psycholinguistic factors."

Soonja Choi expands the contexts to include the cognitive and semantic frameworks of acquisition in her chapter, "Language-Specific Input and Early Semantic Development: Evidence From Children Learning Korean." Using her work on Korean, in comparison with work on English, she tries to sort out relations between language and cognition, coming to new conclusions about the very early influence of specific linguistic forms on the development of the child's semantic systems. She concludes that "children's semantic systems related to verbs are language-specific from the beginning of their language production. . . . These studies . . . suggest that language-specific aspects of grammar influence children's language from early on, perhaps even before language production begins."

Ann Peters expands the contexts in a different direction in a chapter titled, "Language Typology, Prosody, and the Acquisition of Grammatical Morphemes." She makes use of two bodies of data: the acoustic characteristics of languages and infants' abilities to perceive acoustic properties of speech. The chapter deals with individual differences between languages, elaborating the thesis that "languages afford different paths for acquiring grammatical morphemes" and that "this process is . . . influenced by phonetic and prosodic factors." Peters explores such factors in depth, sorting languages into types on the basis of the interplay between acoustic and morphological factors that bear on tasks of perception and learning. At the same time, she begins to sort learners into types on the basis of how they confront such tasks.

Elena Lieven carries on this second theme in her chapter, "Variation in a Crosslinguistic Context." She examines all of the data in the preceding volumes of this series, in a detailed attempt "to demonstrate that variation between children learning the SAME language" can illuminate the processes of acquisition "in often very similar ways to the study of crosslinguistic variation." Her thesis is that "variation between children might inform us about the problems that a particular language presents to language learners." She expands the contexts to consider types of child learners as well as types of child-directed speech, and seeks explanations on the levels of neuropsychology, cognition, temperament, and environment.

The reader might sense a gap in the book at this point. Although Choi, Peters, and Lieven raise some issues of cultural factors, particularly with regard to patterns of adult–child interaction, an expansion of the contexts to include society and culture will have to be found elsewhere. Such an expansion is clearly in the spirit of the present endeavor, and should play an important role in the further development of the field of child language. (See, for example, recent papers in Slobin, Gerhardt, Kyratzis, & Guo, 1996.)

Social factors do come to the fore in my concluding chapter, "The Origins of Grammaticizable Notions: Beyond the Individual Mind." There I argue that we have been hampered in our attempts to account for the innate component of language in that we have ignored the fact that language is shaped, over time, in processes of communication between individuals. Drawing on recent work in grammaticization (or grammaticalization) theory, I argue that some of the structure that has been attributed to the individual mind/brain of the child can be better accounted for as the result of diachronic linguistic processes. In so doing, I revise earlier accounts (Slobin, 1985) based on a division between the semantics of "open" and "closed" classes, and opt for general principles of learning and cognition that apply across the lexicon. I suggest: "Once we have established a social–historical, rather than an individual–mind source of grammaticized notions and their means of expression, we can abandon the search for an innate form-function module . . . The reanalysis of the learning task places 'grammaticizable notions' in the more general domain of concept formation."

These are the expanded contexts that the reader will encounter in the following five chapters. This volume would not have been possible without the great labors of the authors who contributed to the preceding four volumes. We have drawn on their work extensively. Without the energetic help and devoted support of Larry Erlbaum, in Mahwah, New Jersey, and Judi Amsel, now in Ogden, Utah, the project of the entire series would have never come to fruition. The authors and readers of these volumes owe them, and their skilled and friendly staff at Lawrence Erlbaum Associates, sincere thanks. I also appreciate technical support provided by the University of California at Berkeley (Department of Psychology, Institute of Cognitive Studies, Institute of Human Development) and the Max Planck Institute for Psycholinguistics, Nijmegen, The Netherlands.

—Dan Isaac Slobin
Berkeley, California
1997

REFERENCES

Slobin, D. I. (1985). Crosslinguistic evidence for the Language-Making Capacity. In D. I. Slobin (Ed.), *The crosslinguistic study of language acquisition: Vol. 2. Theoretical issues* (pp. 1157–1256). Hillsdale, NJ: Lawrence Erlbaum Associates.

Slobin, D. I., Gerhardt, J., Kyratzis, A., & Guo, J. (Eds.). (1996). *Social interaction, social context, and language: Essays in honor of Susan Ervin-Tripp*. Mahwah, NJ: Lawrence Erlbaum Associates.

Contributors

Soonja Choi
Department of Linguistics
San Diego State University
San Diego, CA 92182
USA
schoi@mail.sdsu.edu

Elena V. M. Lieven
Department of Psychology
University of Manchester
M13 9PL
United Kingdom
lieven@psy.man.ac.uk

Ann M. Peters
Department of Linguistics, Room 569
1890 East-West Road
Honolulu, HI 96822
USA
ann@hawaii.edu

Dan I. Slobin
Department of Psychology
University of California
3210 Tolman #1650
Berkeley, CA 94720-1650
USA
slobin@cogsci.berkeley.edu

1
The Universal, the Typological, and the Particular in Acquisition

Dan I. Slobin
University of California at Berkeley

1. INTRODUCTION: BETWEEN UNIVERSALS AND PARTICULARS

The first volume of this series begins with the following statement: "It is the burden of the present collection of studies to demonstrate that crosslinguistic study does more than reveal uniformities of development, because properties of individual languages influence the course of development. . . . One cannot study universals without exploring particulars" (Slobin, 1985b, p. 4). This theme is amply demonstrated in the 35 chapters of these five volumes. However, in recent years, a third term has been added to the old pair, "universal and particular." This term is TYPOLOGICAL. It appears explicitly in the title of Ann Peters' chapter in this volume, "Language Typology, Prosody, and the Acquisition of Grammatical Morphemes," and it is implicit in chapters in other volumes: Eve Clark's chapter on Romance languages (Clark, 1985), Kim Plunkett and Sven Strömqvist's chapter on Scandinavian languages (Plunkett & Strömqvist, 1992), Lisa Dasinger's chapter on Finno-Ugric languages (Dasinger, 1997), and Robert Van Valin's chapter on ergative languages (Van Valin, 1992). Underlying all of these chapters is a common position with regard to the limits on linguistic diversity: It is, by now, taken as given that the languages of the world represent a varying collection of exemplars of a single universal pattern. However, it has also become evident that the universal pattern allows for systematic constraints on variation. The results of such constraints make it possible to group languages into types, defined by their positions on various parameters or dimensions. This insight is as central to the principles-and-parameters approach as it is to functionalist-typological linguistics.

The pairing of universal and typological is evident in the titles of two important textbooks: Bernard Comrie's (1981) *Language Universals and Linguistic Typology* and William Croft's (1990) *Typology and Universals*. Linguistic typology has become an increasingly active field. In 1982, John Benjamins Publishing Company initiated a major series under the heading "Typological Studies in Language"; more recently, in 1994, Oxford University Press announced a new series, "Oxford Studies in Typology and Linguistic Theory." In the same year, a new linguistic association arose, the Association for Linguistic Typology, which attracted a rapidly growing membership even before it became formally organized, and which has launched a new journal, *Linguistic Typology*.

In a charter statement for the association, Frans Plank and Johan van der Auwera (e-mail, March 1994) succinctly state the central mission as "the charting of crosslinguistic diversity and the empirical determination of its principled limitations." Thus the detailed description of particular languages must also attend to universal principles of variation. These principles, then, become part of the theory of human language. I would phrase the mission of the crosslinguistic study of child language in like terms: THE CHARTING OF CROSSLINGUISTIC DIVERSITY IN LANGUAGE ACQUISITION and THE EMPIRICAL DETERMINATION OF ITS PRINCIPLED LIMITATIONS. The second clause has important methodological consequences: Any proposed explanation of the course of acquisition of a linguistic system in a particular language must be tested in languages that contrast on dimensions relevant to that system. Furthermore, any predicted replication of the phenomenon in question must be sought in languages that do not contrast on such dimensions. That is, one must determine if the explanation applies to typologically comparable languages only or to a broader range of languages. The status of the explanation in an overall theory of language acquisition will vary accordingly. Some acquisitional principles will turn out to have comparable effects across languages—perhaps universally. Other principles will turn out to be sensitive to the type of input provided to the child, with different consequences for different types of languages. One consequence may well be that certain principles are never brought to bear on the acquisition of particular languages.

A typological approach to acquisition requires something of the child and something of the investigator. The child must be sensitive to typologically consistent characteristics of the input language, and the investigator must know how to describe and classify such characteristics in ways that are relevant to acquisition. Let us look briefly at each of these requirements.

These five volumes are full of evidence that children are sensitive to recurrent grammatical patterns in their language. In Volume 2, I summarized this evidence in terms of an Operating Principle for "strengthening": "Whenever an attempted solution succeeds, apply the same strategies to similar problems" (Slobin, 1985a, p. 1193). The evidence, across languages, showed that "the more pervasive a morphological category is in a language, the more readily will it be learned" (p. 1194). A clear example was provided by Berman's (1985) presentation of the acquisition of gender in Hebrew, a language in which gender must be marked in almost every utterance (on verbs, nouns, demonstratives, adjectives, and numerals). Berman generalized this finding to a typological proposal for acquisition (1985, p. 358): "Crosslinguistic consideration of Hebrew data suggests that it might be profitable for each language or language type to establish certain areas of 'language as a formal problem-space for children' (in the sense of Karmiloff-Smith, 1979) as criterial or in some sense particularly central to the task of acquisition." Another example, also from Hebrew, came from children's acquisition of the pervasive morphological pattern of consonant frames with intercalated vowels. I concluded, with regard to the Operating Principle of Strengthening: "Repeated problem solutions along similar lines reinforce the Semitic-speaking child's sense of learning a language of a particular TYPE, thus strengthening and maintaining the typologically consistent characteristics of the language" (p. 1195). My Introduction to Volume 3 (Slobin, 1992) summarizes a number of typological tendencies revealed in the data of that volume; and Ann Peters' chapter in this volume is full of similar examples, which need not be repeated here. On another front, connectionism is providing statistically explicit models of the facilitation of repeated solutions to a class of similar problems.

"Similar problems" can be defined on every level of linguistic analysis. Repeated attention to the distinctive features of PHONOLOGY, RHYTHM, and INTONATION focus the child on language-specific acoustic and temporal patterns, such as the Bantu-speaking child's early segmentation of prefixes, and early attention to vowel harmony in languages such as Finnish, Hungarian, and Turkish. SEMANTIC dimensions underlying morphological choice come to structure the child's space of grammaticized notions, such as aspect in Slavic languages and transitivity in ergative languages. As shown in a large number of GB-inspired studies, children come to organize their SYNTAX in terms of such parameters as dominant branching organization (left versus right) and obligatoriness of explicit subjects. And uses of PRAGMATIC markers, such as Japanese and Korean sentence-final particles, orient the child to language-specific marking of discourse factors.

In order for the investigator to carry out typological developmental analysis, it is necessary to classify languages along dimensions that might be relevant to the proposal at hand. Further research can then determine which particular dimension or collection of dimensions seem to be relevant to the particular pattern of acquisition.

An instructive recent example comes from Dasinger's (1995) research on the development of definite referring expressions in Finnish. Earlier investigations had shown a common developmental pattern in English, French, and German—all languages that have definite articles. Finnish provides a useful comparison, in that the language does not have definite articles. Thus there is a typological contrast that might be relevant to the child's capacity to mark definiteness in discourse. Dasinger found both general and language-specific patterns, studying children aged 3–9 in a referent disambiguation task (like that used by Karmiloff-Smith, 1979, in French) and a narrative task (like that used by Hickmann, 1991, in German and other languages). Overall, Finnish development parallels that of children learning article-bearing languages. Only after about age 5 do children gradually become able to clearly identify referents in discourse, using intralinguistic means; earlier, they rely on referential expressions that are tied, in one way or another, to the extralinguistic context. The typological control thus points to crosslinguistically general factors of conceptual and social development—rather than the availability of particular grammaticized means of expression—in the development of definite reference. However, Dasinger also found a particularly Finnish pattern. Unlike Karmiloff-Smith's French-speaking children, Finnish children were less successful in tasks requiring definite reference to one of a group of identical objects, although words like 'same' and '(an)other' are available in both languages. Here Dasinger makes a suggestion based on a typological constraint: "The apparent lack of the Finnish-speaking child's realization of the necessity of explicitly marking intralinguistic relationships in certain situations may very well be the result of the absence of the obligatory expression of definiteness in the language" (p. 283). That is, the repeated grammatical marking of a particular contrast—as in the use of definite articles—may orient the child to the conceptual or discourse dimensions underlying that contrast (as discussed by Berman & Slobin, 1994, with regard to the development of various form–function relations). Such suggestions, of course, call for further typologically organized research—in this case, attempting to replicate these findings in other languages that do not have definite articles.

To repeat the methodological theme: Studies of a particular phenomenon must be appropriately situated with regard to potentially influential dimensions of language variation. In the Introduction to Volume 3 (Slobin, 1992), I categorized the languages investigated in these volumes with regard to three sorts of classification: genetic language family, geographical area, and Hawkins' (1983) list of possible types of word-order patterns across grammatical constructions. I pointed to the need for a typologically responsible research program, referring to gaps in those taxonomies where child language data were sparse or nonexistent: "Future investigators of child language would do well to study the gaps . . . in seeking promising new research sites. Our theories of acquisition and learnability need to be challenged by the widest range of typological diversity if they are to lay claim to factors of innateness and universality" (pp. 3–6). That is, of course, still true. However, as Dasinger's study illustrates, languages can be typologically contrasted on many different dimensions beyond those considered in that Introduction. In her case, the relevant contrast was "article-bearing" versus "non-article-bearing" languages. Other theoretical issues require different classifications. For example, in Volume 3, Van Valin (1992) argues that acquisition theories using parameter setting and semantic bootstrapping as explanatory devices need to attend not only to ergative versus accusative languages, but also to the types of split ergativity within the set of ergative languages. Later in this chapter, I present evidence for the importance of comparing "satellite-framed" versus "verb-framed" languages (Talmy, 1991). And, in fact, every systematic linguistic classification will turn out to have implications for acquisition: topic-oriented versus subject-oriented, head-marking versus dependent-marking, configurational versus nonconfigurational, fixed versus free word order, prefixing versus suffixing, and so on. Every claim in the child language literature can profitably be lined up against relevant typological contrasts and dimensions, such as these. And, if this is done seriously, it will be seen that almost all of our claims should be seen as quite tentative and limited until the necessary controls have been carried out in a sample of typologically appropriate languages for any given claim.

Attention to typology lends itself to two kinds of crosslinguistic methodology, represented by research carried out either WITHIN or BETWEEN defined groups of languages. The first approach takes advantage of typology as a means of holding many factors constant, exploring fine-grained differences between similar languages. I will call this the INTRA-TYPOLOGICAL APPROACH, and will present four examples, from Slavic, Germanic, and Bantu languages. The second approach compares languages of different types, seeking universals, on the one hand, and typologically specific factors, on the other. I will call this the CROSS-TYPOLOGICAL APPROACH, and will present an extended case study drawn from recent work on spatial conceptualization and narrative discourse in two types of languages.

2. THE INTRA-TYPOLOGICAL APPROACH

In the intra-typological approach, one selects a group of languages that share a collection of typological features, thus making it possible to focus on variation along specified dimensions. By selecting languages that belong to one typological grouping, it is often possible to pull apart features that co-occur in any particular language of the type. That is, one hopes to hold most factors constant in order to explore the role of variation on a particular dimension. In other cases, one might succeed in holding all relevant factors constant, thus testing for replication of a developmental pattern across languages. Most typically, the languages are genetically related, though they need not be. Where common ancestry has led to similar, but slightly varying patterns, we can often make use of such variation to our advantage in studying mechanisms of acquisition. The Slavic and Germanic case studies presented below demonstrate the role of variation WITHIN types, while the Bantu example demonstrates replication within a type category and variation ACROSS types. (What is important about a language family, is, of course, not the historical fact of common ancestry, but the contemporary remainder of that common ancestry in the form of common typological features across languages, along with slightly different solutions to common problems.)

2.1. Slavic Case-Inflectional Paradigms

Perhaps the best case study in intra-typological research is Magdalena Smoczyńska's comparison of the acquisition of the case inflectional paradigms of Russian and Polish in Volume 1 (Smoczyńska, 1985). The paradigms look almost identical on paper. In an early summary of Russian acquisition (Slobin, 1966), I had found that it takes children a very long time to differentiate all of the grammatical forms of each case suffix. There are six cases and three genders, with different forms in singular and plural, and with special forms for some types of animate nouns (not to mention a host of irregularities and exceptions). Russian children go through many stages of simplification and overgeneralization of the paradigm from about age 2 to 5 years (El'konin, 1958; Gvozdev, 1949; Zakharova, 1958). I had suggested that the Slavic paradigm was difficult to acquire for at least two types of reasons: (1) There is a great deal of homophony—for example, the suffix -*u* is not only a singular feminine accusative, but also a dative and a locative for other genders. (2) Gender and animacy are irrelevant to notions of case; therefore, such distinctions should pose a problem in separating out the semantic and formal aspects of case forms in a language like Russian. Similar problems seemed to occur in the acquisition of the Serbo-Croatian case paradigm (Mikeš, 1967; Mikeš & Vlahović, 1966; Radulović, 1975); and so I made a general claim about the course of acquisition of this type of system—on the basis of limited intra-typological evidence (Slobin, 1982).

Subsequently, Smoczyńska carried out the first detailed comparison of the acquisition of two Slavic languages: Polish and Russian. The Polish case-inflectional paradigm is almost identical to the Russian paradigm, and should present the same problems to children—but it does not. When Polish children acquire grammatical cases, they tend to use the correct form for each gender and case from the very beginning, without the kind of massive overgeneralization that one finds in Russian children. This is an ideal example of the value of intra- typological comparison, because it makes it possible to isolate the specific variables that seem to be involved.

As a demonstration, Table 1.1 presents a limited comparison of the two systems, showing only the nominative/accusative contrast for the most frequent forms of singular nouns. The words are given in their orthographical form, with stressed

TABLE 1.1
Russian and Polish Paradigms Compared
(Orthographic; NOMINATIVE/ACCUSATIVE SINGULAR)

	Masculine Animate	Masculine Inanimate	Feminine	Neuter
RUSSIAN				
NOM	*syn*	dom	*roza*	*jabloko*
ACC	*syna*	dom	*rozu*	*jabloko*
POLISH				
NOM	*syn*	dom	*róza*	*jabłko*
ACC	*syna*	dom	*różę*	*jabłko*
	'son'	'house'	'rose'	'apple'

vowels indicated by boldface. Russian and Polish look identical: except for irregulars, masculine nouns end in a consonant, feminine nouns end in -*a*, and neuter nouns end in -*o*. In both languages there are distinct accusative forms for masculine animate and feminine, but not for masculine inanimate and neuter. However, Smoczyńska noted a critical PHONOLOGICAL factor: unstressed vowels are reduced to schwa in Russian, but not in Polish. Thus, for example, feminine *róza* and neuter *jabłko* have perceptually distinct final vowels in Polish, but the corresponding Russian words do not: *rozə* and *jabləkə*. The declensional paradigms that look identical on paper are not identical in the ears of the child. The Polish child is immediately given a way to identify the gender of a noun, because masculine, feminine, and neuter nouns have perceptually different endings. The Russian child has a more difficult task. Because feminine and neuter nouns are often not phonologically distinguished, it is necessary to attend to factors that correlate with gender, such as: the forms of accompanying adjectives, the gender of the pronoun that corresponds to a particular noun, and the overall patterning of the forms of a noun in the paradigm. This is obviously a more difficult task (see Pinker's procedures for inflectional paradigms [1984, pp. 180–192]; Slobin's Operating Principle for Morphological Paradigms [1985a, pp. 1214–1219]). Comparing the two languages, Smoczyńska (1985, p. 65) comes to the following conclusion about the "apparently minor fact" of vowel reduction:

> While most of the nouns ending in -*a* to which Polish children are exposed are regular feminine nouns, the input to the Russian child contains different declension and agreement patterns [for nouns ending in schwa] . . . Such an inconsistent input makes it impossible for the Russian child to discover the criteria of grammatical gender, while Polish children can tolerate the limited amount of inconsistency to which they are exposed, simply regularizing irregular instances according to the tripartite gender distinction.

What is especially important in this analysis is not the fact that Russian is difficult, but that Polish is easy. We have here a clear demonstration that an inflectional paradigm based on arbitrary phonological criteria can be acquired by 2-year-olds if the criteria are transparent and consistent. Evidently, every distinction in form does not have to correspond to a distinction of meaning. This is an important theoretical finding, and it came from detailed comparison WITHIN a typological category of languages—in this instance, both genetic (Slavic) and inflectional (fusional) classifications. As Peters points out in her chapter in this volume, typological comparisons present a wealth of potential case studies of this sort.

2.2. Scandinavian Verb-Particle Constructions

Models of the acquisition of grammatical morphemes pay close attention to factors of acoustic salience (see discussion and references in Peters' chapter in this volume). An ongoing "inter-Nordic project" makes it possible to examine such factors in beautiful detail (Strömqvist et al., 1995). The mainland Scandinavian languages—Swedish, Danish, and Norwegian—all have VERB + PARTICLE constructions, but with systematic differences in word order and prosody (Plunkett & Strömqvist, 1992). The basics can be seen in Table 1.2, using examples of locative particles. In Swedish and Danish, the particle is prosodically prominent, whereas in Norwegian, it is the verb that is prominent. In Danish and Norwegian, the particle is in final position, separated from the verb, whereas in Swedish, it is in medial position, contiguous with the verb. As the inter-Nordic researchers point out, these variations make it possible to test the roles of both prosodic prominence of a particle and its placement in relation to the verb. Preliminary results show that these variations have differing effects on acquisition (Strömqvist et al., 1995; Strömqvist, personal communication, 1995). In Danish, the postposed, stressed particles emerge early as one-word utterances (as they do in English, also). In Swedish, the particles emerge later, and in amalgams with verbs, reflecting their syntactic position following the verb. And in Norwegian, it would seem that verbs first emerge as separate items, with later development of particles. All of the data are not in yet, but it is evident that intra-typological comparisons of this sort are a powerful means of establishing the roles of operating principles and perceptual strategies that deal with perceptual salience and placement of linguistic elements.

TABLE 1.2
Differences in the VERB + PARTICLE Construction Between the Minimally
Different Languages Swedish, Danish, and Norwegian (Strömqvist et al., 1995)

Properties of PRT	Swedish	Danish	Norwegian
	ta **út** det	ta det **úd**	**tà** det ut
Prosodic prominence	+	+	−
Contiguity to V	+	−	−

2.3. Semantics of Spatial Prepositions in English, Dutch, and German

Intra-typological comparisons can also help to reveal the conceptual dimensions used by children in establishing the semantics of grammatical morphemes. For example, it has long been known that notions of containment and support are among the first locative notions to receive linguistic expression across a wide range of languages (e.g., Johnston & Slobin, 1979). More recently, however, Melissa Bowerman and several co-workers have found important crosslinguistic variation in the organization of semantic space underlying locative morphemes (Bowerman, 1993; Bowerman, 1996a, 1996b; Bowerman & Gentner, in preparation; Bowerman & Pederson, 1992; Choi, this volume; Choi & Bowerman, 1991). The child must not only attend to the relevant grammatical forms, but must also learn how those forms relate to language-specific meanings. Consider one example from the realm of locative prepositions in several Germanic languages.

Bowerman (1993) discusses spatial situations such as those described by the English preposition *on*. She notes that in English, *on* is used for various types of support, regardless of the means of support or the type of attachment; for example: *a cup on a table, written words on a page, a handle on a door, a coat on a hook*, and even *a fly on a wall*. In German and Dutch, by contrast, the same semantic range is divided between two prepositions: *auf* and *an* in German, *op* and *aan* in Dutch. Table 1.3, from Bowerman and Pederson (1992), gives a summary of the differences. German and Dutch are "more concerned" about means of support than is English. In both German and Dutch, for example, a hanging object is described by a different preposition than an object that is resting on a surface with gravitational support—compare, for example, Dutch *op de tafel* 'on the table' versus *aan de muur* 'on the wall'. Taking a very fine-grained approach, there are even differences between the uses of German *an* and Dutch *aan*. In Bowerman and Pederson's summary to their table, they note that German is especially concerned about whether the ground object is vertical or horizontal, whereas Dutch is more concerned about whether the attachment is at a point or over a more extended area.

This kind of detailed intra-typological analysis shows that syntactically and acoustically comparable forms present different problems for semantic analysis. Bowerman (1993, p. 11) reports that she and Gentner, in a production task, found that children under age 3 could easily distinguish containment—encoded by *in* in all three languages—from all of the other situations. And English-speaking children correctly contrasted *in* and *on* across a range of situations. Dutch children, however, learned *op* more easily than *aan*, and sometimes overextended *op* to other support relations, though not to containment relations. (Data have not yet been reported for German-speaking children.) The crosslinguistic comparison thus shows that the overall containment/support distinction seems to be readily accessible to children, while the more particular distinctions marked by Dutch (and probably also German) take more time to acquire. Given the simi-

TABLE 1.3

Expansion of Intermediate Categories of *on/in* Continuum; Relevant to Some West Germanic Languages (Bowerman & Pederson, 1992)[a]

	Horiz. support	*Marks (writing, freckles . . .) on non-horiz. surface*	*bugs on non-horiz. surface of manipulable objects (bottle, cup . . .)*	*smeary stuff on non-horiz. surface of manipulable objects*	*bugs on non-horiz. surface of fixed objects (wall, window . . .)*	*smeary, drippy stuff on walls or ceiling*	*Hanging, or other attachment to non-horiz. surface* ↑
English	on	on	on	on	on	on/from	on/to/from ↑
Dutch	op	op	op	op/aan	op	op/aan/tegen	aan ↑
German	auf	auf	auf	auf	an	an	an ↑

[a]The following are examples of the locative domains summarized in Table 2: HORIZONTAL SUPPORT: pencil on table, apple on table, cat on mat; MARKS ON SURFACE: address on envelope, design on T-shirt, writing on blackboard, freckles on cheeks; SMEARY STUFF: raindrops, mud; HANGING: picture on wall, coat on hook, apple on twig; OTHER ATTACHMENT: handle on cupboard, telephone on wall.

larities between the three languages on many other relevant dimensions, this kind of INTRA-typological analysis can clearly reveal the role of semantic features in the acquisition of locative prepositions. And, more generally, the method is a valuable tool for revealing the meanings that children assign to grammatical morphemes.

2.4. Passives in Bantu

Demuth (1992), in Volume 3, discusses the exceptionally early acquisition of passives in Sesotho, in comparison with English and other languages. She suggests that a typological factor is at work in this case. Sesotho is a topic-oriented language (by contrast with subject-oriented languages, like English). That is, the subject position is restricted to old or given—that is, topical information. There are several important syntactic and discourse consequences of this restriction. For example, a subject must be questioned in a passive or a cleft construction—the equivalent of, for example, 'The food is wanted by who?' or 'It's who that wants the food?', rather than the disallowed, 'Who wants the food?'. Dative and accusative objects can passivize; consequently, most verbs can passivize. Demuth concludes that in languages with topic-oriented subjects, "the passive will be a more canonical rather than a marked construction. Thus, whereas the passive in languages such as English is used for certain pragmatic purposes of demoting agency, the passive in languages such as Sesotho is used to maintain the topicality of subjects" (Demuth, 1992, p. 612). This proposal calls for both intra-typological replication and cross-typological disconfirmation, and Demuth presents both kinds of evidence. Another Bantu language, Zulu, is also topic-oriented, and Demuth cites Suzman's (1985, 1987, 1991) similar data on early acquisition of passives. Chichewa presents a valuable contrast case, in that it is also Bantu, but is not topic-oriented (i.e., it allows for questioning of subjects *in situ*). This case makes it possible to hold morphosyntactic factors constant, while determining the role of topic-/subject-orientation. Demuth reports preliminary findings in research by Chimombo (personal communication to Demuth [1990, p. 80]) that passives are acquired later in Chichewa than in Sesotho and Zulu. This case, comparing topic- and subject-oriented languages, moves us from the intra- to the cross-typological approach.

3. THE CROSS-TYPOLOGICAL APPROACH

3.1. Implicational Universals

Cross-typological research begins with the study of one or more individual languages and then works outward, making comparisons along typological dimensions, as in the Bantu example. As a starting point, therefore, one needs to determine dimensions along which languages can vary.[1] Every kind of typological analysis seeks to classify languages according to particular distinctive features, but a classification is of little interest if each distinctive feature is independent of all others. Following Greenberg's (1963, 1966) pioneering work on language universals, typologically oriented research is aimed at the discovery of IMPLICA-TIONAL UNIVERSALS—that is, regular and constrained cooccurrences of particular linguistic features. This sort of research is psycholinguistically interesting if it has the following two characteristics:

- The features constitute an EXHAUSTIVE set along some universal dimension. (In parameter-setting theory, the features are typically binary, but they can also include more choices than two, and they can be scalar as well as absolute.)
- The features CO-DETERMINE each other. There should be psycholinguistic reasons for such co-determination—i.e., an explanatory model is called for.

Consider a very simplified example: Languages can be classified as INFLEC-TIONAL versus NONINFLECTIONAL, in terms of whether or not grammatical relations and categories are directly marked on nouns or verbs. For example, Latin is inflectional, with casemarked nouns, and English is noninflectional. Languages can also be classified in terms of the functions of word order as PRAGMATIC WORD-ORDER LANGUAGES, in which word order is varied for discourse purposes, versus GRAMMATICAL WORD-ORDER LANGUAGES, in which word-order patterns express grammatical relations. In this regard, English is a grammatical word-order language and Latin is a pragmatic word-order language. These two typologies are each exhaustive, in that each defines a dimension on which languages vary, and most languages tend toward one or another end of each dimension. Thus the first psycholinguistic criterion is met. But, as the example shows, the second criterion is also met: Latin is classified as both an inflectional and a pragmatic word-order language; English is classified as both noninflectional and grammatical word-order. If we were to examine a large number of languages in terms of these two dimensions, we would find a crosslinguistic tendency towards filling only two of the four cells of this two-by-two matrix, following the example of Latin and English. And we would seek a psycholinguistic explanation—in this instance, perhaps, the availability of word-order variation to express pragmatic distinctions when grammatical relations are encoded directly on content words. As Hawkins has suggested (1983, p. 125):

> [T]hose languages which encode more pragmatic distinctions explicitly will exhibit correspondingly less pragmatic ambiguity . . . I would expect the more extensive

---

[1]Another term for "dimension" is "parameter." I will avoid this term, since it has become a technical term in GB syntax, and my goal is to make a general presentation, independent of any particular syntactic model. As in phonology, I will use the term DISTINCTIVE FEATURE to refer to ways in which languages differ systematically from one another along a typological dimension.

pragmatic use of word order to correlate quite generally across languages with a richer morphology, with greater surface structure disambiguation, less semantically diverse grammatical relations, less raising, fewer extractions, and fewer deletions, while the more grammatical use of word order will correlate with just the reverse . . .

There are various sorts of possible explanations for implicational universals. Following Chomsky (e.g., 1981), some implicational universals may be an automatic consequence of the innate structure of language, resulting from particular parameter settings as triggered by the input language. In this model, if the subtheories of universal grammar interact in specifiable ways, sets of grammatical properties will emerge with the setting of parameters in each subtheory. In one formulation (Chomsky, 1988, pp. 62–63):

> [T]he principles of universal grammar have certain PARAMETERS, which can be fixed by experience in one or another way. We may think of the language faculty as a complex and intricate network of some sort associated with a switch box consisting of an array of switches that can be in one of two positions. . . . Each permissible array of switch settings determines a particular language. Acquisition of a language is in part a process of setting the switches one way or another on the basis of the presented data, a process of fixing the values of the parameters.

However, this approach, if valid, would only tell part of the story.[2] Most of the issues dealt with in this chapter, and these volumes, lie beyond the purview of this school of formal grammar. Parameter setting pertains to only a segment of the acquisition and use of language, as underlined by Edwin Williams in his introduction to an edited book with Tom Roeper, *Parameter Setting*. After discussing the possibility that parameters may not be independent of one another, Williams comments (Roeper & Williams, 1987, pp. xi–xii):

> The second point I would like to raise in connection with the parameter setting model in acquisition studies has to do with a neglect of those aspects of language that do not lend themselves to parameterization. . . . [T]he extent of linguistic structure for which the parameter setting model is inappropriate may be wider than is recognized. . . . For example, nearly every language has some kind of nominal or verbal paradigm, which is essentially an n-dimensional matrix of forms, mapped in a systematic (but not necessarily bi-unique) way onto a set of morphological distinctions. The number of dimensions of this matrix, the size of each dimension, and the mapping of the matrix onto the set of distinctions are all subject to great variation from language to language, and the idea of 'setting parameters' seems to be of no help here. Another domain apparently beyond parameter setting would be the identification of affixes. . . . There is probably room for low level 'concept

---

[2]The approach itself may be on the wane. In a recent two-volume work on the acquisition of syntax in a crosslinguistic and Chomskian framework (Lust, Suñer, & Whitman, 1994), the editors conclude: "One striking result across both volumes is an apparent diminished role for parameters both in the explanation for cross-linguistic variation and for language acquisition" (Vol. 1, p. xxvii).

formation' as well—languages seem to have language particular categories . . . It would be quite surprising if parameter setting exhausted the possibilities—knowledge of language involves a number of different types of knowledge, and acquisition will proceed most efficiently if the means of learning each type is tailored to that type.

Hyams (1989) agrees with Williams that there is more to language acquisition than parameter setting, but considers language beyond core grammar to be "idiosyncratic or peripheral" (p. 215):

Of course, in addition to fixing the parameters of UG, the child must also acquire the idiosyncratic or peripheral aspects of his language, which may be unrelated or only loosely connected to the parameters. However, it is assumed that once the child has set all the parameters, he will have acquired the 'core' component of the adult grammatical system.

One goal of these five volumes is to show how much fruit there is beyond the core.

Whereas Chomsky's parameters are limited to "core grammar," and are innately specified, the broader typologically oriented approach to acquisition presented here concerns itself with the full range of linguistic phenomena, without prejudging the architecture and structural constraints of the language faculty. These are issues of empirical and theoretical investigation within broader frameworks of linguistic and cognitive structure, psycholinguistic processing, and discourse analysis. In the principles-and-parameters approach to generative grammar, patterns of cooccurrences of linguistic forms may be attributed to the ineluctable interaction of the subtheories of universal grammar. Typological patterning, on this view, is seen as an automatic consequence of the possible types of parameter setting, and the child's task is reduced to one of deduction. On the other hand, many (or all) of such patterns may be explainable in terms of a number of interacting processes.

Hawkins (1983), for example, attempts to explain implicational word-order universals on the basis of a set of processing principles, such as the need to quickly recognize the head of a construction. Using such processing factors, Hawkins arrives at a principle of "Cross-Category Harmony" which accounts for apparently universal tendencies to harmonize the placement of operators and operands across phrasal categories in a language. This kind of functional model explains, for example, the fact that languages with rigid verb-final order also tend to be noun-final within the NP. In a recent book, *A Performance Theory of Order and Constituency*, Hawkins (1994) provides detailed evidence for "the grammaticalization of processing principles." With regard to implicational universals, he concludes (p. xii):

Implicational related properties such as "if SOV, then postpositions in PP" co-occur because they are optimal for processing and involve minimal complexity: fewer computations are required over smaller number of entities in order to reach a given parsing decision, involving in this case the recognition of constituent structure.

Similar functional explanations could be offered for the repeated finding that languages only allow subject ellipsis ("null subject") if they provide sufficient structural information to allow for identification of the subject by other means (e.g., Jaeggli & Safir, 1989). Diachronically, languages lose "processing cues" such as rich inflection or recruit lexical items to provide such cues through processes of grammaticalization (e.g., Hopper & Traugott, 1993; Traugott & Heine, 1991). As a result, a language can change in typology—or even present a mixed picture at some stage in its history, as in the case of modern Hebrew. This is a "null-subject language" in the past and future tenses, which have full person/number marking on the verb, but is a "non-null-subject language" (i.e., has obligatory subjects) in the present tense, where only number is marked (Berman, 1990).[3] This is a confusing pattern for parameter setting, but a consistent one for processing.

The picture that emerges from diachronic crosslinguistic research is one of grammars that reconstitute themselves under shifting balances of online processing constraints rather than grammars that are prespecified as autonomous formal systems (see Slobin, this volume). Indeed, Croft, in his 1990 textbook, *Typology and Universals*, devotes an entire chapter to "External motivation and the typology of form–function relations," summarizing the contributions of economic motivation, iconicity, and communicative motivation. He surveys a number of preliminary, but provocative analyses arising from "the functional-typological approach to language," which he summarizes in the following terms (p. 155): "Functionalism seeks to explain language structure in terms of language function. It assumes that a large class of fundamental linguistic phenomena are the result of the adaptation of grammatical structure to the function of language."

The child language researcher should be cautious, realizing that both formalist and functionalist explanations have inadequacies at the present time, and recognizing that the current polarization in the field seems to reflect institutional and temperamental determinants as much as reasoned argumentation from data— which, in many cases, are compatible with a range of theories. Thus, even with regard to "core grammar," it is far from obvious what portion, if any, of systematic crosslinguistic variation need be attributed to an innate system of parameters and their consequences for syntactic typology.

In any case, these are arguments about forces that shape THE FORM OF THE LANGUAGE TO BE ACQUIRED; they are not explanations of THE PROCEDURES THAT A CHILD MIGHT USE TO ACQUIRE SUCH FORMS. The fact that languages have

---

[3]In fact, as Yonata Levy (personal communication, 1996) has pointed out, the situation in Hebrew is even more complex, in that subject omission is not allowed in third persons in past and future tenses, despite the fact that the verb is fully marked for person and gender. She and Anne Vainikka (in preparation) suggest that this mixed pattern is based on pragmatic distinctions between first/second versus third persons in conversational discourse.

particular "shape" need not be attributed to the acquisition mechanism itself, unless one assumes that the forms that define an individual language are determined by parameters whose setting is merely "triggered" by experience and elaborated by deductive processes. At this point in the science, our understanding of form–function relations is still limited, and it seems premature to opt for such a solution. Rather, the task of child language theory should be to make serious use of the facts of typological variation as a challenge for the development of more adequate theories of the PROCESSES of language acquisition.

In any event, the goal of this chapter—and most of the writing in these five volumes—is not to arrive at The Definitive Acquisition Theory, but rather to illustrate the importance of attending to crosslinguistic and typological factors in preparing the groundwork for such a theory. Therefore, leaving these unresolved theoretical issues aside, I turn to an extended case study of one set of implicational universals that goes well beyond core grammar, and that is realized across a span of later language development. My purpose is to cast light on the interlocking of factors of lexicalization patterns, syntax, and discourse functions in the course of language development. And, from a psychological point of view, the important term is DEVELOPMENT, rather than ACQUISITION. Much attention has been paid to the initial state and the endstate, while the processes of change over time have been too often slighted, ignored, or explained away. The following case study deals with children between the ages of 3 and 9, pointing to continuing change across this age span.

3.2. Motion Descriptions in Satellite-Framed and Verb-Framed Languages

As a case study in cross-typological research, I will focus on verbs of motion in two types of languages, beginning with English and Spanish as examples of the two types, and then making comparisons with other languages of both types. Consider the two equivalent sentences in (1) and (2):

(1) *The man ran into the house.*

(2) *El hombre entró corriendo a la casa.*
    'The man entered running to the house.'

In English, the verb, *ran*, only indicates that motion has occurred, in a particular manner, with no information about the direction of the motion. That information is provided by the verb particle, *in*. By contrast, the verb in Spanish, *entró* 'entered', indicates that motion has occurred in a particular direction, with no indication of manner. That information is optionally provided by a separate verbal element, the gerund, *corriendo* 'running'. And in both languages, additional information about the path of movement can be provided by a prepositional phrase, *to the house, a la casa.* As described in detail by Talmy (1985, 1991), these two patterns are characteristic of English and Spanish overall. In fact, they constitute a basic typological distinction that may be applicable to all languages. Talmy defines the distinction on the basis of the part of a clause that frames the "core meaning" of MOVEMENT ALONG A PATH. In English this information is conveyed by a SATELLITE to the verb, the particle *in*, and so Talmy calls this type of language SATELLITE-FRAMED. In Spanish, it is a verb that frames the core meaning—thus this is a VERB-FRAMED language. In English there is a large collection of verbs of manner of movement, such as *run, walk, fly, swim, crawl, creep*, and they can all be combined with a collection of path satellites, *in, over, up to, across, down from*, and so forth. In Spanish, there is a small collection of verbs of inherent direction, such as *entrar* 'enter', *salir* 'exit', *subir* 'ascend', *bajar* 'descend', and the like. These verbs can be combined with manner expressions when manner is relevant to the discourse, as in (2). According to Talmy (1991), within Indo-European, all languages are satellite-framed except for the Romance languages, which are verb-framed. Finno-Ugric languages and Chinese are also satellite-framed; Semitic and Turkic languages, as well as Japanese and Korean, are verb-framed.[4]

On the basis of this typology, a new kind of implicational universal can be proposed. The proposal is based on studies of narrative discourse, suggesting that the distinction between satellite-framing and verb-framing has implications for the organization of text. The data come from stories elicited by a picture storybook, *Frog, Where Are You?* (Mayer, 1969), in English, German, Hebrew, Spanish, and Turkish (Berman & Slobin, 1994). Consider, first, English and Spanish, as prototypical satellite- and verb-framed languages.[5] The events depicted in *Frog, Where Are You?* invite a rich collection of motion descriptions: A pet frog escapes from its jar and a boy and his dog go looking for the lost frog. Their search involves climbing, falling, running, flying, throwing, dropping, carrying, entering, and exiting. A detailed analysis of all of the motion events in the English and Spanish

---

[4]Talmy's (1991) typological analysis goes far beyond lexicalization patterns for the expression of motion events; the bipartite classification embraces aspect, change of state, realization, and action correlation. Consider, for example, the satellite-framed typology of English constructions such as *eat up, burn out, slam shut, walk along with someone*. A verb-framed language uses separate verbs in corresponding constructions; compare, for example, *The leaves withered away*, with Spanish, *Las hojas se desintegraron al secarse* 'The leaves disintegrated by withering'. Revisions of Talmy's typology have been suggested by Aske (1989) and Slobin and Hoiting (1994), and I am preparing a more detailed typological approach to linguistic descriptions of motion events.

[5]English stories were gathered in Berkeley, California by Virginia Marchman and Tanya Renner. Spanish stories were gathered in Spain by Eugenia Sebastián, and in Chile and Argentina by Aura Bocaz. Narrators were preschoolers (3–5 years), school-age children (7–11 years), and adults. Research reported here was designed in collaboration with Ruth A. Berman, Tel Aviv University, Israel, with support from the U.S.–Israel Binational Science Foundation (Grant 2732/82, to R. A. Berman and D. I. Slobin), the Linguistics Program of the National Science Foundation (Grant BNS-8520008, to D. I. Slobin), the Sloan Foundation Program in Cognitive Science (Institute of Cognitive Studies, University of California, Berkeley), the Max-Planck-Institut für Psycholinguistik (Nijmegen, The Netherlands), and the Institute of Human Development (University of California, Berkeley).

stories reveals major differences at the levels of lexicon, syntax, and narrative organization. In other words, the analysis provides a preliminary approach to what could be called A TYPOLOGY OF RHETORIC. I will summarize some of the differences briefly, attending only to descriptions of change of location.

In order to compare two equal-sized groups of narrators, a comparison can be made between data gathered in California and Spain. There were 12 subjects in each of five age groups: 3, 4, 5, 9, and adult; that is, a total of 60 stories in each language. A major typological difference can be found in comparing the verb lexicons of the two languages. Consider the entire collection of motion verbs used in all 60 stories combined. These include verbs of self-movement and caused movement. The verbs are listed in (3):

(3a) **English verbs:** buck+, bump+, buzz+, carry, chase+, climb+, come+, crawl+, creep+, depart, drop+, dump+, escape, fall+, float+, fly+, follow, get+, go+, head+, hide, hop+, jump+, knock+, land, leave, limp+, make-fall, move, plummet, pop+, push+, race+, rush+, run+, slip+, splash+, splat+, sneak+, swim+, swoop+, take+, throw+, tip+, tumble+, walk+, wander+

(3b) **Spanish verbs:** *acercarse* 'approach', *alcanzar* 'reach', *arrojar* 'throw', *bajar(se)* 'descend', *caer(se)* 'fall', *correr* 'run', *dar-un-empujón* 'push', *dar-un-salto* 'jump', *entrar* 'enter', *escapar(se)* 'escape', *hacer-caer* 'make-fall', *huir* 'flee', *ir(se)* 'go', *llegar* 'arrive', *llevar(se)* 'carry', *marchar(se)* 'go', *meterse* 'insert-oneself', *nadar* 'swim', *perseguir* 'chase', *ponerse* 'put-oneself', *regresar* 'return', *sacarse* 'remove-oneself, exit', *salir* 'exit', *saltar* 'jump', *subir(se)* 'ascend', *tirar* 'throw', *traspasar* 'go-over', *venir* 'come', *volar(se)* 'fly', *volver(se)* 'return'

The first striking difference is simply in terms of variety: 47 verb types were used in English, in comparison with 27 in Spanish. This is due to the collection of English verbs that conflate the expression of motion with manner of motion—verbs like *crawl, creep, plummet, splat, swoop,* and the like. But the imbalance between the two languages is even greater when one considers the resources of a satellite-framed language like English. Recall that satellites, in English, are verb particles such as *in* and *out.* In (3a), the verbs marked with a plus-sign occurred with satellites. If one lists the English verbs together with all of the satellites that accompanied them in the stories, there is a total of 123 verb types, shown in (4):

(4) **English verbs + satellites:**
buck + off
bump + down
buzz + out
chase + after, in
climb + down, on, out, over, up, up in, up on
come + after, down, off, on, out, over, up
crawl + out, over, up
creep + out, up

drop + down, off
dump + in, off
fall + down, in, off, on, out, over
float + off
fly + after, away, off, out, over, up
get + away, down, in, off, on, out, over, past, up, up on
go + down, down out, home, in, off, out, outside, over, through, up
head + for, to
hop + in, on, out, over
jump + down, off, out, over, up
knock + down, down out, in, off, out
limp + in
pop + out, up
push + down, off, off in, out
race + after, away
run + after, along, away, by, from, in, off, out, over, through
rush + out
slip + on, over
sneak + out, over, up
splash + in
splat + in
swim + out, over
swoop + down
take + away, off with
throw + down, down in, in, off, over, over in
tip + off over
tumble + down, out
walk + along, down, over to
wander + out

English differs from Spanish then, not only in its satellite-framing typology, but also in terms of its lexicalization resources: There are more types of motion verbs; many of these verbs conflate motion and manner; and they can be flexibly combined with a range of satellites to produce a large, open set of VERB + SATELLITE constructions. In terms of a typology of rhetoric, we can ask whether these differences have any implications for the narration of motion events in the stories. To simplify the presentation, consider only descriptions of paths of movement, ignoring manner.

A satellite-framed language invites the speaker to elaborate path descriptions by appending several satellites to a single verb of motion. For example, in describing a scene in which an owl leaves its hole in a tree, an English-speaker might say:

(5a) *The owl flew down from out of the hole.*

The satellites trace out a complex trajectory, along with a single verb: the path is *down from out*, and a prepositional phrase specifies the source, *of the hole*. There is no compact way to express this information in a single clause in a verb-framed language. A Spanish-speaking narrator, for example, is more likely to either use a single clause, omitting the fact of downward movement:

> (5b) *El buho salió volando del agujero.*
> 'The owl exited flying of.the hole.'

or the narrator may break up the complex path into two clauses:

> (5c) *El buho salió del agujero y bajó volando.*
> 'The owl exited of.the hole and descended flying.'

That is, there is a tendency to append path segments to a single verb in a language like English, versus a tendency to either simplify path descriptions with one verb or to analyze the path in several verbs in a language like Spanish. This sort of IMPLICATIONAL RELATION between lexicalization patterns and rhetorical style is reflected in the narrative data in several ways.

One might expect English speakers, following this typological tendency, to provide more information about the GROUND of movement—that is, to make more mention of source and goal and landmarks passed along a path, with regard to a verb of motion, because several bits of path and ground information can easily be appended to a single verb, which is, itself, not a path verb. One way to check for this tendency is to count the number of verbs that occur with some specification of ground. These are found in clauses like those in (6b), as opposed to the use of simple directional expressions, such as those in (6a):

> (6a) *The owl flew out.*
> *El buho (se) salió.*
> 'The owl exited.'
> (6b) *The owl flew out of the hole.*
> *El buho (se) salió del agujero.*
> 'The owl exited from the hole.'

Table 1.4 presents figures based on all verbs of motion in the frog stories, along with comparable figures from a study of novels written in English and Spanish, discussed below. The figures are the percentages of such verbs which are accompanied by one or more prepositional phrases that encode source, goal, or landmarks along a path. The overall tendency is for English narratives to use more ground adjuncts with regard to verbs of motion than Spanish narratives. Interestingly, the differences between the languages are most marked for mature speakers/writers: for adult frog-story narrators the comparison between English and Spanish shows 82% versus 63% of motion verbs with mention of ground,

TABLE 1.4
Percentages of Verbs with Mention of Ground

Age	English	Spanish
3–4 yrs	54	48
5 yrs	60	50
9 yrs	62	61
Adult	82	63
Novels	96	81

and for novel writers the contrast is 96% versus 81%. These figures suggest that the endstate model is rather different for the two types of language—even in the case of literary fiction, where novelists are not constrained by the pre-established pictures of an elicited narrative task (for details, see Slobin, 1996b). The developmental patterns reinforce this impression. The American preschoolers provide more ground information than the Spanish preschoolers. There is also a hint of some development during the preschool period in English, but not in Spanish. At school-age the two groups are comparable, though the Spaniards have advanced from the preschool to the 9-year-old level, whereas the Americans were already at that level at age 5. And there is essentially no further development in Spanish, whereas there is continuing development in English until adulthood. Overall, then, it appears that English-speaking narrators may pay more attention to path details than do Spanish-speakers.

Another way of comparing the two types of languages is to look at an extended motion event in detail. As an example, consider the series of changes of location that occur in one particular scene—the dramatic highpoint of the frog story. The scene is shown in a series of six pictures, in the course of which the main protagonist, the boy, endures the following change of location:

Picture 13: The boy, fleeing from an owl, starts to climb a large rock.

Picture 14: The boy is standing on top of the rock, holding on to what appear to be branches.

Picture 15: The boy is lying between the antlers of a deer that is standing just behind the rock. Apparently he unwittingly held onto the antlers, the deer stood up, and the boy became ensnared in the antlers.

Picture 16: The boy is still on the deer's head, as the deer runs toward the edge of a cliff. The boy's pet dog runs along ahead of the deer, turning back to bark.

Picture 17: The deer stands at the edge of the cliff. The boy and the dog are in mid-fall from the cliff to a pond below.

Picture 18: The boy and dog have apparently just fallen into the pond, with their feet sticking up out of the water.

Let us focus just on the boy's journey from the deer's head to the water. One technique, typical of a satellite-framed language, is to compact the journey into a single clause. As shown in (7), this is available to both preschool and school-age English-speaking children:

(7a) *He threw him over a cliff into a pond.* [age 5]

(7b) *He* [=deer] *starts running and he tips him off over a cliff into the water.* [age 9]

Another technique is clause chaining, as in (8). This technique is available in both types of languages. As shown in (8), it is available to Spanish preschoolers.

(8) *Un ciervo le cogió al niño, y le llevó al agua, y le tiró. Se cayó al agua.*
    'A deer picked up the boy, and carried him to the water, and threw him. (He) fell to the water.' [age 5]

Note that in (8) there are two instances of a verb with a prepositional phrase indicating the ground: *le llevó al agua* 'he carried him to the water' and *se cayó al agua* '(he) fell to the water'. There seems to be nothing about verb-framed typology that should prevent Spanish speakers from using compact expressions, like those in (7), in situations where more than one ground element can be associated with a verb. Such expressions are highly frequent in English at all ages. But they are vanishingly rare in Spanish. This can be clearly seen in a combination of Eugenia Sebastián's Madrid data (Sebastián & Slobin, 1994) with stories gathered in Chile and Argentina by Aura Bocaz, covering the ages of 3, 4, 5, 7, 9, 11, and adult (Slobin & Bocaz, 1988). In this entire corpus of 216 Spanish frog stories, there are only three instances of a clause in which both source and goal are mentioned in relation to a single verb: two from Spain and one from Chile. They come from a 5-year-old, a 9-year-old, and an adult, suggesting that this is not a developmental issue, but rather a consequence of verb-framing typology:

(9a) *Se cayó de la ventana a la calle.*
    '(He) fell from the window to the street.' [age 5: Spain]

(9b) *Lo lleva campo a través hasta un barranco.*
    '[The deer] carries him across (the) field to a cliff.' [age 9: Spain]

(9c) *El perro . . . hace un movimiento tal que se precipita al suelo, desde la ventana. . . .*
    'The dog . . . makes a movement such that he plummets to the ground, from the window . . .' [adult: Chile]

It appears, then, that Spanish speakers tend to limit themselves, when using a prepositional phrase with a verb of motion, to one piece of information about the ground (source, goal, or medium).

The same is true of novels. I have examined five novels in each of the two languages (Slobin, 1996b). (See listing of novels in the references following this chapter.) From each novel I selected, at random, 20 descriptions of a protagonist moving from one place to another—that is, 100 motion events for each language. As shown in Table 1.4, above, a ground element is mentioned in 96% of such events in the English novels and 81% in the Spanish novels. Furthermore, as in the frog stories, English writers mention more ground elements per motion event than do Spanish writers—even though novelists are free to be as expressive and creative as they please. On average, English writers mention 2.24 ground elements in each description of a motion event, whereas Spanish writers mention 1.52.

As shown in Table 1.5, when an author does make reference to ground— source, goal, medium, landmarks—English-language authors are far more likely than Spanish-language authors to refer to two or more ground locations, and Spanish-language authors never refer to more than two. Thus the novels, like the frog stories, show English narrations to be richer in encoding path details. I suggest that satellite-framing typology orients speakers to path descriptions outside of the verb. Learning a verb-framed language, by contrast, locates path information in verbs, and each verb can convey only a particular type of path.[6]

Returning to the frog stories, one might ask, then, if Spanish provides other means for providing details of paths, rather than associating ground elements with a single verb of motion. Up to this point, the data presented here have taken the CLAUSE as the unit of analysis for motion description. Most work in linguistic typology focuses on lexicon and grammar, and does not concern itself with larger units. However, in narrative discourse, the movements of a protagonist from place to place are situated in a physical setting and temporal flow of events. Narrators need not limit a path description to a single verb and its adjuncts. In describing realworld or fictional events, a narrator may present a series of linked paths or a path with way-stations. Perhaps Spanish speakers prefer to analyze a motion event into separate clauses, as in (8). The frog story is useful here because we can compare narrations of the same event. Consider the scene of the fall from the cliff again. It consists of six narrative segments, each of which are mentioned in one narration or another:

NARRATIVE SEGMENTS OF THE FALL FROM THE CLIFF: deer starts to run; deer runs, carrying boy; deer stops at cliff; deer throws boy (off of antlers/down); boy and dog fall; boy and dog land in water

Perhaps Spanish narrators mention MORE SEGMENTS of the event, rather than expressing it compactly in English fashion. But this is not the case. The relevant

---

[6]Continuing crosslinguistic study of novels also demonstrates the predicted patterns: German, Dutch, and Russian (satellite-framed) resemble English, while French, Turkish, and Japanese (verb-framed) resemble Spanish with regard to descriptions of motion events (Slobin, in preparation). Note that genetic relationship and common culture have nothing to do with these patterns; the typology of lexicalization patterns divides languages on a different basis than common ancestry, culture, or literary tradition.

TABLE 1.5
Percentages of Motion Events with Ground References in Novels

	Number of Ground Elements Referred To			
Language	0	1	2	3+
English	4	61	26	9
Spanish	19	73	8	0

data come from 9-year-olds and adults, since preschoolers do not tend to provide many details in their stories. The data are shown in Table 1.6, using only the Madrid stories. Only 40% of the Spanish 9-year-olds provided three segments, and none of them provided more than three. In contrast, 92% of the American 9-year-olds provided three or more segments, and, of these, almost half provided more than three segments. Of the adult narrators, 100% of the Americans and only 75% of the Spaniards provided three or more segments of the motion event. In sum, Spanish speakers do not seem to "compensate" for minimal use of source-goal clauses by means of a series of separate action clauses that analyze an event into a number of its components. There may be a narrative pressure against elaboration of a path in a series of clauses, with each clause presenting a bit of foregrounded information. A series of path verbs is "heavier" than a single verb with a series of path satellites and prepositional phrases, and narrators probably avoid this "heaviness" in verb-framed languages.

To sum up thus far: In comparison with English-speakers, Spanish narrators use a smaller set of motion verbs; they mention fewer ground elements in individual clauses; and they describe fewer segments of a motion event. Yet their frog-story narratives, overall, seem to "tell the same story" as English accounts. Although the analysis has been extended from verbs of motion to include associated locative phrases, and has gone from individual motion verbs to series of clauses, the focus has remained on descriptions of MOVEMENT. However, movement always takes place within a physical SETTING. The two languages seem to differ, further, in relative allocation of attention to movement and setting. English, with its rich means for path description, can often leave setting to be inferred; Spanish, with its sparser path possibilities, often elaborates descriptions of settings, leaving paths to be inferred. For example, the trajectories

TABLE 1.6
Percentage of Narrators Mentioning 3+ Segments

	Age Group	
Language	9 yrs	Adult
English	92	100
Spanish	40	75

in (7a) and (7b), above, allow one to infer that there is a cliff located above some water: *over a cliff into a pond, over a cliff into the water*. Compare this to the following Spanish narrative segments:

(10a) *Los tiró a un precipicio donde había harta agua. Entonces se cayeron.*
'[The deer] threw them at a cliff where there was lots of water. Then they fell.'
[age 7: Chile]

(10b) *El ciervo le llevó hasta un sitio, donde debajo había un río. Entonces el ciervo tiró al perro y al niño al río. Y después, cayeron.*
'The deer took him until a place, where below there was a river. Then the deer threw the dog and the boy to the river. And then they fell.' [age 9: Spain]

(10c) *Lo tiró. Por suerte, abajo, estaba el río. El niño cayó en el agua.*
'[The deer] threw him. Luckily, below, was the river. The boy fell in the water.'
[age 11: Argentina]

In these accounts, we are told that the deer 'threw' them and that they 'fell', ending up in the water. We can infer that the trajectory went from some elevated place to the river because of the STATIC descriptions: 'a cliff where there was lots of water', 'a place where below there was a river', 'below was the river'. In comparison with English, Spanish frog stories have an abundance of such static descriptions of settings, suggesting a different allocation of attention between description of movement and description of states. In a sense, the Spanish narrators ARE providing ground information—but it is in separate clauses rather than adjoined to verbs of motion. However, it should be noted that even by this criterion, Spanish frog stories devote less explicit attention to movement and ground, broadly conceived, than do English versions. Table 1.7 summarizes the percentages of the 12 narrators in each age group in Spain and the United States who provided static scene setting descriptions in the scene of the fall from the cliff. There is essentially no development in English, and this option is not taken by any adult narrators at all. In Spanish there seems to be a major development from ages 5 to 9, although only three of the adult narrators take this option.

In sum, analysis of the frog stories reveals a distinct contrast in RHETORICAL STYLE between English and Spanish. English-speakers may devote more narrative attention to the dynamics of movement along a path because of the availability

TABLE 1.7
Percentage of Narrators Providing Extended Locative
Elaboration in Describing the Fall from the Cliff

| | Age Group | | |
Language	5 yrs	9 yrs	Adult
English	8	8	0
Spanish	8	42	25

of verbs of motion (often conflated with manner) that can readily be associated with satellites and locative prepositional phrases to trace out detailed paths in relation to ground elements. Spanish speakers, by contrast, seem to be led (or constrained) by their language to devote less narrative attention to the path dynamics and perhaps somewhat more attention to static scene-setting.

As a result of this broad cross-typological analysis, comparing a satellite-framed and a verb-framed language, it is possible to propose an implicational universal on the level of the typology of rhetoric:

> **IMPLICATIONAL UNIVERSAL:** Narratives in verb-framed languages will tend to devote relatively more attention to scene-setting and relatively less attention to details of paths of motion, in comparison with satellite-framed languages.

This claim can be tested by gathering data from other languages of the two types. That is, having established a pattern in languages belonging to different typological classifications, it is time for replication INTRA-typologically, seeking evidence from additional languages of each type. Additional data from the frog-story project support the implicational universal. There is another satellite-framed language in the sample—German, and two more verb-framed languages—Hebrew and Turkish. Example (11), from German, shows the pattern of event compacting familiar in the English data:

(11) **German:** *Der Hirsch nahm den Jungen auf sein Geweih und schmiß ihn den Abhang hinunter genau ins Wasser.*
'The deer took the boy on his antlers and hurled him down from the cliff right into the water.' [age 9]

Hebrew and Turkish, like Spanish, show the rhetorical style of stage setting: 'a cliff that had a swamp underneath'; 'Just in front of them there was a cliff. Below there was a lake':

(12a) **Hebrew:** *Ve ha'ayil nivhal, ve hu hitxil laruts. Ve hakelev rats axarav, ve hu higia lemacok she mitaxat haya bitsa, ve hu atsar, ve hayeled ve hakelev naflu labitsa beyaxad.*
'And the deer was startled, and he began to run. And the dog ran after him, and he reached a cliff that had a swamp underneath, and he stopped, and the boy and the dog fell to the swamp together.' [age 9]

(12b) **Turkish:** *Ancak önlerinde bir uçurum vardı. Altıda göldü. Çocuk hız yaptığı için, geyiğin başından köpeğiyle birlikte düştü.*
'Just in front of them there was a cliff. Below there was a lake. Because the boy was making speed, he fell from the deer's head together with his dog.' [age 9]

The satellite-framed languages allow for compact presentation of a path of motion, clustering around a single verb, as in the case of *schmeißen* 'hurl' in

TABLE 1.8
Percentage of Narrators Providing Extended Locative
Elaboration in Describing the Fall from the Cliff

	Age Group	
Language	*5 yrs*	*9 yrs*
English	8	8
German	0	17
Spanish	8	42
Hebrew	0	42
Turkish	10	42

(13), or *throw* and *tip* in (7). This means of expression is already available to some preschool-age children, as shown in the 5-year-old English example in (7a). By contrast, in verb-framed languages, where the verb indicates only directionality, the narrator is faced with the task of providing enough stage-setting information for the details of the trajectory to be inferred, as in the Spanish examples in (10) and the Hebrew and Turkish examples in (12). Hardly any preschool-age narrators show this level of proficiency in verb-framed languages.

Table 1.8 expands the data presented in Table 1.7 to include all five languages of the Berman/Slobin study. The table shows the percentages of 5- and 9-year-olds who provide the kind of extended locative elaboration shown in (10) and (12)—that is, descriptions of the static locations of landmarks, such as cliff and water, enabling the listener to infer the source and goal of movement. It is evident that this sort of locative elaboration is rare in the preschool texts in Spanish, Hebrew, and Turkish, but that it develops in school age. By contrast, it is not an option that is exploited in English and German, where satellite-framed devices are available from early on.

More recently it has been possible to ascertain the presence of these patterns in a much larger collection of languages. In a 1995 frog-story workshop we were able to compare nine satellite-framed and seven verb-framed languages.[7] The languages are listed below, with the names of the investigators who gathered the data:

SATELLITE-FRAMED LANGUAGES:

Dutch (Jeroen Aarssen, Petra Bos, Ludo Verhoeven, Carla Zijlenmaker)
English (Virginia Marchman, Tanya Renner)

---

[7]The workshop was supported by the National Science Foundation and was held at the University of New Mexico in conjunction with the Linguistic Institute of the Linguistic Society of America. Participants in the workshop were Jeroen Aarssen, Ayhan Aksu-Koç, Michael Bamberg, Edith Bavin, Ruth A. Berman, Petra Bos, Nancy Budwig, Harriet Jisa, Catalina Johnson Herrera, Sophie Kern, Åsa Nordqvist, Barbara Pearson, Hrafnhildur Ragnsarsdóttir, Judy Reilly, Svenka Savić, Dan I. Slobin, Magdalena Smoczyńska, Anat Stavans, Sabine Stoll, Sven Strömqvist, and Ludo Verhoeven.

German (Michael Bamberg, Mary Carroll, Christiane von Stutterheim)
Icelandic (Hrafnhildur Ragnarsdóttir)
Swedish (Åsa Nordqvist, Sven Strömqvist)
Polish (Magdalena Smoczyńska)
Russian (Yana Anilovich, N. V. Durova, N. M. Yurieva)
Serbo-Croatian (Svenka Savić)
Warlpiri (Edith Bavin)

VERB-FRAMED LANGUAGES

French (Harriet Jisa, Sophie Kern)
Italian (Margherita Orsolini, Franca Rossi)
Portuguese (Isabel Hub Faria)
Spanish (Aura Bocaz, Eugenia Sebastián)
Moroccan Arabic (Petra Bos, Ludo Verhoeven)
Hebrew (Ruth A. Berman, Yoni Neeman)
Turkish (Ayhan Aksu-Koç, Aylin Küntay)

So far we have examined ten adult frog stories in each of these languages. In describing the fall from the cliff, 21% of narrators in the verb-framed languages provide static scene-setting, in comparison with 8% in the satellite-framed languages. In fact, there are no instances at all of such elaboration in Dutch, German, English, Polish, or Russian. By contrast, there are instances in each of the verb-framed languages. The patterns represented in Table 1.6 for English and Spanish are also replicated in the larger sample. Adult narrators in the satellite-framed languages mentioned, on average, more segments of the fall from the cliff, and were far more likely to mention three or more segments, in comparison with narrators in the verb-framed languages. The expected typological differences also hold up on the level of the individual clause. On average, comparing the nine satellite-framed with the seven verb-framed languages, adult narrators mentioned more ground elements per verb of motion in the satellite-framed languages. Thus the predicted patterns of rhetorical style seem to be replicable across languages, based on their typology alone.

The child, of course, must LEARN such patterns—though we have no adequate model of this sort of complex, interactive learning. The patterns are not prescribed by the grammar, but they are consequences of the set of options made available by the grammar. The form of the discourse that children are exposed to is, of course, also determined by the same forces. But children do not simply copy those discourse forms, as evidenced by age differences in the frog stories, across the five languages of the original sample. As noted above, children learning satellite-framed languages provide elaborate path descriptions in the preschool years, using combinations of satellites and prepositional phrases. But children learning verb-framed languages do not manage scene-setting until school age.[8] This is part of a general development of intralinguistic skills, as reflected also in the development of definiteness discussed earlier. The emergence of such skills then has consequences for the mastery of a range of syntactic forms, such as relative clauses, definite referring expressions, anaphora, and temporal subordination (Berman & Slobin, 1994). Explanation of learning processes of this sort requires attention to a number of interlocking factors, going beyond current "domain-specific" approaches to development.

3.3. Intra-Typological Contrasts in Motion Verbs

Returning to verbs of motion, it is profitable to look at patterns of development in similar languages. As in Bowerman's studies, detailed intra-typological comparisons can reveal the roles of additional factors in this domain. Here a comparison of German with English is useful (Bamberg, 1994). As in English, there is a rich collection of verbs of motion and caused motion, most of them simultaneously expressing manner. We have data from four age groups in German—3, 5, 9, and adult—with 12 narrators in each group. Across this age range, in all 48 narrations, there are 37 types of verbs of motion, as shown in (13).

(13) *sich-entfernen* 'distance-oneself', *erklimmen* 'climb', *fallen* 'fall', *fliegen* 'fly', *gehen* 'go', *hoppeln* 'hop', *hüpfen* 'hop', *jagen* 'chase', *klettern* 'climb', *kommen* 'come', *krabbeln* 'crawl', *kriechen* 'creep', *landen* 'land', *laufen* 'run', *plumpsen* 'plop', *purzeln* 'tumble', *rasen* 'speed', *rennen* 'run', *reiten* 'ride', *schieben* 'push', *schleichen* 'creep', *schlittern* 'glide', *schlüpfen* 'slip', *schmeißen* 'hurl', *schubsen* 'shove', *schwimmen* 'swim', *springen* 'jump', *steigen* 'ascend', *sich-stellen* 'stand.up', *stürmen* 'dash', *stürzen* 'tumble', *tauchen* 'plunge', *tragen* 'carry', *treten* 'step', *verfolgen* 'chase', *werfen* 'throw', *ziehen* 'pull'

Similar to English, the diversity of verbs of manner is impressive, and we find far more attention to manner of movement in the Germanic languages than in Romance, Semitic, and Turkic. This is also evident in the analysis of the novels, where English writers pay more attention to manner—whether writing originally in English or translating from Spanish (Slobin, 1996b).[9]

---

[8]The larger sample includes preschool and school-age children, but the child data have not been fully analyzed yet. A volume on the larger project is forthcoming.

[9]The novels mentioned in footnote 6—written in German, Dutch, Russian versus French, Japanese, Turkish—also show the expected difference with regard to descriptions of manner of movement. In fact, it may be the case that verb-framed languages have smaller lexicons of manner-of-movement verbs, in comparison with satellite-framed languages, where manner verbs fill a core syntactic function while supporting associated satellites which encode path of movement.

In addition, as in English, each of the verbs in (13) can be combined with a large range of path satellites, expressed as verb particles in German. For example, using a simple motion verb with no indication of manner—*kommen* 'come'—all of the following occur in the German texts:

(14) *an-kommen* 'arrive', *raus-kommen* 'exit', *rein-kommen* 'enter', *zu-kommen* 'arrive'.

On the other hand, we can pick a German path satellite and note its occurrences with a range of verbs of motion. For example, all of the following verbs of motion are combined with the particle *raus* 'out' in the frog stories:

(15) **raus-** *-fallen* 'fall out', *-fliegen* 'fly out', *-gehen* 'go out', *-gleiten* 'slide out', *-hüpfen* 'hop out', *-klettern* 'climb out', *-kommen* 'come out', *-laufen* 'run away', *-rennen* 'run out', *-schlüpfen* 'slip out', *-springen* 'jump out', *-steigen* 'climb out'.

As in the English sample, then, when all of these possibilities are taken into consideration, there are far more than 37 types of verbs of motion in the German texts.

Path satellites in German encode directionality, as in English. But, in addition, they encode deictic viewpoint by means of the particles *hin* 'thither' and *her* 'hither', which can combine with the directional particles. The range of possibilities is thus considerably greater than in English, allowing for expression of VIEWPOINT PERSPECTIVE along with directionality of motion. Compare, for example, the two descriptions of the dog's fall from the window shown in (16). In (16a) the narrator's eye is outside of the house, at ground level, as indicated by the satellite *her* 'hither', while in (16b) the satellite *hin* 'thither' traces a path downward from the viewpoint of the windowsill.

(16a) *Da fiel der Hund zur Erde **her**-aus.*
'There the dog fell **hither**-out to the ground.' [age 9]

(16b) *Als er sich auf die Fensterbank setzte und **hin**-unter-fiel, zerbrach das Glas in tausend Stücke.*
'When he got onto the windowsill and **thither**-down-fell, the glass broke into a thousand pieces.' [age 9]

German thus provides rich possibilities for detailed description of motion in a given direction in a given manner, and from a particular viewpoint. And a child learning this type of language must learn to attend to all of these features of motion. Table 1.9 shows the range of satellites that were combined with verbs of motion by the children in the German sample (from Bamberg, 1994, p. 221). The translations are only an approximation: Here the richness of German exceeds English. Note that even the 3-year-olds command a large number of verb-satellite

TABLE 1.9
Particles Used with Verbs of Motion by German Children
(Bamberg, 1994, p. 221)

Particle	3 yrs.	5 yrs.	9 yrs.
her 'hither'		+	
daher 'thence'		+	
hin 'thither'	+	+	+
dahin 'thither'			+
aus 'out'		+	+
heraus 'hither-out'			+
raus 'hither-out'	+	+	+
hinaus 'thither-out'		+	+
rein 'inward'	+	+	+
drin 'therein'	+		
runter 'down'	+	+	+
hinunter 'thither-down'			+
hinab 'downwards'			+
rauf 'thereon'	+	+	+
darauf 'thereon'	+		+
rüber 'over'	+		
darüber 'thereover'			+
an 'to'			+
dran 'thereon'	+	+	
ran 'thereon'		+	
nach 'after'			+
hinterher 'behind'	+	+	+
vor 'in-front'		+	
weg 'away'	+	+	+
davon 'away-from'		+	
lang 'along'			+
um 'around'		+	+
rum 'around'			+
hoch 'high-up'	+	+	+

combinations. The distinction between *hin* and *her* is present by age 5 (and probably earlier).

As in English, this range of motion-manner expressions has consequences for the particular rhetorical style that characterizes German frog stories (and German narrative generally). There is an elaboration of spatial movement and location, with attention to the three dimensions of direction, deictic viewpoint, and manner. Prepositional phrases combine freely with verb-satellite constructions to trace out complex trajectories. And there is far more attention to the dynamics of movement than to static descriptions of locations. It seems, then, that learning the available options for describing motion events in a particular language pushes the child to attend to particular features of such events. The lexicalization patterns lead not only to the development of a range of syntactic devices, but also to a sort of "thinking for speaking" (Slobin, 1991, 1996a) that is characteristic of the input language.

3.4. Cross- and Intra-Typological Consequences of Rhetorical Style

Research of this sort points to the development of an overall rhetorical style that emerges from the interplay of a number of interacting factors in each type of language. Consider again the importance of static locative descriptions in a verb-framed language like Spanish. Increased attention to stage-setting has a number of consequences for syntactic development. For example, stage-setting is background information, and in a competent narrative, such information should be presented in subordinate clauses. Note the use of relative clauses in the 9-year-old Spanish examples in (10): *donde había harta agua* 'where there was lots of water', *donde debajo había un río* 'where below there was a river'. The same is true of the 9-year-old Hebrew example in (12a): *macok she mitaxat haya bitsa* 'a cliff that had a swamp underneath'. Dasinger and Toupin (1994), analyzing the frog-stories, have found that Spanish and Hebrew speakers use relative clauses earlier, and for a wider range of functions, than speakers of the other languages in our sample. Relative clauses have a heavier functional load in narratives told in verb-framed languages— at least of the Romance and Semitic type. (Turkish is different, for reasons discussed below.) Here, again, we can seek a network of implicational universals.

Spanish has been described as a "topic-dominant" language, in contrast to English, which is "subject dominant." That is, in English the subject role tends to be assigned to the highest or most agentlike semantic argument of the verb, whether or not it is the discourse topic. Spanish tends to reserve grammatical subjects for established or given discourse topics (Bates & Devescovi, 1989, p. 238).[10] As a consequence, another function of relative clauses in Spanish is the introduction of protagonists in nonsubject position, as the following 5-year-old example:

(17a) *Salió un buho que le tiró al niño.*
'(There) came.out an owl that threw the boy.' [age 5]

Compare this to an English-speaking 5-year-old, describing the same scene:

(17b) *And then he goes up there, and then an owl comes out. And he falls.* [age 5]

The new protagonist, *an owl*, is introduced in subject position, and the following event is presented in an independent clause.

---

[10]This pragmatic typology is different from Demuth's syntactic typology discussed above. In the "topic-oriented" languages of her analysis, it is grammaticality that is at issue; *in situ* questions such as the equivalent of 'Who wants the food' are not licensed. Such questions are grammatical in a "topic-dominant" language like Spanish. What is at issue is the normal discourse function of grammatical subjects in declarative sentences.

Here we have a complex interweaving of typological factors that work together to influence syntactic acquisition: the discourse functions of relative clauses in a language that is both verb-framed and topic-dominant conspire to accelerate the acquisition of both the construction and its functional range.

The examples in (17) also implicate another typological dimension: the so-called "null subject parameter." Spanish is a "pro-drop language"—that is, the use of subject pronouns is optional, apparently because verbs are clearly marked for person and number. Sebastián and Slobin (1994) have suggested that relative clauses in Spanish play a discourse role comparable to the use of null pronouns in English in conjoined constructions. Consider various ways of reporting the situation in which the owl emerges and knocks the boy out of the tree. In both Spanish and English, it is possible to conjoin two clauses with 'and', as shown in (18). Note that the null subject in the second clause is obligatory in Spanish, whereas an explicit pronoun is used in the English version. (An explicit subject pronoun in the second clause in Spanish would have to be contrastive: an owl came out, and some other known participant threw the boy.)

(18a) *Salió un buho y le tiró al niño.*
'(There) came.out an owl and Ø threw the boy.'

(18b) *An owl came out and he threw the boy.*

Both versions in (18) present the emergence of the owl and his subsequent action as temporally separate events: the owl emerged, and then he did something. By contrast, the Spanish example in (17a), with a relative clause, is more tightly packaged. It presents the two events as phases of a single, larger event. Comparable event packaging is achieved in English by subject ellipsis in the second clause. Compare the two versions in (19), repeating (17a) as (19a), with its functional equivalent in English:

(19a) *Salió un buho que le tiró al niño.*
'(There) came.out an owl that threw the boy.'

(19b) *An owl came out and Ø threw the boy.*

The null pronoun is the default in Spanish, and so another construction, the relative clause, is called upon for tighter event packaging. In English, where an explicit subject is the default, an elliptical construction serves the same purpose.[11]

---

[11]Sebastián and Slobin (1994) discuss the situations in which an explicit subject pronoun is required in Spanish, noting that the acquisition task in a "pro-drop" language involves attention to such factors as reference maintenance versus shift, contrastive emphasis, and the like. They note: "It strikes us as anglocentric to refer to a language like Spanish as 'pro-DROP'. What the Spanish-speaking child has to learn is not when to drop a subject pronoun, but rather when to ADD one appropriately" (p. 281). . . . "We would conclude, accordingly, that the Spanish-speaking child has to learn a 'pro-add' language, whereas the English-speaking child has to learn when to stress or delete pronouns that are otherwise obligatory and unstressed" (p. 283).

Thus the functions of syntactic constructions—and the course of their acquisition—cannot be understood outside of a typological framework. And such a framework obliges us to examine the set of contrasting grammatical forms and their discourse roles in order to explain the course of acquisition of any particular form. Relative clauses in Spanish and English, though syntactically similar, have distinctly different roles, given a range of typologically defined and interacting discourse functions.

Following the intra-typological approach further, relative clauses should have similar functions and a similar course of acquisition in the other Romance and Semitic languages (with the exception, perhaps, of French, at least for the role that Sebastián and I have proposed for pro-drop, since French is not a pro-drop language). And, in fact, Bates and Devescovi (1989) have found some Italian uses of relative clauses that are like our Spanish data. Both languages avoid beginning a sentence with a new topic in sentence-initial position, which pulls for the use of some kind of introducer followed by a noun and a relative clause that predicates some activity of the new topic. For example, in describing a picture of a monkey eating a banana, Italian speakers prefer (20a), while English speakers most often provide something like (20b):

(20a) *C'è una scimmia che mangia una banana.*
　　　'There's a monkey that's eating a banana.'
(21b) *A monkey is eating a banana.*

Bates and Devescovi conclude with an important suggestion about rhetorical style, which they call a "descriptive habit" (p. 252):

> If a surface form serves a wider range of functions in one language . . . then it will be called into service more often. The more often it is used, the lower its threshold of activation. . . . The relative clause difference that we have documented here may reflect the joint effects of function and frequency, operating synergistically to create a "descriptive habit" in native speakers of Italian. The combined availability and reliability of the Italian relative clause also makes it an attractive linguistic object for small children, whether or not they have fully grasped the topic-marking function that justifies frequent use of this object in the adult language.

We can now add another typological factor, based on discourse function. Looking across genetic classifications, a major reason why relative clauses have similar discourse functions in Spanish and Hebrew is due to factors of INFOR-MATION FLOW, conditioned by word-order typology. Both Spanish and Hebrew are SVO languages. Turkish, however, is SOV, and, as a consequence, the role of relative clauses is rather different. Here, again, cross-typological research is important: although Turkish is verb-framed, like Romance and Semitic, it belongs to a different word-order typology. Relative clauses precede the noun they modify in an SOV language, as part of an overall cross-category harmony of construction types (along with postpositions, postverbal auxiliaries, etc., as discussed by Hawkins [1983]). As Dasinger and Toupin (1994, p. 488) point out, "the sequence MAIN CLAUSE–RELATIVE CLAUSE allows the speaker to FIRST introduce a new referent in nonsubject position and THEN assert a proposition about it." This natural information flow preserves topic-comment order. However, the Turkish order is RELATIVE CLAUSE–MAIN CLAUSE. Consider how strange it would be to say something like: 'A that-threw-him-down owl came out'. In other words, the order of information flow in an SOV language would require the narrator to predicate something of a protagonist that has not yet been introduced into the scene. As a consequence, relative clauses are not a frequent option in Turkish frog-stories. Here another kind of typological constraint—word order—impacts on the availability of a construction type for a particular discourse function.

4. CONCLUSION

These patterns of implicational relations—syntactic and pragmatic—underline the Leitmotif of this chapter: ONE CANNOT MAKE CLAIMS ABOUT THE ACQUISITION OR USE OF A GRAMMATICAL FORM WITHOUT SITUATING IT TYPOLOGICALLY, IN A NETWORK OF INTERACTIVE PSYCHOLINGUISTIC FACTORS. Some of these factors are a consequence of online information processing at the clause level, while others require attention to the organization of information in connected discourse. As a result, the acquisition and development of any linguistic form or construction must be considered in the light of its "functional load" within the language and speech community. A full theory of language acquisition and development will thus have to attend to three levels of analysis: UNIVERSALS and TYPES and FUNCTIONS. A tremendous amount of basic work remains to be done before we can approach such a theory.

REFERENCES

Aske, J. (1989). Path predicates in English and Spanish: A closer look. *Proceedings of the Fifteenth Annual Meeting of the Berkeley Linguistics Society*, 1–14.
Bamberg, M. (1994). Development of linguistic forms: German. In R. A. Berman & D. I. Slobin, *Relating events in narrative: A crosslinguistic developmental study* (pp. 189–238). Hillsdale, NJ: Lawrence Erlbaum Associates.
Bates, E., & Devescovi, A. (1989). Crosslinguistic studies of sentence production. In B. MacWhinney & E. Bates (Eds.), *The crosslinguistic study of sentence processing* (pp. 225–256). Cambridge: Cambridge University Press.
Berman, R. A. (1985). The acquisition of Hebrew. In D. I. Slobin (Ed.), *The crosslinguistic study of language acquisition: Vol. 1. The data* (pp. 255–371). Hillsdale, NJ: Lawrence Erlbaum Associates.
Berman, R. A. (1990). Acquiring an (S)VO language: Subjectless sentences in children's Hebrew. *Linguistics, 28,* 1135–1166.

Berman, R. A., & Slobin, D. I. (1994). *Relating events in narrative: A crosslinguistic developmental study*. Hillsdale, NJ: Lawrence Erlbaum Associates.

Bowerman, M. (1993). Typological perspectives on language acquisition: Do crosslinguistic patterns predict development? In E. V. Clark (Ed.), *The Proceedings of the Twenty-fifth Annual Child Language Research Forum* (pp. 7–15). Stanford, CA: Center for the Study of Language and Information.

Bowerman, M. (1996a). Learning how to structure space for language—a crosslinguistic perspective. In P. Bloom, A. M. Peterson, L. Nadel, & M. F. Garrett (Eds.), *Language and space* (pp. 385–436). Cambridge, MA: MIT Press.

Bowerman, M. (1996b). The origins of children's spatial semantic categories: Cognitive vs. linguistic determinants. In J. J. Gumperz & S. C. Levinson (Eds.), *Rethinking linguistic relativity* (pp. 145–176). Cambridge: Cambridge University Press.

Bowerman & Gentner. (in preparation).

Bowerman, M., & Pederson, E. (1992, December). *Crosslinguistic perspectives on topological spatial relationships*. Paper presented at Annual Meeting of the American Anthropological Association, San Francisco.

Choi, S., & Bowerman, M. (1991). Learning to express motion events in English and Korean: The influence of language-specific lexicalization patterns. *Cognition, 41,* 83–121.

Chomsky, N. (1981). *Lectures on government and binding: The Pisa lectures.* Dordrecht: Foris.

Chomsky, N. (1988). *Language and problems of knowledge: The Managua lectures.* Cambridge, MA: MIT Press.

Clark, E. V. (1985). The acquisition of Romance, with special attention to French. In D. I. Slobin (Ed.), *The crosslinguistic study of language acquisition: Vol. 1. The data* (pp. 687–782). Hillsdale, NJ: Lawrence Erlbaum Associates.

Comrie, B. (1981). *Language universals and linguistic typology.* Chicago: University of Chicago Press.

Croft, W. (1990). *Typology and universals.* Cambridge: Cambridge University Press.

Dasinger, L. (1995). *The development of discourse competence in Finnish children: The expression of definiteness.* Unpublished doctoral dissertation, University of California, Berkeley.

Dasinger, L. (1997). Issues in the acquisition of Estonian, Finnish, and Hungarian: A crosslinguistic comparison. In D. I. Slobin (Ed.), *The crosslinguistic study of language acquisition: Vol. 4.* Mahwah, NJ: Lawrence Erlbaum Associates.

Dasinger, L., & Toupin, C. (1994). The development of relative clause functions in narrative. In R. A. Berman & D. I. Slobin, *Relating events in narrative: A crosslinguistic developmental study* (pp. 457–514). Hillsdale, NJ: Lawrence Erlbaum Associates.

Demuth, K. (1990). Subject, topic and Sesotho passive. *Journal of Child Language, 17,* 67–84.

Demuth, K. (1992). The acquisition of Sesotho. In D. I. Slobin (Ed.), *The crosslinguistic study of language acquisition: Vol. 3* (pp. 557–638). Hillsdale, NJ: Lawrence Erlbaum Associates.

El'konin, D. B. (1958). *Razvitie reči v doškol'nom vozraste.* Moscow: Izd-vo Akademii Pedagogičeskix Nauk RSFSR. [pp. 34–61 trans. by D. I. Slobin: (1973). General course of development in the child of the grammatical structure of the Russian language (according to A. N. Gvozdev). In C. A. Ferguson & D. I. Slobin (Eds.), *Studies of child language development* (pp. 565–583). New York: Holt, Rinehart & Winston.]

Greenberg, J. H. (1963). Some universals of grammar with particular reference to the order of meaningful elements. In J. H. Greenberg (Ed.), *Universals of language* (pp. 58–90). Cambridge, MA: MIT Press.

Greenberg, J. H. (1966). *Language universals.* The Hague: Mouton.

Gvozdev, A. N. (1949). *Formirovanie u rebenka grammatičeskogo stroja russkogo jazyka.* Moscow: Izd-vo Akademii Pedagogičeskix Nauk RSFSR. [Reissued in Gvozdev, A. N. (1961). *Voprosy izučenija detskoj reči* (pp. 149–467). Moscow: Izd-vo Akademii Pedagogičeskix Nauk RSFSR.]

Hawkins, J. A. (1983). *Word order universals.* New York: Academic Press.

Hawkins, J. A. (1988). Explaining language universals. In J. A. Hawkins (Ed.), *Explaining language universals* (pp. 3–28). Oxford: Blackwell.

Hawkins, J. A. (1994). *A performance theory of order and constituency.* Cambridge: Cambridge University Press.

Hickmann, M. (1991). The development of discourse cohesion: Some functional and cross-linguistic issues. In G. Piéraut-Le-Bonniec & M. Dolitsky (Eds.), *Language bases . . . discourse bases: Some aspects of contemporary French-language psycholinguistics research* (pp. 157–185). Amsterdam: John Benjamins.

Hopper, P. J., & Traugott, E. C. (1993). *Grammaticalization.* Cambridge: Cambridge University Press.

Hyams, N. (1989). The null subject parameter in language acquisition. In O. Jaeggli & K. J. Safir (Eds.), *The null subject parameter* (pp. 215–238). Dordrecht, Netherlands: Kluwer.

Jaeggli, O., & Safir, K. (1989). The null subject parameter and parametric theory. In O. Jaeggli & K. J. Safir (Eds.), *The null subject parameter* (pp. 1–44). Dordrecht, Netherlands: Kluwer.

Johnston, J. R., & Slobin, D. I. (1979). The development of locative expressions in English, Italian, Serbo-Croatian and Turkish. *Journal of Child Language, 6,* 529–545.

Karmiloff-Smith, A. (1979). *A functional approach to child language.* Cambridge: Cambridge University Press.

Lust, B., Suñer, M., & Whitman, J. (Eds.). (1994). *Syntactic theory and first language acquisition: Cross-linguistic perspectives: Vol. 1. Heads, projections, and learnability; Vol. 2. Binding, dependencies, and learnability.* Hillsdale, NJ: Lawrence Erlbaum Associates.

Mayer, M. (1969). *Frog, where are you?* New York: Dial Press.

Mikeš M. (1967). Acquisition des catégoires grammaticales dans le langage de l'enfant. *Enfance, 20,* 289–298.

Mikeš, M., & Vlahović, P. (1966). Razvoj gramatičkih kategorija u dečjem govoru [Development of grammatical categories in child language]. *Prilozi proučavanju jezika, II.* Novi Sad, Yugoslavia.

Plunkett, K., & Strömqvist, S. (1992). The acquisition of Scandinavian languages. In D. I. Slobin (Ed.), *The crosslinguistic study of language acquisition: Vol. 3* (pp. 457–556). Hillsdale, NJ: Lawrence Erlbaum Associates.

Radulović, L. (1975). *Acquisition of language: Studies of Dubrovnik children.* Unpublished doctoral dissertation, University of California, Berkeley.

Roeper, T., & Williams, E. (Eds.). (1987). *Parameter setting.* Dordrecht: Reidel.

Sebastián, E., & Slobin, D. I. (1994). Development of linguistic forms: Spanish. In R. A. Berman & D. I. Slobin, *Relating events in narrative: A crosslinguistic developmental study* (pp. 239–284). Hillsdale, NJ: Lawrence Erlbaum Associates.

Slobin, D. I. (1966). The acquisition of Russian as a native language. In F. Smith & G. A. Miller (Eds.), *The genesis of language: A psycholinguistic approach* (pp. 129–148). Cambridge, MA: MIT Press.

Slobin, D. I. (1982). Universal and particular in the acquisition of language. In E. Wanner & L. R. Gleitman (Eds.), *Language acquisition: The state of the art* (pp. 128–172). Cambridge: Cambridge University Press.

Slobin, D. I. (1985a). Crosslinguistic evidence for the Language-Making Capacity. In D. I. Slobin (Ed.), *The crosslinguistic study of language acquisition: Vol. 2. Theoretical issues* (pp. 1157–1256). Hillsdale, NJ: Lawrence Erlbaum Associates.

Slobin, D. I. (1985b). Why study acquisition crosslinguistically? In D. I. Slobin (Ed.), *The crosslinguistic study of language acquisition: Vol. 1. The data* (pp. 3–24). Hillsdale, NJ: Lawrence Erlbaum Associates.

Slobin, D. I. (1991). Learning to think for speaking: Native language, cognition, and rhetorical style. *Pragmatics, 1,* 7–26.

Slobin, D. I. (1992). Introduction. In D. I. Slobin (Ed.), *The crosslinguistic study of language acquisition: Vol. 3* (pp. 1–13). Hillsdale, NJ: Lawrence Erlbaum Associates.

Slobin, D. I. (1996a). From 'thought and language' to 'thinking for speaking'. In J. J. Gumperz & S. C. Levinson (Eds.), *Rethinking linguistic relativity* (pp. 70–96). Cambridge: Cambridge University Press.

Slobin, D. I. (1996b). Two ways to travel: Verbs of motion in English and Spanish. In M. Shibatani & S. A. Thompson (Eds.), *Grammatical constructions: Their form and meaning* (pp. 195–219). Oxford: Oxford University Press.

Slobin, D. I. (this volume). The origins of grammaticizable notions: Beyond the individual mind. In D. I. Slobin (Ed.), *The crosslinguistic study of language acquisition: Vol. 5, Expanding the contexts.* Mahwah, NJ: Lawrence Erlbaum Associates.

Slobin, D. I., & Bocaz, A. (1988). Learning to talk about movement through time and space: The development of narrative abilities in Spanish and English. *Lenguas Modernas* (Santiago, Chile), *15*, 5–24.

Slobin, D. I., & Hoiting, N. (1994). Reference to movement in spoken and signed languages: Typological considerations. *Proceedings of the Twentieth Annual Meeting of the Berkeley Linguistics Society, 487*–505.

Smoczyńska, M. (1985). The acquisition of Polish. In D. I. Slobin (Ed.), *The crosslinguistic study of language acquisition: Vol. 1. The data* (pp. 595–686). Hillsdale, NJ: Lawrence Erlbaum Associates.

Strömqvist, S., Ragnarsdóttir, H., Engstrand, O., Jonsdóttir, H., Lanza, E., Leiwo, M., Nordqvist, Å., Peters, A., Plunkett, K., Richtoff, U., Simonsen, H. G., Toivainen, J., & Toivainen, K. (1995). The inter-Nordic study of language acquisition. *Nordic Journal of Linguistics, 18*, 3–29.

Suzman, S. (1985). Learning the passive in Zulu. *Papers and Reports on Child Language Development, 24*, 131–137.

Suzman, S. (1987). Passives and prototypes in Zulu children's speech. *African Studies, 46*, 241–254.

Suzman, S. (1991). *Language acquisition in Zulu.* Unpublished doctoral dissertation, University of the Witwatersrand, Johannesburg, South Africa.

Talmy, L. (1985). Lexicalization patterns: Semantic structure in lexical forms. In T. Shopen (Ed.), *Language typology and semantic description: Vol. 3. Grammatical categories and the lexicon* (pp. 36–149). Cambridge: Cambridge University Press.

Talmy, L. (1991). Path to realization: A typology of event conflation. *Proceedings of the Seventeenth Annual Meeting of the Berkeley Linguistics Society, 480*–519. Berkeley, CA: Berkeley Linguistics Society.

Traugott, E. C., & Heine, B. (Eds.). (1991). *Approaches to grammaticalization: Vol. 1. Focus on the theoretical and methodological issues; Vol. 2. Focus on types of grammatical markers.* Amsterdam: John Benjamins.

Van Valin, R. D., Jr. (1992). An overview of ergative phenomena and their implications for language acquisition. In D. I. Slobin (Ed.), *The crosslinguistic study of language acquisition: Vol. 3* (pp. 15–37). Hillsdale, NJ: Lawrence Erlbaum Associates.

Zakharova, A. V. (1958). Usvoenie doškol'nikami padežnyx form. *Doklady Akademii Pedagogičeskix Nauk RSFSR, 2*(3), 81–84. [Trans. by G. Slobin: (1973). Acquisition of forms of grammatical case by preschool children. In C. A. Ferguson & D. I. Slobin (Eds.), *Studies of child language development* (pp. 281–292). New York: Holt, Rinehart & Winston.]

NOVELS

English:

du Maurier, D. (1938). *Rebecca.* New York: The Modern Library.

Fowles, J. (1969). *The French lieutenant's woman.* Boston: Little, Brown & Co.

Lessing, D. (1952). *A proper marriage*. New York: New American Library.
Michener, J. A. (1978). *Chesapeake*. New York: Fawcett Crest (Random House, Inc.).

Spanish:

Allende, I. (1982). *La casa de los espíritus* [The house of the spirits]. Barcelona: Plaza & Janes, S.A.
Donoso, J. (1983). *Coronación* [Coronation]. Barcelona: Editorial Seix Barral, S.A. (Biblioteca de Bolsillo).
García Márquez, G. (1967/1982). *Cien años de soledad* [One hundred years of solitude]. Madrid: Espasa-Calpe, S.A.
Sabato, E. (1988). *El túnel* [The tunnel]. Barcelona: Editorial Seix Barral, S.A. (Biblioteca de Bolsillo).
Vargas Llosa, M. (1977). *La tía Julia y el escribidor* [Aunt Julia and the script-writer]. Barcelona: Editorial Seix Barral, S.A. (Biblioteca de Bolsillo).

2

Language-Specific Input and Early Semantic Development: Evidence From Children Learning Korean

Soonja Choi
San Diego State University

1. INTRODUCTION

Every normal child learns the language spoken around him/her, whether English, Turkish, or Korean. One way to look at this phenomenon is to argue that children have an innate capacity to learn the grammar of the human language. This approach would lead the researcher to investigate grammatical properties that are common to all languages. Another way to approach this phenomenon, however, is to point out that children acquire the specific grammar of the language that is spoken to them, and not of any other language. This chapter is about how the latter happens: How do children acquire the specific language that they are exposed to?

In "Cognitive Prerequisites: The Evidence From Children Learning English" (Volume 2 in this series of books on crosslinguistic studies of language acquisition), Johnston (1985) reviews data on the acquisition of several semantic aspects in English and concludes that children's initial language development is guided by their cognitive development. For example, children rely on nonverbal strategies to interpret unfamiliar linguistic input (e.g., interpreting the word *less* as the concept of *more*); they also acquire members of some form classes (e.g., spatial morphemes) in a predictable order (e.g., *in/on* before *under*), and they often systematically underextend words (Halpern, Corrigan, & Aviezer, 1981; Johnston, 1984) or overextend them (Clark, 1973) according to nonlinguistic concepts or perceptual features. Thus, Johnston concludes: "The observations suggested the priority and guiding influence of nonverbal thought. . . . Taken together, these lines of evidence provide a firm basis for the theoretical claim that nonverbal knowledge guides and constrains some aspects of language growth" (1985, p. 992). Johnston cautions, however, that the English evidence for conceptual prerequisites invites replication with crosslinguistic data. She also suggests that cognitive prerequisites may operate for only some aspects of language. In particular, Johnston proposes that verbs may be a class of words whose meanings may emerge WITH language, and she suggests that research on verb acquisition may shed light on the relation between language and cognition. Indeed, to begin to sort out the relation between linguistic input and cognitive development, crosslinguistic studies are needed.

Many crosslinguistic studies have been done during the last two decades, and we now know a lot more about how children learn languages other than English. But only a few studies have compared different languages in a systematic way with the goal of sorting out the relation between language and cognition (e.g., Johnston & Slobin, 1979; Slobin, 1982). Until very recently, claims about the relation between language and cognition have still been based mostly on analyses of English acquisition.

In this chapter, I present my research on the acquisition of various semantic aspects of Korean at an early period of language acquisition. I have investigated how Korean children acquire language-specific forms and functions in particular semantic domains (e.g., spatial terms, modality), and compared the Korean acquisition patterns to those of children learning other languages (most typically with English). A larger goal of the crosslinguistic comparisons is to understand the extent to which language-specific input on the one hand, and cognitive development on the other, influence children's early semantic development.

After a brief overview of theories on the relation between language and cognition, I will present my previous findings along with some new data. The chapter will focus on the following questions: (1) What kinds of similarities and differences are there in early semantic development in English and Korean? (2) In what semantic domains do we see language-specificity and how early does it begin? (3) To what extent do language-specific input and cognitive development influence semantic development? In examining the nature of input, I will analyze both language-specific grammatical features and caregiver's speech to children.

2. THEORIES ON THE RELATION BETWEEN LANGUAGE AND COGNITION

Several hypotheses have been proposed about the relations between linguistic and cognitive development. The dominant one over the last two decades has been the cognitive prerequisite view, which was already mentioned in the introduction. This view has been largely influenced by Piaget's work. According to Piaget (1962), children develop a variety of concepts related to objects and events from infancy and these nonlinguistic cognitive concepts are prerequisite to linguistic development. For example, children begin to talk when they have developed symbolic representation of objects, for example, the concept of object-permanence (see also Bates, 1979). Also, children produce temporal and causal expressions when they have an understanding of time and causality. In this view, the course of conceptual development is assumed to be universal. For example, all children develop concepts of space and location before time, and consequently they talk about space and location before time. This view suggests, then, that conceptual development precedes and is mapped onto semantic development.

A second, opposing hypothesis is the Whorfian view. Although Whorf himself did not investigate the relationship between language and cognition in children, his view on adult language has had significant implications for language acquisition. In his work on the semantic structure of American Indian languages, Whorf (1956) proposed that languages differ significantly in the way they categorize the world. Given the magnitude of crosslinguistic semantic differences, he suggested that language-specific semantic organization affects the way we perceive and categorize the world. In this view, the role of nonlinguistic conceptual development would play a much smaller role than the influence of linguistic input on children's semantic development.

These two views suggest a rather unidirectional perspective regarding the relation between language and cognition. But perhaps semantic and conceptual development interact in a bidirectional and complex way. On the basis of experimental data, Gopnik and Meltzoff (1986b, 1996) show that at around 18 months, children begin to use words that encode concepts that they are actively exploring and trying to understand. For example, as children become interested in solving relatively difficult problems related to object permanence (e.g., serial invisible displacement tasks), they begin to produce words denoting disappearance, such as *gone*. Also, children produce words like *uh-oh* or *there* as they try to solve means-ends problems (see Section 3.1.1.5 below). On the other hand, children's acquisition of the words *gone* or *there* enhances further understanding of related cognitive concepts. Thus, argue Gopnik and Meltzoff, semantic and conceptual development influence each other in a bidirectional way.

In the 1970s and in the early 1980s, several studies provided support for the Piagetian view (e.g., Slobin, 1973, 1985). Although many studies that served as evidence for the cognitive prerequisite view were on English (see Johnston, 1985, for a review), Slobin's work on the crosslinguistic development of functors (Slobin, 1973, 1985) and spatial terms (Johnston & Slobin, 1979; Slobin, 1982) have been very influential in supporting the view. As noted earlier, Johnston and Slobin (1979) found that children learning different languages acquire spatial terms in a consistent order. This order is hypothesized to reflect primarily the sequence of the emergence of nonlinguistic spatial concepts. Whereas the order of acquisition is consistent, the timing of the acquisition is different across languages. For example, children learning Turkish produce functors for spatial location at a much earlier age than children learning Serbo-Croatian. Slobin (1982) explains this by positing that although the cognitive prerequisites for such learning are in place at an early age, the linguistic complexity of the Serbo-Croatian system causes a gap between the cognitive and linguistic achievements. Slobin (1982) proposed the metaphor of waiting room in which cognitive achievements must wait for linguistic ones. That is, whereas cognitive development is universal, the timing of the acquisition of morphemes may differ from one language to another, depending on the linguistic complexity.

More recently, based on acquisition data of a number of languages (Volume 2 in this series of books on crosslinguistics studies of language acquisition), Slobin (1985) has proposed the Language Making Capacity (LMC), which consists of particular types of cognitive capacity and strategies that guide the young child in what to look for in the semantic mapping between grammatical elements and a particular meaning. He argues that children, guided by LMC, pay attention to particular types of events and notions, and acquire the grammatical forms that encode them. For example, at an early stage of language acquisition, children, regardless of what language they are learning, focus on expressing "Manipulative Activity Scenes"—caused motions that result in a change of state. Within the set of salient scenes, children also have a privileged set of cognitive notions that are readily mapped onto grammaticized forms (i.e., functors) if the language clearly marks them (e.g., agent, patient, path, and location in the Manipulative Activity Scenes). The mapping between a universal set of cognitive notions and the grammaticized forms corresponding to those notions make up what Slobin (1985) calls "Basic Child Grammar" at the initial stage of language development. According to Slobin, then, children start from a universal conceptual starting point, and their initial language is guided by universally shared cognitive concepts. In this view, semantic notions that are specific only to a particular language would be acquired later than universally shared ones, because children would need much more linguistic input to develop language-specific semantic notions than the universal ones:

> When functors are first acquired, they seem to map more readily onto a universal set of basic notions than onto the particular categories of the parental language. Later in development, of course, the language-specific uses of particular functors will train the child to conceive of grammaticizable notions in conformity with the speech community . . . At first, however . . . children discover principles of grammatical marking according to their own categories—categories that are not yet tuned to the distinctions that are grammaticized in the parental language. (Slobin, 1985, p. 1174)

Slobin also suggests, however, that even though children may be initially guided by nonlinguistic concepts, "eventually language-specific patterns may well have a Whorfian effect on the organization of Semantic Space" (1985, p. 1172). Thus, Slobin allows for conceptual development to be molded by language-specific semantic structure, but only after the basic set of universal nonlinguistic concepts have provided the initial semantic structure.

In his more recent work on children's narratives, Slobin found that language-specificity may begin quite early. Berman and Slobin (1987) found that in narratives, 3-year-olds learning different languages (e.g., English, German, Hebrew, and Spanish) already show their sensitivity to language-specific aspects of grammar (e.g., tense/aspect features). Their studies showed that by age 3, the syntactic patterns used by English- and German-speaking children to describe spatial events, like falling down or jumping out, differed strikingly from those used by Spanish- and Hebrew-speaking children. Three-year-olds' narratives also reflect language-specific configurations about which element in the event (e.g., Manner or Path of Motion) should be consistently encoded onto a particular lexical class (e.g., VERB or PARTICLE).

The view that children actually attend to language-specific syntactic and semantic properties from early on—much earlier than the cognitivists claim—and therefore that children have a flexible starting point, has been emphasized by Bowerman (1980, 1985, 1989, 1995) for a number of years. She argues that language-specific aspects of grammar and lexicon influence children's semantic development virtually from the BEGINNING of language development. Bowerman draws her argument by looking at both adult and child grammars across languages. Pointing out significant differences in syntactic and semantic categorizations across languages, Bowerman (1989, 1995) analyzes children's data in a careful and detailed manner relating them to the corresponding adult systems. And, her analyses indeed reveal interesting and significant differences in children's grammars across languages rather than uniformity—differences that reflect differences in the adult languages.

For example, Bowerman (1985) points out that studies of children learning nominative-accusative languages (e.g., English) and those learning ergative languages (e.g., Samoan) show evidence for language-specificity from an early stage. English-speaking children readily use "actor-action" combinations for both actors that initiate actions on objects (a subset of transitive subjects; e.g., *Kendall break*) and actors that initiate self-movement (a subset of intransitive subjects; e.g., *Mommy come*). However, this is not the case for children learning Samoan; they use a particular construction for agents of caused motion that is not extended to subjects of self-movement. These differences can be explained by positing that children pay attention to language-specific correlations of syntactic patterns with semantic distinctions. Analyses of children's early and late errors show that their semantic categories are also linguistically motivated from early on. Bowerman thus concludes that "children are prepared from the beginning to accept linguistic guidance as to which distinctions they should rely on in organizing particular domains of meanings" (1985, p. 1284), and that the structure of initial semantic space is MORE FLEXIBLE than cognitivists would like to claim.

There is a growing body of evidence that by age 3 or 4, children do home in on language-specific principles of spatial categorization. For example, Bavin (1990) showed that 4-year-old children learning Warlpiri, an Australian language, differ from children learning English in the meanings they associate with spatial terms. Also, as noted earlier, Slobin and Berman (1987) found language-specific patterns in the narratives of 3-year-olds. But, by age 3 or 4, children have already mastered the basic structure of the language they are learning. Thus, these studies do not tell us much about the relative contribution of language-specific input and nonlinguistic cognitive development at the beginning of language development. In other words, we still do not know whether language specificity is present from the outset, or emerges only gradually with divergence from a shared starting point. To answer this question, we need to examine children's language from the earliest period possible, particularly because conceptual development in children begins before their language begins. It is also necessary to examine languages that are structurally and semantically quite different from one another. So comparisons between English and Korean, two languages that are quite different, are likely to give us some insight into the issue.

My research focuses on morphological and semantic development related to the verb phrase in Korean (from now on, I will use the word VERBS to mean both verbs and verb phrases). Although verbs are significant in a number of ways for crosslinguistic investigations, they have until very recently received much less attention than nouns in research on the early lexicon (Tomasello, 1992; Tomasello

& Merriman, 1995). One reason why nouns are investigated more than verbs is that for many children (again, most studies have been on English), nouns are acquired first among early words. Furthermore, many semantic categories of nouns are "natural" categories and refer to concrete objects that can be readily identified in terms of their perceptual features (Gentner, 1982). There is also more crosslinguistic consistency in nouns than verbs. In all languages, nouns have a hierarchical structure, for example, superordinate and basic-level categories. And basic-level nouns (e.g., *cat, ball*) often refer to the whole object and not to its parts (Markman, 1990). In contrast, semantic categories of verbs (e.g., *run* vs. *walk*) are not coherently packaged categories that are merely based on what we holistically perceive in an event (Gentner, 1982). For example, verbs like *run* and *walk* contrast only in one component of the movements referred to, that is Manner of Motion. Furthermore, meaning components of verbs are crosslinguistically more diverse and more complex than nouns, and languages differ in the kinds of aspect (of an event) they select as semantically relevant (see Section 3.2 for some concrete examples comparing English and Korean). Johnston makes an insightful remark in this regard. She suggests that nouns and verbs may involve different types of relations between language and cognition. She notes that whereas nouns are based on the notion of similarity, which is well established prelinguistically (see also Mandler, 1992, for a discussion of infants' ability in perceptual analysis), verb probably are not. "Verb meanings seem to entail conceptual notions beyond mere similarity, notions which may or may not be available to the child just learning to speak" (Johnston, 1985, p. 994).

In this chapter, I will be concerned with differences in grammatical features of verbs in Korean and English (i.e., verbs, prepositions/particles, locative case markers, and verb suffixes). Korean and English differ in their semantic categorization of verbs in interesting ways. They also differ in the syntactic and morphological features of verb phrases. Thus, data on the acquisition of verbs in Korean may shed some light on the relation between language-specific input and semantic development during the early stages of language development.

In the following, each section will focus on a particular aspect of Korean grammar and relevant acquisition data will be presented. In Section 3.1, I present longitudinal data showing that verbs are acquired very early in Korean. In Section 3.2, I discuss the syntax and semantics of motion verbs in particular; and in Section 3.3, I discuss the development of locative case markers that categorize nouns and verbs into distinct types. Finally, in Section 3.4, I examine the early acquisition of sentence-ending modal suffixes, and illustrate how caregiver-child interaction plays an important role. The Korean data will be compared to acquisition data in English whenever it is relevant (in Sections 3.1 and 3.2 in particular). Overall, the Korean data I present here suggest strongly that, from the earliest stages of language acquisition, language-specific input influences children's syntactic and semantic development, and that it interacts with children's general cognitive development in a complex bidirectional way.

3. THE DATA

3.1. Early Acquisition of Verbs in Korean

Several researchers have put forth a view that children acquire nouns before acquiring verbs and that nouns form the dominant lexical category at the earliest stages of language development. This view comes from two types of data that have primarily been in English. First, several researchers have reported the phenomenon called the "naming explosion" or "vocabulary spurt" (Nelson, 1973; Halliday, 1975; McShane, 1980), a rapid growth of nouns in a short period of time. For example, Nelson (1973) found that at around 1;6, when children rapidly increase their productive vocabulary, most of these words are nouns. Similar observations were made by Halliday (1975) and McShane (1980) in their detailed case studies. Goldfield and Reznick (1990) showed that in children who showed a vocabulary spurt, the majority of the new vocabulary items were nouns. The second type of evidence is that nouns are found to be predominant in children's early lexicons. In a crosslinguistic survey, Gentner (1982) found that between 1;0 and 2;6, nouns make up 50%–85% (average 66%) of children's early lexicons, whereas verbs/predicates only make up 0%–35% (average 22%). In a large scale study of early lexical development in English which used caregivers' reports on a standardized vocabulary checklist as database, Bates et al. (1994) found that nouns increase at a higher rate than predicates during the acquisition of the first 100 words. More specifically, they found that the predicates, consisting mostly of closed class particles, are rare at the beginning of the one-word period, and gradually grow during the vocabulary acquisition of 100 to 400 words. Such differences found in developmental patterns between nouns and verbs, and mor-pho-semantic differences that exist in the two classes of words have led several researchers to posit a universal pattern of nouns being acquired before verbs. These researchers explain the phenomena by equipping young children with specific innate cognitive and/or perceptual constraints. For example, according to Gentner (1982), concrete nouns universally form natural categories in that there is a perceptually transparent relation between objects and the nouns that label them. CONCRETE NOUNS usually refer to objects which children have already isolated perceptually from their surroundings. Therefore, children do not have to rely much on language-specific input to acquire the semantic categories of noun. Gentner observes that this is not the case for verbs. Verbs generally denote activity and change of location or state, and languages differ in their selection of the features of a particular action or state to include in verb meanings. For example, English expresses change of location (i.e., Motion) together with Man-ner of motion and it is consistently encoded in the main verb (e.g., *The child walked/ran/crawled into the room*), whereas in Spanish, Motion is conflated consistently with the Path in the main verb (e.g., *El niño entró al cuarto caminando/corriendo/gateando* 'The child entered the room walking/running/

crawling') (see also Section 3.2.1 below). According to Gentner (1982), because verb semantics are language-specific, children must have some language input to acquire their meanings, and therefore require more time to learn them.

Markman (1990) has also proposed that there are preexisting and possible innate constraints which guide children's decisions about which meanings to encode. One such constraint, called the WHOLE OBJECT CONSTRAINT, leads children to assume initially that all words refer to objects, and furthermore that they refer to a whole object and not to any of its parts. Children must override this initial constraint in order to acquire verbs and other words that encode actions and relations; so these words are acquired later.

Before we accept the noun primacy phenomenon as universal and accept these constraints as innate, however, we need to look at the English data more closely and also at crosslinguistic data. First, recent studies that carefully analyzed the meaning of early nouns in English-speaking children's lexicons have shown that concrete object nouns (i.e., basic-level object nouns) occupy a smaller proportion in the children's lexicons than previously thought (Bloom, Tinker, & Margulis, 1993; Nelson, Hampson, & Kessler Shaw, 1993). Second, there is evidence that English-speaking children use a set of non-nominal words from a very early stage of their development, for example, *no, more, uh-oh, there, up,* and *down.* Many of these words encode relational concepts such as non-existence, disappearance, success, failure, and location (Bloom, 1973; Gopnik, 1982, 1988; Tomasello, 1992). Although these non-nominal words are not as numerous in types as nouns, they are frequently and consistently used by children from early on (i.e., the type-token ratio is higher for non-nominal words than for nouns), and in some cases non-nominal words appear before nouns in children's lexicons (Gopnik, 1988). Thus, the observation that English-speaking children produce only a limited number of non-nominal words does not necessarily lead to the conclusion that in general children acquire predicates later than nouns.

It is true, however, that in English most of early-acquired, non-nominal words are not verbs, but belong to closed-class categories such as particles (e.g., *up, down*), adverbs (e.g., *there*), or interjections (e.g., *uh-oh*). Indeed, when we restrict our definition of verbs to a morphosyntactic one, we find that English-speaking children produce them far less than nouns. But there is reason to believe that the relatively late onset of verb learning in English may be at least in part the result of its language-specific input. For example, analysis of the degree of perceptual saliency of nouns and verbs in utterance structure shows that nouns have higher perceptual saliency than verbs in English. More specifically, nouns in English occur at the beginning or the end of the sentence, whereas verbs occupy the middle position. Furthermore, subject and object noun phrases are grammatically obligatory (except for imperative sentences where the subject NP is deleted). Thus, children learning English hear an abundance of noun phrases in a salient position. Therefore, to see whether the acquisition of nouns is universally earlier than verbs, it is necessary to examine languages which grammatically treat verbs differently from English. Korean is one such language. In Korean, which is an SOV language, verbs, rather than nouns, occupy the ends of sentences. Also, a verb (or a verb phrase) often occurs alone as a complete clause, and subject and object noun phrases are often deleted in a clause when they are given information in discourse (Clancy, 1994).

3.1.1. *Longitudinal Study of Lexical Development in Korean*

In a longitudinal study, I followed the lexical development of nine monolingual Korean-speaking children from 1;2 to 1;10 (five girls and four boys).[1] The original goal of the data collection was to investigate the relation between early lexical and cognitive developments with the methodology used by Gopnik and Meltzoff (1986b). At the beginning of the study, the total number of words that each child produced was less than ten (5.2 on average). The children were visited in their homes regularly, about once every 3 to 4 weeks (average interval = 26.3 days). For cognitive measures, tests assessing the child's level of object-permanence, means–ends skill, and categorization were administered. For linguistic measures, we used two types of methods. First, the mother reported her child's new words since the last recording session by filling out a standardized Early Language Questionnaire (see Gopnik & Meltzoff, 1986b; Gopnik, 1988; Gopnik & Choi, 1990), and through an interview concerning the new words. The language questionnaire asks (1) what the child says in specific contexts which may elicit the use of relational words or verbs (e.g., when the child wants something; when he/she finishes a meal); (2) what words the child uses to name objects and people; and (3) all other words that the child produced during the period since the last report. For all the words reported in the questionnaire, the parent was asked to provide different contexts (as many as three) in which the child produced each word. The mother's description of the contexts was used to identify the child's meaning (or the referent) of the word, and also to evaluate the productivity of the new word.

After the interview with the mother, we also recorded about 15 minutes of the child's spontaneous speech during free play with the investigator and the mother. During the free play, the child often spontaneously produced the new words that the mother had reported in the questionnaire. This combination of questionnaire and spontaneous speech during free play was designed to elicit as much accurate information about the child's early language as possible. For our

---

[1]All the data reported here come from Korean families living in Southern California. Five of the nine children were first-born, and the remaining four children were the second child of the family. All parents of the subjects were Korean speakers and they only spoke Korean to their children. The older siblings of the latter four children also spoke Korean to the children. The parents' social contacts (largely through Korean churches they go to) are restricted to Korean families. Most of the Korean parents graduated from college and are in lower-to-mid middle class.

purposes, this type of data collection would work better than using a predefined checklist such as the MacArthur Communicative Development Inventories (MCDI) (see Dale, Bates, Reznick, & Morisset, 1989). Furthermore, an inventory specifically designed for English (e.g., MCDI) is not appropriate for a language such as Korean. As our semantic analysis of early words in the next sections will make it clear, there are no straightforward English translations for the early verbs in Korean.[2] (See Tardif, 1996, for a discussion of methods of data collection for crosslinguistic studies of lexical development.)

Our criterion for a new word was that the child had been observed by the mother or the investigator or both to use a given word spontaneously on more than three different occasions. In determining whether a word was a noun or a verb, we used both semantic and morphosyntactic criteria. For nouns, the word must refer to an object (e.g., *dog, milk*) or a person (e.g., *mommy, daddy*) (cf. Gentner, 1982). However, we excluded pronouns and onomatopoeic words (e.g., *twit-twit*) from the noun category. For verbs, the semantic criterion was that the meaning of the verb refers to action, state, or change of state, and that it approximates adult meaning of the verb. We accepted both over- and under-extended uses of words as long as they made sense. For example, several children said *mwul* 'water' for different kinds of liquid (e.g., water, milk, juice), or *ppay* 'take something off of/out from a tight-fitting relation' for taking Legos apart as well as taking their T-shirt off. (For taking a T-shirt off, an adult Korean speaker would use a particular verb for taking clothes off, i.e., *pesta* [cf. Section 3.2.2].) In these cases, *mwul* and *ppay* were coded as noun and verb respectively. Our morphological criterion for a verb was that it have a sentence-ending (SE) mood and modality inflectional suffix. (See Section 3.4 on the development of SE suffixes in Korean.) A SE INFLECTIONAL SUFFIX is an obligatory element of the predicate in Korean (H. B. Lee, 1989). This morphological criterion includes not only action verbs (e.g., *mekta* 'eat') but also stative/adjectival verbs (e.g., *ipputa* 'be pretty'). (For more detailed description of our methodology, see Choi & Gopnik, 1995.)

Our Korean data show two patterns that have not been reported for development in English:

1. We examined whether the Korean children show patterns of vocabulary spurts in the noun and verb categories, that is, acquisition of ten new nouns or verbs during the 3- to 4-week interval between sessions. Of the nine children we studied, seven children showed verb spurts as well as noun spurts. Furthermore, six of the seven children showed a verb spurt BEFORE their first noun spurt. Also, of the seven children who showed a verb spurt, three children had their first verb

---

[2]However, Au, Dapretto, and Song (1994) used a revised version of MCDI for their investigation of early lexical development in Korean. Differences in results between our study and the Au et al. study may be at least in part due to differences in the methods used for data collection.

spurt before they had acquired 50 words. For the other four children, the first verb spurt occurred between the acquisition of 50 and 80 words. This is comparable to the occurrence of the noun spurt in English, which has also been observed to occur at around the 50-word mark (Nelson, 1973; Goldfield & Reznick, 1990).

2. The proportion of verbs in these children's lexicons was as significant as that of nouns throughout the developmental period observed. That is, verbs and nouns were developed in parallel and at the same time.

Table 2.1a shows the proportions of nouns and verbs at the 50-word vocabulary mark (mean age 1;7.24) in Korean (i.e., the session in which the child's cumulative vocabulary size is closest to 50 words). Overall, the table shows that from an early stage of lexical development, verbs are acquired on a par with nouns in Korean. (For the last two children, SA and YN, the study period ended at their first noun spurt before a verb spurt could be observed. We do not know whether or when these children would have developed a verb spurt.) In fact, at the time of the verb spurt, four children had a higher percentage of verbs than that of nouns in their lexicon. Table 2.1b shows the proportion of nouns and verbs over time in five children whose lexical development continued to be followed for several months after their first vocabulary spurts. The proportions of nouns and verbs in these five children are remarkably consistent throughout the developmental period, with nouns consistently comprising between 38% and 45% of the lexicon and verbs between 31% and 41%.

TABLE 2.1a
KOREAN: Percentages of Nouns and Verbs in
Children's First 50 Words (Mean Age: 1;7.24)[a,b]

Child	Nouns %	Verbs %	Adjs./Advs. %	Total Number of Word Types
1 AN	39	41	9	56
2 JY	41	31	17	58
3 JS	38	32	9	47
4 MK	40	36	10	58
5 SN	44	36	8	50
6 TJ	45	31	4	49
7 YJ	33	44	8	48
8 SA	53	12	9	34[c]
9 YN	58	16	9	57
Average	44	31	9	51

[a]The verb category includes stative/adjectival verbs.

[b]The session in which the child's cumulative vocabulary size is closest to 50 words.

[c]SA was observed until her first noun spurt which occurred before she acquired 50 words.

TABLE 2.1b
KOREAN: Percentages of Cumulative Nouns and Verbs of Five
Children Who Were Observed Four or More Sessions After Their
First Noun Spurt (Mean Age at the End of Study: 1;11.28)[a]

Child	Nouns %	Verbs %	Adjs./Advs. %	Total Number of Word Types
3 JS	50	31	5	189
4 MK	41	39	9	143
5 SN	41	39	8	124
6 TJ	41	41	6	178
7 YJ	42	41	7	121
Average	43	38	7	151

[a]The verb category includes stative/adjectival verbs.

Neither early verb spurts of this sort nor the equally predominant statuses of nouns and verbs have been reported in the English-speaking literature. In Choi and Gopnik (1995), we compared the Korean data with the data previously collected from eight English-speaking children ages 1;3 to 1;9, using the same method (Gopnik & Meltzoff, 1986b; Gopnik, 1988). We found that the number of verbs acquired by English-speaking children was significantly lower than Korean children. Even with a broad definition of verbs that includes all relational words (see below), only one of the English-speaking children showed a verb spurt in addition to the noun spurt. She did so at a relatively late age, 1;8.14, which was 3 months after her noun spurt.

Table 2.2a shows the proportions of nouns and verbs in English-speaking children at the 50-word mark. Comparison between Tables 2.1a and 2.2a shows that only 6% of the English-speakers' words were verbs on average, in contrast

TABLE 2.2a
ENGLISH: Percentages of Nouns and Verbs in
Children's First 50 Words (Mean Age: 1;6.22)

Child	Nouns %	Verbs %	Particles/ Adjs./Advs. %	Total Number of Word Types
1 Stephanie	62	4	9	45
2 Natalie	61	5	18	44
3 Ali	59	11	11	56
4 Caitlin	66	9	16	55
5 Melissa	71	6	10	51
6 Michael	60	6	13	48
7 Tama	77	4	12	69
8 Blair	60	6	17	53
Average	65	6	13	53

TABLE 2.2b
ENGLISH: Percentages of Nouns and Verbs
at the End of the Study (Mean Age: 1;8.5)

Child	Nouns %	Verbs %	Particles/ Adjs./Advs. %	Total Number of Word Types
1 Stephanie	66	5	9	65
2 Natalie	67	3	16	69
3 Ali	59	14	11	65
4 Caitlin	68	11	14	99
5 Melissa	55	24	14	138
6 Michael	70	5	11	81
7 Tama	71	6	17	89
8 Blair	60	6	17	53
Average	64	11	13	82

to an average of 31% of the Korean-speakers' vocabulary. We also calculated the proportion of predicates in English that include not only verbs but also adjectives, adverbs, and particles since these encode relational concepts (e.g., *It's cold, It's there, The lights are on*), and compared it with the proportion of verbs in Korean children's lexicons. Even with this broader criterion, the English-speakers used fewer predicates (i.e., verbs plus particles, adjectives, and adverbs) than the Korean-speakers: only 19% on average at the 50-word mark, compared to 40% on average for the Korean-speakers. In contrast, the English-speakers used a greater proportion of nouns than the Korean-speakers. At the 50-word mark, on average, 44% of the Korean vocabularies—less than half—were nouns, in contrast to 65% of the English-speakers' vocabularies. These differences are all statistically significant (Choi & Gopnik, 1995). Because there is a difference in mean age at which the two groups of children acquired 50 words (1;7.24 for Korean compared to 1;6.22 for English), we also measured the proportions of nouns at a later period in English-speaking children. This is shown in Table 2.2b. At the mean age of 1;8.4, comparable to the age when the Korean children acquired 50 words (Table 2.1a), English-speaking children showed the same pattern as that shown at their 50-word mark.

In sum, our study shows that verbs appear in the lexicon of Korean children in parallel with nouns from the one-word stage. Interestingly, early acquisition of verbs has recently been reported for young Mandarin-speaking children (Tardif, 1996). Tardif found that, like the Korean children in our data, Mandarin-speaking children develop nouns and verbs in parallel, and that they show neither noun nor verb bias. After considering several possibilities, Tardif concludes that the early acquisition of verbs in Mandarin Chinese is the result of a variety of language-specific and sociocultural input factors. Before we discuss the factors that influence such early acquisition of verbs, however, I would like to examine the morphological and semantic properties of the early verbs in Korean.

3.1.1.1. *Morphological Unity of Verbs.*   The Korean data show that verbs form a morphological category that is distinct from nouns. This feature is particularly interesting because Maratsos (1991) has suggested that whereas the core of the noun category involves semantic coherence (i.e., reference to entity), that of verbs involves morphological unity (tense, aspect, and negative markers). In my Korean data, four of the seven children who had a verb spurt showed clear productivity in verb morphology during or before their first verb spurt, that is, they used different sentence-ending (SE) modal suffixes on the same verb, inflecting it appropriately for requests, questions, statements, and in some cases, tenses, as shown below (also see Section 3.4). Also, two children used different negative morphemes preceding the same verb at this stage.

Onset of productive uses of verb inflections: examples.

Sentence-ending suffixes (VS = verb spurt session)

TJ 1;8.22 (VS):

(1) (Bringing toys to Mother)
    mantul-ca.   'Let's make (something).'
    make-SE (cohortative)

(2) (After making a car with bristle-blocks, TJ asks M)
    mantul-ess-ci?   '(I) made (it), right?'
    make-PAST-SE (shared information)

SN 1;6.26 (VS):

(3) (After putting a Lego piece on another)
    tway-ss-ta.   'Done'
    become-PAST-SE (new information)

(4) (SN put all the objects on the investigator's hand as requested. SN looking at the Inv.)
    tway-ss-e?   'Done?'
    become-PAST-SE (question)

Negative particles

JS 1;3.8 (VS):

(5) (Giving M a piece of apple)
    mek-e.[3]   'Eat'
    eat-SE (request)

(6) (M give Yoplait to JS, but JS doesn't want it)
    an mek-e.   '(I) don't (want to) eat (it).'
    not eat-SE (statement)

---

[3]The SE form -*e* can be used for both request and statement (cf. Choi, 1991).

(7) (Seeing a baby spitting some food out)
     mos mek-e.   '(He) can't eat (it).'
     can't eat-SE (statement)

The morphological structure of nouns was different from that of verbs. Nouns mostly occurred in bare form at this early period, that is, without any productive bound morphology such as case or plural markers. (Note that the plural marker *-tul* [e.g., *salam-tul*, person-PL, 'people'] in Korean is optional.) The only pattern was that six of the nine children productively and appropriately used the possessive suffix *-kke* after a noun referring to a person, to encode the possessor, for example, *ike emma-kke*, this mommy-Poss, meaning 'This (is) mommy's'. It is important to note that in adult colloquial speech, when labeling an entity (*ike say-(i)-ta* this bird-(COP)-SE 'This is a bird.'), the copular verb stem *i* 'to be' is often deleted when the noun ends with a vowel (e.g., *say* 'bird'). This results in SE markers being directly suffixed to the noun at the surface level, as in *say-ta* '(It's) bird (new information)', *say-ci* '(It's) bird (shared information)'. Thus, children do hear nouns followed by SE suffixes in the input. However, none of the children in this study inflected nouns in this way during early lexical development. These data strongly suggest that nouns and verbs are acquired as distinct morphological categories from this early stage. The data also suggest that children acquire verbs as a category that can be negated or affirmed, and can be inflected for tense and modality.

3.1.1.2. *Closed Versus Open Class.*   As discussed earlier, in English nonnominal words are particles which are members of a closed class. In our English data, the same set of relational words, for example, *in, on, off*, occur with little variation across children. In Korean, relational concepts are expressed primarily by verbs, an open class in the adult language. If relational concepts corresponding to English *in, on*, and so on, are constrained initially by a finite set of cognitive notions (e.g., containment, support), then we might expect that Korean children would pick up a small set of verbs that seem to denote these notions from the input and use them frequently. Furthermore, we would not see much variation across children in the kinds of verbs they acquire. To examine these possibilities, I have compared the degree of diversity of verb types with that of noun types acquired across children. Of the total of 131 verb types, only 31% (42 types) were produced by more than three children. This is remarkably similar to the percentage of nouns produced by more than three children: 36% (59 types) out of 164 nouns. This similarity suggests that verbs form an open class to the same degree as nouns in the acquisition of Korean. Such a high degree of diversity of verb types across children suggests strongly that different children pick up different forms and meanings of actions and states as a result of caregiver-specific and context-specific input. The Korean data suggest that children do not develop a finite set of nonlinguistic relational concepts and then simply try to express those concepts through language, but rather acquire language-specific non-nominal meanings with appropriate morphological forms.

3.1.1.3. *Semantic Content of Early Verbs and Nouns.*   What kinds of verbs do Korean children acquire at this stage? The verbs acquired by the nine children were 131 types in total, and are listed in Table 2.3 (for more detailed information about the productivity of individual verbs, see Choi & Gopnik, 1995). The kinds of verb meanings expressed were, in general, similar to those of the early relational words reported for English (Bloom, 1973; Nelson, 1973; Gopnik, 1982; Gopnik & Meltzoff, 1986a; Tomasello, 1992): They encoded success/failure, disappearance, locative action, state or change of state. Among these, the most predominant categories were verbs related to change of location and motion, for example, *kkita* 'put in/on tightly', *nehta* 'put in loosely'. While, overall, the Korean children talked about the same general domain of actions and relations as English-speaking children, they made finer and different distinctions within that domain: From early on, the Korean children acquired specific verbs of locative actions that related to different body parts and to different types of figure-ground relations. In Section 3.2, I analyze in detail semantic meanings of these motion verbs. Also, at this early stage, the Korean children acquired several verbs of breaking: *kkayta* 'break into pieces', *ppwulecita* 'a long stick-like thing is broken', *kocangnata* 'something doesn't function properly' (e.g., radio), *mangacita* 'something has fallen apart' (e.g., toy). These verbs were used appropriately most of the time.

As for nouns, there were 164 noun types (excluding proper nouns) in total produced by the nine children. The major semantic categories of the noun types were: food (e.g., *wuyu* 'milk'), animals (e.g., *say* 'bird'), clothing items (e.g., *yangmal* 'socks'), kinship terms (e.g., *appa* 'daddy'), concrete objects (e.g., *chayk* 'book') (see Choi & Gopnik, 1995, for more detail). These categories are similar overall to previous reports on English-speaking children (Nelson, 1973; Dale, Bates, Reznick, & Morisset, 1989).

3.1.2. *Relation Between Caregiver's Input and Early Acquisition of Verbs*

How can we account for the early acquisition of verbs and the verb spurts in Korean? Several recent studies lead to the hypothesis that caregivers' speech to children plays an important role in the development of children's early lexicon. As noted earlier (cf. Section 3.1.1), Tardif (1996) found a verb-bias in young children learning Mandarin Chinese. In that study, Tardif also found that Mandarin-speaking caregivers consistently produced more verbs (both in types and tokens) than nouns in their speech to children. A relation between caregivers' input and early lexicon has also been found within the English-speaking community: Goldfield (1993) found a variation among English-speaking mothers in

TABLE 2.3
Verbs Acquired by One or More Children During
the Study Period[a] (-*ta* is a Citation Form)

Word	Gloss	Word	Gloss
Disappearance/Existence Verbs			
epsta	'not exist'	*issta*	'exist'
Success/Failure Verbs			
twayssta	'done'		
Request/Rejection Verbs			
cwuta	'give'	*silhta*	'don't want'
Change of Location/Motion Verbs			
ppayta	'take off/out of a tight-fitting base'	*kkita*	'put on/in to a tight-fitting base'
ancta	'sit down'	*kata*	'go'
ttelecita	'fall off from a base'	*ota*	'come'
anta	'hold in arms'	*epta*	'carry on back'
kka(k)ta	'peel off/take wrapping off'	*tatta*	'close'
pesta	'take clothes off'	*nakata*	'go out'
nehta	'put in a loose-fitting container'	*ilenata*	'get up'
milta	'push'	*yelta*	'open'
thata	'ride'	*pwuthita*	'put/stick on a surface'
kkocta	'put a long stick-like thing tightly on/in a base'	*pikhita*	'get/go away'
pelita	'throw away'	*ollakata*	'go up'
naylyekata	'go down'	*nohta*	'put loosely on a surface'
ipta	'put clothes on'	*sinta*	'put shoes on'
chiwuta	'put away'	*naota*	'come out'
nwupta	'lie down'	*kacta*	'to take/hold'
tteyta	'take off of a surface'	*tephta*	'cover'
nemecita	'fall down'	*pwusta*	'pour in'
ssotta	'pour in large quantity'	*tollita*	'turn'
seywuta	'make stand up'	*naylita*	'take down'
capta	'hold by hand'	*naynohta*	'take out'
ollita	'put something up'	*tolakata*	'go around'
tamta	'put several small things loosely in a container'	*kkenayta*	'take something out of a container'
twuta	'leave something at a particular location'	*ppaysta*	'take something away from a person'
ttwuita	'jump/run'	*kelta*	'hang something on a hook'

(Continued)

TABLE 2.3
(Continued)

Word	Gloss	Word	Gloss
tencita	'throw'	*epsecita*	'disappear'
ttuta	'float'	*cwusta*	'pick up'
ileseta	'stand up'	*tulekata*	'go in'
ssuta	'put hat on'	*swumta*	'hide'
ssahta	'pile up'	*nwuluta*	'push down'
ppacita	'get loose'	*open*	'open'
jump	'jump'	*sit down*	'sit down'
chwumchwuta	'dance'	ccicta	'tear'

Activity Verbs

Word	Gloss	Word	Gloss
hata	'do'	*pota*	'look'
takkta	'wipe'	*mekta*	'eat'
cata	'sleep'	*chata*	'kick'
mantulta	'make'	*caluta*	'cut'
ccikta	'take pictures'	*ppalta* (homonym)	'wash'
ppalta (homonym)	'suck/sip'	*phata*	'dig'
nolta	'play'	*chilhata*	'color/paint'
siksahata	'eat (honorific form)'	*tusita*	'eat (honorific form)'
masita	'drink'	*kkusnata*	'finish'
ssata	'to make stool/poop'	*pista*	'comb'
phwulta	'untangle'	*ilhata*	'work'
mmaymmayhata	'spank'	*shawehata*	'take a shower'
chita	'hit'	*mayta*	'tie'
shihata	'wet' (literally 'do pee')	*camkuta*	'lock'
stop	'stop'	*kwuk*	'cook'
hagu	'hug'		

Change of State Verbs

Word	Gloss	Word	Gloss
kkuta	'turn off electricity'	*kkhita*	'turn on electricity'
ppwulecita	'be broken (for a long stick-like thing)'	*kocangnata*	'be broken (= something doesn't function properly)'
kkayta (homonym)	'wake up'	*cecta*	'get wet'
elta	'be frozen'	*tachita*	'get hurt'
mangkacita	'be broken (= something falls apart)'		
kkayta (homonym)	'break into pieces'		

(Continued)

TABLE 2.3
(Continued)

Word	Gloss	Word	Gloss
Stative/Adjectival Verbs			
aphuta	'(it) hurts'	*chwupta*	'be cold' (used for weather)
tepta	'be hot' (used for animate beings)	*chakwupta*	'be cold' (for things)
		ttukepta	'be hot' (for things)
sikkulepta	'be noisy'	*mwusepta*	'be scary'
ipputa	'be pretty'	*masepsta*	'be not tasty'
masissta	'be tasty'	*sita*	'be sour'
maywupta	'be spicy'	*ccata*	'be salty'
khuta	'be big'	*cakta*	'be small'
sinnanta	'be excited'	*cohta*	'be good'
ttokkathta	'be same'	*mwukepta*	'be heavy'
manhta	'be a lot'		
Other			
moluta	'not know'		

ªTotal number of verbs: 131 types.

how much they emphasized naming. In particular, variation in frequency of nouns in the mothers' speech was positively correlated with the proportion of nouns in children's early lexicon.

As pointed out in Kim's chapter in Volume 4, Korean is a verb-final language. Kim further notes that in acquisition, Korean children show a predominant pattern of putting the verb in the final position, and that this pattern correlates with the predominant word-order pattern of Korean caregivers. Furthermore, in colloquial speech, verbs can occur alone, and subject and object nouns can be deleted when the referents are old/shared information. These features suggest that verbs are perceptually more salient in Korean than in English. Such structural differences as well as possible semantic/pragmatic differences between the two languages in the caregivers' input may be important influential factors for the early development of verbs in Korean. To examine whether children in the two cultures indeed receive different types of linguistic input, Gopnik and I conducted a systematic comparison of caregivers' input in English and Korean (Choi & Gopnik, 1995; Gopnik & Choi, 1995).

In our study of caregivers' input, we asked 20 Korean and 20 American mothers to interact with their children, ages between 1;5 and 1;7. The stimuli used for all interactions were a toyhouse with furniture and figurines and two wordless books. We analyzed the caregivers' input both morphologically and pragmatically. In our morphological analysis, we were interested not only in the overall frequency of nouns and verbs, but also in the kinds of nouns and verbs produced by the caregivers. A number of researchers have suggested that in children's early lexicons, there is asymmetry in the proportions of different types of nouns (e.g., Gentner, 1982; Maratsos, 1991). For example, Maratsos (1991) noted that early nouns are predominantly names of concrete objects. Adapting Maratsos' (1991) categories, we subcategorized nouns into object (i.e., *bed, car*) and non-object (e.g., *way, household*) nouns, and verbs into action (e.g., *put in*) and non-action (e.g., *know*) verbs. The results are shown in Tables 2.4a and 2.4b. We found that American mothers produced significantly more object nouns (both in type and token) per utterance than Korean mothers. The pattern is reversed for verbs: The Korean mothers produced more action verb types and tokens per utterance than the English-speaking mothers. However, the English-speaking mothers produced more non-action verbs than the Korean mothers—specifically, they used significantly more attention-getting verbs (e.g., *see, look*), and mental verbs like *know, think, guess*. The same pattern was shown within individual caregivers; the English-speaking mothers produced significantly more object nouns than action verbs while the Korean mothers provided significantly more action verbs than object nouns.

TABLE 2.4a
Average Number of Different Types of Nouns Per 100 Utterances
in Caregivers' Speech (From Choi & Gopnik, 1995)

	Object Ns		Non-Obj. Ns		Total	
	type**	token*	type	token	type**	token
English	22.8	40.9	1.9	2.3	24.7	43.2
Korean	10.2	29.1	1.7	3.0	11.9	32.1

$*p < 0.05$, $**p < 0.001$ (Paired-sample t-tests (two-tailed)):
Object Nouns: specific object or person (e.g., *baby, ball*).
Non-object Nouns: abstract nouns (e.g., *opportunity*), locative nouns (e.g., *front*), and non-specific nouns (e.g., *thing*).

TABLE 2.4b
Average Number of Different Types of Verbs Per 100 Utterances
in Caregivers' Speech (From Choi & Gopnik, 1995)

	Action Vs.		Non-action Vs.		Total	
	type**	token***	type***	token***	type	token*
English	11.2	20.2	14.5	30.9	25.8	51.1
Korean	16.2	48.2	3.7	14.1	19.8	62.3

$*p < 0.05$, $**p = 0.01$, $***p < 0.001$ (Paired-sample t-tests [two-tailed])
Action Verbs: specific action/activity (e.g., *eat, put X in Y*).
Non-Action Verbs: stative verbs (e.g., *like, feel*), mental verbs (e.g., *think, know*), and attention-getting verbs (e.g., *look, watch*).

A pragmatic analysis also shows a significant difference between the two groups of mothers. In this analysis, utterances were coded as naming or activity-oriented utterances. Utterances that encourage the child to name an object, e.g., *What is it?*, or that label the object explicitly, e.g., *That's a ball*, were coded as naming-oriented utterances, whereas utterances that encourage the child to do something, e.g., *What are you doing?*, or that explicitly describe the impending or completed action, e.g., *You put the car in the garage*, were coded as activity-oriented utterances. We found that Korean mothers direct their children to engage in activities (48%) significantly more often than they label objects (10%). They also do this significantly more often than English-speaking caregivers. In contrast, American mothers label objects (21%) as often as they direct activities (25%), and they produce naming-oriented utterances significantly more often than the Korean mothers.

In summary, Korean children receive different types of input from English-speaking children. Korean children hear more action verbs and are more prompted to talk about action than English-speaking children. These differential aspects of input are probably related to the difference in the acquisition patterns of nouns and verbs between Korean- and English-speaking children.

3.1.3. *Relation Between Specific Cognitive Development and Specific Linguistic Expressions*

Does the early acquisition of the verb in Korean have any relation with aspects of cognitive development? Earlier, I mentioned that in our study, we collected both linguistic and cognitive developmental data from the nine Korean children. In this section, I present a brief report of our study of the relation between the two types of development.

A series of studies by Gopnik and Meltzoff (1986b, 1987) have found that, in English-speaking children, there is a specific relation between a specific type of cognitive development and the acquisition of words that encode it. More specifically, as children solve problems related to the concept of object-permanence, words like *gone* are acquired. Similarly, means–ends skills are closely related to the acquisition of relational words like *there*, and success in object categorization is related to the naming explosion. This specificity hypothesis (Gopnik & Meltzoff, 1986b) has also been supported by our Korean data (Gopnik & Choi, 1990). That is, similar to English learners, learners of Korean show a specific relation between the three types of cognitive achievement and the acquisition of linguistic expressions that encode them. However, the typical order in which the three types of development occurred differed between Korean- and English-speaking children: The majority of the Korean children solved means–ends tasks significantly earlier than categorization tasks, whereas in English, no particular order was found between the two types of tasks (Gopnik & Choi, 1995). The same patterns were shown for the development of corresponding linguistic expressions. Comparison between the two languages showed that Korean children were significantly more advanced in their development of means-ends abilities (and corresponding linguistic expressions) than English-speaking children. On the other hand, they were significantly delayed in their performance on the categorization tasks and naming explosion relative to English-speaking children. Gopnik and Choi (1995) suggest that these crosslinguistic differences are related to the differences in the acquisition patterns of nouns and verbs in the two languages. That is, just as Korean children used verbs earlier, so they acquired means–ends skills relevant to actions and relations earlier. Similarly, just as the English-speaking children show a more elaborated naming vocabulary earlier, so they also show an earlier understanding of object categorization. However, these results do not mean that the direction of influence simply goes from children's linguistic patterns to their cognitive development. As Gopnik and Meltzoff (1996) suggest, Korean children acquire verbs not only because they are salient in the input and frequently provided by caregivers but also because meanings of the early-acquired verbs relate to their current cognitive interests and therefore are within the limits of their cognitive understanding. Thus, there seems to be an intimate bidirectional relation between a particular type of cognitive development and a particular set of words. We will come back to this issue in the conclusion.

In the next section, I present Korean data on the locative expressions which children learning different languages acquire from early on.

3.2. Semantic and Morphosyntactic Aspects of Motion Verbs in the Acquisition of Korean

Children express locative actions from an early stage (Bloom, Lightbown, & Hood, 1975). Gopnik (1982) and Tomasello (1987, 1992) have particularly noted that many of children's non-nominal words—for example, particles such as *up, down, on,* and *off*—express spatial notions. Korean children also acquire many words that encode locative actions at an early stage. As shown in Table 2.3, half of the verbs that nine Korean children acquired (64 out of 131 verb types) during their first two years express an aspect of Motion (Manner, Cause, or Path of Motion, see below for details) and change of location. In collaboration with Melissa Bowerman at the Max Planck Institute for Psycholinguistics, I have systematically examined similarities and differences in the way Korean and English children express Motion events, and how children learning the two languages develop spatial expressions. Our data show that children's spatial expressions are organized according to language-specific grammatical principles virtually from the beginning of language development. Before discussing children's spatial expressions, let us review the adult systems of the two languages.

3.2.1. *Lexicalization Pattern of Motion Events:*
Spontaneous Versus Caused Motion

Talmy (1985) defines a MOTION event as follows: "a situation containing movement of an entity or maintenance of an entity at a stationary location" (p. 60). A MOVEMENT refers to a directed motion that results in an overall change of location (e.g., going in and out of something or going up and down). LOCATION refers to either a static situation or "contained" motion that results in no overall change of location (e.g., jumping up and down). In Choi and Bowerman's study (1991), we were particularly concerned with identifying the characteristic patterns of expressions of dynamic motion events, thus, our analysis of the adult systems and children's early locative words was restricted to "directed" motion. We also included in our analysis verbs of posture changes (e.g., *sit down, stand up*), which refer to "contained" motion. Children talk about these events from the one-word stage.

Motion events can be divided into two subclasses: CAUSED MOTION and SPONTANEOUS MOTION. Caused motion refers to an event in which an agent (typically animate) causes another entity (typically inanimate) to move from one place to another, as in *John put the cup on the table*. Spontaneous motion refers to an event in which an animate being spontaneously initiates his own movement resulting in a change of location, as in *John ran into the store*.

According to Talmy, a Motion event has four basic components:

Motion: Presence of Motion.
Figure: The moving object.
Ground: The reference object with respect to which the Figure moves.
Path: The Course followed by the Figure with respect to the Ground.

These components can be identified in a straightforward way in the following English sentence:

(1) *John   went   into   the room.*
    [Figure] [Motion] [Path] [Ground]

A motion event can also have a Manner (e.g., *run/walk/swim*) or a Cause (e.g., *push/throw*) as a distinct external event. We also include the component Deixis (e.g., motion towards the speaker vs. motion away from the speaker) in the set of meaning components for motion events, as it plays an important role in the lexicalization of motion events at least in some languages (see DeLancey, 1985; Wienold, Dehnhardt, Kim, & Yoshida, n.d.). Talmy has found that languages differ in the way they characteristically lexicalize these components. For example, in some languages, the components lexicalized in the main verb are Motion and Manner (e.g., *walk, run*), while in others, they are Motion and Path (e.g., *enter, exit*). Building on Talmy's analysis of typological differences, I briefly describe our analysis of Korean and English patterns of lexicalizations.

3.2.1.1. *English.*   In English, as in most Indo-European languages and Chinese, Motion is characteristically conflated with Manner, Cause, or Deixis in the main verb, and Path is expressed separately by a "satellite" to the verb (i.e., particles in English) (Talmy, 1974, 1985). Talmy (1985) calls languages of this type "satellite-framed." In English, this conflation pattern is consistent for both spontaneous and caused motions, as shown in the following examples.

   i. Conflation of [Motion + Manner/Cause].
      Spontaneous motion: *John **walked/skipped/ran** in(to) the room*,
      Caused motion: *John **slid/rolled/bounced** the keg into the storeroom.*
      *John **blew/pushed** the napkin off the table.*
   ii. Conflation of [Motion + Deixis].
      Spontaneous motion: *John **came/went** into the room.*
      Caused motion: *John **took/brought** the keg into the storeroom.*

As the above sentences illustrate, in English, there is consistency in the kinds of components that are expressed in the main verb. It is also important to note that Path is marked in the same way in sentences of both types, with prepositions and particles like *in(to), out (of), on(to), off, up, down,* and *away*.

3.2.1.2. *Korean.*   In the second class of languages in Talmy's typology, which includes Romance, Semitic, Turkic, Japanese, and Polynesian, the main verb characteristically expresses Path. In languages of this type, which Talmy terms "verb-framed" languages, Manner can be optionally expressed with a gerund or an adverbial phrase. As the following Spanish examples illustrate, Motion and Path are consistently conflated in the main verb, regardless of whether the motion event is spontaneous or caused:

Conflation of [Motion + Path].

Spontaneous motion:
   *La botella **entró/salió** a/de la cueva (flotando).*
   'The bottle **entered/exited** to/from the cave (floating)'

Caused motion:
   *Juan **metí** el barril a la bodega (rodándolo).*
   'John **inserted** the barrel to the storeroom (rolling it)'

Spanish has several verbs that conflate Path with Motion, e.g., *subir* 'ascend', *bajar* 'descend', and *pasar* 'pass'. Transitive Spanish verbs of the same type include *meter* 'insert', *poner* 'put', *juntar* 'join', and *separar* 'separate' (Talmy, 1985).

Korean is, like Spanish, a verb-framed language. In Korean, Path, Manner, and Deixis are encoded by separate verbs. When all of these components co-occur in a clause, they follow a particular order with a connective *-e/-a* between verbs (see below). Korean is also similar to Spanish in that most Path information is encoded by verbs for both spontaneous and caused motions. Korean lacks a system of morphemes dedicated to Path marking like the English spatial prepositions and particles. However, it does have several locative case markers, such as *-ey* 'at, to', *-kkaci* 'to', *-lo* 'toward', and *-eyse* 'from', which, when suffixed to a Ground nominal, designate general notions such as goal or source of motion. Unlike the prepositions/particles *in* or *on* in English, they do not encode the particular spatial relationship between Figure and Ground.

Korean differs from Spanish (and also from English in this respect) in that the characteristic conflation patterns for caused and spontaneous motions are different. In transitive clauses expressing caused motion, Motion is typically conflated with Path, as in Spanish. But in intransitive clauses expressing spontaneous motion, Motion, Path, and (optionally) Manner are expressed by separate constituents. Let's take a look at the two types of clause in more detail

3.2.1.2.1. Spontaneous motion. In expressions of spontaneous motion, the final verb is typically a deictic verb (*kata* 'go' or *ota* 'come') (*-ta* is a citation form) that specifies the agent's movement away from or toward the speaker. This verb is preceded by a Path verb, which, in turn, may be preceded by a Manner verb. The order of verbs is thus [Manner] [Path] [Motion + Deixis], as illustrated in (2):

(2)   *John-i pang-ey (ttwui-e) tul-e ka-ss-ta.*
      John-NOM room-LOC (run-CONN) enter-CONN come-PAST-DECL[4]
      [Figure]   [Ground]   ([Manner])   [Path]   [Motion + Deixis]
      'John went in(to) the room (running).'

In example (2), *John* is the Figure, and *pang* 'room' is the Ground. The locative suffix *-ey* 'to, at' on *pang* indicates simply that *pang* represents the Goal of the event. The first verb, *ttwui-* 'run', which is optional, specifies Manner of Motion. The next verb, *tul-* 'enter' (or more precisely 'be.in'), specifies Path with respect to the Ground. In other words, *tul-* specifies that John ended up inside the room. The Path verb thus describes the spatial relationship between Figure and Ground as the result of the motion. Other Path verbs include *olu-* 'ascend', *nayli-* 'descend', *na-* 'exit', *nem-* '(go) over', *cina-* 'pass', *kennu-* 'cross', *ttalu-* 'follow/along'.

---

[4]In this chapter, SE refers to a sentence-ending modal suffix used in colloquial speech, and DECL refers to an unmarked ending suffix used as citation form for a sentential example.

Although the Path morpheme *tul-* 'enter' is a verb, it encodes path in a rather pure sense, and does not refer to the dynamic movement itself. This is shown by the fact that Path verbs like *tul-* 'enter' can sometimes be used alone or combined with the stative verb *iss-* 'to be located' to express static location of an entity, to focus on the result of the action rather than the action itself, or to present the situation in a rather abstract and holistic way.[5] In fact, for verbs like *tul-* 'enter' and *na-* 'exit', the use of a deictic verb, *ka-* 'go' or *o-* 'come', is obligatory in expressions of spontaneous dynamic motions that involve a certain amount of distance; i.e., without a deictic verb sentence (2) would be ungrammatical.[6] (See also Wienold, Dehnhardt, Kim, & Yoshida, n.d., and for more discussion of the semantics of Korean deictic verbs and similar patterns in Japanese, see Choi & Kita, 1997).

A deictic verb is also obligatory when the agent (the causer in this case) not only moves an entity but also moves along with it. For example, when someone takes or brings something while moving, this can be expressed by combining *kaci-* 'have' with *ka-* 'go' or *o-* 'come'. For example, 'John took/brought a book to the library'

---

[5]For example, when *tul-* 'enter' is used alone (1) or with *iss-* 'be.located' (2), a stative meaning is conveyed. In (3), *olu-* 'ascend' is the main verb. This sentence conveys the event of John's climbing the mountain as a whole; the fact that he had to move is backgrounded and not central to the meaning.

(1) *sakwa-ka sangca-ey tul-ess-ta.*
     apple-NOM box-LOC enter-PAST-DECL
     'Apples are in the box.'

(2) *sakwa-ka sangca-ey tul-e iss-ta.*
     apple-NOM box-LOC enter-CONN be.located-DECL
     'Apples are in the box.'

(3) *John-i san-ey oll-ass-ta.*
     John-NOM mountain-to ascend-PAST-DECL
     'John climbed the mountain.'

[6]Use of *kata* 'go' and *ota* 'come' denotes a change of location that involves a certain amount of distance and physical movement, such as going (or coming) upstairs or going (or coming) into a room. But, if the change of location involves minimal distance or involves only one step (1, 2) or one jump (3), then a deictic verb is not needed. In such cases, the Path verb may be the final verb (3), or it may be combined with a posture verb (1, 2) (Choi & Kita, in preparation):

(1) *John-i mwun-ey tul-e se-ss-ta.*
     John-NOM door-LOC enter-CONN stand-PAST-DECL
     'John stepped in the door (= one step inside the room).'

(2) *John-i tan-ey ol-la se-ss-ta.*
     John-NOM podium-LOC ascend-CONN stand-PAST-DECL
     'John stepped up on the podium.'

(3) *John-i changmwun-eyse matang-ulo ttwui-e nayli-ess-ta.*
     John-NOM window-from garden-to run-CONN descend-PAST-DECL
     'John jumped down to the garden from the window.'

is rendered as *John-i chayk-ul tosekwan-ey kaci-e ka-/o-ass-ta* 'John-NOM book-ACC library-LOC have-CONN go-/come-PAST-DECL' (= John went/came to the library having a book). Thus, in these sentences, *kaci-* expresses the action of 'getting' the book and *ka-* 'go' or *o-* 'come' expresses the agent's (or causer's) movement to the Goal along with the book. In the same manner, if someone moves a desk into the room, the final verb is a deictic verb denoting the spontaneous and dynamic change of location of the agent, e.g., *John-i chayk-sang-ul pang-ey tul-i-e o-ass-ta* 'John-NOM desk-ACC room-LOC enter-CAUSE-CONN come-PAST-DECL' (= John brought the table into the room).

In summary, in expressions of spontaneous motion, the final verb is characteristically a deictic verb that encodes dynamic Motion along with deixis, and separate verbs preceding it express Path and Manner.

3.2.1.2.2. *Caused motion.* Caused motion is expressed differently from spontaneous motion in two important ways. First, as shown in (3), a deictic verb is not needed for a caused motion, thus the Path verb is typically the final verb.[7] In this case, Motion is usually conflated with Path, as in Spanish, rather than Deixis.

(3) *John-i kong-ul sangca-ey (kwul-li-e)* **neh-ess-ta.**
     John-NOM ball-ACC box-LOC (roll-Caus.-CONN) put.in-PAST-DECL
     [Agent]   [Figure] [Ground]   ([Manner])   [Motion + Path]
     'John put the ball in the box (rolling it).'

Second, most of the Path verbs used for caused motion are morphologically distinct from intransitive Path verbs (compare the Path verbs in (2) and (3) above). They are inherently causative transitive verbs which incorporate Motion and often Ground and Figure as well. Table 2.5 lists some of the frequently used transitive Path verbs.

In contrast to Korean, recall that in English, Path is marked the same way whether a motion is spontaneous or caused (cf. *The ball rolled **into** the box* vs. *John rolled the ball **into** the box*). In particular, the same particle or preposition is used for both types of context with constant meaning. For example, *in* is used for a containment relationship between the Figure and Ground whether the motion is spontaneous or caused, whether the Figure is animate or inanimate, or whether it is liquid or solid object.

In Table 2.5, note that the only verb roots that are used both for spontaneous and caused motion with the same Path meaning are *olu-* 'ascend' and *nayli-* 'descend'. (*-(l)i* is a causative suffix. When the stem ends with *i* then the causative suffix is zero as in the case of *nayli-*.) The causative forms of *tul-* 'enter' and

---

[7]As noted earlier, when the agent not only causes the Figure to move, but also moves with the Figure him/herself, the final verb would be a deictic verb to denote the agent's own movement.

TABLE 2.5
Transitive Verbs for Caused Motion in Korean

Verb	Meaning (Examples)

Cause to ascend/descend

ollita Cause something to move up. (Move a poster upward on the wall)

naylita Cause something to move down. (Move a poster downward on the wall)

Join

kkita 'Fit' a three-dimensional object tightly to another. (Lego pieces, earplugs-ears, cassette-cassette case, top-pen, ring-finger)

nehta Put things loosely into a container or around a longish object. (wallet-handbag, ball-box, furniture-room, ring on pole)

pwuthita Join a flat surface to another flat surface. (sticker-book, poster-wall, two table sides)

kkocta Put a solid object elongated in one dimension into/onto a base. (flower-vase, book-shelf, dart-board, hairpin-hair)

tamta Put multiple objects in a container that one can carry. (fruits-basket, candies-bowl, toys-box)

pwusta Pour liquid (or a large quantity of tiny objects) into a container. (milk-cup, sand-pail)

nohta Put something loosely on a surface. (pen-table, chair-floor)

Separate

ppayta Take off/out/apart a three-dimensional object from a base that holds it tightly. (Lego pieces, earplugs-ears, top-pen, ring-finger)

kkenayta Take out things from container. (wallet-handbag, toys-basket)

phwuta Scoop liquid (or a quantity of tiny objects) out of a container. (water-bucket, sand-pail)

tteyta Separate two-dimensional flat object from surface. (sticker-book, poster-wall)

kkata Take off a covering layer or wrapper. (shell-nuts, peel-banana, wrapper-candy)

kkakta Take off a covering layer with knife. (skin-apple, planing a board, sharpening a pencil)

Put clothing item onto one's own body part

ipta Trunk of body (dress, shirt, pants)

ssuta Head (hat, umbrella)

sinta Feet, legs (socks, shoes)

(*Pesta* is the reverse of all of these.)

Put something onto/into one's own body part in order to support or carry it

anta Arms (a person, an object, e.g., baby, package)

epta Back (a person, e.g., a baby or child on mother's back)

cita Back (an object, if *not* also supported by shoulder)

ita Head (an object, e.g., a pot)

tulta Hand (an object, e.g., briefcase, suitcase)

mwulta Mouth (an object, e.g., a cigarette)

na- 'exit', e.g., *tul-i* 'enter-CAUSE', and *nay-* 'exit.CAUSE', are also possible in some contexts to express caused motion. However, the distribution of the contexts for *tul-* and *na-* and their transitive counterparts, *tul-i-* and *nay-*, differ. Contexts in which the transitive form *tul-i-* is used are much more restricted than those in which the intransitive form *tul-* is used (cf. Wienold et al., n.d.).[8]

As Table 2.5 illustrates, many transitive Path verbs for caused motion incorporate not only the notion of Path, but also specific type of Ground (particularly concerning putting something onto different body parts), and sometimes Figure (e.g., *kkocta* 'put an elongated stick-like figure to a base'). Also, in some cases, a particular manner is incorporated into the Path verb, e.g., *kkita* requires a certain amount of force. Thus, these Path verbs for caused motion differ significantly from the Path verbs used for spontaneous motion. Whereas the former conflate several components of motion events along with path, the latter primarily express paths alone.

3.2.2. *Semantic Categories of Path in English and Korean*

As noted earlier, the kinds of information incorporated in the path morphemes are different in the two languages: English path morphemes express paths in a rather pure sense (e.g., they are not conflated with Manner or Cause), while Korean path morphemes used for caused motion incorporate not only Motion but often also Ground, Figure, or Manner.

Korean path verbs differ from English path particles in another important way: the categorization of spatial relationships. Consider notions of joining and separation (bringing an object into or out of contact with another), which are typically expressed in English with phrases like *put in/on/together* and *take out/off/apart*. In English, these Path markers (particles and prepositions) apply to a broad range of spontaneous and caused motion events. The choice among them is governed primarily by notions like containment, support/attachment, or symmetrical movement between Figure and Ground. Thus, *in* is used when the Figure ends up completely or partially contained by the Ground object (e.g., *put*

---

[8]For example, *tul-i*, enter-CAUSE, is used when the agent moves with the Figure.

> *John-i chayksang-ul pang-ey tul-i-e o-ass-ta.*
> John-NOM desk-ACC room-LOC enter-CAUSE come-PAST-DEC
> 'John brought the desk into the room.'

If the agent only causes the Figure to move into something, and the agent himself/herself does not go in with the Figure, *nehta* is typically used.

> *John-i kong-ul sangca-ey tency-e neh-ess-ta.*
> John-NOM ball-ACC box-LOC throw-CONN put.in-PAST-DECL
> 'John threw the ball into the box.'

the candle in the candle holder, or *put the doll in the bathtub*). *On* is used when the Figure: (1) ends up in contact with the surface of the Ground (*put the suitcase on the table/the stamp on the envelope*), (2) is in contact with and envelops (or encircles) the Ground object completely or partially (*put the pillowcase on the pillow/the ring on your finger, put hat/shirt/pants on*), or (3) becomes attached to the Ground (*Put one Lego piece on another*). *Together* is used when two objects are similar in size and are both moved relative to each other, and the contrast between *on* and *in* is lost: **put** *two magnets/two pop-beads* **together**. The encoding of the converse actions of taking things *out, off,* and *apart* are governed by similar considerations.

Korean employs quite different semantic categories of spatial relations. The verb *kkita* and its opposite *ppayta* is a case in point. The Path denoted by *kkita* 'fit the Figure object tightly with the Ground object' is a tight fit/three-dimensional meshing, and it is indifferent to whether the Figure goes INTO, ONTO, OVER, or TOGETHER with the Ground. It is routinely used to express putting earplugs into ears, one Lego piece onto or together with another, and the top of a pen onto (= over) the pen. *Kkita* is also used for both putting a ring onto a finger and putting a finger into a ring, because both involve a tight-fitting relationship. The reversal of these actions is specified by *ppayta* 'unfit'.[9] The *kkita/ppayta* category refers specifically to a three-dimensional tight-fitting relationship; different verbs are used for loose containment (*nehta* 'put in a loose containment'/*kkenayta* 'take out') and surface contact (*nohta* 'put something loosely on a surface'/*cipta* 'pick something up'). Figure 2.1 shows schematically how the semantic categories of *kkita* cross-cut the categories of *in/on/together*.

Transitive Path verbs of joining and separation also incorporate aspects of Figure and Ground. For example, different verbs are used for solid vs. liquid Figures (e.g., *nehta* 'put in' vs. *pwusta* 'pour in') and for flat versus elongated Figures (e.g., *pwuthita* vs. *kkocta*). Fine distinctions are made when the human body is the Ground object: Different verbs are used for putting clothing onto different body parts, and also for putting people or objects into/onto different body parts for purposes of support or carrying. For example, *ipta* is used for putting clothes onto the trunk of the body, and *sinta* is used for putting shoes/socks on feet; *anta* is used for putting something in arms. Acts of putting a Figure onto the back are distinguished according to whether the Figure is animate (*epta*) or inanimate (*cita*).

Words like *oluta* 'ascend' and *naylita* 'descend' seem at first glance to have the same meanings as *up* and *down* in English. But they do not: In English, *up* and *down* are used not only for overall changes in the Figure's location (e.g., *go up, run down*) but also with posture verbs to indicate "in place" changes in the Figure with respect to the vertical axis, e.g., *She suddenly sat up* (from a lying posture)/*sat down* (from a standing posture); *she lay down* (to take a nap);

---

[9]*Ppayta* 'take off/out/apart' is used more generally for separation than for *kkita* 'put on/in/together'. For example, *ppayta* can be used for taking out a sweater from a drawer if it involves some difficulty.

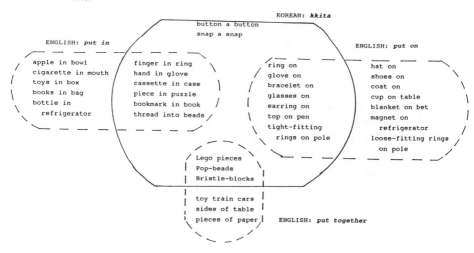

FIG. 2.1. The category of *kkita* 'put into relationship of tight fit or attachment' compared to English *put in/on/together*.

He stood up (and left the room). (Posture verbs plus *up* or *down* also express static postures, e.g., *he sat down all during the concert*; see Talmy, 1985.) Korean, in contrast, expresses posture changes with monomorphemic verbs, e.g., *ancta* 'sit down', *nwupta* 'lie down', *(ile)seta* 'stand up', *ilenata* 'get up', *kkwulhta* 'kneel down', *kitayta* 'lean against'. When these posture verbs are preceded by the Path verbs *olu-* 'ascend' and *nayli-* 'descend' (e.g., *nayli-e ancta*, descend-CONN sit), the resulting phrase does not have the same meaning as English 'stand up', 'sit down', etc.: It specifies that the Figure first gets up onto a higher surface or down onto a lower surface, and then assumes the specified posture.

To summarize, English uses the same verb conflation patterns in both intransitive clauses expressing spontaneous motion and transitive clauses expressing caused motion, and it encodes Path separately with the same Path markers (particles and prepositions) whether the clause is transitive or intransitive. Korean, in contrast, typically uses different lexicalization patterns for spontaneous motion and caused motion, and many of its Path markers (verbs) in the two cases are distinct. Even when the same verb root is used for both types of events (e.g., *tul-* 'enter' vs. *tul-i-* 'cause to enter'), their meanings are not the same, e.g., the kinds of Figure and Ground each verb requires are often different. In addition, many Korean Path verbs have a narrower range of uses than the English Path markers that translate them. Furthermore, the two languages differ in the way the Manner/Cause component is typically used (see Section 3.2.3.2).

3.2.3. *Development of Expressions for Motion Events*

Choi and Bowerman (1991) studied how English- and Korean-speaking children develop expressions for motion events at an early age, from 14 to 24 months. Given our analysis of the spatial expressions in adult English and Korean, we were primarily interested in two questions: (1) Do English- and Korean-speaking children show language-specific patterns in their lexicalization patterns? (2) What are similarities and differences in their semantic categorization of spatial relations? Our database for English is Bowerman's diary study of her two children. For Korean data, I examine here the spatial expressions of nine Korean children whom I followed longitudinally, which include the four children of the younger age group that was reported in Choi and Bowerman (1991).

Early in language development, most references to action take place in the immediate context of the action. We considered only utterances produced while an action was taking place, just after it had occurred, or just before it occurred. In the last case, the utterances expressed intentions, desires, or expectations of particular motion events. Both the English- and Korean-speaking children began to use words to encode motion in such situations in the same age range—around 14 to 16 months. We classified their utterances into spontaneous motion and caused motion according to whether the motion was (or would be, in the case of anticipated events) spontaneous or required an agent's causal action. Utterances classified as spontaneous motion were used for self-initiated motion by animate beings, usually the child herself (see Huttenlocher, Smiley, & Charney, 1983), for example, a child says *na ka* 'exit go' when he wants to go outside. Utterances classified as caused motion were used for a motion brought about by an external agent, for example, a child says *neh-e* '(I am) putting in' while putting a ball into a box. (For a more detailed description of the coding criteria, see Choi & Bowerman, 1991.)

One remarkable similarity between the two sets of children was the kinds of events that they were interested in talking about. For example, children using both languages often commented on their own changes of posture or location, such as sitting down or climbing up onto chairs; they talked about wanting to go outside; they asked adults to pick up or carry them; and they referred to donning and doffing clothing and to object manipulations of many kinds, for example, putting things into a bag and taking them out and putting Lego pieces or popbeads together and taking them apart. These similar preoccupations are probably driven by children's general cognitive development, including what they are interested in talking about (Gopnik & Choi, 1990; Gopnik & Meltzoff, 1986b). Although the topics referred to by the two sets of children were remarkably similar, the patterns of linguistic expressions of learners of the two languages differed systematically. Our analysis of the differences shows a clear influence of language-specific properties, both morphological and semantic, on children's early expressions of motion events.

3.2.3.1. *Morphosyntactic Differences.*

3.2.3.1.1. *English-speaking children.* The two English-speaking subjects in our data show the following patterns: Path particles are used productively from the one-word stage to express both spontaneous and caused motions, and Manner/Cause verbs and Path particles are also combined productively to express both types of motion events in the period of two-word combination (Bowerman, 1994; Choi & Bowerman, 1991).

Both children began producing path particles like *on, off, out, up,* and *down* from 14 months. During the first few months (between 14–16 months for C and between 14–18 months for E) the Path particles tended to be context-bound (e.g., saying *out* only for going out), and tended to be used for either spontaneous or caused motion, but not for both. (E, however, used *down* for both types of Motion at 16 months.) Over the next few months, the children began to use Path particles increasingly for both spontaneous and caused motion. By 19–20 months, they used almost all Path particles in both types of context, and for a wide variety of spontaneous and caused motion events. For example, they used *on* for spontaneous motions such as sitting or standing on things, and for caused motions such as putting on clothing of all kinds, attaching tops to pens and stickers to surfaces, and putting objects down on surfaces. They used *off* for the reverse of these actions. They used *in* for going into houses, bathtubs, and the child seat of a shopping cart (i.e., spontaneous motions) and for putting things into various containers (i.e., caused motions), and *out* for the reverse of these actions (see Gopnik, 1980, and Gopnik & Meltzoff, 1986a, for similar uses by other children). They used *back* for their own or another person's spontaneous return to an original location, for putting objects back where they were usually kept (e.g., watch on arm, books on shelf), and for rejoining parts of an object (e.g., top on pen, lid on bottle). The following utterances illustrate such productivity:

Spontaneous motion:

    16 mos. *Down.* (climbing down from doll's crib).
    18 mos. *On.* (trying to climb to the top of a whole pile of toys).
    19 mos. *Get up.* (as the child climbs on a chair).
    19 mos. *Out.* (wanting to go out).
    20 mos. *Daddy out.* (waiting for father to get out of car).

Caused motion:

    17 mos. *Down.* (pushing a cat's head down).
    19 mos. *Up bottle.* (when the child places a bottle up on a pillow on the couch).
    17 mos. *That on.* (requesting the removable bar of the child's crib to be put on).
    19 mos. *Out.* (trying to take pegs out of pounding bench).

The two children began to produce Manner verbs between 17 and 18 months. Manner verbs they produced during these months include *walk, run, jump, push, pull.* Between 19 and 21 months, the two children began to combine Manner verbs and Path particle (e.g., *run out, pull down*) productively for both spontaneous and caused motion (see Section 3.2.3.2 for more detail).

3.2.3.1.2. *Korean children.*   The nine Korean children I followed longitudinally produced many spatial expressions from a young age (14–16 months) and their spatial expressions developed steadily. In Table 2.6, I summarize the development of Path and Posture verbs in the Korean children. The verbs included in Table 2.6 are produced by at least two children. The first pattern to note is that distinct verbs are used for spontaneous and caused motions. The only two verb roots that appear in both columns in Table 2.6 are those that adults also productively use in spontaneous and caused motions in the adult grammar: *oluta* 'ascend'/*ollita* 'cause to ascend' and *naylita* 'descend/cause to descend'. One child used the intransitive form *oluta* 'ascend' for caused motion, and the transitive form *ollita* 'cause to ascend' for spontaneous motion. All the other verbs were used for either spontaneous or caused motion following the adult pattern.

Second, there was a strong tendency for children to begin expressing verbs for caused motion before spontaneous motion. Between 14–16 months, six of the nine children began using verbs appropriately for caused motion, and by 19 months all nine children did so. For seven of these children, the first caused motion verb was either *kkita* 'fit' or *ppayta* 'unfit'. Typical contexts in which the two verbs were used included putting Lego pieces together or taking them apart, fitting plastic shapes into or out of the holes of a shape box, and trying to take a bib or shirt off. In all these cases, the child (or the caregiver) caused an object to be joined to or separated from a Ground object.

The number of Path verbs for caused motion increased steadily at each developmental period: Between 17–18 months, children acquired *kka(k)ta* 'peel off', and *nehta* 'put into a loose container', *naylita* 'cause to go down', the carrying verbs *anta* 'hold/carry in arms' and *epta* 'hold/carry on back', and the clothing verb, *pesta* 'take off clothes'. By 22 months, verbs like *kkocta* 'put elongated object to base' and *tteyta* 'remove from surface attachment' were added to the list, along with additional clothing verbs. By 24 months, the list included 13 transitive Path verbs. (The list would be longer if we include the verbs produced by one child.)

While Path verbs for caused motion developed early, Manner verbs expressing caused motion did not. Also, there were more individual differences among the types of Manner verbs produced by children. Whereas one child produced *tencita* 'throw' at 17 months, and one said *tollita* 'cause to turn' at 18 months, most children started producing Manner verbs at around 21 months. Between 21 and 24 months, several children produced *ssotta* 'pour', *milta* 'push', *chata* 'kick', and *tencita* 'throw'.

Let's now turn to intransitive verbs for spontaneous motion. For seven of the nine children, the first such verbs to appear were either the posture verb *ancta* 'sit down' or the deictic verbs *kata* 'go' or *ota* 'come'. The deictic verbs were used only for spontaneous motion. The deictic verb *kata* 'go' was typically used when the child wanted to go out, or when he/she wanted the addressee to go away. *Ota* 'come' was generally used for asking somebody to come toward the child. The average age of onset of a deictic verb (either *kata* 'go' or *ota* 'come')

TABLE 2.6
Development of Posture and Path Verbs in Korean

14–16 months

Spontaneous	Caused
Path: -	Path: *kkita* (2) 'fit' *ppayta* (5) 'unfit'
Posture: *ancta* (2) 'sit down'	Put X on body part: *anta* (2) 'in arms' *epta* (2) 'on back'

17–18 months

Spontaneous	Caused
Path *oluta/*ollita* (2) 'ascend/ cause to ascend'	Path: *kka(k)ta* (4) 'peel off' *kkita* (7) 'fit' *nehta* (3) 'put in' *ppayta* (6) 'unfit' *naylita* (2) 'cause to descend' **oluta/ollita* (2) 'ascend/cause to ascend'
Posture: *ancta* (5) 'sit down' *ilenata* (2) 'stand up'	Carry: *anta* (3) 'in arms' *epta* (3) 'on back'
Deixis: *kata* (3) 'go'	Clothing: *pesta* (2) 'take off'

19–20 months

Spontaneous	Caused
Path + Deixis: *na kata* (3) 'go out' *olla kata/ota* (3) 'go/come up'	Path: *kka(k)ta* (6) 'peel off' *kkita* (7) 'fit' *nehta* (3) 'put in' *ppayta* (9) 'unfit' *tteyta* (2) 'separate two surfaces' *naylita* (2) 'cause to descend' *ollita* (2) 'cause to ascend'
Posture: *ancta* (5) 'sit down' *ilenata* (5) 'stand up'	Carry: *anta* (4) 'in arms' *epta* (6) 'on back'
Deixis: *kata* (5) 'go' *ota* (4) 'come'	Clothing: *pesta* (3) 'take off' *sinta* (3) 'on feet'
Manner: *naluta* (2) 'fly'	

(Continued)

TABLE 2.6
(Continued)

21–22 months

Spontaneous	Caused
Path + Deixis:	Path:
na kata (5) 'go out'	*kka(k)ta* (8) 'peel off'
naylye kata (2) 'go down'	*kkita* (8) 'fit'
olla kata/ota (3) 'go/come up'	*kkocta* (2) 'put elongated object to base'
	nehta (3) 'put in'
	ppayta (9) 'unfit'
	ollita (3) 'cause to ascend'
	naylita (4) 'cause to descend'
Posture:	Carry:
ancta (6) 'sit down'	*anta* (6) 'in arms'
ilenata (6) 'stand up'	*epta* (4) 'on back'
Deixis:	Clothing:
kata (5) 'go'	*ipta* (4) 'on trunk'
ota (5) 'come'	*pesta* (4) 'take off'
	sinta (4) 'on feet'
	Manner/Cause
	ssotta (3) 'pour carelessly'
	milta (3) 'push'

23–24 months

Spontaneous	Caused
Path + Deixis:	Path:
na kata (6) 'go out'	*kka(k)ta* (8) 'peel off'
naylye kata (5) 'go down'	*kkita* (8) 'fit'
olla kata (4) 'go up'	*kkocta* (2) 'put elongated object to base.'
tule kata (4) 'go in'	*nehta* (3) 'put in'
	nohta (3) 'put on'
	ppayta (9) 'unfit'
	pwusta (2) 'pour in'
	pwuthita (2) 'joining two surfaces'
	tamta (2) 'put multiple objects in a container'
	tteyta (2) 'separate two surfaces'
	ollita (3) 'make ascend'
	naylita (4) 'make descend'
Posture:	Carry:
ancta (8) 'sit down'	*anta* (7) 'in arms'
ilenata[a] (6) 'stand up'	*epta* (6) 'on back'
ileseta[a] (2) 'stand up'	
nwupta (3) 'lie down'	

(Continued)

TABLE 2.6
(Continued)

23–24 months *(Cont.)* Spontaneous	Caused

Deixis:
  kata (7) 'go'
  ota (5) 'come'
	Clothing:
	  ipta (8) 'on trunk'
	  pesta (6) 'take off'
	  sinta (7) 'on feet'
	  ssuta (4) 'on head'
	Manner/Cause:
	  chata (3) 'kick'
	  milta (5) 'push'
	  ssotta (4) 'pour carelessly'
	  tencita (2) 'throw'

Note. Numbers in parentheses refer to the number of subjects who produced the verb during the given period.

[a]*ilenata* focuses on the process of getting up from a non-standing posture (e.g., lying or sitting down), whereas *ileseta* focuses on the result of posture change, that is, standing up.

was 19 months. This is relatively late compared to 16 months, which is the average onset of the verbs for caused motion, *kkita/ppayta* 'fit/unfit'.

Between 17–18 months, the Path verb *oluta* 'ascend' was used without a deictic verb by two children when they were trying to climb up to a chair or bed.[10] The combination of Path and Deictic verbs, *na kata* 'exit go' and *olla kata* 'ascend go', began to be produced at around 19 months. The Path verbs that children acquired during the study period consisted of four Path verb stems: *olu-* 'ascend', *nayli-* 'descend', *na-* 'exit', and *tul-* 'enter'. The average onset of a path verb (one of the four verbs) for spontaneous motion was 21 months, which is much later than the onset of the caused motion verb *kkita/ppayta* 'fit/unfit'. It is interesting to note that the Path form *tul-* 'enter' was acquired at a relatively late period compared to the English-speaking children: Only four out of the nine Korean children began to produce *tul-* at around 24 months. *Tul-* 'enter' denotes the notion of containment, which many researchers believe to be one of the basic, early-acquired cognitive concepts, and the two English-speaking children in our data produced *in* to express spontaneous motion at around 19 months.

Manner verbs for spontaneous motion were limited in number and also slow to develop. In the cumulative lexicon of the nine children, only four Manner verbs are found for spontaneous motion between 20 and 24 months. One child said *ketta* 'walk'; two produced *naluta* 'fly'; one child said *ttwuita* 'jump' and *tolta* 'turn'.

___

[10]There were greater individual differences in the acquisition of terms for spontaneous motion than for those for caused motion. For example, there was one child who produced *oluta* 'ascend' as she was trying to get up onto her bed from 15 months, but, as Table 2.6 shows, it was not a typical pattern in Korean children; most children produced the Path and Deictic verbs between 19 and 24 months.

During the developmental period observed, the Korean children made lexical distinctions between spontaneous and caused motion. For example, they used *kkita* 'fit' and *kkenayta* 'take out' only for caused motion and did not overextend these verbs to spontaneous motion, such as, they did not say *kkita* when they crept into a narrow space or *kkenayta* when they got out of the bathtub. Similarly, the children used verbs like *na kata* 'exit go' only for spontaneous motions, such as going out of the house and getting out of the bathtub. They also used *kata/ota* 'go/come' only for spontaneous motion in which an animate being spontaneously moved from one location to another. Thus, they did not violate the distinction between spontaneous and caused motion along a Path throughout the developmental period observed. The only verb roots used for both spontaneous and caused motions were the verbs of vertical path: *olu-* 'ascend'/*ol-li-* 'cause to ascend', and *nayli-* 'descend/cause to descend'. In adult Korean, the two verbs are productively used in both types of motion events with equivalent Path meaning.

In summary, at the morphosyntactic level, a major difference between children learning English and Korean is in their willingness to extend Path words across the transitivity boundary. English-speaking children use Path particles for both spontaneous and caused motion in a productive way, whereas Korean children use distinct verbs for the two types of events. These developmental patterns reflect the characteristic pattern of lexicalization of dynamic Motion events in English and Korean. We have also seen that the two English-speaking children began to produce Manner verbs somewhat earlier than the Korean children. This may also have to do with the adult grammar. In English, Manner verbs are the main verbs of the sentence, whereas in Korean they are optional elements and often do not occupy the main verb position.

3.2.3.2. Early Two-Word Combinations Expressing Motion Events. In expressing Motion events, English uses a combination of a main verb and a particle: The main verb expresses Manner (or Deixis), and the particle expresses Path. The two English-speaking children used this combinatory rule productively at an early age (from 19 months for E, and from 21 months for C). That is, they began to combine Path particles with a variety of verbs specifying the Manner of a motion event. (Combinations of particles with nouns naming the Figure, e.g., *Christy in*, started earlier.) Many of the children's verb-particle combinations are also common in adult speech, but there is evidence that they understood the underlying combinatorial principle and were not simply imitating. First, they produced novel combinations such as *carry up* (picking up and righting a fallen-over stool; E 21 months), *close in* (trying to stuff a jack-in-the-box down into the box and shut the lid; E 20 months), and *catch in* (asking M to go capture her between two boxes; E 24 months). Second, they freely combined particles and Manner verbs with each other as independent components. For example, they used *out* to express a Figure's exit from containment and combined it freely with different Manner verbs as in *run out* or *pull out*, *get out*, while also combining the various Manner verbs such as *run* appropriately with different Path particles to express different trajectories, for example, *run up, run down, run out*. They followed this pattern for both spontaneous and caused motions. For example, Bowerman's subject E produced the following combinations between 21 and 24 months, among many others (Bowerman, 1994):

> *pour + down/out/in/on me*
> *pull + down/up/out*
> *push + down/in/off*
> *put + down/on/in/back*
> *get + down/up/out*
> *come + down/out/in/off/back*

In Korean, the final verb in transitive clauses expressing caused motion is a Path verb, such as *kkita/ppayta* 'fit/unfit'. Manner verbs can precede this verb, such as *tol-li-e ppayta* 'turn-CAUS-CONN unfit' (= take Figure from its tightly fitting Ground by turning it, i.e., twist out/off/apart), or *mil-e nehta* 'push-CONN' (= put something in a container by pushing it, i.e., 'push in'). However, these combinations are less frequent than constructions like *twist/pull/cut/roll off* and *push/throw/kick/slide in* in English. This is because the two languages differ in what information must be expressed and what can be left to inference.

In English, it is often obligatory to spell out Path rather completely, even when it can be readily inferred from context. For example, in English one must specify the Path when expressing a change of location, such as *John threw a pebble into the river*. In this sentence, the relationship between Figure and Ground is easily inferred by the specification of the Ground, *river*. In Korean, a Path verb can be omitted in such contexts if a transitive verb expressing the Manner or Cause of the motion is supplied. Thus, in Korean, *John-i tol-ul kangmwul-ey tency-ess-ta* 'John-NOM stone-ACC river.water-LOC throw-PAST-DECL' (= John threw a stone to the river) is a perfectly acceptable sentence. Note that, unlike English prepositions/particles, the locative case marker *-ey* 'at, to' encodes only the notion of goal and does not specify the spatial relation between the Figure and the Ground. In cases like the above example, where the Figure-Ground relation is pragmatically implied, locative case endings on the Ground nominal are sufficient, and a Path verb often sounds redundant.

Recall that for expressions of spontaneous motion along a bounded path, Korean typically combines a Path verb with a deictic verb, as in *tule kata* 'go in' or *na kata* 'go out'. Manner verbs can optionally precede the Path verb. When the Motion is unbounded (i.e., the endpoint of the Motion is not known), Manner verbs can occur alone or in combination with a deictic verb, such as *John-i cip-ulo ttwui-ess-ta* 'John-NOM house-toward run-PAST-DECL' (= John ran toward the house) or *say-ka nal-a ka-ss-ta* 'bird-NOM fly-CONN go-PAST-DECL' (= The bird flew away).

I examined the pattern of two-word combinations in our nine Korean subjects. Compared to the high productivity of Manner + Path pattern produced by the English-speaking children, two-word combinations involving Manner in Korean-speaking children were observed infrequently, and also with individual differences. Furthermore, the Korean children used different types of combinations for caused and spontaneous motion. For spontaneous motion, they productively combined Path with a deictic verb:

Path + Deixis

olla + kata/ota	'ascend go/come'	(= go/come up)
naylie + kata/ota	'descend go/come'	(= go/come down)
na + kata/ota	'exit go/come'	(= go/come out)
tule + kata/ota	'enter go/come'	(= go/come in)

Combinations of Manner with Deictic verbs occurred only occasionally. One child who acquired the verb *ketta* 'walk' early, said *kele ka* 'walk go' as she was walking with her mother (the stem form *ket-* 'walk' changes to *kel-* before the connective *-e*). Another child said *nala ka* 'fly go' when seeing a bird fly away. Another child said *tola ka* 'turn go' when looking at the record player turning around.

For caused motion, Path verbs or Manner verbs tended to occur alone, and not together—a pattern characteristic of adult Korean as well, as discussed earlier. In cases where either a Path or Manner verb was combined with another verb, the other verb was typically an auxiliary verb. Hence, the combination pattern was Path/Manner verb + auxiliary verb. The auxiliary verbs used most often were *cwuta* 'do something for somebody' to ask help from the caregiver, or *pota* 'try, attempt' to ask the caregiver to perform the action. Here are some examples:

Path + Auxiliary

ppay + cwue	'unfit + help'	(= take out/off for me)
kki-e + cwue	'fit + help'	(= put in/on for me)
kka + cwue	'unwrap/peel.off + help'	(= unwrap or peel off for me)
naylie + cwue	'descend + help'	(= take me down)
ppay + poa	'unfit + try'	(= try taking (it) out/off)
nehe + poa	'put.in + try'	(= try putting (it) on)

Manner + Auxiliary:

tencie + cwue	'throw + help'	(= throw (it) for me)
mile + cwue	'push + help'	(= push (me or it) for me)

While, for spontaneous motion, the Korean children readily combined Manner and Deixis (e.g., *olla kata* 'up go'), they did not do so for caused motion. We do not see combinations of the following type: *mile kata* 'push go' (= move away from the speaker pushing (it)), *kwullie ota* 'roll.CAUSE come' (= move toward the speaker rolling (it)), *cha kata* 'kick go' (= move away from the speaker kicking (it)). (Recall that in adult Korean, *kata/ota* 'go/come' is not used for caused motion unless the agent moves with the Figure.) Thus, the Korean children in our study used distinct combination patterns for spontaneous and caused motions.

During the period of two-word combinations, the Korean children produced few of the combinations of Manner and Path that we typically see in English-speaking children. They did not produce combinations such as *cha nehta* 'kick insert', *mile nehta* 'push insert', *mile ollita* 'push ascend.CAUSE' (= push up), *tollie ppayta* 'turn.CAUSE take out/off' (= taking (it) out/off by turning (it)). In two-word combinations, then, the kinds of information that English-speaking children and Korean-speaking children encoded were not the same. Furthermore, whereas English-speaking children used the same combinatory patterns for both spontaneous and caused motion, Korean-speaking children used distinct patterns for spontaneous vs. caused motion.

3.2.3.3. *Semantic Categorization of Spatial Relations.*   Our spontaneous data show that children are sensitive to the language-specific meaning of Path morphemes from early on. For joining and separating objects, the Korean children used *kkita* 'put onto/into a tight-fitting base' and *ppayta* 'take off/out from a tight-fitting base' respectively for Figure and Ground objects that have tight-fitting relationship regardless of whether the relationship is containment, support, or attachment, such as putting Lego pieces together and taking them apart, or putting plastic shapes into matching holes and taking them out. Interestingly, the children often overextended the two verbs for situations that, although involving tight fit, would be encoded with different verbs by adults. For example, they overextended the verb *ppayta* to taking a T-shirt or shoes off before learning the appropriate verb, *pesta* 'take clothes off'. One child also said *ppayta* when asking his mother to release him when she was holding him tight in her arms. This is not an appropriate use of *ppayta* for adult speakers. Adult speakers would use the verb phrase *noh-a cwuta* 'release give'[11] for this situation, since the mother does not take the child out from her arms that surround him, but rather lets go of the child by releasing her arms from a holding position.

For putting objects loosely into a container, such as when putting toys into a basket or when putting an object into a plastic bag, the children used either *nehta* 'put something loosely in or around' or *tamta* 'put relatively small things loosely in a container'. For putting objects loosely on a surface such as a table or floor, children appropriately used *nohta* 'put something loosely on surface'.

As discussed earlier, many transitive motion verbs in Korean conflate Motion not only with Path but also with information about Ground and sometimes Figure.

---

[11]*Noh-* has two rather different meanings: 'put something loosely on surface' and 'release'.

From the beginning of lexical development, the children's use of these verbs was generally appropriate, showing that they were sensitive to the incorporation of these elements. The sense that Ground may be a component of a motion verb's meaning seems to become particularly strong between 17 and 20 months. At this time the children distinguished two verbs of supporting/carrying according to the body part that serves as Ground (*anta* 'put into arms to support/carry' vs. *epta* 'put on back to support/carry'), and began to use appropriate clothing verbs according to the body part (*ipta* 'put clothes on trunk' and *sinta* 'put shoes or socks on feet'). They also began to use the verb for removal of clothes, *pesta* 'take clothes off'.

Learners of English also use Path particles according to the adult system of their language. Our two subjects distinguished systematically in their spontaneous speech between *in/out* and *on/off* on the basis of whether the Figure goes into/out of a container or onto/off of a surface. Their use of the two Path particles was indifferent to whether the Figure fit the Ground object tightly or loosely, or—in the case of clothing—what part of the body the Figure ended up on.

These spontaneous data strongly suggest that English- and Korean-speaking children acquire language-specific semantic categories from the beginning of the one-word stage. Since there is much variation in contexts in which children spontaneously produce words, Bowerman and I conducted a controlled elicited production experiment with young children learning English or Korean (or—in a third group of children—Dutch). On the basis of our analysis of children's spontaneous speech data and of the adult systems of English, Korean, and Dutch, we selected a standardized set of actions of joining and separating two objects: putting a cassette in case (tight containment relationship); putting toys in a bag (loose containment relationship); and donning and doffing clothing of different kinds (carried out with a doll). The experimenter presented the two objects in either a joined or separated state (e.g., a cassette presented in a fitted case or a cassette in one hand and a case in the other) and asked the child to prompt her what to do with them. Our goal was to see whether children would categorize the actions similarly across languages, as would be predicted by the theoretical approach that emphasizes cognitive bases, or in a language-specific way. For each language we had 40 subjects: 10 adults and 30 children, 10 each in the age ranges 2;0–2;5, 2;6–2;11, and 3;0–3;5. Even the children in the youngest group responded well to our procedure. Here, I focus on the English and Korean data (see Bowerman, 1995, for a three-way comparison that includes Dutch).

A systematic comparison of English and Korean shows clearly that, from at least age 2 (the youngest children in our study), children's semantic categorization is already being shaped by the language-specific system they are exposed to. But their sensitivity to the language-specific system interacts with nonlinguistic strategies of categorizing spatial relations in a complex way.

Figures 2.2 through 2.4 display the data from most of the joining actions in Venn diagrams. The first figure shows how the youngest children learning English or Korean predominantly categorized the actions; the second shows the oldest

Semantic categories of joining actions by the youngest age group (2;0–2;5) in Korean (K) and English-speaking [E] children.

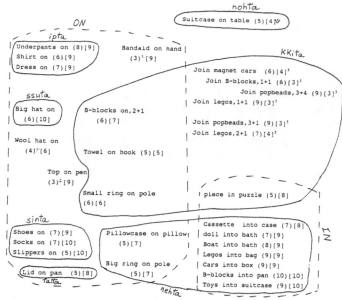

[1] For putting a wool hat on, four Korean children said *ssuta* 'put on head', and three said *kkita* 'put in/on tightly'.

[2] For putting a top on pen, three Korean children said *kkita* 'put in/on tightly', two said *nehta* 'put in/around loosely' and two said *tatta* 'close'.

[3] For putting a bandaid on, three Korean children said *pwuthita* 'join two surfaces'.

[4] For putting a suitcase on table, four English-speaking children said *on*.

[5] For joining magnet cars, B-blocks, Legos, and popbeads, three or four English-speaking children said *on*.

Figure 2.2

Figures 2.2–2.4. The actions in Figures 2.2 through 2.4 are all joining actions expressed by *in*, *on*, or *together* by English-speaking children. The position of each action is constant in all three figures, except putting a towel on hook, and putting a top on pen.

Solid lines—Korean
Broken lines—English

1. Numbers in parentheses and brackets show the number of Korean and English-speaking subjects respectively who responded with the word (labeled outside the category line), i.e. (Korean subjects) [English subjects].

2. Approximate meanings for the Korean semantic categories in the Figures are as follows:

kkita	'put in/on/together tightly to the Ground'
nehta	'put in/around loosely'
nohta	'put on surface loosely'
pwuthita	'joining two surfaces'
ipta	'put [a clothing item] on trunk'
ssuta	'put [a clothing item or umbrella] on head'
sinta	'put [a clothing item] on foot'
tatta	'close'
kelta	'hook'
tephta	'cover'

Semantic categories of joining actions by the oldest group (3;0–3;5)
in Korean (K) and English-speaking [E] children.

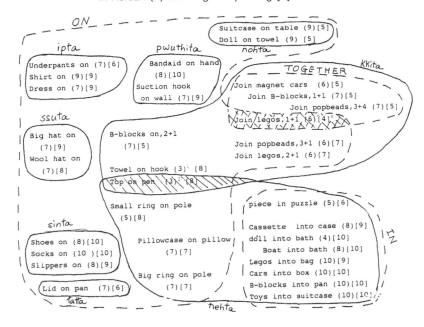

[1]For putting a towel on a hook, three children said *kkita* 'fit tightly' and three said *kelta* 'hook'.
[2]For putting a top on pen, three children said *kkita* 'fit tightly', three said *nehta* 'put in/around loosely', and three said *tatta* 'close'.
[3]For joining two Legos together, four children said *together* and four said *on*.

XXX   Overlapping area of *together* and *on*.
\\\   Overlapping area of *kkita* and *nehta*.

Figure 2.3

children; and the third shows the adult speakers of the two languages. The figures include the actions for which most English-speaking adults said *in, on,* or *together* (33 actions out of the total of 40 joining actions). The position of each action in these diagrams is constant (except for one stimulus: putting a lid on pan), so that we can compare how the actions were categorized across age groups. The categories reflect the dominant response to each action in each age group. (The criterion for the dominant response is the use of a particular word by five or more of the ten subjects in the group.) The dominant responses are labeled outside the relevant category lines. Numbers in parentheses show the number of Korean subjects who responded with the word shown outside the category lines, and numbers in brackets give the same information for the English subjects. For example, Fig. 2.2 shows that 'putting underpants on' was expressed with *ipta* by eight Korean-speaking children and with (*put*) *on* by nine English-speaking

Semantic categories of joining actions by adult
speakers in Korean (K) and English [E].

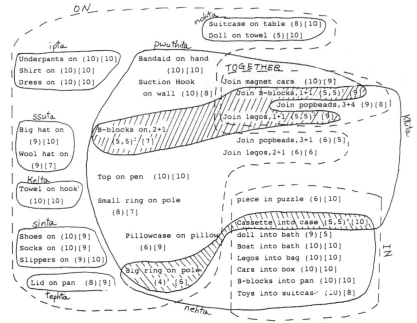

[1]For putting a towel on hook, Korean adults used a specific verb *kelta* 'hook'.

[2]For these items, five adults said *kkita* 'fit tightly' and five said *pwuthita* 'join flat surface to surface'.

[3]For putting a big ring on pole, four adults said *kkita*, three said *nehta*, and three said *kelta*.

[4]For putting an audio cassette into a case, five adults said *kkita* and five said *nehta*.

///: Overlapping area of *kkita* and *pwuthita*.

\\\: Overlapping area between *kkita* and *nehta*.

Figure 2.4

children. In the cases where there was a competition between two words, for example, five subjects said *kkita* and five subjects said *nehta*, I have indicated the competing responses and made notes in the figures. In other cases, there was one dominant response for each action.

Analyses of the data at both general and specific levels reveal several interesting patterns:

1. From the youngest age group, 2;0–2;5 (Fig. 2.2), there is significant agreement among the children learning the same language about categorizing spatial actions. More specifically, dominant patterns could be identified for about 80% of the joining actions.

2. The semantic categories of the youngest age group in each language are significantly more similar to those of the adult group of the corresponding

language than to same-age group learning the other language.[12] That is, the categories of Korean 2-year-olds are significantly more similar to those of the adult Koreans than of English-speaking 2-year-olds.

Patterns of categorization in 2-year-old Korean- and English-speaking children are in fact quite different. For example, Korean-speaking children distinguish clothing verbs appropriately, such as *ipta* for trunk of body, *ssuta* for head, and *sinta* for feet. Also, Korean children say *kkita* for tight-fitting relations regardless of whether the Figure ends up being contained in the Ground (e.g., piece in jigsaw puzzle) or supported by the Ground (e.g., one bristle block on top of another). The word is indifferent as to whether there is a symmetrical or asymmetrical movement between the Figure and the Ground (e.g., putting two magnetic train cars together vs. adding one popbead to a string of popbeads).

The 2-year-old Korean subjects distinguish between tight-fit and loose-fit relations. For example, they say *kkita* for putting a ring on a pole that just fits the ring's hole, whereas they say *nehta* for putting a bigger ring on the pole. Also, whereas they say *kkita* for putting one Lego piece tightly on another, they say *nohta* for a loose support relation, such as putting a suitcase on a table. In the case of *nehta*, children not only use it for loose containment such as putting a boat into a bathtub or putting toys into a suitcase, but also for covering/enveloping relations such as putting a pillowcase on a pillow. (The latter use of *nehta* is an error on the child's part, and is discussed in (3) below.)

In contrast to the several categories distinguished by Korean 2-year-olds for these actions, English-speaking 2-year-olds distinguish only two major categories, *in* and *on*. The 2-year-old learners of English use *in* only for a containment relationship whether it is tight or loose, such as putting a piece in a jigsaw puzzle and a boat into bathtub. Unlike the Korean 2-year-olds' *nehta* category, the *in* category formed by the English-speaking children of the same age excludes relations in which the Figure encircles or covers the Ground, such as putting a loose ring on pole and putting a pillowcase on a pillow (see (3) below).

Unlike the way Korean children use *kkita*, English-speaking children use *on* for all types of attachment (e.g., putting a top on a pen), encirclement (e.g., putting a small/big ring on a pole) and covering (e.g., putting a pillowcase on a pillow), including putting clothes on all parts of the body. Interestingly, they do not readily use *on* for what adults would think of as prototypical instances of the meaning of

---

[12]This analysis involved comparing the similarity matrices of speakers of different groups (i.e., whether the speakers used the same morphemes or morpheme combinations for a given action). We first constructed an aggregate matrix for the adult speakers of each language. We then correlated the similarity matrix of each child with the aggregate adult matrix for all three languages (English, Korean, and Dutch) and with the matrices of all the other children. (The cells of the matrices, for example, action 1 paired with action 2, action 2 paired with action 3, and so on, constitute the list of variables over which the correlation is carried out.) Finally, we tested whether the children in the youngest age group for each language correlated significantly better with the adult aggregate matrix for their own language (and for the other two languages), or with same-age children speaking each of the other two languages.

on—putting something down on surface (e.g., a suitcase on table). The majority of the children simply said *here* or didn't know what to say, although they probably recognized the anticipated spatial relation between the suitcase and the table.

The actions that could be considered as central members (those actions for which eight or more children said a given word) of the 2-year-olds' *on* category have some specific attachment or contact relationship between Figure and Ground. The Figure and Ground in these cases are perceptually distinct from each other, e.g., putting clothes (= Fig.) on a part of body (= Gr.), putting a top (= Fig.) on pen (= Gr.) (see Gopnik & Meltzoff, 1986a, for an insightful discussion of the early uses of *on* in English).

There is some overlap between the *on* and *kkita* categories formed by English- and Korean-speaking children (see Fig. 2.2). But, the two categories differ in what can be considered as their central members. The central members of the *kkita* category for Korean 2-year-olds are the Figure-Ground objects that are similar in size and shape, and that have natural tight-fit relations, such as putting magnets, bristle blocks, and Legos together (the categories in the upper right corner in the figures). However, for English-speaking 2-year-olds, these actions do not form a clear category yet: Only three or four children said *on*. The children's unwillingness to use *on* for these actions suggests their sensitivity to the adult system: English-speaking adults do not use *on* for the symmetric joining of two objects that are similar in size and shape, but rather use *together*.

3. A closer look at the categories of *in* and *on* in English and *nehta* and *kkita* in Korean reveals similarities and differences among these categories. One type of similarity is that the children in both groups respond very consistently to the situations that involve loose containment. That is, in both languages, the response patterns are clear for situations such as putting a boat into a bathtub and putting toys into a suitcase. These actions form the central members of the categories *in* and *nehta* 'put something loosely into a container'.

The difference between the two categories is that English-speaking children restrict their use of *in* to containment and Korean-speaking children extend the category *nehta* to encircling and covering relations. For example, 2-year-olds say *nehta* for putting a pillowcase on pillow as well as for putting a big ring on pole, and 3-year-olds say *nehta* for putting either a small or big ring on pole as well as for putting a top on pen.

There is evidence that these extensions (and overextensions) are influenced by the adult system in Korean. In the adult system, the category *nehta* is both similar to and different from the category *kkita*. First, the two categories overlap to some extent (see Fig. 2.4)—for putting a cassette into a cassette case, half of the adults said *kkita* and half said *nehta*. Thus, when a relatively tight-fit relation involves a complete insertion of the Figure (= moving object) to the Ground, and when the Ground can be seen as a prototypical container (as a cassette case can, but a slot in a jigsaw puzzle can not) speakers say either *nehta* or *kkita*.

Second, Korean adults use *nehta* to refer not only to putting things loosely into containers but also to loose encirclement (e.g., putting a big ring on a pole).

In this use, *nehta* is similar to *kkita*: Both are indifferent as to whether the Figure encircles or is encircled by the Ground. Thus, *nehta* is used for putting both a big ring on a pole and a pole into a big ring. Similarly, *kkita* is used for putting both a ring on a finger and a finger into a ring. The same reversibility is seen in the use of *kkita* when the Figure tightly covers or is covered by the Ground: For example, *kkita* is used both for putting a top tightly on a pen or a pen into its top. Crucially, however, when *nehta* is used for covering rather than encircling situations, the Figure must be covered by—not covering—the Ground (e.g., *nehta* can refer to putting a pillow into a pillowcase, but not putting a pillowcase on a pillow).

With such adult patterns in mind, let's go back to children's overextension examples. Two- and 3-year-old Korean children overextended *nehta* to putting a pillowcase on a pillow. (The experimenter made sure that the Figure was the pillowcase and not the pillow, and adult subjects consistently interpreted the pillowcase appropriately as the Figure saying *kkita* 'put tightly on' or *ssiwuta* 'cover'.) Also, the 3-year-olds overextended *nehta* for putting both a tight and a loose ring on a pole. The children's erroneous use of *nehta* in *kkita* contexts may be derived in part from adults' overlapping uses of the two words. Additionally, the overextension of *nehta* to situations in which the Figure covers the Ground may be influenced by adult patterns in which the same verb is used regardless of whether the encircling or the encircled object is treated as the Figure (and the covering or the covered object, in the case of *kkita*).

In contrast to the Korean children, only one child in the second age group (2;6–3;0) said *in* for putting a tight or loose ring on pole. For putting a pillowcase on pillow, a few children (two in the youngest age group, one in the second group, and three in the oldest age group) said *in*, but the predominant answer in all three age groups was *on*. These data suggest that English-speaking children distinguish between Figure and Ground quite well (and better than Korean children) from early on.

4. We have seen that 2-year-olds are already acquiring the language-specific spatial semantic system. But, the categorizations of the 3-year-olds are even closer to the language-specific system than that of the 2-year-olds. In other words, there is a progression toward the adult categorization from the youngest to the oldest age group of children. In both languages, 3-year-olds make finer categorizations than 2-year-olds, more closely approaching the adult categorization. For example, the development of the category *pwuthita* (typically used for two-dimensional attachments such as putting a bandaid on a hand) emerged between 2;6 and 3;0: 2-year-olds did not use the word, e.g., they either overextended *kkita* (a word for three-dimensional tight-fit relations) to two-dimensional attachment, or said nothing, whereas most of the 3-year-olds used *pwuthita*.

In English, a major difference between 2- and 3-year-olds is the treatment of symmetric and asymmetric movement. For symmetrical actions like putting two magnets or two Lego pieces together, the youngest group of English-speaking children either overextended the word *on* or did not respond. The distinction between the two types of movement began to develop between 2;6 and 3;0, with half of the 3-year-olds distinguishing the two types of joining actions. (There was a parallel transition between *off* and *apart* for separation, but *together* tended to be acquired earlier than *apart*.) These developmental orders can be attributed to the degree of perceptual and cognitive complexity.

3.2.4. *Summary*

Korean- and English-speaking children talk about similar locative events and situations (e.g., going up and down, putting things in and taking them out of containers). But a closer examination of children's language shows that the two groups of children differ systematically in their early syntactic and semantic structure and that these differences reflect language-specific patterns of the adult language. Bowerman's and my data show that from an early stage children develop language-specific lexicalization patterns of motion events. They also attend to a number of criterial features in the adult system that distinguish one semantic category from another. We have seen that the criterial features often differ across languages. For example, English systematically distinguishes containment vs. support while Korean does not. Conversely, Korean systematically distinguishes tight- vs. loose-fit relations, while English does not. Out data show that English- and Korean-speaking children are able to extract these language-specific distinctive features and use them productively from an early stage.

3.3. Acquisition of Locative Casemarkers

In this section, I focus on how Korean-speaking children acquire a set of grammaticized morphemes, locative casemarkers. These morphemes, which are suffixed to nouns, are part of locative expressions in that they express goal, location, and source of a motion event. However, locative casemarkers are different from the spatial verbs discussed in the preceding sections in that they form a closed set (i.e., functors), and operate at a syntactic level. Between 1;0 and 3;0, Korean children acquire four locative casemarkers: *-ey, -eyta, -hanthey, -eyse*. The four markers overlap in the thematic roles they specify, but they contrast in that they make distinctions of the following types: animacy vs. inanimacy of the goal argument, stative vs. process verbs, and intransitive vs. transitive verbs. These distinctions must be made for the locative markers to be used appropriately. Let's look at the adult system more closely before turning to acquisition data.

3.3.1. *Locative Casemarkers in Korean*

The four locative casemarkers, *-ey, -eyta, -hanthey, -eyse*, mark the following thematic functions:

Casemarkers	Thematic functions
-ey	Goal, Location
-eyta	Goal
-hanthey	Goal, Location (= entails Possession)
	Indirect Object
-eyse	Source, Location

-Ey expresses Goal as in (1a), and static location as in (1b).

(1a) *John-i hakkyo-ey ka-n-ta.* (*-ey*: Goal)
John-NOM school-**to** go-PRES-DECL
'John goes to school'.

(1b) *John-i hakkyo-ey iss-ta.* (*-ey*: Location)
John-NOM school-**at** be-DECL
'John is at school'.

-Hanthey expresses goal, as in (2a), location or possession as in (2b), and indirect object as in (2c). This last use of *-hanthey* contrasts with the accusative marker *-(l)ul* which marks the direct object (theme/patient).

(2a) *Aki-ka emma-hanthey ka-n-ta.* (*-hanthey*: Goal)
Baby-NOM mommy-**to** go-PRES-DECL
'The baby goes to mommy'.

(2b) *John-hanthey hyeng-i iss-ta.* (*-hanthey*: Location/Possession)
John-AT/TO older brother-NOM be-DECL
'John has an older brother'.

(2c) *emma-hanthey senmwul-ul cwu-n-ta.* (*-hanthey*: Goal (Indirect Object))
Mommy-**to** present-OBJ give-PRES-DECL
'(Somebody) Gives Mommy a present'.

-Eyta also expresses goal, as in (3a).

(3a) *Aka-ka cup-eyta uyu-lul pwu-ess-ta.* (*-eyta*: Goal)
Baby-NOM cup-**to** milk-OBJ pour-PAST-DECL
'The baby poured milk into the cup'.

Finally, *-eyse* also expresses source, as in (4a), and location of an activity, as in (4b).

(4a) *John-i hakkyo-eyse tolawa-ss-ta.* (*-eyse*: Source)
John-NOM school-**from** return-PAST-DECL
'John returned from school'.

(4b) *John-i hakkyo-eyse kongpwu ha-n-ta.* (*-eyse*: Location)
John-NOM school-**at** study do-PRES-DECL
'John is studying at school'.

These examples show that several forms are used to express the same thematic roles. For example, *-ey, -hanthey*, and *-eyta* are all used to express goal, and *-ey* and *-eyse* both mark location. But a closer look at these forms shows that each represents a specific semantic or syntactic category related either to the noun they are suffixed to or to the main verb of the clause.

First, *-ey* and *-hanthey*—both used to mark goals—make a distinction on the basis of animacy: *-ey* is used when the goal argument is an inanimate object, whereas *-hanthey* is used when it is an animate being. This distinction is obligatory, as shown in (5).

> (5) *-ey* vs. *-hanthey*: inanimate vs. animate noun
> *hakkyo-ey/-*hanthey kata* 'school-to go' (= go to school)
> *emma-*ey/-hanthey kata* 'mommy-to go' (= go to mommy)

Second, *-ey* and *-eyta*—both used to mark goals—make a distinction on the basis of transitivity: *-ey* is used with both intransitive and transitive motion verbs, whereas *-eyta* is used only with transitive motion verbs, as shown in (6).

> (6) *-ey* vs. *-eyta*: intransitive vs. transitive motion verbs
> *table-ey/-*eyta olla kata* 'table-to ascend go' (= go up on the table)
> *table-ey/-eyta cup-ul nohta* 'table-to cup-do put-on' (= put the cup on the table)

Third, the two markers expressing the location of an event make an obligatory distinction between stative verbs (*-ey*) and activity/process verbs (*-eyse*), as shown in (7).

> (7) *-ey* vs. *-eyse*: stative vs. activity/process verbs
> *hakkyo-ey/*eyse issta* 'school-at be.located' (= be at school)
> *hakkyo-*ey/-eyse nolta* 'school-at play' (= play at school)

The stative verbs in Korean are restricted to adjectival verbs (e.g., *ipputa* 'be pretty', *maypta* 'be spicy') and a small set of verbs which denote locations and postures: *epsta* 'not.exist', *issta* 'be.located', *swumta* 'hide', *namta* 'remain', *sokhata* 'belong', *tulta* 'be.in', *ancta* 'sit', *seta* 'stand', *kitayta* 'lean', *nwupta* 'lie down'. These verbs do not take the progressive form *-ko issta*, whereas activity/process verbs do (Kim, 1990). However, to express duration of a state, the stative verbs take the resultative form *-e issta*, e.g., *John-i mwun twui-ey swum-e issta* 'John-NOM door behind-LOC hide-CONN be.located-DECL' (= John is hiding behind the door). (*Epsta* 'not.exist/not.be.located' and *issta* 'be.located', however, take neither the progressive form nor the resultative form.) The Korean stative verb category differs from its English counterpart at least in two aspects: In Korean, posture verbs, e.g., *ancta* 'sit' or *seta* 'stand', do not take the progressive, whereas in English they do (e.g., *John is standing in front of* *the theater*).[13] Further, the kinds of verbs considered as stative differ in the two languages: Korean stative verbs consist of a small set of locative and posture verbs (perhaps with the exception of *sokhata* 'belong'), and adjectival verbs (e.g., *ipputa* 'be pretty'), whereas English stative verbs are existential verbs (e.g., *be*), possession verbs (e.g., *have*), and also include psych verbs like *love* and *need*.

To summarize, several semantic/syntactic distinctions are made with locative casemarkers in Korean: animate vs. inanimate nouns, transitive (caused) vs. intransitive (spontaneous) motion verbs, and stative vs. process/activity verbs. For example, when *-ey* expresses goal, it is used with an inanimate goal argument with an intransitive verb; thus, it contrasts with both *-hanthey* (used with an animate goal) and *-eyta* (used with a transitive verb). When *-ey* expresses location, it occurs with stative verbs, thus contrasting with *-eyse* (used with an activity verb).

Many other languages also make these distinctions, although the morphological rules are, of course, language-specific. Several researchers have examined how children acquire them, and have made specific claims:

1. *Animacy Versus Inanimacy.* In Russian and Polish, the choice of locative case suffixes are determined partly by the animacy vs. inanimacy of the noun, but young children do not make the distinction (Slobin, 1985). Also, Bowerman (1978, 1985) reports that her two daughters made errors with *put* and *give*, using *put* inappropriately when the goal is animate (e.g., **You put me just bread and butter*), and *give* when the goal is inanimate (e.g., **Don't give those next to me*). Based on these data, Slobin concludes that ANIMACY is not "a Notion that children readily attend to in establishing mapping for functors—or at least the functors we have been considering" (1985, p. 1186).

2. *Transitive Versus Intransitive Action Verbs.* Rispoli (1987) has observed that Japanese children rarely make errors on this distinction from an early period in their spontaneous speech: They correctly use transitive action verbs for caused motion and intransitive action verbs for spontaneous motion. As discussed in Section 3.2, Choi and Bowerman (1991) also found that Korean children clearly distinguish transitive verbs for caused motion from intransitive verbs for spontaneous motion.

3. *Stative Versus Process Verbs.* Bickerton (1984) has argued that this distinction is innate in children. He bases this claim on his study of creole grammars in which the distinction between stative and process verbs is consistently made. A number of studies have evaluated this claim: Cziko and Koda (1987) report that Japanese children also make a distinction between state versus process verbs by using the present progressive form only with process verbs. On the other

---

[13]When a posture verb takes the progressive suffix (*-ko issta*), it only means that the person is in the process of getting into a particular posture, such as *anc-ko issta* 'sit.down-PROG' (= be in the middle of sitting down).

hand, Li (1989) shows that the kinds of verbs considered as stative in Chinese and English are different and that there is little evidence that Chinese children distinguish between stative and process verbs.

Acquisition data in Korean will allow us to further evaluate these claims, since its locative casemarking system makes the relevant distinctions. In the next section, I will analyze the development of locative markers at an early period as well as errors that occur at a later period.

3.3.2. *Development of Locative Markers in Korean Children*

I have analyzed the development of the locative markers in four children observed longitudinally (Choi, 1991). The period of observation ranged from 1;8 to 4;8. I found that (1) the locative markers tended to occur at first with specific nouns or verbs, generalizing only later; and (2) certain distinctions were made early and without error, whereas other distinctions were acquired later after a period of reorganization.

The four locative forms emerged in the following sequence: *-ey* > *-eyta* > *-eyse*, *-hanthey*. *-Ey* was acquired first by all children; *-eyta* was typically acquired within 1 or 2 months. A few months later, *-eyse* and *-hanthey* were acquired around the same time. This order of acquisition is consistent with the pervasive finding that children express the goal of motion before the location of an event. For example, Clancy (1985) reports that Japanese children acquire the marker for Goal (*ni*) before the marker for location of an activity (*de*) (see also Bloom et al., 1975). However, the Korean children acquire *-hanthey*, which also expresses goal, relatively late. This may be due to its plurifunctionality: the marker expresses location, possession, and indirect object. In the following section, I look at the development of these markers by pairs that contrast in a particular way.

3.3.2.1. *-ey and -eyta.*   The children initially used *-ey* correctly, to express goal, but with a restricted set of verbs, mostly *kata* 'go' and *ota* 'come'. *-Ey* was used much less frequently to express location at this early stage. When it expressed location, however, it typically occurred with the stative verb *issta* 'be.located'. See (8) through (11).

(8) (TJ 2;2)
appa hakkyo-ey ka-ss-ta.
daddy school-**to** go-PAST-SE
'Daddy went to school'.

(9) (TJ 2;7)
cip-ey wa-ss-e.

home-**to** come-PAST-SE
'Came home'.

(10) (WJ 1;8)
pwuek-ey ka-ss-e.
kitchen-**to** go-PAST-SE
'(Mommy) went to the kitchen'.

(11) (WJ 2;1)
cip-ey iss-e.
home-**to** be.located-SE
'(Somebody) is at home'.

When *-eyta* (denoting goal with a transitive verb) emerged, it contrasted correctly with *-ey*. That is, it was always used with a transitive motion verb denoting caused motion (see [12]–[13])—most frequently *nohta* 'put an object on a surface' as shown in (12)—*nehta* 'put an object in a container', and the light verb *hata* 'to do something'. The children made only occasional errors in their choice between *-ey* and *-eyta* during the development period studied.

(12) (HS 1;11)
yeki-(ey)ta nwa.
here-**to** put.on
'Put it on here'.

(13) (WJ 1;9)
cecpyeng-eyta pwue.
bottle-**to** pour.in
'Pour (it) in the bottle'.

As noted earlier, the early distinction between transitive verbs for caused motion and intransitive verbs for spontaneous motion is consistent with Choi and Bowerman's (1991) finding that Korean children restrict transitive verbs, such as *kkita* 'put an object tightly onto/into something', to situations of caused motion. It is also consistent with Rispoli's finding (1987) that 2-year-old Japanese children distinguish between the two types of action. In the case of locative markers, it should be recalled that the *-eyta* case marking for caused movement is optional, that is, it is grammatical to use *-ey* for both spontaneous and caused motions. But, the children acquired *-eyta* early, and used it only for caused motions. This suggests that the spontaneous vs. caused motion distinction is highly salient to young Korean children.

3.3.2.2. ***-ey* and *-hanthey.*** Turning to the acquisition of *-ey* (used for inanimate goals) vs. *-hanthey* (used for animate goals), the distinction is clearly grasped from the beginning: The children produced *-ey* first, using it only with inanimate nouns only, and when they acquired *-hanthey*, they used it only with animate nouns, typically human (see [14]–[16]). Initially the two markers were used with a small set of inanimate and animate nouns: *-Ey* was used with *cip* 'house' and *hakkyo* 'school', and *-hanthey* with *emma* 'mommy'. Later, the distinction became more productive, and it was observed consistently throughout the developmental period observed.[14]

(14) (TJ 2;11)
    *nwukwu-**hanthey** ka?*
    who-**to** go
    'go to who?'

(15) (WJ 1;10)
    Adult: *eti ka?*
             where go
             'Where are you going?'
    Child: *emma-**hanthey**.*
             mommy-**to**
             'To mommy'.

(16) (HS 2;5)
    *na-**hanthey** cwe.*
    I-**to** give
    'give (it) to me'.

The early and errorless distinction on the basis of animacy in Korean contrasts with the relatively late acquisition of the distinction in Polish and Russian. But it is important to note that in Polish and Russian, the distinction is combined with gender and number in a complex way (e.g., in Polish, the animate vs. inanimate distinction is made for masculine singular nouns in accusative case (Smoczyńska, 1985)), and it is not always obligatory. In contrast, the distinction in Korean is systematic, morphologically transparent, and obligatory. The Korean data suggest that when the input language makes a morphologically clear and obligatory distinction between two categories, children readily acquire it without error.

So far, we have seen two distinctions that were made appropriately by Korean children from early on: animate versus inanimate nouns, and transitive versus intransitive motion verbs. Interestingly, the two distinctions seem to be closely related in sentence construction: In expressions of spontaneous motion, which is typically encoded by an intransitive verb, the entity that moves is typically animate as in '***John ran to the store***'. In contrast, in expressions of caused motion encoded by a transitive verb, the entity moved is typically an inanimate noun, as in *John put **the cup** on the table*. It is possible, therefore, that in Korean, the

---

[14]Of all the instances of *-hanthey* in all children, only three errors have been detected.

early distinction between animacy vs. inanimacy interacts with the early differentiation between transitive and intransitive sentences. In fact, Rispoli (1987, 1989) found the two types of distinctions to be related in the speech of Japanese children and caregivers: Japanese children predominantly use intransitive sentences when an animate being undergoes a change of location; conversely, they predominantly use transitive sentences when the entity moved is inanimate. Furthermore, Rispoli (1989) found that this pattern is mode.ed in Japanese caregivers' sentences.

To see whether the same is true for Korean, I looked at the speech of the mothers of two children between 22 and 24 months. Similar to Rispoli's data, Korean caregivers show systematic and distinct usage of transitive and intransitive locative construction based on animacy and inanimacy of the Figure of Motion. Based on these data, it can be hypothesized that, from the Korean child's perspective, the acquisition of one distinction (i.e., distinction of animacy or verb types) reinforced the acquisition of the other, and that such an intimate relationship between the two played an important role for the early and error-free learning of the two types of distinctions.

3.3.2.3. *-ey and -eyse.*   Let's now turn to the distinction between stative and activity verbs made by *-ey* and *-eyse* respectively. Recall that initially the children used *-ey* correctly for prototypical stative verbs, such as *issta* 'be.located' (cf. (11) above). Similarly, at the beginning, the children used *-eyse* correctly with a few activity verbs, as shown in (17) and (18).

(17) (SB 2;11)
      *nay-ka hakkyo-**eyse** mantul-ess-e.*
      I-NOM school-**at** make-PAST-SE
      'I made it at school'.

(18) (HS 2;3)
      *pang-**eyse** hay-ss-e.*
      room-**at** do-PAST-SE
      'I did (something) in the room'.

Later on, however, the children began to make a number of errors confusing *-ey* and *-eyse*. Examples of errors of substituting *-eyse* for *-ey* are shown in Table 2.7a. In these examples, children made errors by using *-eyse* with stative verbs. The errors involving the reverse pattern, that is, the use of *-ey* where *-eyse* would be appropriate, are shown in Table 2.7b. In these examples, children incorrectly used *-ey* with process/activity verbs, such as *nolta* 'play' and *takkta* 'clean'. Although such errors were not predominant in their uses of the two markers, they were more substantial than errors of other kinds (e.g., *-ey* vs. *-eyta*). For example, in TJ's speech produced between 3;0 and 3;6, 20% of her *-ey* and *-eyse* uses were incorrect. It is striking that during the error period the children used

TABLE 2.7
Examples of Errors Involving **-ey** and **-eyse**

a. *-eyse* substituted for *-ey*. (i.e. *-eyse* is inappropriate with stative verbs.)

1. TJ (3;1): *chimtay-*eyse swumesse.* (to hide)
'(Somebody) hid in the bed.'

2. TJ (3;5): *yeki-*(ey)se swumesse thokki-ka.* (to hide)
'The rabbit hid here.'

3. TJ (3;6): *Mr. Bump yeki-*(ey)se epsse.* (not-be located)
'Mr. Bump is not here.'

4. TJ (3;8): *os-un Tops-*eyse epsci.* (not-be located)
'There are no dresses at Tops.' (Tops = a supermarket)

5. TJ (3;10): *cip-*eyse issci.* (to be located)
'(Somebody) is at home.'

6. SB (2;10): *kyohwey-*eyse ike isse.* (to be located)
'This is in the church.'

7. HS (2;8): *chimtay-*eyse nwue.* (to lie down)
'Lie down on bed.'

8. HS (2;8): *Baby yeki-*(ey)se nwupca.* (to lie down)
'Baby lies down here.'

9. WH (2;1): *echung-*eyse issci.* (to be located)
'(Mommy) is on the second floor.'

b. *-ey* substituted for *-eyse*. (*-ey* is inappropriate with process verbs.)

10. TJ (3;2): *cip-*ey theyleybi pwa.* (to watch)
'(I) watch TV at home.'

11. TJ (3;2): *chyeta poko isse, changmwun-*ey.* (to look)
'(Somebody) is looking at the window.'

12. TJ (3;3): *eti-*ey cwukesse?* (to die)
'Where did (she) die?'

13. TJ (3;5): *ichung-*ey chengso-hay.* (to clean)
'(She) is cleaning on the second floor.'

14. SB (2;11): *canti-*ey campwu-hay.* (to jump)
'(Somebody) is jumping on the grass.'

15. WJ (2;0): *PL-cip-*ey ike kacko nolketun.* (to play)
'PL plays with this at home.'

16. WJ (2;2): *appa pang-*ey nolassketun.* (to play)
'(I) play in daddy's room.'

17. WJ (2;2): *Baby acwumma cip-*ey [pota].* (to see)
'I saw it at the aunt's.'

18. WJ (2;3): *na ce pang-*ey [cata].* (to sleep)
'I slept in that room.'

19. WJ (2;6): *cip-*ey mwe hana?* (to do)
'What (does she) do at home?'

Note. 1. In parentheses, the main verb of the utterance is indicated.
2. The verb in brackets has been mentioned in the preceding discourse, and is the implicit predicate of the child's utterance.

-*eyse* even with the most prototypical stative verbs, *issta* 'be.located' or *epsta* 'not.be.located'.

These errors suggest that the initial correct use of -*ey* and -*eyse* with a limited set of stative vs. process verbs is not readily generalized to the categories defined in the adult language. These error data thus do not support Bickerton's (1984) Language Bioprogram Hypothesis (LBH). According to the LBH, the distinction between stative and process verbs is innate. Contrary to Bickerton's claims, data of Korean children show that the grammatical distinction between stative and process/activity verbs is learned over time with a period of errors and reorganization.

3.3.2.4. **-*hanthey* and -*(l)ul*.** In examining children's errors with the four locative markers, another type of error was striking, that involving -*hanthey*. As noted above, -*hanthey* is used with an indirect object of verbs such as *cwuta* 'give' and *ponayta* 'send'. (Note that the indirect objects of these verbs are animate beings.) However, during the developmental period observed, the children made a number of errors, using -*hanthey* for patient/theme role where the direct object marker -*(l)ul* would be appropriate. Some examples are shown in Table 2.8. Particularly interesting errors are those uses of -*hanthey* for prototypical transitive verbs such as *mekta* 'eat' and *mwulta* 'bite', since the actions referred to by these verbs result in a clear change of state of the patient. These error data provide evidence that are counter to nativistic views (e.g., Pinker,

TABLE 2.8
Examples of Errors Involving Substitution of -*hanthey*
(Indirect Object Marker) for -*(l)ul* (Direct Object Marker)

1. TJ (3;6):	*nwukwu-*hanthey [ttaylita]?* (to hit)
	'Whom (did she hit)?'
2. TJ (3;6):	*mwune-ka Mr. Bump-*hanthey meknuntay.* (to eat)
	'The octopus ate Mr. Bump.'
3. TJ (3;6):	*yay-*hanthey [meke].* (to eat)
	'(He's eating) it.'
4. TJ (3;6):	*Lalary-*hanthey [ttaylita].* (to hit)
	'(She hit) Lalary.'
5. TJ (3;6):	*mengmeng-ika yay-*hanthey ttalaka.* (to follow)
	'The doggie is following her.'
6. TJ (3;8):	*HJ-ka Lalary-*hanthey yeki mwulesse.* (to bite)
	'HJ bit Lalary here.'
7. TJ (4;7):	*emma-*hanthey manasse.* (to meet)
	'(He) met mommy.'
8. HS (2;5):	*nay-ka yoke-*hanthey haysse.* (to do something)
	'I did this.'
9. HS (2;8):	*pise, acwumma-*hanthey.* (to comb)
	'I comb the aunt.'
10. WJ (2;6):	*cow-*hanthey man/*(self-corrected) *cow-lul manasse.* (to meet)
	'(It) met the cow.'

1984; Gropen, Pinker, Hollander, & Goldberg, 1991) that suggest an innate linkage between a semantic role (e.g., affected patient) and a syntactic role (e.g., direct object). Rather, the data presented here suggest that the argument structure of even prototypical transitive verbs must be at least in part learned from the input (Bowerman, 1990; see also Brinkmann, 1993) (see Section 5 for more discussion).

3.3.3. *Summary and Discussion*

In summary, the data on locative casemarkers show that children initially make correct distinctions for all four locative markers with a small set of nouns and verbs. Thus, at the beginning, children acquire casemarkers piecemeal, associating each marker with individual verbs or nouns. Consider for example, TJ, whose development was followed for a long time. At first, TJ used each locative marker with only one or two verbs.

Marker	*Co-occurring verbs*
-ey:	*kata* 'go', *ota* 'come', *issta* 'be.located'
-eyse:	*cata* 'sleep'
-eyta:	*nohta* 'put.on loosely', *nehta* 'put.in loosely'
-hanthey	*kata* 'go', *cwuta* 'give'.

For some markers, co-occurring nouns were also restricted, for example, *-ey* occurred mostly with *cip* 'house' or *hakkyo* 'school', and *-hanthey* with *emma* 'mommy'. Similar to TJ, the other children's early combinations of a particular locative marker and particular verbs or nouns often seemed like unanalyzed chunks (e.g., *cip-ey ka-ss-e*, house-to go-PAST-SE, 'went home'; *emma-hanthey*, mommy-to, 'to mommy') taken from their caregivers' speech.

As children moved into a linguistically more complex period, however, their developmental patterns for the four markers diverged: Whereas they continued to maintain almost error-free uses for some distinctions, for others, they went through late error periods (i.e., periods of reorganization). Analysis of both types of data suggests, however, that linguistic input is important for the acquisition of these markers.

The distinctions that continued to be error-free in the children's speech are the animacy versus inanimacy and transitive versus intransitive distinctions. Earlier, I suggested that the two types of distinctions may interact with each other and that the early acquisition of these rules may be facilitated by several types of cues provided in the linguistic input. First, in Korean, transitive and intransitive locative verbs have distinct morphology. Second, in my data, caregivers typically use intransitive sentences when an animate being spontaneously changes location, whereas they use transitive sentences when the entity moved is inanimate. Third, animacy is consistently distinguished from inanimacy by a locative case marker, such as *-hanthey* vs. *-ey*. Compared to children learning some other languages (e.g., English, Polish), Korean children are exposed to an input that provides a relatively high degree of semantic and morphological transparency concerning animacy and transitivity of locative verbs. Following Slobin's operating principle on semantic transparency (1973), Korean children seem privileged to acquire the two types of distinction early.

For the distinctions between stative and process/activity verbs, and between direct and indirect objects, however, periods of error were observed. What do these errors tell us? Let's first look at when the errors began. Table 2.9 shows the development of the four markers in three children as well as their error period. (The observation of the fourth child began at 2;10, when he already produced all four markers.) The table shows that the amount of time it took children to produce all four forms varied from two to nine months. But all three children were similar in that they began making errors one to three months after all four markers were acquired. The error period lasted about three to six months; after that, only occasional errors were detected.

Thus, the data show a U-shaped learning curve for these markers. Such learning curves, and in particular those in which errors appear relatively late, have been reported by Bowerman (1981, 1982) in her studies of English-speaking children's acquisition of syntax and word meaning. Bowerman explains that errors occur as children begin to compare forms and discover regular relationship between them. The Korean data on locative markers support this view. The timing of the error period, that is, after the acquisition of all four markers, suggests that the children make errors as they attempt to formulate rules that govern the locative case marking system as a whole, and discover regular relationship among the markers.

Also important to note is that the error period occurred when there was a rapid increase in the number of verbs with which the children used locative markers. Consider again TJ's development. At the initial stage, TJ combined the four locative markers with only seven verbs in total. However, during the error period, the number of verbs that TJ used with the markers increased to 53 verb types. Similar patterns are shown in the other children. This suggests that errors may occur as children construct some general underlying rules about the locative markers in order to deal with many verbs. For example, as children acquire several locative markers and use them with many verbs, they may discover that

TABLE 2.9
Development of Locative Markers and Error Periods in Three Korean Children

Child	Study Period	Onset of Casemarking	Production of All Four Markers	Frequent Error Period
TJ	1;9–4;8	2;2	2;11	3;0–3;6
HS	1;11–2;10	1;11	2;3	2;5–2;8
WJ	1;8–2;8	1;8	1;10	2;1–2;6

both -*ey* (locative marker for stative verbs) and -*eyse* (locative marker for activity/process verbs) share the function of expressing location of an event. This discovery could motivate them to use the two markers interchangeably for the location of an event, since they are not yet clearly differentiating between stativity and activity. Even when children do acquire the distinction between stativity and activity, they may still make errors if they have not learned how the input language categorizes the two types of verbs. For example, events denoted by verbs like *pota* 'see' and *cata* 'sleep' are not dynamic (i.e., nothing happens when one sees or is sleeping), and yet in adult Korean they are categorized as activity verbs and take -*eyse* as their locative marker. Korean children have to learn through further linguistic experience that -*ey* is restricted to verbs that express location, such as *issta* 'be.located', *namta* 'remain', *swumta* 'hide', *epsta* 'not.exist', and to posture verbs.

Similar explanations can be given for the errors with -*hanthey* (indirect object marker). Children initially seem to correctly restrict -*hanthey* to animate goals and -*(l)ul* to inanimate patients. For example, they initially use -*hanthey* for the animate goal of a few intransitive verbs, such as *kata* 'go', and to animate indirect objects of transitive verbs of transfer, such as *cwuta* 'give' (see examples [14]–[16] above). But, as children become able to acquire a large number of verbs and nouns and combine them syntactically, they also produce sentences in which an animate being is the patient of the main verb, for example, *Mary-lul ttaylita* 'Mary-ACC hit' (= hit Mary). Using the animacy versus inanimacy distinction that they have developed, children may continue to use -*hanthey* for animate nouns even when the language requires these nouns to be expressed as direct objects, that is, patients (cf. examples in Table 2.9). This would result in errors. Furthermore, as is well known, the degree of affectedness or change of state does not always provide cues for determining whether the argument is direct or indirect object (Schlesinger, 1977; Brinkmann, 1993). For example, in *John-i Mary-lul ttâl-a ka-n-ta* 'John-NOM Mary-ACC follow-CONN go-PRES-SE' (= John is following Mary), the patient Mary is not obviously affected. Nevertheless, Korean uses the direct object marker -*(l)ul* (cf. example 5 in Table 2.9). Korean children have to learn that -*hanthey* is often used as a formal dimension for dative or goal roles determined by language-specific verb-argument structure. Thus, the errors made during the reorganization period suggest that children are constructing rules based on their previous linguistic experiences, and that they need further linguistic input to assimilate the adult rules.

3.4. Acquisition of Sentence-Ending Modal Particles

In this last section of data presentation, I focus on the acquisition of sentence-ending (SE) modal suffixes in Korean. My main goal in this section is to present a qualitative analysis of the caregiver–child interactions that seem to be crucial in the acquisition of the meanings of a class of grammatical morphemes in

Korean. Such analysis will shed light on not only what children acquire but also HOW children acquire language-specific grammar.

As discussed in Kim's chapter in Volume 4 (1997), children begin to use a few modal suffixes BEFORE 2 years, and by 3;0, children productively use a number of suffixes (see Table 2.7 in Kim, 1997). In Choi (1991) I have shown that many of these suffixes denote epistemic/evidential meanings (see also next section). In my data, between 1;8 and 2;2, children acquire four epistemic modal suffixes, *-ta, -e, -ci,* and *-tay,* in a consistent order. Furthermore, from this early period, they use the suffixes with clear pragmatic distinctions that relate to old versus newly acquired knowledge (expressed by *-e* and *-ta* respectively), certainty of information (*-ci*), and source of information (*-tay*). Choi (1991, 1995) shows that both the child's cognitive understanding of the world and the discourse-interactional aspects of context play an important role in the child's early acquisition of these modal suffixes. In the following, I will briefly describe the Korean modal system in adult grammar, and will present a detailed analysis of acquisition data of three children.

3.4.1. The Modal System in Korean

Korean has two types of modal forms: SE modal suffixes and modal auxiliary verbs. Table 2.10 shows a list of modal forms in the two categories with approximate meanings in English. SE suffixes are bound morphemes and occupy the final position among the inflections on the predicate (verb or adjective). Since Korean is a verb final (SOV) language, the suffixes occur typically at the end of the sentence, as in (1). SE suffixes form an obligatory grammatical category, that is, a sentence must have an SE suffix.

(1) *Younghi-ka Seoul-ul ttena-ss-e.*
     Younghi-SUBJ Seoul-OBJ leave-PAST-SE
     'Younghi left Seoul.'

In contrast, modal auxiliary verbs are free morphemes which can optionally occur after the main verb, as in (2). An auxiliary verb must be connected to the main verb by a specific connecting suffix on the latter to express a given modal meaning. For example, the connective *-ya* followed by the auxiliary verb *twayta,* that is, *-ya twayta,* expresses obligation, whereas the connective *-to* with *twayta* expresses permission.

(2) *Younghi-ka Seoul-ey ka-ya/to tway(-e).*[15]
     Younghi-SUBJ Seoul-to go-CONN AUX(-SE).
     'Younghi must/can go to Seoul.'

---

[15]*-e* is deleted when the verb stem ends with a vowel.

TABLE 2.10
Modal Forms and Meanings in Korean
(Frequently Used in Caregivers' Speech to Children)

Form	Meaning
A. Sentence-Ending Modal Suffixes	
EPISTEMIC	
-ta	Newly perceived information for the speaker
-e	Assimilated information, unmarked form
-ci/-cyana*	Certainty of proposition, shared information
-kwun(a)	Newly made inference
-tay	Reported speech, hearsay/story telling
-ney	Information based on factual evidence
-ni	Uncertainty and negative bias of proposition
DEONTIC/EPISTEMIC	
-llay	desire, future
-kkey	intention, future, prediction
B. Modal Auxiliary Verbs	
EPISTEMIC	
-ci moluta	possibility (weak)
-kes kathta	possibility (strong)
-tus hata	possibility (strong)
-(u)l kesita	probability
-na pota	inference
DEONTIC	
-swu issta	ability
-to twayta	permission
-ya hata/twayta	obligation
-ko siphta	desire

**-cyana* is the suffix *-ci* followed by the negative marker *-ana*. The two morphemes, when combined, express a stronger commitment to the truth of the proposition than *-ci*.

Other examples include the connective *-ko* and the auxiliary *siphta* expressing desire, and *-swu issta* expressing ability. Thus, connectives are an integral part of the whole auxiliary modal system in Korean. A list of combinations of frequently used connectives and auxiliary verbs in Korean is shown in Table 2.10B. Note that each form denotes either agent-oriented or epistemic meaning, and there is no overlap of the two types of modality on the same verb, except the verb *hata* 'to do'.

In contrast to the auxiliary verbs, SE suffixes have more abstract meanings, and their functions have been an area of investigation in recent studies of Korean linguistics. Several studies (Choi, 1991; H. S. Lee, 1991; K. Lee, 1986) have suggested that many of the SE suffixes code the differential status of information in the speaker's knowledge system. H. S. Lee (1991) states the functions of SE suffixes as follows:

> What is differentiated by sentence-terminal suffixes is various epistemic modality categories, including the speaker's knowledge status, background expectation, evidentiary sources of the information conveyed, and the speaker's assumption about the addressee's point of view. (H. S. Lee, 1991, p. 471)

Several SE suffixes code degrees of integration of information in the speaker's mind. The contrasts among the three suffixes, -ta, -kwun, and -e, illustrate this point. The suffix -ta is often used by the speaker when he/she has just perceived something noteworthy in the present context, "either because it is about the accomplishment of awaited events or states of affairs at the very moment of speaking" (H. S. Lee, 1993). Consider the following context: John and his wife are waiting for a friend at a restaurant. Their friend is late. Upon seeing the friend finally appear at the restaurant door, John would say:

(3) *o-ass-ta.*
     come-PAST-SE
     '(He) has come.'

The use of -ta is appropriate in this context, in which John has just seen the friend and registers the information in his mind for the first time. Comments made with -ta may not be directed to the listener; they can be noteworthy remarks to the speaker himself. Once the speaker has registered this new information, in subsequent conversations, for example, when the speaker repeats the information again to his wife, or when he tells this experience later to another friend, he would use the SE form -e:

(4) *o-ass-e.*
     come-PAST-SE
     '(He) came.'

In this latter context, the use of -ta, that is, *o-ass-ta* is ungrammatical. The use of -ta is not restricted to the perception of the outside world. It can also occur with an internal state of mind. For example, adult Koreans often say *al-ass-ta*, know-PAST-SE '(I)'ve got (it)' when they have just come to an understanding of something. (It should be noted that -ta is not an aspectual marker denoting perfective aspect. One can use -ta when describing a state of affairs as well as an ongoing activity if it draws the speaker's attention for the first time, e.g., *ippu-ta* pretty-SE '(she's) pretty', or *o-n-ta* come-PRES-SE '(They) are coming').

The suffix *-kwun* is similar to *-ta* in that it is also used for newly acquired information. However, the information marked by *-kwun* (or *-kwuna*) is often an INFERENCE based on what the speaker has just seen, as in example (5).

(5) (The mother, upon seeing her daughter, notices that her eyes are red. The mother says,)
ne wul-ess-kwuna.
you cry-PAST-SE
'You cried.'

By using *-kwun*, the mother expresses that she has just realized what happened by inference from indirect evidence. In this case, Korean speakers would not use *-ta*. As H. S. Lee (1985, 1993) argues, both *-ta* and *-kwun* are used for knowledge that has not yet been assimilated into the speaker's knowledge system. The difference between the two suffixes is that *-ta* is used with knowledge obtained through direct experience, whereas *-kwun* is often used with knowledge obtained through inference.

In contrast to *-ta* and *-kwun*, *-e* is used when the information has already been assimilated into the speaker's knowledge system: the speaker acquired the information in the past, therefore has known it for some time. As mentioned above, once newly perceived information is encoded with *-ta* or *-kwun*, *-e* must be used in subsequent mentions of the information. In H. S. Lee's survey (1991), *-e* is the most frequent suffix (58%) in spontaneous discourse interactions. This is not surprising, since in conversations participants often contribute to the topic by offering information that they already have about the topic. Indeed, one can conclude that *-e* is the unmarked suffix in conversations.

In discussing *-kwun* above, we have seen how a particular status of knowledge is related to an evidentiary source, for example, direct experience or inference. There are a few other suffixes that differentiate evidential sources in Korean. The difference between *-tay* and *-ney* is a case in point. Whereas *-tay* marks hearsay or reported speech, *-ney* signals that the event was directly witnessed by the speaker.

All of these suffixes are used only in informal conversational interactions where participants, familiar to one another, freely and spontaneously exchange information about the current topic. Probably due to this characteristic, the meanings of many suffixes incorporate the speaker's assumption about how much the listener knows. That is, the speaker's choice of a specific SE suffix reflects his assumption about the listener's status of knowledge of the proposition (H. S. Lee, 1991). For example, the suffix *-ci* (or *-cyana*) is used when the speaker commits himself to the truth of the proposition; it expresses certainty (*-cyana* expresses a stronger commitment than *-ci*) regardless of whether the information comes from direct experience or from inference. At the same time, *-ci* denotes that the information is also known to the listener or can be readily inferred by the listener. This is confirmed by the use of -*ci* in questions. The suffix -*ci*? is used in a question when the speaker is certain about the truth of the proposition and at the same time wants to confirm that the listener also believes (or knows) it's true. This is shown in (6). (Thus, in the case of (5) above, if the mother is certain of her inference, she can say *ne wul-ess-ci*? 'You cried, didn't you?') Considering the context of (6), the meaning conveyed by -*ci* is that the speaker is certain that Mary is pretty and also believes that the listener has the same opinion. The speaker expects agreement from the listener. Compare this with the suffix -*ni*? in (7). When -*ni*? is used, it conveys the speaker's assumption that the listener knows more than the speaker about the matter (since only the latter saw Mary).[16] By using -*ni* the speaker expresses a desire to know what the listener believes to be true.

(6) (Possible context: Both speaker and listener saw Mary and both liked her. The speaker later asks,)
Mary-ka ippu-ci?
Mary-SUBJ pretty-SE?
'Isn't Mary pretty?'

(7) (Possible context: The speaker heard from someone that Mary was pretty. The speaker asks the listener, who has seen Mary,)
Mary-ka ippu-ni?
Mary-SUBJ pretty-SE?
'Is Mary pretty?'

Thus, -*ci* and -*ni* express different degrees of certainty which also relate to what the speaker assumes about the listener's knowledge.

In summary, I have discussed several examples to show that a number of SE modal suffixes in Korean express evidentiality and different statuses of knowledge in which the speaker's and the listener's beliefs about an event or state are involved. Probably because of the requirement of incorporating what the listener believes about a particular situation, these modal suffixes are neither used in formal situations (e.g., a formal speech), nor in contexts where the speaker/writer does not have a particular listener/reader in mind, such as in newspapers. (-*Ta* is an unmarked SE form for these contexts.) In other words, these suffixes are used only in interactive contexts (e.g., a conversation, a personal letter to a friend) in which the speaker knows what and how much the listener knows. As we will see below, the Korean acquisition data of modal suffixes suggest that such discourse-interactional features and nonverbal contextual cues that accompany them facilitate and enhance the acquisition of epistemic/evidential modal suffixes.

---

[16]-*ni* can also express the speaker's negative opinion about the proposition. Thus, sentence (7) can be said when the speaker thinks that Mary is not pretty and asks the listener about the latter's opinion of Mary.

3.4.2. Development of SE Suffixes
in Korean-Speaking Children

A growing body of research on communicative competence in children shows that children learn to be good participants in conversations from a young age. Several studies (Shatz, 1983, 1984; Pellegrini, Brody, & Stoneman, 1987) have shown that even 2-year-olds are capable of giving enough information and keeping their linguistic contributions truthful and relevant to the topic of discourse. Bloom, Rocissano, and Hood (1976) have also shown that before children reach 2 years, they have learned a basic rule of discourse, that of conversational turns, and that between 2 and 3 years, children increase the amount of information they contribute to the shared topic. Furthermore, Shatz, Hoff-Ginsberg, and Maciver (1989) have suggested an important role that linguistic input plays in the acquisition of modal auxiliaries (see also Hoff-Ginsberg, 1986; Shatz, 1991).

Modal suffixes in Korean express a variety of epistemic/evidential notions (except perhaps -*kkey* and -*llay*),[17] such as the degree of newness of information and direct and indirect sources of information. However, the meanings of these modal particles are closely tied with the pragmatics of discourse interaction as shown in the previous section. Given the findings that children develop communicative competence early on, the modal functions of SE suffixes in Korean may be within children's cognitive grasp and linguistic capacity from an early age. Furthermore, there are several characteristic morphological features of SE suffixes that may facilitate early acquisition of SE suffixes in Korean, particularly when we consider Slobin's operating principles (1973). First, SE suffixes occur at the ends of sentences (most often with one syllable consisting of a consonant and a vowel), and therefore are perceptually salient. Second, the SE suffixes constitute an obligatory category in that all sentences in discourse interactions must end with a SE suffix. During interactions with children, the caregiver provides a variety of SE suffixes appropriate to specific discourse contexts. From the acquisition perspective, this means that children hear different SE suffixes frequently from their caregivers. Third, there is a relatively high degree of semantic transparency in that agent-oriented and epistemic meanings are distinguished morphologically, and SE suffixes denote epistemic meanings most of the time.

As noted earlier, the general developmental pattern is that children acquire the suffixes -*ta, -e*, and -*ci* (in this order) before the suffixes indicating future (i.e., -*llay* and -*kkey*) and then the suffix -*tay* is acquired along with some agent-oriented modal auxiliaries. These SE suffixes are acquired before 3 years in all three children. In investigating the mechanisms of such an early acquisition

---

[17]-*Kkey* and -*llay* denote intention and desire respectively. It should be noted, however, that, as discussed in a number of studies, constructions that express intention and desire often develop a use for prediction, which can be considered epistemic (Bybee, 1985; Bybee & Pagliuca, 1985; H. S. Lee, 1991).

of modality, I would like to note that the frequency of the suffixes in caregivers' speech to children correlated only partially with order of acquisition. Whereas the input frequencies of -e and -ci correlated with the acquisition order (i.e., the caregivers used -e more frequently and the children acquired it earlier than -ci), those of -e and -ta did not (i.e., the caregivers used -e more frequently than -ta but the children acquired the latter first). This evidence suggests that Korean children did not learn the modal suffixes simply because of the high frequency of the forms in the input. Understanding the acquisition process of these suffixes requires more detailed study of the meanings expressed by children.

To identify the meanings of these suffixes in the children's speech, I found it necessary to examine linguistic aspects as well as nonlinguistic contexts in which the suffixes are used. Concerning linguistic aspects, I have analyzed the structure of discourse interactions between the child and the caregiver. This includes an analysis of discourse contingency (i.e., whether or not the child's utterance maintains the shared topic) and the effect of preceding utterances on the child's selection of a particular SE suffix. Since an SE suffix is a verb inflection, I have also examined the kinds of verbs to which children attach a particular suffix in their speech. As for nonlinguistic contexts, I have analyzed the events, states, and entities that the children refer to in their propositions. I have also examined the types of context which provide the child with particular information, that is, their sources of information. I analyze the modal meanings encoded by -ta, -e, -ci, and -tay in the three children's speech. Examples come mostly from TJ's speech, who I followed closely from 1;8 till 3;0.

3.4.2.1. *Acquisition of the Suffixes -ta and -e: Distinction Between Newly Perceived and Old Information.*   During the first phase, -ta was used to describe events as well as states of affairs, whereas -e was restricted to requests. Examples are shown in (8) and (9).

(8) TJ (1;9)
     (TJ looks inside her doll house and sees that it's empty.)
→ TJ: *eps-ta.*
          not-exist-SE
          'There is nothing.'

(9) TJ (1;9)
     (TJ says to a friend)
→ TJ: *ilwu o-a.*
          here come-SE
          'Come here.'

In (8) TJ describes a state of affairs, and in (9) TJ asks her friend to come closer. All three children used the two suffixes in this contrastive way, -ta for statements and *-e* for requests. The distinction between statements and requests is parallel to the mood distinction between declarative and imperative: *-ta* for the declarative mood, which expresses the speaker's assertion of propositions, and *-e* for the imperative mood, which directs the listener to do something. It seems therefore that at the beginning the two suffixes distinguish mood in the children's speech. This supports Stephany's finding (1986) that mood distinction occurs early.

At this early period of language development, verbs attached to *-ta* were limited in number and were restricted to those that reflected the child's cognitive interests in trying to understand the world. That is, the kinds of events and states of affairs that the children described (all with *-ta*) were about the here-and-now, and closely related to cognitive concepts that children develop at this developmental stage, for example, existence of an entity, success/failure, and change of state/location (Gopnik & Choi, 1990; Gopnik & Meltzoff, 1986a; Slobin, 1985). This is revealed in the analysis of the types of events/states referred to as well as specific verbs used by children:

Events/states	*Verbs* (used by more than two children)
i. existence/disappearance:	*iss-ta* 'exist', *eps-ta* 'not-exist'
ii. success:	*twayss-ta* 'have become'
iii. state:	*can-ta* 'sleeping', *kath-ta* 'be same'
iv. completed action:	*hayss-ta* 'done', *olla kass-ta* 'went up'.

The children expressed all four types of events/states with the suffix *-ta* repeatedly (whenever these contexts occurred) during the first few weeks, typically using the specific verbs noted above. This suggests that statements made by the children with the suffix *-ta* at this stage reflect the kinds of concepts they are trying to assimilate into their general cognitive system. This probably explains why Korean children acquire the form *-ta* early even though the relative frequency of the input for this form is much lower than suffixes such as *-e*.

Within 1 to 6 weeks (depending on the child) from the time *-e* was first used for requests, both *-ta* and *-e* were used in declarative statements. (*-e* also began to be used appropriately in questions.) Within the same mood, however, the two suffixes systematically contrast different degrees to which a proposition (i.e., event or state to be encoded in language) had been assimilated into the child's knowledge system. Specifically, the children used *-ta* for newly perceived information which was not fully assimilated into their knowledge system or their general cognitive system, whereas they used *-e* for information that had been integrated into their body of knowledge.

First, we will discuss the use of *-ta*. The contexts of *-ta* were similar to those noted above. Observe examples from (10)–(12).

(10) TJ (2;0)
       (Looking at a picture of Mr. Bump fallen down on the ground)

→   TJ: *nemecye-ss-ta.*
           fall-PAST-SE
           '(He) fell down.'

(11) HS (1;10)
      (HS puts a Lego person in a chair.)
→   HS: *tway-ss-ta.*
           become-PAST-SE
           'Done.'

(12) TJ (1;11)
      M: *Mickey eti iss-ni?*
             Mickey where exist-SE
             'Where is Mickey?'
      (TJ pointing to a picture of Mickey Mouse on her doll house)
→   TJ: *Mickey yeki iss-ta.*
           Mickey here exist-SE
           'Mickey is here.'

The events described in (10)–(12) above occur in the children's immediate context and are newly registered in their mind. In (10), TJ describes the scene which has drawn her attention: falling down is not a normal posture. In (11), HS marks the completion of her goal as the action was just accomplished, and in (12), TJ has just found the picture of Mickey. These examples illustrate typical contexts in which *-ta* is used, and they can be categorized as follows:

(a) describing a scene in a picture as the child is looking at it,
(b) describing events/states that the child has just observed:
     i.   a perfective aspect which results in a particular state,
     ii. an ongoing event/state, e.g., *can-ta* 'sleeping',
(c) commenting on the existence or non-existence of an event/object.

These three types were the dominant types (85% on average) of contexts for *-ta*. This suggests that the semantic content of propositions with *-ta* was something that the children had just perceived through direct experience. The children seemed to describe the event as they became aware of it.

The suffix *-e*, on the other hand, was used in different types of contexts from those for *-ta*. Let's look at some examples first:

(13) TJ (2;1)
      (At the beginning of the recording session, TJ shows the investigator a cushion that her mother made a few days ago.)
→   *emma mantul-ess-e.*
      mommy make-PAST-SE
      'Mommy made (it).'

(14) TJ (2;2)

(TJ is in the middle of a book, but doesn't want to read anymore. TJ closes the book.)

→   TJ: *eps-e.*
           not-exist-SE
           'no more.'

(15) TJ (1;11)

(TJ is in another room. M asks TJ to bring a color book.)

     M: *ppalli kac-ko o-a. illwu o-a.*
           quickly take-and come-SE here come-SE
           'Bring (it) quickly. Come here.'

→   TJ: *an ka(-a).* (*-a* is deleted after a vowel.)
           not go (-SE)
           '(I'm) not going.'

(16) HS (2;0)

(HS gives a piece of apple to the Investigator (Inv). Inv. doesn't want it any more. HS holding the apple,)

→   HS: *yoke-nun acci-kke nwu-ka hay(-e)?* (*-e* is deleted after a vowel)
           this-TOP uncle-POSS who-SUBJ do(-SE)?
           'Who will do (= eat) uncle's apple?'
           (By this question, HS implies that it is she who wants to eat the apple. In other words, in her mind 'who' refers to HS herself, and she asks the question to get permission from the investigator.)

In (13) TJ states a past event that is well known to her, and in (14) the child creates a desired state (i.e., because the book is closed, reading is finished) and describes it to convince the adult of its truth. In both (13) and (14), the information that the child conveys has been established in her mind before actually saying it. Example (15) and (16) show that *-e* is used also for negations and questions. In (15), M has asked TJ to come back to the living room, and TJ negates the proposition. In (16), the child asks about a proposition that is on her mind, that is, she wants to eat the apple. In both cases, the proposition negated or questioned has already been established in the child's knowledge system. Thus, *-e* was frequently used in the following types of situations:

(d) to give information about a past event/state;

(e) to convince the listener of an event/state of affairs, or to talk about an event/state which was not occurring at the time of speech (e.g., negation, actions which the child was about to perform, make-believe events while playing with a doll or a toy); and,

(f) in questions to verify the truth of a proposition.

The functional distribution of -*e* was clearly different from that of -*ta*. Whereas -*e* was used in the above three types of contexts (d–f) more than 64% of the time on average, -*ta* was rarely used in those contexts (about 5% of the time). But, there were individual differences on the type of context in which the child used -*e* most frequently: Two children used it most frequently to inform about past events/states (d), whereas one child used it most frequently for type (f), that is, in wh-questions.

-*E* was also used for present events/states (i.e., contexts in which -*ta* is typically used, that is, (a)–(c) above), but such uses amounted to less than half of all -*e* uses (36% on average). Furthermore, a careful analysis of -*ta* and -*e* used in the description of present states/events shows that the two suffixes contrast in a systematic way. One contrast was related to the way the two suffixes were used in repetitions of a proposition. When -*ta* and -*e* occurred within one conversational turn, the first mention of the proposition was marked by -*ta*, and subsequent repetitions then switched to -*e*. That is, -*ta* was used to code information for the first time, whereas -*e* was used in subsequent mention of the information. (See examples in Kim's chapter, Section 5.2.)

Another systematic difference between -*ta* and -*e* related to discourse contingency, that is, whether or not the utterance maintains the current topic and adds new information to it (Bloom, Rocissano, & Hood, 1976). If the function of -*ta* is to register a new and noteworthy event/state that draws the child's cognitive interest, the form would be used in monologue situations where the child tells herself about the meaning of the event. (As mentioned earlier, adult speakers also show this phenomenon.) On the other hand, as H. S. Lee (1985) notes, -*e* would be used to exchange information since the information has become part of the speaker's knowledge system. The analysis of discourse contingency is shown in Table 2.11. The children used -*e* more often than -*ta* as they responded to adult utterances giving more information about the topic. Table 2.11 shows that the proposition with -*ta* was often not related (i.e., non-contingent) to the current topic. Instead, it was used when the child shifted to a different topic that drew the child's attention. An example is (17).

TABLE 2.11
Frequency of Occurrence of -*ta* and -*e* in Relation to the Discourse
Topic During the First 6 Months of Children's Use (from Choi, 1991)

	-*ta*		-*e*	
	Related[a]	Unrelated[b]	Related	Unrelated
HS	9%	91%	65%	35%
PL	19%	81%	57%	43%
TJ	24%	76%	64%	36%

[a]Related to the immediately preceding utterance, or to the current topic.
[b]Unrelated to the current topic, i.e., introduction of a new topic.

(17) TJ (2;0)
 (Investigator points to the girl that she colored)
 Inv.: *i salam ippu-ci?*
   this person pretty-SE?
   'Isn't this person pretty?'
 TJ: *ippu-ci.*
   pretty-SE
   'pretty'.
 Inv.: *i salam ippu-ci?*
   this person pretty-SE?
   'Isn't this person pretty?'
 (TJ hears a baby cry upstairs.)
→ TJ: *aka u(l)-n-ta.*
   baby cry-PRES-SE.
   'A baby is crying.'
 Inv.: *aka ul-e?*
   baby cry-SE
   'Is baby crying?'

In (17), as TJ hears a baby cry, she comments on this, abruptly interrupting the topic of coloring. This non-contingency occurred in 83% (on average) of the children's -*ta* uses. In contrast, the propositions with -*e* showed a much lower frequency of non-contingency (39% on average). In fact, more than half of the time, the propositions with -*e* maintained the current topic. More specifically, -*e* was used to respond to or comment on the preceding adult question or statement as follows:

(18) TJ (2;4)
 (Investigator and TJ are looking at a picture of a boy on a dog's back.)
 Inv.: *yay-nun eti iss-ni?*
   this.child-TOP where be-SE?
   'Where is this child?'
→ TJ: *oll-a ka-ss-e.*
   move.up-CONN go-PAST-SE
   '(He) went up.'

In summary, several types of analysis have shown that the children in the present study used the modal suffixes -*ta* and -*e* for distinct functions. -*Ta* was used to encode a new and noteworthy proposition as the child became aware of its meaning. In the beginning, propositions with -*ta* also reflected cognitive concepts that the children were developing. At a later stage, -*ta* encoded new/un-assimilated information that the child experienced directly in the here and now. In both cases, -*ta* was often used to introduce a new topic during interaction. In contrast, -*e* was used for propositions that were already established in the child's knowledge system, and its function in discourse was to contribute more information to the current topic.

3.4.2.2. *Acquisition of -ci: Shared Knowledge and Certainty of the Truth of the Proposition.* The third modal suffix to be acquired by the children was *-ci*. (The children also acquired *-cyana* around the same time, and the data in this section include both *-ci* and *-cyana*.) In the acquisition of *-ci*, the influence of the caregivers' input played an important role: Initially, *-ci* was produced by the children as complete or partial repetition of adult utterances with the suffix. (For the development of the Japanese particle *-ne* which denotes shared knowledge, Clancy, 1985, also observed that imitation played an important role at an early stage.) For example, when the investigator said *nemecy-ess-ci?* 'fall-PAST-SE' (= fell down?), when a pile of blocks fell, TJ also said *nemecy-ess-ci* as a statement. After a few months of imitation, *-ci* began to be used spontaneously in the following contexts: (a) when reiterating a proposition in the preceding utterance produced either by the child herself or by the interactant (example [19]), or (b) when redescribing an event or state which had been described several times before (example [20]).

(19) TJ (2;2)
    (TJ touches Investigator's record player.)
    Inv.: *ike manci-ci ma. acwumma-kke-ya.*
        this touch-CONN NEG. aunt-POSS-SE.
        'Don't touch this. This is aunt's' (referring to Inv.)
→ TJ: *acwumma-kke-ci.*
        aunt-POSS-SE.
        'This is aunt's.'

(20) TJ (2;3)
    (TJ is telling a story looking at the picture of a teddy bear fallen down on the floor.) (In many previous sessions, TJ talked about the same picture in the same way.)
→ TJ: *khwung nemecy-ess-ci.*
        Boom fall.down-PAST-SE
        'Boom, (it) fell down.'
    Inv.: *Ung?*
        What
        'What?'
→ TJ: *khwung nemecy-ess-cyana.*
        Boom fall.down-PAST-SE
        'Boom, (it) fell down.'

In (19) *-ci* is used when repeating the adult's statement, and in (20) it is used for information which the child said several times before. The characteristic uses of *-ci* suggest that children pay attention to the preceding discourse, and also remember conversations which took place in the past. The repetition of the proposition with -*ci* in this way allows the child to be certain that the information contained in the proposition is shared with the caregiver.

Later in the development, the function of -*ci* included certainty that developed during ongoing discourse. The following example illustrates such a function:

(21) HS (2;9)
    (One coin chip is stuck in toy cash register)
    Inv.: *kelye-ss-cyana.*
        stuck-PAST-SE
        '(It's) stuck.'
    HS: *kelye-ss-e?*
        stuck-PAST-SE
        '(It's) stuck?'
    Inv.: *ung.*
        yes
        'Yes.'
    HS: *ike kocang na-ss-nunka po-a.*
        this obstacle arise-PAST-CONN seem-SE
        'This seems to be broken.'
    Inv.: *kocang an na-ss-e.*
        obstacle NEG arise-PAST-SE
        '(It) isn't broken.'
    HS: *kocang na-ss-e.*
        obstacle arise-PAST-SE
        '(It's) broken.'
    Inv.: *tasi ha-l-kkey.*
        again do-FUT-SE
        '(I')ll do it again.'
    (Inv. tries but it still gets stuck)
    HS: *an tway.*
        NEG become
        '(It) doesn't work.'
    Inv.: *an tway.*
        NEG become
        '(It) doesn't work.'
→ HS: *kocang na-ss-ci.*
        obstacle arise-PAST-SE
        '(It)'s broken.'

In example (21), being broken becomes more and more certain to HS as the coin keeps getting stuck. Also, in (21), the verb phrase *kocang nata* 'be broken' is expressed several times by the child herself before marking it with the suffix -*ci*. This use of -*ci* suggests that the child can pay attention to a stretch of discourse and the development of information over several conversational turns. At this developmental stage, certainty constructed through discourse is often accompanied by perceptual evidence, as shown in (21). At a later time, *-ci* also began to be used for events that are normally done in a particular situation. In this case, *-ci* often co-occurred with the obligation connective *-ya* (or with the nominalizer *-ke(s)*) as shown in the following example:

(22) TJ (2;3)
    (Mother (M) and child are playing with a doll. They have just finished washing the doll.)
    JS: *aki mokyok ta hay-ss-e.*
          baby bath all do-PAST-SE
          'The baby finished taking a bath.'
    M: *aki mokyok ta hay-ss-unika icey mwe ha-ya tway?*
          baby bath all do-PAST-then now what do-CONN must?
          'Since the baby finished her bath, what should she do now?'
→   TJ: *os ipe-ya-ci.*
          clothes put.on-CONN-SE
          'She must put clothes on.'

*3.4.2.3. Acquisition of **-tay**: Indirect Sources of Information.* In the adult grammar, the function of *-tay* is to report hearsay information or to relay someone else's speech (H. S. Lee, 1985). For example, when the speaker reports information that he/she indirectly obtained (e.g., heard from another person, or read in a newspaper), he/she uses the suffix *-tay* to mark the indirect source of the information.

The children in my study used *-tay* much less frequently than the three suffixes analyzed above. Although the sample size is small, the data show a consistent pattern. *-Tay* was used primarily in contexts where the children relayed information whose source was a third party: (a) telling the listener what the child believed a third party said or felt or (b) reporting what a third party just said. All three children used *-tay* in these contexts. (Two of the three children used *-tay* when telling a story from a picture book. The caregivers of these two children modeled the use of *-tay* in the book-reading context.) In both contexts, the child gave the listener information that the child assumed the listener may not know. For example, in (23), TJ infers that Ernie might hurt his feet by jumping many times. In (24), HS reports to the investigator what her sister has just said, appropriately with the suffix *-tay*.

(23) TJ (2;4)
    (TJ looking at a picture of Ernie jumping)
    Inv.: *jumphu-ha-e?*
          jump-do-SE?
          '(Is he) jumping?'
→   TJ: *pal ayaya ha-n-tay.*
          foot ayaya (typical sound made when one is hurt) do-PRES-SE
          'He says his feet are hurt.'

> Inv.: *ung.*
> yes
> 'Oh. I see.'

(24) HS (2;5)
> (HS and her older sister are coloring.)
> HS's sister: *nay-ka saykchil hay cwu-kkey.*
>   I-SUBJ coloring do give-SE
>   'I will color (it) for you.'
> (HS immediately reports to Inv.)

→   HS: *enni-ka saykchil hay cwu-n-tay.*
>   sister-SUBJ coloring do give-PRES-SE.
>   '(My) sister says that she will color (it) for me.'

Because *-tay* is used for information that is only indirectly accessible, the use of *-tay* might indicate that the child is relaying information that the addressee does not know. If this is the case, then, the use of *-ci* and *-tay* taken together suggests that between 2;0 and 2;6 Korean children are learning to be sensitive to what the listener knows. As we saw in the case of *-ci*, this early sensitivity to the discourse situation is probably developed through caregiver-child interaction.

In summary, children's uses of SE suffixes between 1;8 and 3;0 show the following development. First, *-ta* is acquired to denote newly perceived information at the moment of speech that attracts the child's cognitive interest. This use of *-ta* contrasts with *-e* or *-ci* in that the information it codes is unrelated to the preceding discourse. Furthermore, children acquire it first even though it is not as frequent as *-e* in the caregivers' speech. Soon, *-e* is acquired to exchange old information in discourse interaction. Next, the modal form, *-ci*, is acquired that specifically codes the sharing of information with the listener. The characteristic developmental pattern for *-ci* is that it starts as an imitation of the caregiver's immediately preceding use of the modal suffix. Later, children use it to confirm the shared aspect of the information with the caregiver based on their preceding and previous discourses. The propositions with *-ci* in the children's speech predominantly contain information related to the shared topic: 85% of the *-ci* uses have discourse contingency. Later, children acquire *-tay* expressing information that comes from an indirect source. I have suggested that the child may use *-tay* to inform the listener of a proposition the latter may not know.

Explanation for these results has to do with both children's general cognitive development and language-specific input. We have seen that the children acquire their first SE suffixes to express their own knowledge status, and subsequently to incorporate the listener's knowledge status. This conforms to the general view that children's use of language develops from egocentric to decentered (Piaget, 1955). Also, a closer look at the contexts in which particular propositions were expressed suggests that at the earliest stage in the children's development of SE modals, propositions were related to the information in the immediate context. In particular, information with the suffix -*ta* was closely tied to what was going on at the time of speech. Then, the children acquired -*e* and -*ci* to convey information about past events. This parallels children's general cognitive development that goes from an understanding of present events to an understanding of events removed from the present (i.e., past or future). The development of functions reflects underlying cognitive capacity at the time of acquisition, not only across suffixes, but also with respect to a single suffix. For example, the use of -*ci* was first limited to repetitions of the preceding propositions and later expanded to include past events. Also, during the observation period, not all SE suffixes were acquired by the children. For example, they did not produce -*kwun* (unassimilated inference based on newly perceived information) till after 3;0.

Within these limitations, however, it is remarkable to observe that the children acquired a variety of epistemic meanings relating to different degrees of assimilation of knowledge in their minds, different sources of information, and the knowledge status of the listener. As shown in the analyses presented here, the contrasts at issue were made systematically by the children. Early acquisition of these functions in Korean is interesting because research on the acquisition of modality in spontaneous speech has shown that epistemic modality is acquired later than agent-oriented modality (Stephany, 1986). In addition, a number of experimental studies have shown that an understanding of different degrees of certainty about a proposition develops after 3 years in children learning English (Byrnes & Duff, 1989; Hirst & Weil, 1982; Moore, Pure, & Furrow, 1990). But, the epistemic meanings investigated in these studies relate to the status of knowledge that results from reasoning by the child which is relatively independent of a particular discourse-interactional context. For example, the distinction between *must* and *may* in English in *He must/may be home by 5 o'clock* has little to do with the speaker's assumption about how much other participants know about the proposition. Also, in most of the experimental studies on the acquisition of epistemic modality, tests have been designed to understand such context-independent reasoning. For example, in Moore et al. (1990), children (between 3 and 6 years of age) were asked to guess the location of an object hidden in a box solely on the basis of one-sentence cues which varied in epistemic modal auxiliaries, for example, *It must be in the red box* or *it might be in the blue box*. Moore et al. found that ability to find the hidden object on the basis of the modal meaning was shown in children older than 4 years. However, the results of these studies give little indication of how and when children understand modal forms that incorporate discourse-interactional meanings.

Early acquisition of modality in Korean is at least in part due to perceptual saliency of the morphemes referred to at the beginning of Section 3.4.2. above. But more interestingly, I would like to argue that the discourse interactional functions of the suffixes play an important role in the early acquisition of epistemic modality. That is, the understanding that the primary function of the modal suffixes is to exchange information and construct shared knowledge among conversation participants may have enhanced the children's sensitivity to and acquisition of different kinds of information. In particular, we have seen that the distinction between new and old knowledge is related to discourse contingency. Also, the notion of certainty of information is embedded in the expression of shared knowledge.

Early sensitivity to the discourse functions of SE suffixes in Korean correlates well with the findings on the acquisition of discourse-pragmatic phenomena for English-speaking children, as mentioned earlier (cf. 3.4.2.): Children use language in requesting information and answering questions from the one-word period (Dore, 1974; Shatz, 1983). Several studies on discourse contingency between caregiver and child have shown that children imitate caregivers' utterances from early on. One function of imitation is maintaining a shared topic. Bloom et al. (1976) show that imitation is crucial in the development of the discourse skill of contributing new information to a shared topic. Also, Pellegrini, Brody, and Stoneman (1987) demonstrate that 2-year-old children show signs of observing the cooperative principles, such as giving useful and truthful information to construct shared knowledge relevant to the topic of discourse. My analysis presented here on Korean modal suffixes suggests that such an ability in young children, namely, to follow the progression of discourse toward more and more shared knowledge between the speaker and the listener is instrumental to the early acquisition of SE modal suffixes.

4. LANGUAGE-SPECIFIC INPUT AND SEMANTIC DEVELOPMENT

In this chapter, I have presented Korean acquisition data on several different semantic domains related to verbs. The studies presented here show that when we look at children's language development at a global level we see commonalities across languages. For example, between 1;0 and 2;0, Korean- and English-speaking children express similar kinds of situations and events: existence and disappearance of entities, success or failure of planned action, change of location and spatial relations of entities. Like children learning other languages, Korean children are also interested in talking about actions that bring about a change of state in entities (Slobin, 1985). In expressing motion events, both English- and Korean-speaking children acquire expressions for Paths of dynamic motion from early on. These crosslinguistic similarities are probably driven by children's general cognitive interests and understanding of the world at this early stage.

General cognitive development also explains some of the consistent developmental orders of linguistic expressions found in a particular semantic domain. For example, similar to Japanese children (Clancy, 1985), Korean children acquire the markers for goal, -ey/-eyta, earlier than the marker for location of activity,

-eyse. Some of the developmental order of evidential/epistemic modal functions in Korean can also be explained by cognitive development. Children produce their first SE suffixes to express their own knowledge status, and subsequently to incorporate the listener's knowledge status. My earlier crosslinguistic study of the development of negation has shown that linguistic expressions which relate to different functions of negation (e.g., rejection, inability, denial) develop in a similar order in English, French, and Korean (Choi, 1988). In the acquisition of spatial terms, Korean children acquire expressions for containment and three-dimensional attachment (e.g., *nehta, kkita*) earlier than those for two-dimensional attachment (e.g., *pwuthita*).

However, when we take into account the grammatical and lexical differences across languages, and examine children's languages at a detailed level, particularly in the domains where differences are found in the adult grammar (e.g., semantics of verbs), we are struck by children's sensitivity to language-specific features from the very beginning of their linguistic period. The data I presented in this chapter provide evidence for such sensitivity. For example, in the study of the acquisition of verbs, Gopnik and I have found that, unlike English-speaking children, Korean-speaking children often show a verb spurt during the one-word stage. Also, the proportion of verbs in the child's lexicon is significantly larger in Korean than in English throughout the early period of lexical development. Furthermore, Korean-speaking children acquire verbs as a coherent morphological class from an early stage. These data cast doubt on the view that at the initial stage of language acquisition, verbs are cognitively and universally less accessible than nouns. The Korean data suggests that when the input language provides favorable aspects for verb learning (e.g., occurrence of verbs in a perceptually salient position and a relatively high frequency of action verbs by caregivers), children learn a variety of verbs in parallel with nouns from the beginning of their language development.

Early language specificity is also found in children's syntactic and semantic patterns related to expressions of Motion events. In two-word combinations, children in both languages combine a Figure or Ground nominal and a Path morpheme, e.g., *Christy in* (as the child is about to climb into the bathtub) in English, or *Appa tule ka* 'Daddy enter go' (= Daddy go in) (asking the father to go into the shower) in Korean. However, when we examine the areas of grammar in which differences exist in the two adult grammars, that is, lexicalization patterns of Manner, Path, Deixis, and Motion, differences in children's two-word combinations are readily found: Whereas English-speaking children use the same combinatory pattern, verb plus particle (e.g., *push in, go in*), regardless of whether the motion is caused or spontaneous, Korean-speaking children use distinct combinatory patterns for the two types of motion. Furthermore, English-speaking children use a number of Manner verbs in combination with Path particles from an early stage, whereas Korean-speaking children combine them only infrequently with Path verbs.

In the domain of spatial terms, particularly of Path morphemes—which children acquire early—our data show that the semantic categorization of 2-year-old Korean-speaking children is more similar to the Korean adult system than to the categorization of 2-year-old English-speaking children. That is, by 2 years, children have already accommodated themselves quite significantly to the system of the input language. Qualitative analyses of the contexts in which children use individual Path morphemes show early language-specificity rather clearly. For example, Korean-speaking children readily overextend the word *nehta* 'put something loosely in or around' to contexts where a Figure covers a Ground object (e.g., putting a pillowcase on a pillow). In contrast, most English-speaking children do not overextend *in* in this way. As discussed earlier (Section 3.2.3.3), this language-specific overextension of *nehta* by Korean-speaking children reflects the Korean adult speakers' use of *nehta* (and also *kkita*), which is indifferent to whether the Figure goes into or onto the Ground when the spatial relation involves tight-fit or encirclement (e.g., *kkita* is used both when a person puts a ring tightly ONTO a finger, and he/she puts a finger INTO a ring, and *nehta* is used both when a person puts a big ring ON pole or puts a pole INTO a big ring.)

Several cognitivists have claimed that early words are mapped onto universal cognitive notions that are established prelinguistically (Clark, 1973; Nelson, 1974; Mandler, 1992). Evidence for this claim comes both from studies on nonlinguistic perceptual/conceptual development in prelinguistic infants (Baillargeon, 1994; Spelke, 1990), and similarities in the early linguistic expressions of children (mostly learning English). For example, noting that *up* and *down* are acquired from the one-word stage by many English-speaking children, Bloom (1973) and Gruendel (1977) propose that *up* is an early cognized concept. According to this view, children learning different languages start from the same set of nonlinguistic concepts that serve as building blocks for semantic learning. For the linguistic encoding of spatial relations, the building blocks (or underlying nonlinguistic concepts) may include containment, support, contact, and verticality/gravity. For the linguistic encoding of dynamic motions, animacy, causality, and agency may be important prelinguistic concepts (Mandler, 1992). In this view, the child's task is simply to map prelinguistic concepts onto words. This process may involve directly mapping a concept onto a word (e.g., the mapping between the concept of containment and the word *in* in English), or may involve combining or finely subdividing nonlinguistic concepts in accordance with the adult system of the input language (e.g., the categories of *in* and *on* in English are collapsed under one preposition, *en*, in Spanish; conversely a subset of the English *on* category is subdivided by several clothing verbs in Korean).

Our analyses of early words in Korean and in English reveal, however, that the acquisition of word meaning is not simply a matter of mapping universal nonlinguistic concepts onto language, or of assembling them in a language-specific configuration. Rather, our data suggest that children attend closely to language-specific input to formulate the meaning of a word and that, from the very beginning of linguistic development, there is a close interaction between their cognitive capacity and the influence of language-specific input.

One reason for this conclusion is that the crosslinguistic comparisons presented here reveal few nonlinguistic conceptual primitives that are ready-made for linguistic learning such that all children express those concepts by language. For example, the underlying concept for *kkita* is fittedness between Figure and Ground, regardless of whether the relationship is containment, support, attachment, or encirclement, and the semantic category of *kkita* cross-cuts those of *in, on,* and *together* in English (cf. Figs. 2.1 & 2.4). In other words, *kkita* is neither a category in which several categories in English are collapsed, nor is it a subcategory of any one category in English. Similar observations hold for *nehta* and *pwuthita* (cf. Fig. 2.4). Also, clothing verbs like *sinta* and *ssuta*, a subset of the *on* category in English, are subdivided on the basis of a meaning component, that is, body part as Ground, which does not play a role in the English spatial particle system. Despite such complex crosslinguistic differences, children home in on language-specific meanings remarkably early.

Cognitivists might argue that all the Korean categories may be another set of conceptual primitives that have not been discovered yet. This may be true for some of the categories: For example, Mandler (1994) argues that the tight-fit feature expressed by *kkita* in Korean may be a prelinguistic concept. However, this proposal suggests that we ultimately need to credit the child with a large number of conceptual primitives before language begins. This is because the number of language-specific semantic features increases as we add language-specific features of other languages (cf. Bowerman, 1995, for her analysis of Dutch; Bowerman, deLeon, & Choi, 1995, for a three-way comparison between English, Korean, and Tzotzil). Even the *kkita* category in Korean differs in its underlying semantic principles from the closest category in Japanese, *hameru* 'fit tightly', which also denotes a tight-fit relation but which is restricted to surface contact (Bowerman & Choi, 1992). Crediting a prelinguistic child with a large number of conceptual primitives is somewhat against the motivation for hypothesizing a nonlinguistic conceptual basis for language learning, since the conceptual basis is supposedly composed of a relatively limited set of notions that help the child to initiate language learning. Given the extent of crosslinguistic variation in semantic systems, then, the early acquisition of language-specific semantic categories can best be explained if we posit that children attend to the contexts in which adults use individual lexical items and formulate hypotheses about their meanings based on the input, and that children start this process from very early on.

Data on the early acquisition of the epistemic/evidential meanings of sentence-ending suffixes by Korean children also suggest that children extract meaning from interacting with adult speakers rather than relying on prelinguistically established concepts. The meanings of these suffixes are quite abstract, that is, they are not about perceptual objects and events, but about how a piece of information relates to the discourse/pragmatic context at the time of conversation.

The particular meaning-form relation of SE suffixes is language-specific: Many languages, including English, do not have a set of grammaticized morphemes that express modal meanings comparable to those expressed in Korean, and children learning English have not been reported to express evidential/ epistemic modal meanings in a systematic way at an early stage. However, by age 2, Korean children make a linguistic distinction between newly perceived information and old information, and they use a special form (i.e., -ci) for information that is shared with the interactant.

How do Korean children acquire these meanings so early? Do they have prelinguistic concepts that are ready-made to be mapped onto modal suffixes? Probably not. Some of the modal meanings expressed early on may be cognitively driven (i.e., the use of -ta for existence and disappearance). But the discourse analysis of interactions between caregiver and child presented here clearly suggests that Korean children construct much of the semantics of the suffixes by attending to the way adult speakers use them in interaction. That is, children hear a given suffix consistently in a particular context (e.g., the caregiver's consistent use of -ci when repeating/confirming something that she just said, or repeating something that the child already knows about), and they extract the meaning of shared information and certainty from those contexts.

So far, I have argued that a simple mapping between prelinguistic conceptual primitives and lexical items does not explain the early acquisition of language-specific semantic categories. In the domain of spatial terms, the argument was made by examining a variety of contexts (including the contexts of overextension (e.g., *nehta* and *in*)) in which children produce spatial words. However, we might wonder whether the central meanings of the words are similar across languages. That is, perhaps, children learning different languages start producing spatial words with the same core meanings which are driven by pre-established cognitive concepts. For example, Slobin (1985) suggests that early in linguistic development children attend to the same kinds of prototypical scenes/events (e.g., Manipulative Activity Scene) and from these scenes they extract a universal set of notions like Agent, Patient, Path, or Goal. These notions then are mapped onto the first grammatical/linguistic notions that children acquire. Our data show that, within the spatial domain, children across languages indeed start expressing Paths quite early. Taking Slobin's view to a more specific level, we might also expect that, within the domain of Path, children learning different languages attend to the same types of perceptually salient prototypical scenes, and start building word meanings from these prototypical scenes. In learning the meanings of *on* in English and *kkita* in Korean—both words can be used for surface contact and attachment—children in both languages may start from the same type of scenes which serve as their core meaning. For example, prototypical contexts for English-speaking children's production of *on* and Korean-speaking children's production of *kkita* might be scenes of attachments like putting Legos together. (Gopnik [1980; Gopnik & Meltzoff, 1986a] suggests that English-speaking children initially use *on* frequently for attachment actions like putting Legos or magnets together.)

To test this possibility, I have looked at the kinds of actions that the 2-year-old children in our production data readily label with a particular word, and determined the central meaning of a word by picking out those actions for which more than eight children (out of a maximum of ten) used a given word for a particular action. Using this criterion, I found that the meanings of *nehta* in Korean-speaking and *in* in English-speaking children indeed center around the same type of actions: More than eight children in both languages readily labeled the actions involving putting objects loosely into a container, such as, a boat into a bathtub or putting Legos into a bag (cf. Fig. 2.2). Note, however, that these uses are appropriate both in the English and Korean adult systems. So we do not know whether the similarity in central meaning for *in* in English and *nehta* in Korean comes from a nonlinguistic conceptual basis or from attention to the adult system.

On the other hand, the meanings of the spatial words referring to contact, attachment, encirclement, and covering, center around quite different actions in the two languages. More specifically, the core meaning of *kkita* has to do with putting Legos or bristle blocks together, whereas in English the core meaning of *on* has to do with putting a top on pen, putting a lid on a pan, putting a bandaid on, putting clothes on (cf. Fig. 2.2, and Section 3.2.3.3). Thus, there is no overlap between the core meaning of *kkita* and that of *on*. Furthermore, the actions for which Korean children readily named as *kkita* (i.e., joining popbeads and Legos) were those that 2-year-old English-speaking children did not quite know how to label.

This data suggests that children do not start semantic learning by first attending to prototypical scenes—determined by nonlinguistic perceptual saliency—and then acquiring the labels that the adult speakers provide for those scenes. Rather, our data suggests that children attend to language-specific input that the caregiver provides (e.g., the contexts in which the Korean caregiver consistently says *kkita*), and formulate the core meaning of the word on the basis of the input. Of course, the meaning that they induce from the input must be within the child's cognitive grasp and his/her cognitive interest, but it does not mean that the meaning itself is established before the language begins (see also similar discussion in Bowerman, 1980). It seems, then, that attention to prototypical scenes driven by nonlinguistic factors may guide semantic development at a general level (e.g., early acquisition of a set of Path morphemes). But in constructing the meaning of individual spatial words, children attend to the way the language they are learning categorizes space.

So far, I have critically examined the cognitivist claim that there is a direct mapping between nonlinguistic conceptual basis and language learning, and have argued that, from the BEGINNING of the linguistic period, children's word meanings are significantly shaped by the semantics of the input language and not purely by nonlinguistic conceptual categories. In addition to claims about cognitive universals, there are also claims about innate linguistic universals: Children have innate and universal categories that are specifically built for language learning. For example, Bickerton (1984) claims that the distinction between stative and process verbs is innate (i.e., biologically programmed) and therefore universal in linguistic coding. This means that all grammars have such a distinction, and in learning a language, all children make this distinction regardless of the kind of language input they get. An important piece of evidence for this claim comes from creole languages, where the distinction between stative and process verbs is made even when the input (pidgin) language does not distinguish the two types of verbs grammatically (Bickerton, 1984, 1989). Also, it is well-documented that English-speaking children use the progressive form -*ing* appropriately with process/activity verbs and do not overgeneralize it to stative verbs (e.g., Brown, 1973).

Several kinds of crosslinguistic acquisition data, however, have challenged this claim (Li, 1989; Youssef, 1988). For example, contrary to the nativist theory, Li (1989) found that Chinese children overextend the imperfective progressive aspectual marker used only for process verbs to stative verbs. In my Korean data on locative casemarkers, I have found similar types of errors: Korean children overextend the locative marker (-*ey*) that co-occurs only with stative verbs to activity/process verbs, such as *nolta* 'to play', *ttaylita* 'to hit'. Conversely, they overextend the marker (-*eyse*), which co-occurs only with activity/process verbs to stative verbs. During the period of errors, Korean children overextend -*eyse* even to prototypical stative verbs like *issta* 'to be'. These data suggest that the distinction between stative and activity verbs is learned rather than innate.

Errors involving the indirect object marker, -*hanthey*, and the direct object marker, -*(l)ul*, also suggest that a nativistic view such as Pinker's semantic bootstrapping theory (1984, 1989) is too strong. Pinker (1984) argues that children have innate semantic concepts like agent and patient, and as they experience regularities (e.g., word order, case endings) in the input language between a semantic category, say agent, and a syntactic rule, say subject before the verb, children map the agent role to the subject position by innate linking rules. Pinker further suggests that the innate knowledge of agent and patient is strongest for canonical agent-patient verbs like *hit* and *break*, and that these roles should be correctly linked to syntactic rules from early on in children's grammar. The Korean error data, however, show that children make errors involving -*hanthey* and -*(l)ul* even for prototypical transitive verbs, such as *mwulta* 'bite'. These data suggest that children have to learn at least in part the argument structures of the language they are learning.

5. CONCLUSION

In summary, I have shown that children's semantic system related to verbs is language-specific from the beginning of their language production. In recent crosslinguistic acquisition research, an increasing number of studies have shown early influence of language-specific input in language acquisition (Hoff-Ginsberg, 1986; Sera, Rettinger, & Castillo Pintado, 1992; Shatz, 1991; Tardif, 1996; Weist, Wysocka, & Lyytinen, 1991). These studies, as well as those presented here, suggest that the language-specific aspects of grammar influence children's language from early on, perhaps even before language production begins. To the extent that children's grammar is molded at least in part by language-specific grammatical patterns, children's nonlinguistic cognitive systems and possible innate linguistic structures which underlie the acquisition of grammar must be flexible (Bowerman, 1985, 1989). From the child's perspective, our data suggests that, from a remarkably early age, the child actively works on extracting the relevant meaning components of a word by attending to what is consistently present across all the contexts in which a given word is used (e.g., the child discovers that in all the contexts in which *kkita* is used, there is a consistent aspect of tight-fit between Figure and Ground). Given the significant number of crosslinguistic differences in semantic categorization, the identification of a particular feature (e.g., tight-fit) as a critical aspect of word meaning may be an insight (or "discovery") on the child's part after having observed a number of *kkita* contexts in the input, not something that is derived directly from a set of available nonlinguistic concepts. As Gopnik and Meltzoff (1996) discuss, this insight the child makes is undoubtedly within his/her cognitive capacity at a particular developmental stage. In this way, there is an intimate bi-directional relation between language-specific input and cognitive development.

What I have presented in this chapter is in large part the evidence that language-specific aspects of grammar influence children's early SEMANTIC systems. Whether the language-specific semantic system affects the organization of the child's nonlinguistic cognitive system, that is, linguistic determinism (Whorfian hypothesis), is quite a different matter, and has not been systematically explored in developmental psycholinguistic research. In fact, very little is known about the effect of semantic systems on children's conceptual systems; extensive research with sound methodology is necessary to investigate this issue.

However, in our data there is one piece of evidence that suggests the influence of language-specific input on cognitive development at some level. Gopnik and Choi (1990, 1995) found that Korean-speaking children are significantly more advanced in the development of means-ends abilities when compared with English-speaking children. On the other hand, they are significantly delayed in their performance on object categorization tasks. We found that Korean-speaking children show early verb explosions, whereas English-speaking children show early noun explosions. As discussed in Section 3.1.1.5, Gopnik and Choi (1995) suggest that the two types of cognitive development may be related to the differential pattern of acquiring nouns and verbs. That is, the early acquisition of verbs may be related to (or may even influence) the early achievement of means-ends skills in Korean-speaking children, whereas early naming vocabulary in English-speaking children may be related to their more advanced understanding of object categorization. To the extent that the linguistic differences between the two languages are influenced by the language-specific input, our data suggest that the cognitive differences are also influenced by language-specific input.

Finally, the data presented in this chapter suggest that, as insightfully suggested by Johnston (1985), investigations of non-nominal words provide us with valuable data for deepening our understanding of the relation between linguistic input and cognitive development in semantic development. This direction of research seems to have already begun in the field of psycholinguistics: There is a growing interest in studying the development of non-nominal words both within and across languages, and in both adult and child language (Bowerman & Pederson, 1992; Brown, 1994; Levinson, 1997; Naigles, 1990; Sera, Reittinger, & Castillo Pintado, 1991; Shatz, 1991; Tomasello, 1992).

In addition to crosslinguistic studies of semantic development, we need to know more about caregivers' linguistic input in different cultures, and how it relates to children's language development. We also need to know more about possible roles of cultural differences in children's semantic development. For example, in traditional Korean culture, most of the daily activities take place at the ground level (e.g., traditionally, Koreans eat, work, or sleep on the floor), whereas in North America, they take place at a raised level (e.g., chair, high desk, raised bed). These cultural factors probably affect child-raising practices (e.g., presence or absence of high-chairs) and also the contexts in which caregivers use language with children. It is hoped that in another ten years, research in these areas will enable us to sort out the precise nature of the relative contribution of language-specific input and cognitive development to children's semantic development.

ACKNOWLEDGMENTS

I am very grateful to Melissa Bowerman and Alison Gopnik for their extensive comments and corrections on an early version of this chapter. I would also like to thank Charlotte Webb and Rita Jeffries for their editorial help. I would like to express my deep appreciation to Dan Slobin for encouraging me and giving me the opportunity to present my work in this volume. The preparation of this chapter was supported in part by NSF grant #SBR-9310494.

REFERENCES

Au, T. K., Dapretto, M., & Song, Y. (1994). Input vs. constraints: Early word acquisition in Korean and English. *Journal of Memory and Language, 33*, 567–582.

Baillargeon, R. (1994). How do infants learn about the physical world? *Current Directions in Psychological Science, 3*, 133–139.

Bates, E. (1979). *The emergence of symbols: Cognition and communication in infancy.* New York: Academic Press.

Bates, E., Marchman, V., Thal, D., Fenson, L., Dale, P., Reznick, J. S., Reilly, J., & Hartung, J. (1994). Developmental and stylistic variation in the composition of early vocabulary. *Journal of Child Language, 21*, 85–124.

Bavin, E. (1990). Locative terms and Warlpiri acquisition. *Journal of Child Language, 17*, 43–66.

Berman, R., & Slobin, D. I. (1987). Five ways of learning how to talk about events: A crosslinguistic study of children's narratives. *Berkeley Cognitive Science Report, 46*, Berkeley, CA.

Bickerton, D. (1984). The language bioprogram hypothesis. *The Behavioral and Brain Sciences, 7*, 173–188.

Bickerton, D. (1989). The child, the bioprogram and the input data. A commentary on Cziko. *First Language, 9*, 33–37.

Bloom, L. (1973). *One word at a time*. The Hague: Mouton.

Bloom, L., Lightbown, P., & Hood, L. (1975). Structure and variation in child language. *Monographs of the Society for Research in Child Development, 40*, (Serial No. 160).

Bloom, L., Rocissano, L., & Hood, L. (1976). Adult-child discourse: Developmental interaction between information processing and linguistic knowledge. *Cognitive Psychology, 8*, 521–552.

Bloom, L., Tinker, E., & Margulis, C. (1993). Words children learn: Evidence against a noun bias in early vocabularies. *Cognitive Development, 8*, 431–450.

Bowerman, M. (1978). Systematizing semantic knowledge: Changes over time in the child's organization of word meaning. *Child Development, 49*, 977–987.

Bowerman, M. (1980). The structure and origin of semantic categories in the language-learning child. In M. L. Foster & S. Grandes (Eds.), *Symbol as sense* (pp. 277–299). New York: Academic Press.

Bowerman, M. (1981). Beyond communicative adequacy: From piecemeal knowledge to an integrated system in the child's acquisition of language. *Papers and Reports on Child Language Development, 20*, 1–24.

Bowerman, M. (1982). Reorganizational processes in lexical and syntactic development. In E. Wanner & L. R. Gleitman (Eds.), *Language acquisition: The state of the art* (pp. 319–346). Cambridge: Cambridge University Press.

Bowerman, M. (1985). What shapes children's grammars? In D. I. Slobin (Ed.), *The crosslinguistic study of language acquisition: Vol. 2. Theoretical issues* (pp. 1257–1319). Hillsdale, NJ: Lawrence Erlbaum Associates.

Bowerman, M. (1989). Learning a semantic system: What role do cognitive predispositions play? In M. L. Rice & R. L. Schiefelbusch (Eds.), *The teachability of language* (pp. 133–169). Baltimore: Paul H. Brooks.

Bowerman, M. (1990). Mapping thematic roles onto syntactic functions: Are children helped by innate linking rules? *Linguistics, 28*, 1253–1289.

Bowerman, M. (1994). From universal to language-specific in early grammatical development. *Philosophical Transactions of the Royal Society of London B, 346*, 37–45.

Bowerman, M. (1995). Learning how to structure space for language: A crosslinguistic perspective. In P. Bloom, M. Peterson, L. Nadel, & M. Garrett (Eds.), *Language and space* (pp. 385–486). Cambridge, MA: MIT Press.

Bowerman, M., & Choi, S. (1992). *The expression of Motion in Korean and Japanese.* Presented at the Third Annual Southern California Japanese/Korean Linguistics Conference at San Diego State University.

Bowerman, M., deLeon, J., & Choi, S. (1995). *Verbs, particles, and spatial semantics: Learning to talk about spatial actions in typologically different languages.* Paper presented at the Child Language Research Forum, Stanford University.

Bowerman, M., & Pederson, E. (1992, December). *Crosslinguistic perspective on topological spatial relationships.* Paper presented at the Annual Meeting of the American Anthropological Association, San Francisco.

Brinkmann, U. (1993). Nonindividuation versus affectedness: What licenses the promotion of the prepositional object? *The Proceedings of the Twenty-fifth Annual Child Language Research Forum, 25*, 158–170.

Brown, P. (1994). The INs and ONs of Tzeltal locative expressions: The semantics of static descriptions of location. *Linguistics, 32*, 743–790.

Brown, R. (1973). *A first language: The early stages.* Boston, MA: Harvard University Press.

Bybee, J. (1985). *Morphology: A study of the relation between meaning and form.* Amsterdam: John Benjamins.

Bybee, J., & Pagliuca, W. (1985). Cross-linguistic comparison and the development of grammatical meaning. In J. Fisiak (Ed.), *Historical semantics and historical word formation* (pp. 59–83). The Hague: Mouton.

Byrnes, J. P., & Duff, M. A. (1989). Young children's comprehension of modal expressions. *Cognitive Development, 4*, 369–387.

Choi, S. (1988). The semantic development of negation: A crosslinguistic longitudinal study. *Journal of Child Language, 15*, 517–531.

Choi, S. (1991). Early acquisition of epistemic meanings in Korean: A study of sentence-ending suffixes in the spontaneous speech of three children. *First Language, 11*, 93–119.

Choi, S. (1995). The development of epistemic sentence-ending modal forms and functions in Korean children. In J. Bybee & S. Fleischman (Eds.), *Modality in grammar and discourse* (pp. 165–204). Amsterdam: John Benjamins.

Choi, S., & Bowerman, M. (1991). Learning to express Motion events in English and Korean: The influence of language-specific lexicalization patterns. *Cognition, 41*, 83–121.

Choi, S., & Gopnik, A. (1995). Early acquisition of verbs in Korean: A crosslinguistic study. *Journal of Child Language, 22*, 497–530.

Choi, S., & Kita, S. (1997). *Path and deictic verbs in the description of Motion events in Japanese and Korean.* Manuscript in preparation.

Cziko, G. A., & Koda, K. (1987). A Japanese child's use of stative and punctual verbs. *Journal of Child Language, 14*, 99–111.

Clancy, P. (1985). The acquisition of Japanese. In D. I. Slobin (Ed.), *The crosslinguistic study of language acquisition: Vol. 1. The data* (pp. 373–524). Hillsdale, NJ: Lawrence Erlbaum Associates.

Clancy, P. (1994, August). *Acquisition of subject and object particles in Korean.* Paper presented at the Daewoo symposium on linguistic theory and the acquisition of Korean semantics and syntax, Seoul, Korea.

Clark, E. (1973). Non-linguistic strategies and the acquisition of word meanings. *Cognition, 2*, 161–182.

Dale, P., Bates, E., Reznick, J. S., & Morisset, C. (1989). The validity of a parent report instrument of child language at 20 months. *Journal of Child Language, 16*, 239–249.

DeLancey, S. (1985). The analysis-synthesis-lexis cycle in Tibeto-Burman: A case study in motivated change. In J. Haiman (Ed.), *Iconicity in syntax* (pp. 367–390). Amsterdam: John Benjamins.

Dore, J. (1974). A pragmatic description of early language development. *Journal of Psycholinguistic Research, 3*, 343–350.

Gentner, D. (1982). Why nouns are learned before verbs: Linguistic relativity versus natural partitioning. In S. A. Kuczaj II (Ed.), *Language development. Vol. 2: Language, thought, and culture* (pp. 301–334). Hillsdale, NJ: Lawrence Erlbaum Associates.

Goldfield, B. (1993). Noun bias in maternal speech to one-year-olds. *Journal of Child Language, 20*, 85–100.

Goldfield, B., & Reznick, J. S. (1990). Early lexical acquisition: Rate, content, and the vocabulary spurt. *Journal of Child Language, 17*, 171–183.

Gopnik, A. (1980). *The development of non-nominal expressions in 12-24 month old children.* Unpublished doctoral dissertation, University of Oxford, Oxford, England.

Gopnik, A. (1982). Words and plans: Early language and the development of intelligent actions. *Journal of Child Language, 9*, 303–318.

Gopnik, A. (1988). Three types of early word: The emergence of social words, names and cognitive-relational words in the one-word stage and their relation to cognitive development. *First Language, 8*, 49–70.

Gopnik, A., & Choi, S. (1990). Do linguistic differences lead to cognitive differences?: A crosslinguistic study of semantic and cognitive development. *First Language, 10*, 199–215.

Gopnik, A., & Choi, S. (1995). Names, relational words, and cognitive development in English and Korean-speakers: Nouns are not always learned before verbs. In M. Tomasello & W. Merriman (Eds.), *Beyond names for things: Young children's acquisition of verbs* (pp. 63–80). Hillsdale, NJ: Lawrence Erlbaum Associates.

Gopnik, A., & Meltzoff, A. (1986a). Words, plans, things and locations: Interactions between semantic and cognitive development in the one-word stage. In S. Kuczaj & M. Barrett (Eds.), *The development of word meaning* (pp. 199–223). New York: Springer-Verlag.

Gopnik, A., & Meltzoff, A. (1986b). Relations between semantic and cognitive development in the one-word stage: The specificity hypothesis. *Child Development, 57*, 1040–1053.

Gopnik, A., & Meltzoff, A. (1987). The Development of categorization in the second year and its relation to other cognitive and linguistic developments. *Child Development, 58*, 1523–1531.

Gopnik, A., & Meltzoff, A. (1996). *Words, thoughts, and theories.* Cambridge, MA: MIT Press.

Gropen, J., Pinker, S., Hollander, M., & Goldberg, R. (1991). Syntax and semantics in the acquisition of locative verbs. *Journal of Child Language, 18*, 115–151.

Gruendel, J. (1977). *Locative production in the single word utterance period: A study of* up-down, on-off, *and* in-out. Paper presented at the Biennial Meeting of the Society for Research in Child Development, New Orleans.

Halliday, M. A. K. (1975). *Learning how to mean: Explorations in the development of language.* London: Edward Arnold.

Halpern, E., Corrigan, R., & Aviezer, O. (1981). Two types of 'under'? Implications for the relationship between cognition and language. *International Journal of Psycholinguistics, 8-4(24)*, 36–57.

Hirst, W., & Weil, J. (1982). Acquisition of epistemic and deontic meaning of modals. *Journal of Child Language, 9*, 659–666.

Hoff-Ginsberg, E. (1986). Function and structure in maternal speech: Their relation to the child's development of syntax. *Developmental Psychology, 22*, 155–163.

Huttenlocher, J., Smiley, P., & Charney, R. (1983). Emergence of action categories in the child: Evidence from verb meanings. *Psychological Review, 90*, 72–93.

Johnston, J. (1984). Acquisition of locative meanings: "Behind" and "in front of." *Journal of Child Language, 11*, 407–422.

Johnston, J. (1985). Cognitive prerequisites: The evidence from children learning English. In D. I. Slobin (Ed.), *The crosslinguistic study of language acquisition: Vol. 2. Theoretical issues* (pp. 961–1004). Hillsdale, NJ: Lawrence Erlbaum Associates.

Johnston, J., & Slobin, D. I. (1979). The development of locative expressions in English, Italian, Serbo-Croatian, and Turkish. *Journal of Child Language, 16*, 531–547.

Kim, Y. J. (1990). *The syntax and semantics of Korean case: The interaction between lexical and syntactic levels of representation.* Unpublished doctoral dissertation. Harvard University.

Kim, Y. J. (1997). The acquisition of Korean. In D. I. Slobin (Ed.), *The crosslinguistic study of language acquisition, Vol. 4.* Mahwah, NJ: Lawrence Erlbaum Associates.

Lee, H. B. (1989). *Korean grammar.* New York: Oxford University Press.

Lee, H. S. (1985). *Consciously known but unassimilated information: A pragmatic analysis of the epistemic modal suffix "-kun" in Korean.* Paper presented at the First Pacific Linguistics Conference, University of Oregon.

Lee, H. S. (1991). *Tense, aspect, and modality: A discourse-pragmatic analysis of verbal affixes in Korean from a typological perspective.* Unpublished doctoral dissertation. University of California at Los Angeles.

Lee, H. S. (1993). Cognitive constraints on expressing newly perceived information: With reference to epistemic modal suffixes in Korean. *Cognitive Linguistics, 4*, 135–167.

Lee, K. (1986). Pragmatic function of sentence enders. *Immunkwahak (Humanties), 56*, 41–59.

Levinson, S. C. (1997). Relativity in spatial conception and description. In J. J. Gumperz & S. C. Levinson (Eds.), *Rethinking linguistic relativity* (pp. 177–202). Cambridge: Cambridge University Press.

Li, P. (1989). *Aspect and aktionsart in child Mandarin.* Unpublished doctoral dissertation. University of Leiden.

Mandler, J. (1992). How to build a baby: II. Conceptual primitives. *Psychological Review, 99,* 587–604.

Mandler, J. (1994). Precursors of linguistic knowledge. *Philosophical Transactions of the Royal Society of London B, 346,* 63–69.

Maratsos, M. (1991). How the acquisition of nouns may be different from that of verbs. In N. Krasnegor, D. Rumbaugh, R. Schiefelbusch, & M. Studdert-Kennedy (Eds.), *Biological and behavioral determinants of language development* (pp. 67–88). Hillsdale, NJ: Lawrence Erlbaum Associates.

Markman, E. (1990). Constraints children place on word meanings. *Cognitive Science, 14,* 57–77.

McShane, J. (1980). *Learning to talk.* Cambridge: Cambridge University Press.

Moore, C., Pure, K., & Furrow, D. (1990). Children's understanding of the modal expression of speaker certainty and uncertainty and its relation to the development of a representational theory of mind. *Child Development, 61,* 722–730.

Naigles, L. (1990). Children use syntax to learn verb meanings. *Journal of Child Language, 17,* 357–374.

Nelson, K. (1973). Structure and strategy in learning to talk. *Monographs of the Society for Research in Child Development 38* (Serial Nos. 1–2), 1–136.

Nelson, K. (1974). Concept, word, and sentence: Interrelations in acquisition and development. *Psychological Review, 81,* 267–285.

Nelson, K., Hampson, J., & Kessler Shaw, L. (1993). Nouns in early lexicons: Evidence, explanations and implications. *Journal of Child Language, 20,* 61–84.

Pellegrini, A., Brody, G., & Stoneman, Z. (1987). Children's conversational competence with their parents. *Discourse Processes, 10,* 93–106.

Piaget, J. (1955). *The language and thought of the child.* New York: Meridian Books.

Piaget, J. (1962). The role of imitation in the development of representational thought. *Evolution Psychiatrique, 27,* 141–150.

Pinker, S. (1984). *Language learnability and language development.* Cambridge, MA: Harvard University Press.

Pinker, S. (1989). *Learnability and cognition.* Cambridge, MA: MIT Press.

Rispoli, M. (1987). The acquisition of the transitive and intransitive action verb categories in Japanese. *First Language, 7,* 183–200.

Rispoli, M. (1989). Encounters with Japanese verbs: Caregiver sentences and the categorization of transitive and intransitive action verbs. *First Language, 9,* 57–80.

Schlesinger, I. M. (1977). The role of cognitive development and linguistic input in language acquisition. *Journal of Child Language, 4,* 153–169.

Sera, M., Reittinger, E., & Castillo Pintado, J. (1991). Developing definitions of objects and events in English and Spanish speakers. *Cognitive Development, 16,* 119–142.

Shatz, M. (1983). Communication. In J. Flavell & E. Markman (Eds.), *Handbook of child psychology, Vol. 3* (pp. 841–890). New York: Wiley.

Shatz, M. (1984). Answering appropriately: A developmental perspective on conversational knowledge. In S. Kuczaj (Ed.), *Discourse development* (pp. 19–36). New York: Springer-Verlag.

Shatz, M. (1991). Using cross-cultural research to inform us about the role of language in development: Comparisons of Japanese, Korean, and English, and of German, American English and British English. In M. H. Borstein (Ed.), *Cultural approaches to parenting* (pp. 139–153). Hillsdale, NJ: Lawrence Erlbaum Associates.

Shatz, M., Hoff-Ginsberg, E., & Maciver, D. (1989). Induction and the acquisition of English auxiliaries: The effects of differentially enriched input. *Journal of Child Language, 16,* 121–140.

Slobin, D. I. (1973). Cognitive prerequisites for the development of grammar. In C. A. Ferguson & D. I. Slobin (Eds.), *Studies of child language development* (pp. 175–208). New York: Holt, Rinehart & Winston.

Slobin, D. I. (1982). Universal and particular in the acquisition of language. In E. Wanner & L. R. Gleitman (Eds.), *Language acquisition: The state of the art* (pp. 128–170). New York: Cambridge University Press.

Slobin, D. I. (1985). Crosslinguistic evidence for the Language-Making capacity. In D. I. Slobin (Ed.), *The crosslinguistic study of language acquisition: Vol. 2. Theoretical issues* (pp. 1157–1256). Hillsdale, NJ: Lawrence Erlbaum Associates.

Smoczyńska, M. (1985). The acquisition of Polish. In D. I. Slobin (Ed.), *The crosslinguistic study of language acquisition: Vol. 1. The data* (pp. 595–686). Hillsdale, NJ: Lawrence Erlbaum Associates.

Spelke, E. (1990). Principles of object perception. *Cognitive Science, 14*, 29–56.

Stephany, U. (1986). Modality. In P. Fletcher & M. Garman (Eds.), *Language acquisition* (2nd ed., pp. 375–400). Cambridge: Cambridge University Press.

Talmy, L. (1974). Semantics and syntax of motion. In J. P. Kimball (Ed.), *Semantics and syntax, Vol. 4* (pp. 181–238). New York: Academic Press.

Talmy, L. (1985). Lexicalization patterns: Semantic structure in lexical forms. In T. Shopen (Ed.), *Language typology and syntactic description, Vol. III: Grammatical categories and the lexicon* (pp. 57–149). Cambridge: Cambridge University Press.

Tardif, T. (1996). Nouns are not always learned before verbs: Evidence from Mandarin speakers' early vocabularies. *Developmental Psychology, 32*, 492–504.

Tomasello, M. (1987). Learning to use prepositions: A case study. *Journal of Child Language, 14*, 79–98.

Tomasello, M. (1992). *First verbs.* Cambridge: Cambridge University Press.

Tomasello, M., & Merriman, W. E. (Eds.). (1995). *Beyond names for things: Young children's acquisition of verbs.* Hillsdale, NJ: Lawrence Erlbaum Associates.

Weist, R., Wysocka, H., & Lyytinen, P. (1991). A cross-linguistic perspective on the development of temporal systems. *Journal of Child Language, 18*, 67–92.

Whorf, B. L. (1956). *Language, thought, and reality: Selected writings of Benjamin Lee Whorf* (Ed. by J. B. Carroll). Cambridge, MA: MIT Press.

Wienold, G., Dehnhardt, A., Kim, C., & Yoshida, M. (n.d.). *Lexikalische und syntaktische Strukturen japanischer und koreanischer Bewegungsverben* [Lexical and syntactic structures of Japanese and Korean motion verbs]. Unpublished manuscript.

Youssef, V. (1988). The language bioprogram hypothesis revisited. *Journal of Child Language, 15*, 451–458.

3

Language Typology, Prosody, and the Acquisition of Grammatical Morphemes

Ann M. Peters
University of Hawai'i

1. INTRODUCTION

Why is the Turkish inflectional system so much easier for children to learn than the English one or even than the Finnish one? Why are Russian inflections so difficult? Why is French so much harder for children to segment than Chinese? How is it possible for children to acquire West Greenlandic at all? After reading a number of the chapters in these volumes with an eye to how easy or hard it seems to be for children to acquire the grammatical morphemes of each language, one begins to ask such crosslinguistic questions as these. While Slobin (1985) has already addressed some of these questions from the point of view of the regularity and transparency of morphological systems, my own work on children's segmentation of words and morphemes has convinced me that there is a broader perspective from which these questions can be fruitfully approached, namely one that includes phonology.

In my chapter in Volume 2 of this series (Peters, 1985) I considered how children identify linguistic units at the earliest stages of language learning and suggested that they use the phonological properties of the speech they hear to help them extract recognizable and useful chunks which then become available both for production and as aids in further analysis of the language system. The question of how learners identify grammatical morphemes was only briefly touched on in my discussion of segmentation of morphosyntactic frames. I concluded that chapter with a list of too-seldom-reported kinds of information about properties of target languages that might give us a broader range of crosslinguistic information about how learners extract initial units and then segment them into appropriate adult morphemes. In the ten years since that chapter was written, advances have taken place on a number of fronts: we have more descriptions of the acquisition of more typologically diverse languages (especially those in the third volume of this series); new research has been done on the acoustic properties of speech directed to infants; we know more about infants' ability to perceive various acoustic properties of the speech stream as well as about somewhat older children's ability to perceive morphemes within utterances, even before they can produce them; and, several relatively new, prosodically based phonological theories are becoming better known which may prove useful in guiding our understanding of how children extract the building blocks of their language. It therefore seems appropriate to take a new look at some of my earlier questions, but this time with a stronger emphasis on grammatical morphemes, integrating these new developments.[1]

What does the phonological structure of a language have to do with the ease of acquisition of its morphological system? It is easiest to explain this by

---

[1]Although sharp-eyed readers may recognize that I have repeated one or two examples from Peters (1985), I have tried to use new ones whenever possible. The repeats are the best illustrations I have found for their particular phenomena.

considering the kinds of observations that led me to this question. The story begins with the realization that children seem to vary in the amount of attention they allocate to different aspects of the phonetic signal. A particularly dramatic example can be found in Klein's (1978) study of the ways in which young children with MLU between 1.12 and 1.35 (re)produce two to five syllable words. The data from her four subjects suggests that two of them (Stacy and Jason) aimed at reproducing the most salient syllable or pair of syllables with a fair degree of fidelity. A third (Kathy) mostly reproduced the stressed syllable plus those following it, also with a fair degree of fidelity, while the fourth (Jason) usually produced the right number of syllables, but none very accurately (see Table 1). This notion that some children orient to syllables and segments while others orient to prosodic "tunes" is supported in various ways by the work of researchers such as Echols (1993), Lieven (1989), Macken (1979), Peters (1977, 1983), and Plunkett (1990, 1993).

Is this sort of phonetic bias confined to the segmentation of word-like units, or does it carry over into the acquisition of the morphosyntactic system? If so, then how do such phonological biases affect this aspect of language development? The first detailed look at how such differences might influence the acquisition of English morphology has only recently been presented by Peters and Menn (1993), who trace the morphological development of two children. One child, Seth, was a "tune-child," who began approximating grammatical morphemes with rhythmically appropriate schwa-like "filler syllables." Over a six to eight month period, these syllables gradually acquired the phonological forms appropriate to their adult targets. The other child, Daniel, was a "syllable/segment-child" who focused on the word-final Z-morphemes (/s/z/əz/) of English. While his initial hypothesis seems to have been that they were governed by a phonological rule, Peters and Menn show how he slowly converted the basis of their appearance to a morphological one.

To begin to extend this sort of inquiry into the crosslinguistic arena, we have only to note that while the perception and segmentation of words will be an early task for learners of isolating languages such as English, French, or Mandarin that have relatively little inflectional morphology, the segmentation of BOUND MORPHEMES may be important much earlier for learners of highly inflecting languages such as Turkish, Georgian, or West Greenlandic. Moreover, we are beginning to get reports of children who differ in this way in their manner of acquisition of languages other than English. For instance, both word and tune children have been observed acquiring Danish (Plunkett, 1990, 1993), German (Stern & Stern, 1928), and Norwegian (Simonsen, 1990). Tune children have also been reported in data from Italian (Cipriani et al., 1990), and Portuguese (Scarpa, 1990).

Adopting the position, then, that individual differences among learners may influence their acquisition of grammatical morphemes, we may next ask how such variations will interact with both the phonological and the morphological

TABLE 3.1
Individual Differences in Production of Multi-Syllable Words

TARGET	Stacy I	Jason	Kathy	Joshua
2 syllable: / ˘				
BEtty, BUnny	bɛɪ	beɪ	dɛ	
[bɛti bəni]			dɛbi	babi
TIger, HIGHchair	taɪt	daɪ		
[taɪgə haɪtʃer]	taɪtaɪ	daɪjə	daɪtʃi(t)	tada
3 syllable: / ˘ ˘				
Elephant	aɪsɪs	ɛtɪ(t)	awdɪt	wɛwɛ
[ɛləfənt]		awfɪn	ɛwɪt	lɛlɛ
OCtopus	pus			apus
[aktəpus]	adəpus	ʔaʔapu	aʔəpus	adəpus
		gaʔapu	akɪtwus	
MIcrophone	fo(m)	maɪfo	bo(n)	
[maɪkrəfon]		maɪgəfo		mawəwə
TElephone,TElescope	fo(m)		bon	
[tɛləfon tɛləskop]		daɪgo		dadawo
		dɛdo		dɛlɛlo
TRIangle	fegu	taɪju	daɪnu	lalalala
[traɪæŋgl]		biju	faɪnæ	lɛlulɛlu
AStronaut		aɪno	sæso	æːət
[æstrənɔt]			sæso-mɔ	æwæwæ
			æosɪ-tɔs	
3 syllable: ˘ / ˘				
baNAna	baɪ	nænæ	mænɛ	næni
[bənænə]		mæːæ	næna	
3 syllable: ˘ ˘ /				
kangaROO	wuː	kiwu		wuː
[kæŋgaru]		gagewu		dadawu
4 syllable: / ˘ \ ˘				
AlliGAtor	geɪ(k)		gædi	
[æləgetə]		ægejə	gæjedə	ægigi
			dæwədejə	
MOtorCYcle	saɪku	modaɪʔu	saɪgu	muːlalak
[motəsaɪkl]			mokɪsaɪku	mumulalak
TAPEreCORder	kɔɪ		kɔɪ	
[teprəkordə]			tago	
		dekɔə		tetitodɔ
CUddleWUddle	wau		kæwo	
[kədlwədl]		kəuwəwu	kəduwaɪ	
CAterPIllar	paɪ	bəwe		
[kætəpɪlə]		həbəwə		dadabəbe
4 syllable: ˘ / ˘ ˘				
piNOcchio	nogo	bɪŋgo	dəbi	
[pənokio]	nokijo		dəbido(p)	
5 syllable: \ ˘ / ˘ ˘				
HIppoPOtamus	paɪsis	hɪəbaɪ	pamɪs	
[hɪpəpatəməs]		hɪpaudi	ɛwɛsəbɪs	ɪbaba
		paʔɪʔɪʔis	hɪpa amɪs	hɪpopada
				bibibababa
5 syllable: ˘ / ˘ \ ˘				
reFRIgerAtor	wejə	bijə	wejə	
[rɪfrɪgəctə]				

138

characteristics of different languages to produce different profiles for the acquisition of morphemes. We have two focal questions to answer:

1. What phonetic and/or morphological characteristics of a language contribute to words/morphemes tending either to cling together into complex units or naturally to fall apart at the seams (some sort of "clingability index")?
2. How does starting with bigger or smaller units affect a child's progress toward the adult morphological system?

The kinds of phonological features that are likely to be important here include the presence or lack of prosodic highlights (such as strong contrast between stressed and unstressed syllables vs. little stress constant); the degree to which morphophonemic changes or resyllabifications occur at morpheme boundaries (which may serve to obscure these boundaries); the degree to which syllable boundaries and morpheme boundaries coincide; and the degree to which grammatical morphemes draw from a restricted pool of phonemes (e.g., the English *th*-morphemes.

Thus, although this chapter is about morphology, I suggest that it is not really possible to understand the acquisition of morphemes in isolation from phonology. We need to ask how the above-mentioned phonological properties interact with the morphological typology of the language being learned with respect to perceptibility and segmentability. Are the morphemes of isolating languages necessarily easier to discover than those of agglutinative or inflectional languages? Are those of polysynthetic languages necessarily harder to find?[2] Because, as we will see below, we can find a range of variation in the morphological segmentability of languages of a given type, it appears that we have a three- dimensional problem to deal with: (morphological segmentability) × (morphological typology) × (prosodic sensitivity (word vs. tune children)). Figure 3.1 presents a suggestive two-dimensional array attempting to classify a few languages by morphological typology and clarity of morpheme boundaries. The possible influence of prosody upon acquisition is suggested by the labels T and S, which represent known cases of "tune children" and "syllable children."

Although a systematic look at a full array such as this could be expected to provide a thorough understanding of both what children bring to the task and the ways they have available for acquiring a linguistic system at the level of grammatical morphemes, there are two problems with such an approach. First, such an array would clearly be too massive to deal with in a chapter this size. Second, we do not yet have the information to fill many of its cells. Rather than trying to be exhaustive, we will look at selected examples chosen to be maximally suggestive of the kinds of effects that we might expect to find in this arena. To

---

[2]See Section 3.1 for a discussion of morphological typology including agglutination and (poly)synthesis.

```
H                                              WGreenlandic
A                                              Mohawk
R                                              K`iche' S
D                              Hebrew?
B                              Korean
O                                              Finnish
U                                              Hungarian
N                              Russian
D        French     Portuguese
A                              Polish
R                              German TS
I                    Spanish
E                              Japanese
S        English TS            Tagalog?
         Danish TS
         Norwegian TS                          Sesotho
E                                              Turkish
A                    Mandarin
S                    Cantonese
Y                    Vietnamese
         Isolating   Inflecting   Agglutinative   Polysynthetic
```

MORPHEMES/WORD

FIGURE 3.1.   Segmentability versus Morphological Typology.

establish a perspective from which we can understand the evidence from children learning different languages, however, we need to establish an adequate backdrop of phonological and morphological information. Therefore this chapter will proceed as follows: in section two, we will first review certain prosodic characteristics of adult languages and establish a vocabulary for discussing them, and then consider how prosody can affect perception and segmentation; the third section will contain a brief review of relevant dimensions of morphological typology and how these characteristics can affect a learner's ability to perceive grammatical morphemes; in the fourth section, I will present a set of crosslinguistic generalizations, gleaned from the data, about strategies for acquiring grammatical morphemes in different types of languages. As in my earlier chapter, I will conclude by raising some questions for which we still have no answers and proposing some directions for future research.

2. PROSODIC ISSUES[3]

Before tackling the acquisition data from children, we need a framework and some vocabulary for discussing both how prosody varies across languages and

---

[3]I am particularly indebted to the patient feedback and support of Patricia Donegan and Ken Rehg as I struggled with this section of the chapter.

the kinds of characteristics that might affect learners' abilities to segment at the morphological level. As a sort of consciousness-raising exercise, we will first take a quick, and necessarily sketchy, look at certain prosodic properties of adult languages.[4] We will then consider how these characteristics might affect the learner's segmentation task.

2.1. Prosodic Characteristics of Adult Languages

Let us use the term PROSODY to refer to the interplay of changes in four acoustic properties: pitch, duration, rhythm, and intensity. In some languages, changes in these characteristics tend to coincide. For instance, in English STRESSED syllables simultaneously have higher pitch, longer and fuller vowels, and greater loudness. In other languages, however, such changes are dissociated: in TONE LANGUAGES pitch necessarily operates separately from duration and intensity. Even where pitch is not phonemic, many languages make separate use of these properties. In Turkish, "stress" (as manifested by an increase in intensity) falls on the first syllable of a word, but there is also a more salient pitch rise, or "accent," usually on the last syllable of a word. One of our questions here is about how simultaneous or separate changes in these properties might affect the segmentability of a language.

Pitch. An oversimplification that will be useful in our discussion is that although pitch may vary in a continuous manner, from a phonemic point of view it can be considered to have discrete values. In certain Asian tone languages, there may be as many as five phonemic pitch levels; in African tone languages, on the other hand, two to three levels usually suffice. In many languages, it is reasonable to say that pitch has two kinds of values: marked and unmarked. Moreover, the value that is unmarked may be High or Low, depending on the language. For instance, in English, unstressed syllables are lower in pitch than stressed ones, whereas in Eastern Norwegian unstressed syllables are higher in pitch than stressed ones (a situation that is very counter-intuitive for an English-speaker learning Norwegian!). Even in some tone languages, where pitch changes may be lexically contrastive, it can be the case that only the marked tones need be entered in the lexicon with the unmarked tones being filled in by rules (e.g. Demuth, 1993; Pulleyblank, 1986). Finally, in PITCH-ACCENT LANGUAGES, the equivalent of lexical stress is realized by changes in pitch but not in intensity, and pitch changes do not occur so frequently as in tone languages. For example, in Tokyo Japanese, the word *hana* 'flower' carries such an accent, but the word *hana* 'nose' does not. This is illustrated in the following two sentences, where the accent (indicated by ^) is considered to be the point where pitch changes from High to Low):[5]

---

[4]For considerations of space this sketch makes no pretense of being complete. For elaboration of many of the notions introduced here, readers are referred to Hogg and McCully (1987).

[5]A rule assigns low pitch to the first syllable of each of these sentences.

(1) *hana ^ga akai*   'the flower is red'
     L H L L L
     hana ga akai   'the nose is red'
     L H H H H

We see here that not all sentences carry a pitch accent, and also that the "accent" actually affects the pitches of the following word, rather than the marked lexical item itself.

Duration. This property poses a different set of problems. While it, too, can vary continuously, it would be useful to have some sort of basic timing unit for measuring duration. In languages such as Finnish, Hungarian, or Japanese, which have phonemic contrasts in vowel length, the length of a short vowel is usually taken as such a unit. This unit is called the MORA by scholars of Japanese; there are other definitions of the mora also in current usage (for a fuller treatment, see Nagano-Madsen, 1992). We note in passing that syllable weight (heavy vs. light) is also involved with durational phenomena, where the weight of a syllable may be defined in terms of attributes such as: (a) number of vowels (with diphthongs and long vowels counting double), (b) number of consonants (with both clusters and long/geminate consonants counting double), and (c) closure (with CVC being treated as heavier than CV). (See 3.2.2 for further discussion.) Just as with pitch, duration may be dissociated from intensity: in Hungarian, where "stress" (manifested by a slight increase in intensity) falls on the first syllable of each word, long or short vowels can appear in any position in the word (another situation that is very counter-intuitive for English-speaking learners of Hungarian). This is illustrated in (2); on the second line, stressed syllables are capitalized, long vowels are indicated with a colon.

(2) *Kérek   egy kiló paradicsmot.*   'Give me one kilo of tomatoes.'
     KE:rek egy KIlo: PAradicsmot
       L s   s   S l S s s   s
     [L/l = long, S/s = short]

In languages such as English, Portuguese, or Russian, which allow considerable vowel reduction in unstressed syllables as well as lengthening of stressed syllables, it is harder to identify a basic unit of vowel length. Is it the smallest possible value? Or some sort of middle ground from which duration can be both shortened or lengthened? Or is there no such unit? What does seem to be the case is that in the longer (stressed) syllables of these languages, vowels are more fully realized and there are more vowel contrasts in these positions. For instance, according to Major (1985), in Brazilian Portuguese 24 different vowels and diphthongs can occur in tonic (primary stress) positions, 18 can occur in pretonic (secondary stress) positions, but only 8 can occur posttonically (unstressed). In these languages, when a word contains a heavy syllable, that is the one that tends to be stressed, whereas unstressed syllables tend to be lightened even further through vowel reduction.

Intensity. There is little to say about this property as a separate entity. It is related to the subjective perception of loudness, although a syllable may have relatively high acoustic intensity yet not be perceived as especially loud. Outside of its use for emphasis, I am unaware of any language in which intensity operates phonemically independent of its interaction with pitch and duration.

Rhythm. I will define rhythm informally as the (relatively) regular, periodic spacing of perceptual prominences accompanied by changes in pitch, duration, and/or intensity. Rhythm is of psycholinguistic interest because it can provide one kind of organizing framework for an utterance—a framework that seems to be accessible to learners before they have acquired words or grammar. Unfortunately, rhythm is an aspect of language that phonologists and psycholinguists have only recently felt ready to tackle—in the growing field of metrical phonology. (See, e.g., Goldsmith, 1989; Halle & Vergnaud, 1988; Hayes, 1984, 1985; Hogg & McCully, 1986.) Although it seems that rhythm is a universal property of biological behavior, we know very little about how it is exploited by infants in the process of language acquisition.

Given the definition above, units of rhythm will most naturally be the units of timing between perceived prominences. Languages have often been classed as either STRESS-TIMED or SYLLABLE-/MORA-TIMED languages. Eriksson (1991) has shown that in languages traditionally identified as belonging to the former group (such as English or Swedish), stressed syllables tend to be longer (and hence more prominent) than unstressed ones, which are of roughly equal length. Here the principal rhythmic unit is the FOOT, defined as stretching from one stressed syllable up to (but not including) the next stressed syllable. In syllable-/mora-timed languages, on the other hand, it seems that all syllables are roughly of equal duration, whether stressed or not (Eriksson, 1991). This probably contributes to the perception of these languages having a more even, "machine-gun" quality. Here the principal rhythmic unit is the syllable or mora. Whatever its acoustic basis, there does seem to be some sort of "psycholinguistic reality" to the stress-timed/syllable-timed dichotomy. Let us adopt a pair of more neutral terms: RHYTHMIC and ARHYTHMIC languages.

What is the possible role of rhythm in the segmentation of the speech stream? To the extent that the word or morpheme boundaries of a language reliably coincide with its foot boundaries, these latter can provide useful clues to the presence of the former. We will see in 2.1.2, however, that this is not always the case. We know much less about rhythm in syllable- and mora-timed languages. While some of them seem to have surface rhythmic patterns similar to English or Italian, others do not. For instance, line length in Japanese haiku is measured in moras. Are units such as a four-mora-stretch available to the infant learner of Japanese in the same way as the foot seems to be the infant learner of English?

To conclude this introduction, it is important to note that there is more than one structural level at which prosody plays a role: phonological (mora, syllable, foot), morphological (word), syntactic (phrase, clause, sentence), and/or pragmatic (utterance). Because our concern is with understanding how learners segment the phonetic signal, we will consider here only the phonological levels of syllable and foot, and the morphosyntactic levels of word, phrase, and clause.

2.1.1. *The Syllable/Foot/Accent-Group Level*

A syllable tends to be perceived as more prominent than those in its neighborhood when one or more of the following occur: pitch changes from unmarked to marked, duration increases, or loudness increases. Through such changes prosodic contrasts between neighboring syllables are achieved. We could describe this with terms such as High-Low, Long-Short, Loud-Soft, or Strong-Weak. We have introduced the term foot to refer to a minimal group of syllables that contains a single prosodic contrast:

(3)   many   handsome gentlemen
feet: | s w | s   w | s w w |
      where s = strong, w = weak

One dimension along which languages vary has to do with whether such prosodically contrasting syllables occur at regular or irregular intervals.

Rhythms can be superimposed on rhythms. For instance, at regular intervals in stress-timed languages, prominences may be strengthened. We therefore also need a term such as ACCENT GROUP to refer to a set of feet in which the prominence on one foot is stronger than that on the others.

(4)   many   handsome gentlemen
feet: | s w | s   w | s w w |
acc.: || S w | s   w || S w w ||
      where s = strong, w = weak, S = stronger

Hayes (1984) calls this accent group level the "level of scansion"; it is the level at which a rhythmic "beat" is most easily perceived. In contrast, in syllable-timed languages like French or Japanese, the intervals at which prominences occur are more unequal; even though some of these languages have rules that assign secondary stress (e.g., to heavy syllables, so that there are not, in actuality, long stressless sketches), one does not find the kind of scansion beat characteristic of English or Russian.

(5) *la   phonologie autosegmentale*
    | w   w w w s | w w w w S |
    where S = word stress
    s = secondary stress

Kérek   egy kiló   paradicsmot.
KE:rek egy KI lo: PAradicsmot
l L   s   ls l Sl l Ss s   s l
where S = word stress
s = secondary stress

Another characteristic of the rhythmic languages is that they tend not to have vowel quantity contrasts; for them the scansion beat is what is important as can be seen in their poetry. Arhythmic languages, which are more likely to have phonemic contrasts in vowel-quantity, tend to base their poetry on counts of syllables or moras rather than on beats.

How do these observations relate to perception and segmentation? It seems likely that individual segments (phonemes) are not immediately accessible as perceptual units, however, syllables and feet are. And there is growing evidence that, at least in English, feet play a role in segmentation: Cutler's analyses of misperception errors (Cutler & Butterfield, 1992; Cutler, 1990) show that English speakers develop a (probabilistic) strategy of expecting stressed syllables to mark the beginnings of open-class lexical items. This in turn suggests that they may tend to organize the speech stream into trochees (Strong-weak) wherever possible. Psycholinguistically, the phenomenon of stress adjustment, whereby a word's natural stress pattern may be altered when two strong syllables are juxtaposed, is further evidence of the importance of this kind of rhythmic alternation. For example, while English speakers will say *ponTOON* (a borrowed word with an iambic (weak-Strong) structure) in isolation or at the end of an utterance, in combination they may shift to the trochaic *PONtoon BRIDGE* to avoid the "stress clash" of *ponTOON BRIDGE* (Hogg & McCully, 1986, pp. 128–132). While English speakers develop a preference for trochees (Cutler & Carter, 1987), it is still an open question whether speakers of any languages (e.g., those with word-final prominences and perhaps bounded feet) come to prefer Iambs.

I have not been able to find any discussion of what the natural perceptual units are in vowel-quantity languages that have uneven accent groups. Although alternating-stress rules do subdivide the longer feet as in (6), I would guess that these internal feet may be less salient than the feet of stress-timed languages.

(6)   *Három   kiló   paradicsmot   kérek.*
      ll S w ll S w ll S w l s   w ll S w ll

2.1.2. *Morphosyntactic Chunks: Words, Phrases, Clauses*

Let us now look briefly at the kinds of language-specific phonological processes that can either enhance or obscure morphosyntactic boundaries, and thus help or hinder the language learner's perception of morphosyntactic units.

Let us start at the word level. A rough generalization we can make concerns the level at which phonological processes apply. When they apply with the word as their domain, they will respect word boundaries. On the other hand, when they apply with whole phrases or utterances as their domain, they will be more likely to cross word boundaries, and thus obscure them.

Phonological processes which RESPECT word boundaries include:

[A] FIXED STRESS/PITCH-ACCENT/VOWEL-LENGTHENING: Finnish, Hungarian, Turkish, Warlpiri have word-initial stress; Polish has penultimate stress; a number of southern Bantu languages have penultimate lengthening on phonological words.

[B] VOWEL HARMONY that has the (morphologically complex) word as its domain, as in Finnish, Hungarian, or Turkish.[6]

[C] SYLLABIFICATION that produces syllable structures that respect word or morpheme boundaries, for example, by "resetting" to CV at the beginnings of words. Thus in German, when a word begins with a vowel a glottal stop is inserted, clearly marking the beginning of the word. This device is also used in Swedish (Gårding, 1981), and often in English.[7]

Phonological processes which may OBSCURE word boundaries often involve words that begin or end with vowels, and include:

[A] ELISION (coalescence of vowels) In the following Greek example, /o/ followed by /a/ is reduced to /a/ (from Gårding, 1981, p. 148; syllables are marked with /):

(7) lexical: *to mandolino apo tin Madriti*
    syllabic: to ma/do/li/na/ pti/   ma/dri/ti/
                 'a mandolin   from Madrid'

[B] "RE"SYLLABIFICATION, post-syntactic syllabification processes that operate on whole phrases or clauses and thus have the capability of altering some sort of original (or citation) syllable structure. We see a particularly striking example of this in the following Spanish example in which no word boundary after the first coincides with a syllable boundary (from Harris, 1983, p. 43):[8]

---

[6]It is interesting that, while Estonian is closely related to Finnish, it has lost the vowel harmony. Frances Karttunen (personal communication) has suggested that it would be interesting to compare these two languages in this respect.

[7]As an English speaker I have difficulty inhibiting this glottal stop when trying to speak a language where the presence or absence of an initial glottal stop makes a lexical difference, as in Hawaiian *'ala* 'fragrance' versus *ala* 'path'.

[8]Patricia Donegan has suggested to me, however, that a particular phonetic process may either enhance or obscure the presence of morphosyntactic boundaries depending on its status in the

(8) lexical: *Los otros estaban en el avión.*
     syllabic: lo/so/tro/se/ste/ba/ne/ne/la/vion
                'the others were on the airplane'

[C] contraction across word boundaries, as in our Greek example (6), where *apo tin* is reduced to *pti.*

[D] LIAISON, or the insertion of a morphologically determined (and not very transparent) consonant in front of words beginning with vowels in certain syntactic contexts. This occurs in French, where the more common pattern, applying to words beginning with consonants is illustrated in (9).

(9) | | 'cat' | 'a cat' | 'the cat' | 'this cat' | 'the cats' |
|---|---|---|---|---|---|
| lexical: | *chat* | un chat | *le chat* | *ce chat* | *les chats* |
| morphemes: | ša | ʒ ša | lœ ša | sœ ša | le ša |
| syllables: | ša | ʒ ša | lœ ša | sœ ša | le ša |

When words begin with vowels, however, the inserted consonant varies:

(10) | | 'tree' | 'a tree' | 'the tree' | 'this tree' | 'the trees' |
|---|---|---|---|---|---|
| lexical: | *arbre* | un arbre | *l'arbre* | *cet arbre* | *les arbres* |
| morphemes: | arbr | ən arbr | lœ arbr | sɛt arbr | lez arbr |
| syllables: | ar/br | ə/nar/br | lar/br | sɛ/tar/br | le/zar/br |

We note that, as shown here, resyllabification is also involved, further obscuring the boundaries. That this situation poses a segmentation problem is nicely illustrated in Grégoire's (1971) description of a 2-year-old's series of attempts to say *arbre*: each of the child's tries include a different linking consonant: *le beau z-abe, le beau t-abre, un petit n-arpe, au l'arpe* (p. 94).

[E] AFFIXES that shift word-internal stress patterns because stress is assigned after the affix has been adjoined to the word. For example, in Polish, word-stress is penultimate. When suffixes are added, stress falls on the

language, that is, on whether it is phonological or morphophonological. Since phonological processes apply across-the-board and generally operate to ease articulation, children can eventually discover that it is safe to discount their effects when searching for morphosyntactic boundaries or identifying allomorphs. Such processes probably include consonant assimilations that simplify articulation, vowel harmony, and the kind of resyllabification we saw in 2.1.2 which produces a simple across-the-sentence CV syllable structure. Morphophonological processes, however, are morphologically conditioned, and especially when the conditioning is opaque (i.e., involves exceptions) children will have to pay attention to them as they look for morphosyntactic boundaries, particularly when allomorphs are involved. Such processes would include morphologically conditioned consonant changes or "gradations" (as in Finnish or West Greenlandic), vowel harmony that only applies selectively (e.g., some affixes are excepted), and achievement of CV structure via liaison that introduces morphologically determined linking consonants (as in French).

penultimate syllable of the combined form (Bill Johnston, personal communication; stressed syllables are capitalized).

(11) *ROwer*   'bicycle'   (NOM:SG)   *koBIEta*   'woman'   (FEM:NOM:SG)
      roWErem   'by bicycle'   (INSTR:SG) *do KObiet* 'to women' (FEM:GEN:PL)
      roweRAmi   'by bicycles' (INSTR:SG)

K'iche' has clitics that affect the assignment of stress. Because stress is final in the phonological word, one result of adding such a clitic to a word is that stress falls on the clitic rather than on the main word (personal communication, Pye, 1983). Example 12 shows the change in stress assignment resulting from the addition of the clause-final termination marker =*oh*:

(12) *ku/TIJ le WAH* 's/he's eating the food'
      ku/ti/JOH   's/he's eating it'

At higher syntactic levels, clause boundaries can be signaled by phonological cues such as LENGTHENING of the penultimate or ultimate syllable, a tendency toward increased LOUDNESS clause-initially and decreased loudness clause-finally, and a tendency for the PITCH of declarative statements to decline across the clause (Gårding, 1981).[9] We note, however, that languages differ both in the extent to which such signals are present, and in the extent to which duration, pitch, and intensity operate together at these levels (see Gårding, 1981; Hallé, de Boysson-Bardies, & Vihman, 1991; Vassière, 1983). Let us consider two examples that illustrate the kinds of interactions that may affect the usefulness of these sorts of cues for locating morphosyntactic boundaries.

2.1.2.1. *The Interaction of Constituent Structure and Metrical Structure.*   In English, definite and indefinite articles are unstressed and precede their nouns which carry stress. Following Gerken (1991), we note that this means that the article either occupies the weak syllable of a less preferred iambic foot which includes its noun, as in (13), or, perhaps the weak syllable of a preferred trochaic foot which straddles constituent boundaries, as in (13'):

```
        |  v   /  |  /  | v    /  |
(13)  | the/a lamb | kissed | the/a bear |
        [   NP   ] [ VP  [   NP   ]]
        |  v    /  |  /  v   |  /  |
```

---

[9]While this is widely true, it is not universally so. In some languages the pitch of declarative sentences is rising rather than falling and stressed syllables have low rather than high pitch; e.g., East Norwegian (Haugen & Joos, 1972), Chamorro (Topping, 1973).

(13′) | *the/a lamb* | kissed the/a | *bear* |
    [NP] [VP [NP   ]]

In the Scandinavian languages, on the other hand, the situation is slightly, but interestingly different (Plunkett & Strömqvist, 1992). While indefinite articles precede their nouns, as in English, definite articles surface as inflections which follow their nouns: *et lamm* 'a lamb' but *lamm-et* 'the lamb'. The Swedish equivalent to (13) is:

      | /   ˇ | /   ˇ | /   ˇ |
(14) | *lamm-et* | *kyss-te* | *björn-en* | 'the lamb kissed the bear'
    [NP] [VP   [NP]]

While (14) divides nicely into trochees which also coincide with the NP constituents, when indefinite articles are substituted, as in (14′) the metrical structure is not so neat:

     ˇ   /   /   ˇ ˇ   /
(14′) *et lamm*   kyss-te en björn   'the lamb kissed a bear'
    [NP] [VP [NP]]

We can analyze (14′) into feet in a number of ways. Let us first assume that footing in Swedish works similarly to Gerken's (1991) proposals for English. According to her analysis, feet, at least in production, are maximally binary (consisting of at most two syllables) and exhaustive (so that w-S syllables are possible through less preferred). This produces:

     | ˇ   / | /   ˇ | ˇ   / |
(14″) | *et lamm* | *kyss-te* | *en björn* |

A possible alternative assumption is that all feet begin with strong syllables, producing:

    ˇ | / | /   ˇ ˇ | / |
(14‴) *et* | *lamm* | *kyss-te en* | *björn*

The fact that the Scandinavian definite article follows its nouns and is thus more likely to be part of the same foot as the noun may serve both to link the two more tightly for the learner as a single constituent to be analyzed and to position it in a more easily perceptible position relative to the prenominal indefinite article.[10] One

---

[10]See Slobin's Operating Principle: "Pay attention to the last syllable of an extracted speech unit" (1985, p. 1251).

might therefore predict that, at least on a metrical basis, definite articles would be easier for Scandinavian children to grasp, but that there would be no such difference for English learners. This is a question that has yet to be investigated.

2.1.2.2. The Interaction of Constituent Structure and Syllable Boundaries.

A priori we would expect that grammatical morphemes will be difficult to perceive and extract when their boundaries do not coincide with syllable boundaries. As a second illustration of possible interactions between phonology and morphosyntax let us look at the degree to which syllables and morphemes coincide in different languages. At one extreme we find languages such as Mandarin (Erbaugh, 1992) in which syllable and morpheme boundaries are almost perfectly matched. Learners of such languages do not go far astray if they adopt a strategy of assuming that any syllable is a full and free morpheme. At the other extreme are languages in which morphemes and syllables are complexly intermeshed. In these volumes, perhaps the most striking examples are K'iche' (Pye, 1992) and Hebrew (Berman, 1985).

Morphemes in K'iche' tend to be of the form VC, whereas nonfinal syllables are CV. The result of these conflicting requirements is that syllabification runs roughshod over morpheme strings, blurring their boundaries. The examples in (15) show the kinds of mismatches between morpheme and syllable boundaries typical of this language. In the first, the morpheme string *k-aw-il-oh* is syllabified into *ka/wi/loh*; in the second, an epenthetic /a/ is added to the morpheme string *k-war-ik* before it is syllabified into *ka-wa-rik*. The third example we have already seen in (12).

(15) K'iche' (from Pye, 1983, pp. 587–588, personal communication)[11]
Morphemes are separated with -; syllables are separated with /.

Target:	*kawiloh*	kawarik	*kutijoh*
Morphs/Syls:	k-a/w-i/l-oh	k-/wa/r-ik	k-u-/ti/j-oh
Gloss:	I like it	he is sleeping	s/he's eating it

Syllable and morpheme boundaries in Hebrew are also noncoincident, but the morphological reasons are somewhat different. In Semitic languages, lexical roots, which carry the semantic cores of words, are abstract and unpronounceable because they consist of mere skeletons of (usually) three consonants. Word-formation consists of inserting inflectional morphemes between and around these consonants. While prefixes or suffixes may be full syllables, what is inserted BETWEEN the consonants are patterned sequences of vowels which form pronounceable syllables with the consonants of the root, as illustrated in (16). (Note that a regular process of spirantization causes /k/ to become /x/ syllable-finally.)

---

[11]Syllabifications were checked with Pye (personal communication).

(16) Hebrew (adapted from Berman, 1985, pp. 259–260)

Root:	K-T-V	
Inflection:	--a--a--	
Word:	*KaTaV*	'write'
Syllables:	ka/tav	

Inflection:	ni---a--	
Word:	*niXTaV*	'be written'
Syllables:	nix/tav	

Inflection:	hit--a --e--	
Word:	*hitKaTeV*	'correspond' = 'write each other'
Syllables:	hit/ka/tev	

Inflection:	hi----i--	
Word:	*hiXTiV*	'dictate' = 'cause to write'
Syllables:	hix/tiv	

| Inflection: | ----a-- | |
| Word: | *KTaV* | 'script' |

| Inflection: | ----i-- | |
| Word: | *KTiV* | 'spelling' |

Inflection:	mi----a--	
Word:	*miXTaV*	'letter'
Syllables:	mix/tav	

Inflection:	--a----an	
Word:	*KaTVan*	'typist'
Syllables:	kat/van	

Morphemes which are infixed into the middle of a root can also result in mismatches between morpheme and syllable boundaries. This is common in the Filipino languages as well as in some Micronesian languages such as Palauan and Chamorro. Example 17, from the Filipino language Bontoc, shows the disruption of stems that results when a -VC- infix is inserted after the first consonant.

(17) Bontoc (from *Language Files*, p. 148)
    Infix: *-um-* 'is becoming'

Without infix:		With infix:	
fi/kas	'strong'	*fU/Mi/kas*	'he is becoming strong'
ki/lad	'red'	*kU/Mi/lad*	'he is becoming red'

ba/to	'stone'	*bU/Ma/to*	'he is becoming stone'
fu/su	'enemy'	*fU/Mu/su*	'he is becoming an enemy'

2.2. Effects of Prosody on Perception and Segmentation

Now that we have developed a rudimentary framework for thinking about the kinds of prosodic characteristics that might affect the perception and segmentation of grammatical morphemes, we are ready to consider some evidence about how children actually use prosody in the very early stages of language acquisition. We will conclude this section by formulating some working questions, to be considered in Section 4, about how these prosodic strategies might affect the acquisition of grammatical morphemes crosslinguistically. Let us first look at perception, then at production.

2.2.1. *Prosody and the Perception of Linguistic Structure*

When infants begin segmenting the continuous speech stream into manageable chunks—those that are small enough first to remember and then to try to reproduce—they do not seem to extract random pieces (Peters, 1985). On the other hand, neither do they always begin by (re)producing complete morphosyntactically significant units (phrases, clauses, words) of the adult language. On what basis, then, do they operate? Might they be using prosody as a "bootstrap" into morphology? A number of researchers, including Echols and Newport (1992), Gleitman and Wanner (1982), L. R. Gleitman, H. Gleitman, Landau, and Wanner (1988), Morgan, Meier, and Newport (1987), and Peters and Menn (1993), have proposed that prosody may serve to alert learners to pay attention to hitherto undiscovered structural patterns in the target language.

A number of researchers have been looking at babies in their first year of life, focusing on developments in their abilities to perceive different aspects of the speech stream. The evidence seems to support the proposal that babies do attend to prosodic aspects of language very early and in increasingly linguistic ways. On the one hand, Anne Fernald has been looking at the prosodic characteristics of infant-directed speech (IDS) and considering how they might affect babies' awareness of the kinds of information carried by the speech stream. (For a review, see Fernald, 1991.) She proposes the following scenario: in the first few months the prosodic contours of IDS serve in a global way to alert, soothe, please, or warn; in the next few months these contours themselves come to function as identifiable messages, forming the basis of "the first regular sound-meaning correspondences for the infant"; and toward the end of the first year "prosodic marking of focused words helps the infant to identify linguistic units within the stream of speech" (Fernald, 1991).

Other researchers have been investigating whether IDS contains sufficient acoustic cues to syntactic structure to allow babies to use them as a bootstrap into syntactic structure. In their story-reading contexts, Lederer and Kelly (1993) have found that English IDS contains robust and reliable structural cues which are clearer than those in adult directed speech (ADS). Fisher and Tokura (1996) have also found prosodic cues to clause boundaries in both English and Japanese IDS. Like Lederer and Kelly, they conclude that acoustic cues could be used to support bootstrapping into phrase structure. The 1993 "Signal to Syntax" conference held at Brown University has most recently addressed the prosodic bootstrapping question (Morgan & Demuth, 1996).

Peter Jusczyk and his associates have focused on the kinds of speech that babies of different ages prefer to listen to, and then have considered implications for how babies might develop the ability to segment the speech stream. (For an overview, see Jusczyk, 1992.) They have found that by the age of 4½ months, babies seem to be aware of the prosodic patterns that mothers use to segment their IDS into clauses, preferring not to listen to speech in which pauses have been inserted so as to interrupt these patterns. A set of American babies at this age preferred "well-segmented" IDS, whether it was in English or Polish. By 6 months, however, the preference was confined to their mother tongues—they showed no preference for well- vs. mis-segmented Polish (Jusczyk et al., 1993). Jusczyk and his group have also found some evidence that by 9 months American babies are beginning to be sensitive to possible acoustic correlates of English phrasal units (Jusczyk et al., 1992). He suggests that the cues babies use probably include those listed in the previous section: viz. the lengthening of phrase-final syllables and phrase-final pitch contours—combined with the pauses that occur there (Jusczyk, 1992).

Promising as this research has seemed, there are some caveats. Fernald and McRoberts (1995) point out that researchers have not yet paid sufficient attention to the reliability of the cues being investigated for the induction of syntactic structure. Although it can be demonstrated that certain prosodic cues are indeed often present at clause and phrase boundaries, this is not always the case. They ask whether, given the presence of such a set of cues in a particular location, the probability of a syntactic boundary occurring at that same place is high enough for an infant to be able to rely on the co-occurrence in trying to induce phrase structure.

Bernstein-Ratner (1986) has compared the kinds of phonetic cues that American mothers provide about morphosyntactic structure when they are talking to adults and to children at three stages in language development: late preverbal, one-word, and early combinations (MLU 2.5–4.0). She found that, while mothers signaled the existence of phrase and clause boundaries with the expected changes in pitch and the insertion of pauses, the most reliable cue was increased vowel length. Moreover, mothers extended their pre-boundary vowels significantly more when their children were in the late preverbal stage, suggesting that they are (unconsciously) providing syntactic segmentation cues just when their babies are ready for it. Bernstein-Ratner (1984) also found that, when talking to their children, mothers were more careful about how they articulated their vowels in all syntactic contexts. That is, there was less spread for any target and the vowel ranges overlapped less than when talking to an adult. Of particular interest is her finding that the vowels in function words were being made especially clear to the more advanced children who were starting to combine words.

Metrical patterns may also serve as important cues. In some new research, Jusczyk is finding that between 6 and 9 months American babies seem to develop a preference for a language-specific rhythmic pattern. The evidence is that 9-month-olds, but not 6-month-olds, prefer to listen to a list of English words with the typical English Strong-weak trochaic pattern over a matched list of weak-Strong (iambic) English words (Jusczyk, Cutler, & Redanz, 1993). It is possible that this developing preference will eventually help babies segment open class words out of the speech stream. Joyce Tang Boyland points out (personal communication) that in Mandarin an open class word usually contains two morphemes, thus two syllables, that is, a single foot. Moreover, in Mandarin IDS, lexical items often consist of reduplications of just one of these syllables. She notes that this has the effect of reducing phonetic complexity while preserving the rhythmic structure. The English IDS convention of adding the syllable -ie to monosyllabic lexical items can be seen as accomplishing the same ends.

Putting these lines of research together, we have suggestions for the kinds of acoustic cues that babies might actually use (1) to discover the meaningfulness of whole messages (Fernald), (2) to find the boundaries of clauses and phrases (Jusczyk, Bernstein-Ratner), and (3) eventually to extract and identify "words" (all three). But are prosodic cues reliable indicators of meaningful linguistic units (words and morphemes) in all languages for all children? The presence of both syllables and intonation contours in all languages assures us that there are prosodically defined (and hence extractable) chunks that are both short (single syllables) and long (sequences of several syllables). In the absence of sufficient experience to have discovered the morphosyntactic patterns of the target language, using prosodic information would enable children to get started on the process of finding those patterns. It would also give them something to try to say. The importance of syllable-sized units to young infants is supported by Jusczyk's research (summarized in Jusczyk, 1992) on early perceptual abilities. Mehler, Dupoux, and Segui (1990) also argue that both infants (acquiring speech) and adults (processing speech) make use of a perceptual unit that corresponds roughly to the syllable. Certainly, in some languages, such as Mandarin, syllable and morpheme boundaries coincide perfectly and the syllable would be a linguistically useful unit of attack. In languages such as K'iche' (15), however, the mismatch is pervasive. On what basis do learners proceed in these latter languages?

To refocus this question in light of the issues raised at the outset, it is my thesis that

the size of a particular child's initial extractions and the extent to which they coincide with morphosyntactic units of the adult language depends on the interaction of prosodic and (morpho)-phonological characteristics of the language being learned with attentional preferences of the individual child.

This proposal results from a combination of two lines of thought: first, the ways in which both segmentability and prosodic highlighting differ across languages; second, evidence such as Klein's (Table 3.1) that some children seem to be more attuned to segmental details within single syllables, while others focus on prosodic information such as number of syllables, stress pattern, and pitch variation.

There is evidence from the early productions of many children that both syllables and feet are naturally extractable units (Echols & Newport, 1992; Echols, 1993). Which ones? The prosodically salient ones, which are louder, longer, have contrastive pitch, or are utterance-final. It is especially clear that children are reproducing syllables rather than morphemes when the boundaries do not coincide as in the following examples from Mohawk and K'iche':

(18) Mohawk (child aged 1;9, from Mithun, 1989, p. 291)
    Morphemes are separated with -; verb roots are underlined; syllables are separated with /; stressed syllables are in boldface.

Child's try:	ti	ki:(r)	io:
Adult form:	*satita*	shneki:ra	*sewahio:wane'*
Syllables:	sa/**ti**/ta	shne/**ki:**/ra	se/wa/**hio:**/wa/ne'
Morphemes:	s-at-<u>ita</u>	s-<u>hnek</u>-ihra	s-w-<u>ahi</u>-owan-'
	'get in!'	'drink!'	'apple'

K'iche' (child 2;2, from Pye, 1983, pp. 587–588; personal communication)

Child's try:	loh	lik
Adult form:	*kawiloh*	kawrik
Syllables:	ka/wi/**loh**	ka/wa/**rik**
Morphemes:	k-aw-<u>il</u>-oh	k-<u>war</u>-ik
	'I like it'	'he is sleeping'

Because the pitch–accent in Mohawk is penultimate, the final foot of a word consists of two syllables, and this is what a slightly more advanced child succeeds in reproducing:

(19) Mohawk (child aged 2;4, from Mithun, 1989, p. 292)

Child's try:	ta:ti	waest	io:wana
Adult form:	*sata:ti*	wakeras	*sewahio:wane'*
Syllables:	sa/**ta:**/ti	wa/ke/ras	se/wa/**hio:**/wa/ne'
Morphemes:	s-<u>atati</u>	w-<u>akr</u>-as	s-w-<u>ahi</u>-owan-'
	'talk!'	'it stinks'	'apple'

In K'iche', on the other hand, because children begin with the final syllable of the word, they have only one direction in which to move. According to Pye

(1983, p. 589), "As their language developed, the children's verbs gradually increased in the number of syllables contained . . . [They] added new syllables to the front of those they were already producing, in effect working from the back of the verb to the front."

Although infants seem to find that syllables or feet are the first and most easily accessible units within the speech stream, they eventually have to make the transition to morphosyntactic units, such as words, phrases, or clauses (Gleitman et al., 1988; Peters, 1983; Peters & Menn, 1993). This happens very early: Gerken and McIntosh (1993) have now found that, even when children's productive MLUs are less than 1.5, they indicate some awareness of the placement of function morphemes in that they respond better to commands in which such morphemes are correctly placed (*Find the bird for me*) than when they are misplaced (*Find was bird for me*) or when a nonsense syllable is substituted (*Find gub bird for me*).

How do children manage this prosodic-to-syntactic shift? And how does its difficulty vary across languages? *A priori* we would expect the task to be easier to the degree that both kinds of boundaries coincide. More explicitly, we would expect that the reliability with which stress or pitch–accent predicts word, phrase, or clause boundaries would make a difference to how easy it will be for a child to find morphosyntactic boundaries in that language. As an example of the kinds of boundary interactions that may be relevant here, let us briefly revisit the Scandinavian articles.

As we saw in Example 14, Swedish, Norwegian, and Danish indefinite articles precede their nouns, while definite articles follow them. If (as seems likely for Swedish, at least) these languages have a bias in favor of trochees, and if children are indeed biased to extract and operate with whole feet, then the constituent Noun-Definite would be a more natural metrical unit than Indefinite-Noun. This predicts that, controlling for factors such as input frequency, we would expect to find learners of these languages producing definite articles earlier than indefinite ones. There is a little evidence to support this prediction: in her analysis of Strömqvist's Swedish-learning subject, Markus, Nelfelt (1990) found that at 1;11.23, he produced definite articles three times as frequently as indefinites (while the parent produced them about equally often).[12] On the other hand, Plunkett and Strömqvist (1992) report that Plunkett's two Danish-learning subjects produced indefinite articles before definites. Clearly this is an empirical question that needs further investigation.

A somewhat analogous picture can be found in Sesotho, a southern Bantu language (Demuth, 1992b, 1993). Here we find phrase-final penultimate lengthening, which produces trochaic feet. There is a constraint on minimum word

---

[12]Olle Engstrand has told me, however, that it is his impression that young Swedish children at about 1;5 (i.e., in the late babbling/early word stage) are more likely to imitate Indefinite-Noun than Noun-Definite.

length, requiring a prosodic word to contain at least two syllables, i.e., a trochaic foot. Because the most common noun STEMS are disyllabic, they constitute single feet in their own right (Short/Long); with their (monosyllabic) noun-class agreement prefixes (CL) they contain 1½ feet (Short | Long Short). Possessive and demonstrative stems, on the other hand, are monosyllabic; with agreement prefixes they constitute but a single foot, which is also phrase–final because the structure of a Noun Phrase is: CL-Noun CL-Modifier. What is of interest here is that, at early stages, children are more likely to produce classifiers with adjectives (final single foot) than with nouns (nonfinal foot-and-a-half).

(20) Child (2;1):

	˅ | / ˅ | / ˅ |	
	kolo	sa-ne	'that school'
Adult form:	*se-kolo*	sa-ne	
Morphemes:	7-school	7-that	

	˅ | / ˅	| / ˅ |	
Child (2;2):	ponko	la-ne	'that green corn stalk'
Adult form:	*le-phoqo*	la-ne	
Morphemes:	5-gr corn stalk	5-that	(Demuth, 1994)

To take this line of thought one step further, I would like to propose the following Spotlight Hypothesis:

> Prosody may serve the learner, not only as an aid in segmentation, i.e., in finding boundaries, but also to highlight aspects of morphological structure on which to focus.

The reasoning behind this goes as follows: in any language there are too many grammatical morphemes for learners to acquire all at once. They can, however, reduce this problem to a manageable one by initially focusing on those that are both frequent and salient. This includes morphemes that are associated with some sort of prosodic salience as well as those that have a locational salience such as a tendency to appear at the ends of utterances or phrases (Slobin, 1973, p. 185). I will present three suggestive examples which illustrate ways in which prosody may spotlight grammatical morphemes.

1. Shifting Stress in K'iche'. We have already seen that in this agglutinative language stress falls on the last syllable of a word. When verbs are clause-final their last morpheme is a "termination-marker" which is necessarily stressed (Pye, 1983, p. 586). Nonfinal verbs receive no such marker, with the result that they are stressed on the final syllable of the stem, as we saw in (12) (reproduced here for convenience):

(12) *ku/TIJ le WAH*   's/he's eating the food'
     ku/ti/JOH   's/he's eating it'

Thus children hear verbs in two forms, with stress both on and off the stem. Pye describes a relatively early stage in which the children he observed produced multi-word utterances but only produced a single syllable of each word. Furthermore, they produced only the stressed syllable of a verb, but this syllable shifted appropriately with the verb's clause-finality. In Pye's words, "they used the stems in clause-medial contexts, while using only the terminations in clause-final contexts" (1983, p. 597). The fact that the children could shift their target in this way suggests that they were aware of more than one syllable while still in a one-syllable production stage (p. 598). Perhaps the location of stress served as a kind of spotlight which highlighted the presence vs. absence of the termination marker.

2. A "Marked" Tonal Pattern in Swedish. Swedish has two tonal pitch accents, here referred to as Word Accent 1 (WA1) and Word Accent 2 (WA2). These are part of the phonology of open class words (Plunkett & Strömqvist, 1992; Peters & Strömqvist, 1995). While these accents are lexically assigned, and while their domain is the word (rather than, e.g., the phrase), they are affected by sentence accent. In particular, the tonal contour of a word accent is most fully realized on the focused word of the sentence.

The accent WA2 has two properties relevant to the Spotlight Hypothesis. First, unlike WA1, which can occur on one-syllable words, WA2 can only occur on a word that has a syllable following the stressed one. Second, in Stockholm or Gothenburg Swedish the pitch pattern of a WA2 word in focus position in a sentence is extremely salient because, in addition to a fall in the syllable with primary stress, it includes a characteristic rise in the post-stress syllable. Crucially, this highlighted post-stress syllable may include an inflectional morpheme such as plural, definite article, or present tense. Although the occurrence of the post-stress rise is not necessary for the identification of WA2 (indeed, it is the fall on the primary stressed syllable that is the most reliable acoustic correlate of WA2 across contexts), it is nevertheless this rise/high pitch that is particularly salient to the ears (including non-native ones). Some evidence of its salience to young children comes from Engstrand, Strömqvist, and Williams (1991), who found that, as early as 1;5, a set of five children began producing identifiable WA2 contours (but not yet WA1 contours) on appropriate target words. In the production data from these five children, the investigators found that the rise/high pitch on the post-stressed syllable was a more reliable indication of WA2 than the presence of a fall on the stressed syllable.

Of interest here is the following application of the Spotlight Hypothesis: might the coincidence of a prosodic highlight, such as WA2, with the appearance of an inflection facilitate the acquisition of the latter by somehow spotlighting it? Are inflections that cooccur with WA2 acquired earlier than those that cooccur with WA1? Peters and Strömqvist (1995) have begun investigating this question using data from Strömqvist's subject Markus. Markus began producing recognizable WA2 contours at about 17 months, well before his first productions of inflectional morphemes. When these latter began appearing at about 20 months, not only were they produced with WA2, but this tonal pattern tended to be extended to inflectional combinations that should have had WA1. This overgeneralized linking of WA2 with inflections lasted about two months, after which it began to dissociate. We take this as preliminary evidence in favor of the Spotlight Hypothesis.

3. A More Salient Tone in Sesotho. Sesotho verb stems can be described as underlyingly either High or Low.[13] According to Demuth (1993), "tone is predictably associated at the lexical level with the first syllable, and pitch is realized on the remainder of the verb by various lexical tone rules or melodies." In her longitudinal study of a Sesotho child, Demuth found that at 2;1 the majority of both High and Low verbs were produced as High, and that this imbalance persisted at 2;6, not resolving until 3;0. She notes, however, that even at 2;1 the child did produce 35% of Low verbs as Low and concludes that "by this time the distinction between two types of verb classes is already being made." She goes on to suggest that "access to the underlying tone of verbs is difficult to ascertain given the large amount of tonal sandhi found in languages like Sesotho, and that the child may develop a 'default High' strategy for marking verbs until he or she is able to determine that the underlying tone of a particular verb is not H."

It looks as though these Sesotho and Swedish tonal phenomena share a number of interesting features: they both involve the assignment of one of a pair of tonal patterns at the lexical level; the surface realizations of these patterns are influenced by morphological and discourse considerations; one of these patterns is more acoustically salient than the other and it is this one which seems to be produced first by language learners. Because morphology is involved in both cases, perhaps the more salient pattern is also serving as a spotlight on the accompanying morphological phenomena.

To conclude our discussion of the influence of prosody on the perception of language structure, it is necessary to consider the question of possible individual differences. Although the kind of evidence available primarily regards production, which makes it difficult to make inferences about perception, there are some hints that different children pay attention to different aspects of the phonetic signal. In Table 3.1, we have already seen evidence from Klein (1978) that some children seem to focus more on reproducing single stressed syllables and the segments within them, while other children orient to the number of syllables and the overall stress pattern (the prosodic "tune"). I would like to suggest that in employing either of these strategies, children are paying attention to approximately the same AMOUNT of information, but that they are extracting it from different parts of the phonetic signal. Klein (1981) also proposes a contrast between SYLLABLE-REDUCING children, who are likely to omit unstressed sylla-

---

[13]This is a simplification of Demuth's analysis, in which verbs are lexically specified as High or Unmarked for tone, and where surface syllables that are unspecified for tone are ultimately realized as Low.

bles but produce fairly faithful approximations of stressed ones, and SYLLABLE-MAINTAINING children, who keep the number of syllables but use fillers or reduplications to approximate the unstressed ones.

I have found the autosegmental framework (Goldsmith, 1989) useful in thinking about this.[14] The general idea is that different kinds of phonological information, such as stress, pitch, and syllable structure, may be separable from each other to the extent of being stored and, at least partially, processed in separate TIERS. As an illustration of the potential usefulness of this way of thinking, let us return to Klein's data in Table 3.1, and consider just two of the words, *hippopotamus* and *motorcycle*. The top part of Table 3.2 gives a simplified representation of the adult pronunciations of these words, with separate tiers for different kinds of stress, for syllables, and for segments, followed by sets of tiers for consonantal features and then for vocalic features. (In order to simplify the presentation I have omitted many of the features needed for a complete representation, leaving just enough to distinguish the segments in these two examples.) These are followed by my attempts to represent the information incorporated in the pronunciations of two of Klein's subjects, Joshua, a "tune" child, and Stacy, a "syllable-segment" child (again omitting all but the information essential for these two examples).

What we see is that Joshua pays attention to the number of syllables (and presumably to the stress pattern, although Klein does not indicate stress). Every syllable but one is of the form CV, but only the two most stressed syllables (/ba/ and /mu/) reflect very closely their respective adult targets (/pa/ and /mo/). Otherwise he seems to spread the features from each stressed syllable onto the others, ending up with sequences of similar vowels and consonants: *bi-bi, ba-ba-ba, mu-mu, la-lak*.[15] Stacy, on the other hand, only tries to reproduce syllables from the final foot of each word, but her syllables are more differentiated than Joshua's. Thus she seems to be paying more attention to the distinctive features of the segments she does attempt.

These sorts of differences are widely attested, but have not been looked at in this framework. For instance, the two children studied by Peters and Menn (1993) had similar strategies: Seth, like Joshua, was a "tune" child who paid attention to the stress, syllable, and skeletal tiers, while Daniel, like Stacy, was more of a syllable-and-segment child who reproduced individual syllables, perhaps aiming at their skeletal shapes. (He tended to get the C-V-C structure, but used a lot of consonant harmony to accomplish it.) This is yet another way in which the study of the phonological characteristics of children's early productions can help us understand how they acquire morphology.

---

[14]So has Echols, who has proposed an autosegmentally based model for the production of early words (Echols & Newport, 1992; Echols, 1993).

[15]Echols (1993), working within the autosegmental framework, suggests that this sort of phenomenon can be described as the spreading of features to segmentless syllable nodes.

TABLE 3.2
Tiered Phonological Representations

```
                      hippopotamus               |    motorcycle
           {word                x                |    x
stress     [foot     x           x               |    x                 x
syllable             s   s   s   s   s           |    s    s    s    s
skeletal             C V C V C V C V C V C       |    C V  C V  C V V  C V
C  |stop               +   +   +                 |    +    +          +
O  |labial             +   +       +             |    +
N  |alveolar                   +       +         |         +    +
S  |nasal                          +             |    +
   |segments   h   p   p   t   m   s             |    m    t    s    k
V  |high       +                                 |              +
O  |mid            +       +   +                  |    +    +
W  |low                +                          |              +
E  |round                                        |    +
L  |lateral                                      |                     +
S  |segments   ɪ   ə   a   ə   ə                  |    o    ə    a ɪ    l
segments       h ɪ p ə p a t ə m ə s             |    m o  t ə  s a ɪ  k l
```

```
Joshua     + = adult; * = Joshua                 |
stress/foot    x           x                     |    x                 x
syllable       s   s   s   s   s                 |    s    s    s    s
skeletal       C V C V C V C V C V               |    C V  C V  C V  C V C
C  |stop       *   +*  +*  +*  +*                 |    +*   +*   +        *
O  |labial     *   +*  +*  *   +*                 |    +*   +*
N  |nasal                      +                 |    +*        *
S  |lateral                                      |              *        *
consonants     b   b   b   b   b                 |    m    m    l    l k
V  |high       +*      *                          |    *         *    +
O  |low            +*      *       *              |              +*       *
W  |round                                        |    +*        *
segments       b i b i b a b a b a               |    m u  m u  l a  l a k
```

```
Stacy      + = adult; * = Stacy                  |
stress/foot            x                         |              x
syllable           s           s                 |    s         s
skeletal           C V V     C V C               |    C V V  C V
C  |stop           +*                            |              +*
O  |labial         +*                            |
N  |alveolar               *    +*               |    +*
consonants         p           s   s             |    s         k
V  |high                 *          *             |      +*        *
O  |low            +*                            |    +*
W  |round                                        |              *
segments           p a l     s i s               |    s a l  k u
```

2.2.2. *Prosody and the Production of Linguistic Structure*

Turning now to production, if we assume that children perceive more than they are capable of producing, how do they choose exactly what to say? The generally accepted view has been that communicative function is an important determiner: the most communicatively important words are uttered and the others are omitted. Bolinger (1965) suggests that suprasegmentals are also important, characterizing them as "those components of speech that come first for the child but last for the analyst: intonation, accent and stress, and rhythm." He notes researchers' neglect of these features, suggesting that "[i]f the child could paint the picture, these would be the wave on which the other components ride up and down; but the linguist is older and stronger, and has his way—he calls them suprasegmentals, and makes the wave ride on top of the ship" (p. vii).

The neglect has not been total, however, especially with the recent surge of interest in prosody and "non-linear" phonology. For instance, Gerken (1991) is working on a metrically based model of early speech production for children learning English. According to this model, as part of planning an utterance for production, children divide a phrase into trochees (strong-weak), working from left to right. Phrase-initial weak syllables, as well as any other "strays" that cannot be assigned to one of these binary feet, are vulnerable to omission. This model is consistent with the extensive evidence she has collected on children's early productions.

There may be more to add to Gerken's metrical story, however, in that to the extent that different children are sensitive to different aspects of the prosodic portion of the signal, they may make different uses of it. While we might expect that children would start by selecting and producing single syllables and work up to longer and longer sequences of them as their production capacity increases, this seems to be an area for individual differences. In particular, not all children start at the syllable level; some, such as Waterson's (1976, 1978) subject, P, plunge in at the whole word or foot levels, while those like Peters' Minh begin at a multifoot, whole-utterance level (Peters, 1977). These latter children seem to rely on the rhythmic structure of the whole utterance to provide a sort of momentum of speech along which the planned forms can ride. Let us look at some of the evidence that suggests that there are at least three prosodic levels, from syllables to feet to accent groups, at which different children organize their early productions.

1. Syllable-Level Producers. Children such as Menn's Daniel seem to choose to reproduce the most salient syllable of a word or utterance and to omit the others (Menn, 1971, 1973). For some of these children we find further evidence that the syllable is indeed the domain of focus, at least for production, in the appearance of within-syllable consonant harmony (*duck* > /gək/) that suggests a within-syllable spread of features from one consonantal node to another. For these children it appears that the rhythm of the whole word or utterance is not an aspect that they choose to reproduce, nor does it serve as a facilitator of production. Inevitably, children must progress beyond the syllable as a level of organization, but there may be more than one route. Some children may compress information from more than one target syllable into a single output syllable (Echols, 1993) while others extend their attentional preference for stressed syllables to the words of multi-word utterances. For instance, in (21) we see examples of productions in K'iche' where stress on individual words seems to have been the determiner of what was produced.

(21) K'iche' (from Pye, 1983, p. 588; personal communication)

		Child's try:	paj	weh	ma	k'am	taj
Adult form:	a:	kasipaj	chuweh	ma	kink'am	taj

Syllables:	a:	ka/si/**paj**	chu/**weh**	ma	kin/k'am	**taj**
Morphemes:	a:	k-a-<u>sipa</u>-j	chi-w-eh	ma	k-in-<u>k'</u>am	ta-j
		'will you give it to me'			'I won't take it'	

When these children begin producing word combinations, their productions often seem rather jerky and arhythmic with the content words being separated by short pauses rather than filler syllables. (For evidence that these are indeed constructions, rather than successive single word utterances, see Scollon, 1976, who calls them vertical constructions, and Branigan, 1979.)

2. Foot Level Producers. Children working at the foot level choose a salient foot (often the one carrying primary stress or the final one of a longer utterance) including some or all of the weak syllable(s). We have seen examples of this from Klein's Stacy, and from Mohawk, in (17).

3. Accent-Group Producers. These include Klein's Joshua (1978) and Peters' subjects Minh (1977) and Seth (Peters & Menn, 1993). They seem to be sensitive to the rhythmic structure of a whole word or phrase, with even some very early utterances consisting of more than one foot. Productions such as Minh's spontaneous /hO'lUk/gə'dæl/ 'oh-look-at-<u>that</u>' at 0;11.16, consist of entire accent groups including the unstressed syllables. Because of production limitations, however, these latter are likely to be underspecified, either surfacing as schwas or being filled in from neighboring segments, as we saw with Joshua.

Moreover, there are now enough reports in the literature of children who use filler syllables to suggest that, while some fillers may indeed be protomorphemes, with a small set of identifiable targets, others may have been inserted simply to maintain a rhythmic beat. If Gerken (1991) is right that metrical footing is an important organizer of children's early multi-syllabic utterances, then it seems plausible that, while some children might DELETE syllables that fall outside of optimal feet, others might INSERT syllables to fill up otherwise defective feet. In particular, while some children might not mind producing sequences of two strong syllables, others might find it easier to produce alternations of strong and weak syllables. Let us look at some examples.

Simonsen's (1990) Norwegian subject Nora produced quite a number of filler vowels at 2;3.0. While some of these can be identified as protomorphemes, others cannot. On listening to the tape, however, the rhythmic beat of certain utterances is so salient as to suggest that the grammatically unmotivatable vowels may have served a rhythmic function.

(22)

/ ∨	/ ∨		/ ∨	/ ∨
hun e	*datt é*		*den E*	*seng-en.*
she ∨	fell [out of]		that ∨	bed-DEF

/ ∨	/ ∨	/ ∨
ja og	*jeg é*	*lån - en.* [=*lån-er+den*]
yes and	I ∨	borrow(-PRES)+it

Entries in the turn of the century German diary data for Günther Stern (Stern & Stern, 1928/1965, pp. 100–102) suggest that, unlike his older sister Hilde, he, too, produced rhythmic as well as protomorphemic fillers. In the following examples, which show Günther at about 2;5, producing both kinds of fillers, I have superposed what seem to be plausible footings onto the diarist's orthographic renditions of Günther's utterances.

(23) All rhythmic fillers:

```
          |   /  v         v | / v  v | /   v | / v  |
Günther:  hilde          papao ä hilch ä hünter.
Target:   Hilde [trinkt] Kakao, v Milch v Günther.
          'Hilde [drinks]  cocoa, Günther [drinks] milk.'
```

All protomorphemic fillers:

```
          |      v      /  |  v       / | v   v  /  |
Günther:  ä       hut?   ä      handa  ä  hut?
Target:   [Wo ist der]  Hut? [Auf der] Veranda der Hut?
          '[Where is the] hat? [On the]  veranda the hat?'
```

Mixture of rhythmic and protomorphemic fillers:

```
          v |  / v    v | /  v  v | / v    v  |   / v v | / v |
Günther:  E  hosser E heller E hünter   E     heine E hilde.
Target:   Eine grossen v Teller hat Günther, einen kleinen v Hilde.
          'A big plate [has] Günther,         a little [one has] Hilde.'
```

```
2;5-1/2   v |  /   v | /  v v | / v        |  / v | /  v  v | / v|
Günther:  E  buch eheben E  hünter --      süsser junge E hilde.
Target:   DET buch gegeben v  Günther,     "süsser Junge" v Hilde.
          'a/the book [was] given [by] Günther, "sweet lad" [said] Hilde.'
```

It may also be the case that at times filler vowels or syllables simultaneously serve as protomorphemic place holders and as rhythmic organizers. This seems to have been the case in some of the examples we have just seen. The same can be said of certain productions reported in the literature on children learning English, including Bloom's subjects Eric, Gia, and Kathryn (1970) and Peters' subject, Seth (Peters & Menn, 1993). In the following examples from Seth, although plausible morphemic targets can be found for each of his fillers, there seems to be a strong rhythmic structure as well.

```
(24)  |  v    /  | v   /  |
      n   fwo  ə  kəp                      1;10.0
      'want? throw DET cup'
```

ˇ | / ˇ | / ˇ |
m̲ pɪk ə̲ fawis   1;10.2
'w̲a̲n̲t̲? pick D̲E̲T̲ flowers'

| ˇ   / | /ˇ / |
m̲ brəS ə̲ tif   1;11.0
'w̲a̲n̲t̲? brush D̲E̲T̲ teeth'

Researchers studying the acquisition of the Bantu languages Siswati (Kunene, 1979) and Sesotho (Connelly, 1984; Demuth, 1992a) report that agreement prefixes on both nouns and verbs first tend to be approximated by what Connelly first called "shadow prefixes" (1984, p. 79). These morphemes are syllabic, unstressed, and occur word-initially. The examples in (25) are from Sesotho (numbers refer to agreement classes).

(25) Child (2;0): *a̲-sale*   *a̲-hae* 'her earrings'
     Adult form: *ma̲-sale*   *a̲-hae*
     Morphs: 6-earrings 6-POSS-her/his
     (Connelly, 1984)

     Child (2;2):   *kolo*   *y̲a̲-ne* 'that school'
     Adult form: *se̲-kolo*   *s̲a̲-ne*
     Morphs: 7-school   7- that
     (Demuth, 1992a)

Functors which show agreement can also be approximated by fillers as in (26).

(26) Child (2;2): *le-bese ke*   *e̲o̲ e̲*   *papa*
     Adult form: *le-bese ke*   *le̲o̲ le̲*   *papa.*
     Morphs: 5-milk COP 5-DEM CONJ 9-porridge
                 'There's the milk and the porridge.'
     (Demuth, 1992a)

Fillers appear in Turkish as well; Aksu-Koç and Slobin (1985, pp. 847–848) report that, at the earlier stages of development (under about 2;6), children may fill out the prosodic contours of complex verb forms by including "extra, meaningless syllables between the stem and the final person-number affixes." Their interpretation is that "the child attempts to retain some of the rhythmic picture of complex verbs, incomprehendingly inserting morphemes that sound like passive and causative particles" and revealing "a semantically unmotivated analysis of words into combinable syllables."

Finally, there is intriguing new evidence from Mandarin: Twila Tardif finds that several of the Mandarin-learning children she studied were producing sentence-initial filler syllables at 22 months (personal communication). Although Mandarin is a tone language, it is similar to stress-timed languages in the presence of a contrast between full and reduced syllables (Mary Beckman, personal communication). The latter are syllables which carry what is referred to as "neutral tone," and are both shorter and less tonally distinctive than the full-toned syllables. Moreover, a number of function morphemes in Mandarin carry this neutral tone. Although Tardif has not yet done an analysis of these Mandarin fillers, it looks as though here is yet another language in which children can choose a filler-syllable strategy.

There seems, in sum, to be a fair amount of crosslinguistic evidence that rhythm could provide a kind of momentum which facilitates production for at least a subset of children. In reference to K'iche', Pye (1983) has suggested that: "The acquisition of sentence rhythms gives children a framework on which they can build phonological segments. The stressed sentence accents play a central role in keeping the beat, and in defining the over-all rhythmic pattern. The unaccented syllables may then be positioned relative to the accents . . . Before children can talk, they must learn to sing" (p. 599).

This concludes our overview of possible roles of prosody in perception and production for both adults and children. Let us briefly summarize our findings before we begin to consider how we might usefully cross-classify languages in order to address the problem of what children must do to acquire the grammatical morphemes of different languages.

We defined prosody as the interplay of pitch, duration, rhythm, and intensity, and saw that, because these characteristics may or may not vary in concert, depending on the language, different languages can use them in different ways. We looked briefly at suprasegmental phonological units such as syllables, feet, and accent groups, and noted that their degree of correspondence with morpholexical units varies from language to language. We also noted that there seem to be individual differences in how children actually make use of the prosodic structure of the language they are learning. This leaves us with two working questions about how children's prosodically based strategies could affect the acquisition of grammatical morphemes crosslinguistically:

1. When there is too much information present in the phonetic signal to sort out all at once, which parts are most accessible to focus on first? How well do they match the morphological boundaries?
2. What kinds of devices are available to language learners to enable them to identify a useful problem to work on and to narrow their focus to a workable set of forms from which to extract patterns? Do these devices always work?

We will return to these questions in Section 4.

3. MORPHOLOGICAL TYPOLOGY AND THE SEGMENTATION OF GRAMMATICAL MORPHEMES

Before we proceed to a crosslinguistic consideration of the acquisition of grammatical morphemes we need to do two more things. First, we need a framework within which to conceptualize the differences between languages in such a way as to facilitate an understanding of the different problems encountered by children as they acquire these morphemes. Such a framework needs to include both information about the morphological structure of a language (how tightly the morphemes are bound, and how rigidly patterned, or "slotted" its morphological structure is), and enough about its morphophonological characteristics to shed light on how easily segmentable these kinds of morphemes are. Although a preliminary classification was sketched in Section 1, we now need to develop this more fully. Our second task will be to consider briefly the kinds of phonological and morphophonological processes that can affect the perception of grammatical morphemes and again to make some general remarks about which languages have which properties.

3.1. A Minimal Scheme for Morphological Classification[16]

Comrie (1981, p. 43) suggests that at least a two-dimensional scheme is needed to classify languages morphologically. One of his dimensions, the Analytic-Synthetic one, relates to the number of morphemes per word, while the other, the Agglutinating-Fusional one, reflects how easy or hard the morphemes are to segment from each other phonologically.[17] One weakness of Comrie's treatment is that he never seriously addresses a third dimension, that of segmentability of semantic function. For lack of a better term, I will call this the Unitary–Portmanteau dimension.

3.1.1. *Degree of Synthesis: Number of Morphemes per Word*

The extremes of this dimension are represented by analytic or isolating languages on the one hand and synthetic languages on the other.

ANALYTIC LANGUAGES have few or no bound morphemes. There may be no inflection at all, as in southeast Asian languages such as Vietnamese, or very little, as in most Germanic languages. If there is also no derivational morphology, words will be very short, with the limiting case being one morpheme per word.

---

[16]I would like to thank Byron Bender for his helpful and stimulating comments on this section.

[17]The reader is warned first that Comrie (1981) uses these terms somewhat more narrowly than they have traditionally been employed; second, that the scheme presented here is truly minimal, in that to achieve a more accurate classification the introduction of a semantic (form-function) dimension would also be needed. See Comrie, pp. 39–49, for fuller discussion.

This latter state is more closely approximated in Cantonese than in Mandarin, where most words in the major lexical classes actually contain two morphemes (Tseng, 1991). Sometimes, as in Vietnamese, there is also one syllable per morpheme (per word), although the framework places no limitation on the amount of phonetic content per morpheme. One consequence of an absence of inflections is that the burden of marking constituent structure, grammatical functions (e.g., subject, object), and thematic roles (e.g., agent, patient) must be carried by free grammatical morphemes and word order.

At the other end of this continuum are the SYNTHETIC LANGUAGES, in which it is possible for words to be composed of long strings of morphemes. In some of these languages, such as Turkish or Finnish, words contain but a single lexical stem to which are added derivational and inflectional affixes. For instance, Turkish noun and verb stems can carry seven or more suffixes, with three or four being quite common (Hankamer, 1989). In POLYSYNTHETIC LANGUAGES like West Greenlandic Eskimo (WGE) or Mohawk, the concatenation of morphemes is so pervasive that it is possible to express the equivalent of an entire English sentence in a single word. Some of these latter languages are also INCORPORATING, because in them it is possible for a single word to contain, along with grammatical affixes, multiple lexical roots, such as a verb and its noun object or a noun and its adjectival modifier. These languages typically rely on bound morphology to convey grammatical and thematic roles, although both analytic and synthetic ways to express a given grammatical relationship often coexist.

In the middle of this continuum are languages where the typical noun or verb contains a few, but not many, morphemes. Some intermediate languages have considerable derivational morphology, including compounding, despite a relative lack of bound inflections. This is the case in English, German, and the Scandinavian languages where it is possible, though not common, for words to get quite long (e.g., *productivity-enhancing* or *psychopharmacology*). Otherwise, English, French, and German are close to the analytic end, Sesotho and Japanese are in the middle, and Hungarian, Finnish, Georgian, and K'iche' are closer to the synthetic end. Because Hebrew does not typically have very many morphemes per word it is fairly analytic, although sometimes it is possible to express the same grammatical notion both analytically (with free morphemes) and synthetically (with bound morphemes) (Berman, 1985).

Synthesis may involve more or less freedom in the ordering of categories of bound morphemes. Thus, the verbs and nouns in languages such as Georgian or K'iche' are best described as having a fixed sequence of slots before and/or after the root, each one of which carries a specific kind of information (which may be zero). In contrast, WGE, where derivational affixes can be applied recursively,[18] is less of a "slot" language.

---

[18]According to Fortescue and Lennert Olsen (1992, p. 115), "a verbal stem can be nominalized (or a nominal one verbalized) then again verbalized (or nominalized) by successive affixes up to several times within one complex word-form."

3.1.2. Fusion: Segmentability of Morphemes

The endpoints of this dimension are represented by AGGLUTINATING languages at one pole and FUSIONAL languages at the other.

In the most highly AGGLUTINATING LANGUAGES, such as Turkish or Sesotho, it is easy to find the phonological boundaries of the affixes because their edges are not obscured by opaque, morphologically conditioned sound substitutions, as in Hungarian or Finnish.[19] Allomorphy that is governed by regular, across-the-board phonological processes (voicing or nasal assimilation, vowel harmony) does not seem to cause segmentation problems. The existence of a single, easily recognizable form (absence of allomorphs), of course, enhances segmentability. As Comrie notes (1981, pp. 46–47), however, segmentability and invariance are really separate dimensions, because it is possible to have phonologically distinct allomorphs that are nevertheless easy to segment within the speech stream (English go/went; Turkish first person plural -iz/-k).

In FUSIONAL LANGUAGES, such as Polish, Russian, and German, segmentation can be interfered with by morphologically conditioned sound changes that alter, and hence perceptually obscure, morpheme boundaries. It is interesting to note that pairs of languages, such as Polish/Russian or Japanese/Korean or Spanish/Portuguese, that may be quite near each other on the analytic-synthetic scale, may be farther apart on the agglutinating-fusional scale because of differences in boundary-obscuring morphophonological processes.

Diachronically, sound changes may cause inflections to erode away phonologically. When this happens, functional considerations require that they be replaced somehow, often by free morphemes. This seems to be happening in Brazilian Portuguese, where inflections for person and number are increasingly being replaced by subject pronouns. Although in French many of the inflections have also eroded away, some scholars believe that the increasingly obligatory clitic pronouns that precede the verbs actually function like inflections in carrying information about person, number, and case (Kaiser & Meisel, 1990).

One problem with this agglutinative-fusional dimension is that it offers no easy way to classify languages like Hebrew, with its interdigitated morphemes, and Tagalog, with its infixes. We will return to this issue after we look at our third dimension.

3.1.3. Degree of Semantic Fusion: Number of Meanings per Morpheme

Here we are concerned with segmentability of semantic functions: at one extreme each affix expresses a single, clearly distinguishable grammatical notion, while at the opposite pole several semantic functions are inextricably fused into

---

[19]From this point of view extremely analytic languages are similar to agglutinating ones to the extent that their (free) morphemes are easy to segment.

a single phonological form (often referred to as a PORTMANTEAU MORPH). This is the case, for example, in most Indo-European languages (e.g., German, Polish, Russian, Italian, Spanish, Portuguese), where phonologically unsegmentable affixes carry combinations such as person+number+tense, or number+gender.

Comrie (1981, pp. 45–46) notes that there are practical constraints on the amounts of synthesis and fusion that can coexist in a language. The limiting case is a practical impossibility, namely a language that is simultaneously so synthetic (with many morphemes per word), so phonologically fusional (making morphemes hard to segment), and so semantically fusional that "each sentence would simply be totally and unsegmentably distinct from every other sentence of the language." He thinks, therefore, that in practice synthesis tends to vary inversely with fusion. Fortescue (1992) suggests that the combination of polysynthesis with morphophonemic fusion in fact contributes to the typological stability of the languages of the Eskimo-Aleut family. He proposes that a high degree of morphophonemic alternation results in many distinct allomorphs of any morpheme, which the learner must assimilate and keep track of. This requires a large amount of cognitive work which leads to a "more structurally ramified and deeply rooted memory trace for that morpheme than if it had just the one form that behaved in a strictly agglutinative manner" (p. 246). Therefore fusion may "act as a protective measure against the universal tendency toward lexicalization of base-plus-affix combinations, which in the case of a language with rich morphology might threaten to produce an inflated stock of long, unanalyzable bases" (p. 247).

How, now, do we classify interdigitating languages such as Hebrew and Tagalog? Byron Bender has pointed out (personal communication) that traditional morphological typology, which is based in a long history of morphological studies, has a built-in bias in favor of languages where morphemes are simply concatenated, that is, suffixed or prefixed or both. This framework does not provide for languages that build words through extensive modification of roots (through interdigitation of morphemes, like Hebrew, or through infixation and reduplication, like Tagalog or many Micronesian languages). Staying within our three-dimensional schema, the best we can do with Hebrew is to classify it as fusional because of its similarity to Latin in all three dimensions (number of morphemes per word, phonological segmentability of affixes, and degree to which functions can pile up within one morpheme). Tagalog, on the other hand, is quite similar to Turkish in each dimension, suggesting that it is agglutinative. That these categorizations do not fit well with our intuitions about these languages suggests that perhaps we need yet another dimension, that of degree of interdigitation of morphemes. Because it is not the purpose of this chapter to develop a new morphological typology we will simply note these problems and move on. Figure 3.1 presented a rough classification along these lines of some of the languages discussed so far.

3.2. Classification of Languages by Phonological Characteristics Affecting Segmentation

Our next task is to take the phonological and rhythmic characteristics of languages that we discussed in Section 2.1 and to use them to begin to understand how they can affect the perceptual processes involved in segmenting and identifying grammatical morphemes. We would also like to begin to sort languages into groups where grammatical morphemes are easier or harder to perceive.

3.2.1. *Clarity/Blurriness of Morpheme Shapes and Boundaries*

Morphemes tend to have phonological or lexical variants, called allomorphs. These variants present the learner with the problem of how to determine an appropriate base upon which to create new forms through morphological processes such as affixation. To the extent that it is difficult to identify a set of variants as belonging to a single equivalence-class, we have one kind of perceptual blurriness.[20] It is important to bear in mind, however, that the mere existence of allomorphs does not necessarily make it difficult to recognize which morpheme a variant belongs to. Across-the-board sound changes that operate regularly and without exception become so automatic that they are quite transparent. This is the case with voicing assimilation in the English plural and past tense.

In WGE there are regular phonological processes that affect juxtapositions of consonants (Fortescue & Lennert Olsen, 1992). Because this language does not allow consonant sequences other than /ts/ or geminates, when a stem ending in a consonant is juxtaposed to a suffix beginning with a different consonant, a regressive assimilation regularly applies, as in (27):

(27) *ornig+niar+lugu*   come.to-intend.to-CONTEMP
orninniarlugu   'intending to come to him'
[*rl* represents a single segment, the voiceless lateral fricative ɬ]

Such changes do not seem to be difficult for children to handle.

Similarly, Turkish, Hungarian, and Finnish each have vowel harmony, whereby the vowel of a morphological suffix is phonologically conditioned by the vowels of the stem to which it attaches.[21] To the extent that vowel harmony

---

[20]See Slobin (1985, pp. 1207–1219) for a discussion of some of these same issues from the standpoint of how learners organize morphological information once it has been perceived.

[21]In the native words of such languages, all the vowels of a morpheme harmonize, so which vowel is the conditioning one is irrelevant. Stems borrowed from languages without vowel harmony, however, may not have all vowels in harmony, in which case a choice must be made. In Turkish it is the last vowel of the stem to which a suffix harmonizes. (Dan Slobin, personal communication.)

occurs automatically it seems to pose little problem for the recognition of allomorphs: Slobin (1985, p. 1213) and MacWhinney (1985, p. 1085) report that in Turkish and Hungarian children seem to have no difficulty acquiring the harmonized variants of affixes.[22] When, however, vowel harmony is either more limited in its domain and/or more idiosyncratically conditioned it might be expected to cause more difficulty for allomorphic recognition.

Finnish also has a set of consonant alternations (known as gradations) that are morphophonologically conditioned. For instance, the stem that means 'hand' has four allomorphs: *käsi-/käte-/käde-/kät-* (*käsi* 'hand', *käsissä* 'in the hands', *käteen* 'into the hand', *kädessä* 'in the hand' *kättä* 'hand+PARTIT'). The child's problem is to determine from a citation form, such as *käsi*, the appropriate base to use in constructing other inflected forms, such as *kädet* 'hands' or *käteni* 'my hand(s)'. Errors occur when the learner puts an affix on the wrong stem. Toivainen notes (1990, p. 51) that at an early stage children tend to overuse the strong grade of a consonant (producing, e.g., *kengkä-ttae* rather than *kengngä-stä*), and he suggests that it may be easy for them to miss these morphophonological changes. In Estonian, which is closely related to Finnish, the final consonants which condition gradation have been lost, with the result that these alternations are much more opaque. Frances Karttunen reports (personal communication) that for this reason, consonant gradation is much more difficult for second-language learners of Estonian than of Finnish.

In contrast to assimilations which are easy to process because the conditioning elements are present, neutralizations, such as the devoicing of word-final obstruents in German, might be expected to present learners with difficulties in determining stems. If German children ever say such things as *korp-en* instead of *korb-en* 'basket-ACC:SG' it would suggest that they may have a hard time determining the appropriate base form.

The recognition of allomorphs becomes even more difficult when variants are altered by sound changes that operate on only one or a small class of morphemes (English *woman/women, come/came, ring/rang*). The most difficult case of all is when allomorphs are suppletive, that is, where there is arbitrary replacement of one phonological form by a completely unrelated one (English *go/went, is/were/been*). For this reason, suppletive forms remain in a language only when both variants are sufficiently frequent.

Another kind of blurriness results when sound changes operate at morpheme boundaries in such a way that it is hard to know exactly where the boundaries are, that is, when the precise segmentation point is difficult to locate. It is particularly hard to be sure of the precise form of a stem or base form when

---

[22]In Peters (1985, p. 1057) I suggested that, in the presence of regular and pervasive vowel harmony, on the one hand there would be a tendency to perceive affixes which do not harmonize as not being part of the same word as their stem, while on the other hand there would be a tendency to perceive free morphemes which do harmonize as belonging to the word they occur with. So far no further data on these questions have come to my attention.

sound changes at the edges of morphemes result in neutralization, so that a sound encountered on the surface could have resulted from more than one underlying sound, or combination thereof.

Similarly, a learner will have a hard time determining what underlies *a* when both *a+i* and *a+u* reduce to *a*. This happens in WGE, as we see in (28).

(28) Progressive assimilation in WGE (Fortescue & Lennert Olsen, 1992, pp. 116–117)

nuna-u-voq	land-be-3SG:INDIC
nunaavoq	'it is (a) land.'
sana-(u)t(i)-paa	make-do.for.someone-TRANS:INDIC
sannappaa	'he made it for him.'

WGE also has processes which truncate consonants from the ends of morphemes. In (29) we see *gi+vaa* reducing to *gaa* and *q+g* reducing to *r*.

(29) Truncation of consonants in WGE (Fortescue & Lennert Olsen, 1992, p. 116)

arnaq-gi-vaa	mother-have.as-3SG/3PL:TRANS:INDIC
arnaraa	'she is her mother' [q is a uvular stop; r a uvular scrape]

3.2.2. *Timing/Rhythm Characteristics*

Rhythmic characteristics of languages can affect segmentation by providing different kinds of prosodic "handles" for the novice to grasp at. What are the implications for morphological segmentation?

Languages in Which Stresses/Feet Are Prominent. These are characterized, as we have seen, by a tendency for pitch, length, and intensity to be associated in the single kind of highlight we call stress. Salience contrasts between stressed and unstressed syllables result in rhythmical alternations of highlighted and lowlighted syllables in fairly rapid succession. This, in turn, defines a rhythmic beat which prosodically segments the speech stream into naturally graspable units (stressed syllables, feet, accent groups, phonological words). Languages of this type include English, German, Danish, Russian, Polish, Italian, Portuguese, Warlpiri.

In many of these languages there are correlations between stress and syllable structure, particularly with the amount of phonetic material contained in a syllable. In her survey of stress rules in over 140 languages in the Stanford phonology archive, Ohsiek (1978) found that the weights of syllables figure in the determination of stress in at least 30 of these stress-timed languages. In particular, heavy syllables, which contain final consonants and/or long vowels or diphthongs, seem to attract stress, while light syllables, which contain only short vowels with no consonantal coda, tend to receive stress only when a word contains no heavy syllables. She suggests that putting stress on the syllables with more material may enhance the perceptual contrast between stressed and unstressed syllables.

This same effect may also be achieved by the tendency for unstressed syllables to be further lightened through vowel reduction (e.g., in English, Russian, and Portuguese).

Finally, let us note that in many stress-timed languages grammatical morphemes tend to be unstressed, whereas major lexical items tend to have at least one stressed syllable. In the present context, it looks as though, in these languages, stress and syllable weight together help define potential segmentation handles that favor units that are prosodically defined and include at least parts of open-class items. In other languages with stress-timing, however, it is possible for grammatical morphemes to be more prosodically highlighted. This happens in both Italian and Hebrew, in which certain inflections are not only clause-final but are stressed and/or lengthened. Leonard and his colleagues (Leonard, Bortolini, Caselli, McGregor, & Sabbadini, 1992; Dromi, Leonard, & Shteiman, 1993) have found that children with selective language impairments have less trouble acquiring such morphemes than those which are not prosodically highlighted in this way. Pizzuto and Caselli report that three normal children learning Italian tended to acquire "obligatory bound replacive morphemes such as main verb inflections, earlier and with less difficulty than free suppletive morphemes such as copulas, pronouns, and most notably articles" (1992, p. 545).

Languages Where Syllable-/Mora-Timing Is Predominant.   In Section 2.1 we saw that there is a group of languages in which length, intensity, and pitch tend to operate separately rather than in concert. Vowel quality tends to be quite clear in these languages because they are reduced relatively little; vowel quantity (length) also tends to be contrastive. For reasons suggested in Section 2, however, sequences of syllables have less of the kind of rhythmic character typical of stress-prominent languages, thus offering the novice less in the way of rhythmically defined units for segmentation. Even in French, which has strong phrase-final stress, the rest of the syllables in a phrase tend to be even, without local highlights (Gårding, 1981). Some syllable- or mora-timed languages, such as Spanish and Japanese, are characterized by a rat-a-tat-tat of predominantly light or open syllables, while others, such as Thai (Patricia Donegan, personal communication) contain sequences of heavy syllables uninterrupted by light ones.

A force that may conspire in achieving a relatively uniform sequence of syllables is the tendency in some languages to elide vowel sequences that occur through the juxtaposition of a word (or morpheme) ending in a vowel with a word (or morpheme) beginning with a vowel. Similar coalescences may happen with consonant sequences. If resyllabification then takes place, the margins of words (morphemes) can be lost.[23] Example 30 shows the following coalescences in Greek: *e+e>e, o+a>a, po+ti>pti; m+m>m, n+m>m* (from Gårding, 1981, p. 148). The resulting syllable structure is quite uniform.

---

[23]We saw an example of resyllabification without coalescence in Spanish in Example 7.

(30) lexical: *i madam marian malarmé exi to mandolino apo tin madriti*
      syllable: i/ma/da/ma/riam/ma/lar/me/xi/to/ma/do/li/na/pti/ma/dri/ti
      'Madame Marianne Mallarmé has a mandolin from Madrid.'

Some languages "avoid" this problem by inserting "buffer" consonants whenever the juxtaposition of two morphemes would result in a sequence of two vowels. If, as in Turkish, each inflection carries its own distinctive buffer (e.g., -*n*-GEN, -*y*-ACC), extra cues as to morphological class are also provided (Aksu-Koç & Slobin, 1985, p. 840).

A morphologically controlled process which may incidentally contribute to uniformity of syllable structure is liaison. While most analyses of French (e.g., Selkirk, 1981) describe liaison as the surfacing of an underlying consonant in certain syntactic contexts, from the standpoint of a learner, liaison may appear to be the insertion of a rather arbitrary consonant. This takes place following a (closed-class) morpheme that ends in a vowel but only when the next word also begins with a vowel (and is part of the same syntactic phrase). Because resyllabification then takes place, so that the inserted consonant is perceived as belonging to the same syllable as the vowel that follows it, liaison simultaneously helps maintain an ideal CV(C) syllable structure and makes it difficult for the learner to determine the underlying form of the vowel-initial morpheme. We immediately see the difficulty if we look again at Examples 9 and 10, which show the pattern for consonant-initial words, the pattern for vowel-initial words, and the attempts of Grégoire's two-year-old subject to say the vowel-initial word arbre (1971, p. 94).

(9)		'cat'	'a cat'	'the cat'	'this cat'	'the cats'
	lexical:	*chat*	un chat	*le chat*	*ce chat*	*les chats*
	morphemes:	ša	ɜ ša	lœ ša	sœ ša	le ša
	syllables:	ša	ɜ ša	lœ ša	sœ ša	le ša

(10)		'tree'	'a tree'	'the tree'	'this tree'	'the trees'
	lexical:	'tree'	'a tree'	'the tree'	'this tree'	'the trees'
	lexical:	*arbre*	un arbre	*l'arbre*	*cet arbre*	*les arbres*
	morphemes:	arbr	ən arbr	lœ arbre	sɛt arbre	lez arbr
	syllables:	ar/br	ə/nar/br	lar/br	sɛ/tar/br	le/zar/br

(31) 2-yr-old: narp, larp, tabr, zab

In our search for the kinds of segmentation handles afforded by different languages, we have been implicitly working with an opposition of stress-languages (those in which extra length and intensity, together with change in pitch, all tend to cooccur in a single stressed syllable), with syllable/mora-languages (in which length, intensity, and pitch are dissociated). Although such a dichotomy is tempting, the distinction is more heuristic than absolute, because languages actually fall along a continuum rather than congregating at the poles. There is space here only to offer two suggestions about what can be found in the middle. First, there are languages in which length is dissociated from stress, which is achieved through a combination of increased intensity and change in pitch; these include Swedish, Norwegian, Danish, and German, which all have vowel-length contrasts. Second, there are languages, such as Polish, in which, although the presence of stress is marked by changes in length, pitch, and intensity, the absence of stress is not accompanied by reduction of vowels, as in Russian or English.

The possibility that stress plays a role in segmentation raises a number of questions. It has already been suggested that the rhythmic beat of stress-languages may offer the learner one kind of segmentation handles (accent group, foot, stressed syllable). What might be some implications for segmentation in sylla-ble-/mora-languages? Is rhythm less likely to be used than other kinds of prosodic cues? Although Fisher and Tokura (1996) have found reliable differences in three prosodic features (pause duration, pitch excursion, and F_0 amplitude) of clause-final syllables in the IDS of three Japanese mothers, rhythm as English-speakers know it may not play a role. What sorts of strategies will help learners of these languages focus on grammatical morphemes? Are they more likely to be "syllable children" than "tune children" (2.2.2)? One possibility is that, for whatever kind of prosodic highlighting exists, any regularly recurring grammatical morpheme that closely follows a highlighted syllable is in position to get picked up as part of an unopened package. We will have to leave these questions for future research.

4. STRATEGIES FOR ACQUIRING GRAMMATICAL MORPHEMES

4.1. The Focus Problem

We are at last ready to consider how children acquire grammatical morphemes in different languages. To what extent do children follow a universal path in this regard? To what extent do they employ strategies which vary from language to language and/or from child to child? What is the crosslinguistic evidence? To the extent that we find different paths, we need to distinguish those that are due to typological attributes, such as those sketched in the previous section, from those that are due to individual differences among learners. Before we can address the crosslinguistic question, we need to consider what kinds of evidence we can find about what children might be paying attention to.

We already noted that different acquisition paths (e.g., the TUNE PATH, the FOOT PATH, the SYLLABLE/SEGMENT PATH) have been found among learners of Danish, English, Finnish, German, Norwegian, and Portuguese. We suggested that one crucial difference among these paths—a difference lying near their starting points—might involve the size of phonetic unit that children choose to reproduce and the role of prosody in the organization of their early productions. Researchers have reported two kinds of evidence that, in their early utterances, children reproduce only part of what they perceive: first, the systematicity of certain omissions, and second, the predictability of positions in which phonologically underspecified fillers are inserted. As for omissions, Gerken, Landau, and Remez (1990) have shown that, when children with MLUs under 2.0 are asked to imitate sentences that contain either real or pseudo-functors, they are significantly more likely to leave out the real morphemes than the pseudo ones. (The pseudofunctors are similar to real functors in positioning and lack of stress.) Gerken et al. conclude that this systematic omission is evidence that even at this early stage children in fact are aware both of where many real functors belong and of what they sound like. Following up this study, Gerken and McIntosh (1993) investigated the ability of English-learning children to respond to commands formed with grammatical morphemes used grammatically (*Find the bird*), grammatical morphemes used ungrammatically (*Find was bird*), and pseudomorphemes (*Find gub bird*). They found that even children with productive MLUs less than 1.50, who spontaneously produced no articles at all, responded significantly better to commands containing grammatical morphemes than to those containing ungrammatical or nonsense ones. Gerken and McIntosh conclude that children are aware of functors and use them in comprehension well before they produce them.

Turning now to the evidence provided by fillers, we have already suggested that, while some of these may be rhythmically determined, others seem to be protomorphemic in nature. We have also noted that different children employ different kinds of protomorphemes. Tune children, who insert syllables, include Adam (Brown, 1973, CHILDES transcripts), Eric (Bloom, 1970), and Seth (Peters & Menn, 1993). Somewhat intermediate is Scollon's subject Brenda (1976), who at 2;0.12 sometimes inserted a pause or an intake of breath for a "missing" morpheme.[24] Dan Slobin's son Shem, who inserted protomorphemic segments rather than syllables,[25] may have been following a path where he focused more on the phonetic content of single syllables than on the prosodic structure of sequences of syllables (see Peters & Menn, 1993, for discussion). Evidence that protomorphemes can be other than syllabic raises the possibility that there might be other ways in which children signal awareness of a missing morpheme, such as by adding length to the syllable to which it should be attached.[26]

---

[24]From my own analysis of Scollon's tape.

[25]Between 2;1 and 2;2, Shem added final sibilants (/s,z/) to many nouns. Shem did seem to have acquired the notion of marking plural and possessive, and in many cases plural, possessive, auxiliary, or copula were plausible targets. Nevertheless, Slobin reports (personal communication) that it was often not possible to determine their function. It is for this reason that they seem to be somewhat PROTOmorphemic.

[26]Such possibilities point up the need for greater PHONETIC awareness on that part of researchers interested in the early development of morphosyntax!

At the end of Section 2.2 we suggested that one reason for the existence of these different paths is that there is too much information present in the acoustic signal for learners to pay attention to all at once.[27] We can reformulate this as a problem faced by all language learners.

> **Focus Problem.** When there is too much information present in the phonetic signal to sort out all at once, which parts are most accessible to focus on first? What kinds of strategies are available to enable learners to identify a useful problem to work on and to narrow their focus to a workable set of forms from which to extract patterns?

The data (both already cited and to be cited) are consistent with the view that, in the absence of clear segmentation cues, the units which children do in fact focus on are those that are phonologically defined; from these they try to extract patterns of occurrence at both morpholexical and phonological levels.[28]

This focus problem can be viewed as a figure-ground problem, reflecting the fact that learners have to "decide" which aspects of the signal to pay attention to. From a morphosyntactic point of view it looks as if tune children tend to perceive sentences as frames with slots to be filled, where the frames are composed of functors or proto-functors (including "pivots"), and the slots contain open-class items (nouns, verbs, and adjectives). Syllable children, on the other hand, tend to pay less attention to the frames (the closed-class bits) and focus on the slots, that is, the open-class items, which they juxtapose in their early utterances. It is thus possible that, at early stages, functors play different roles for different children, serving as phonologically defined frames with fillable slots for FORMULAIC children and as segmentation cues for JUXTAPOSERS. In this way grammatical morphemes can be seen as a kind of bridge between two aspects of language, the phonological/rhythmic and the morphosyntactic.

4.2. Some Generalizations About Strategies for Acquiring Grammatical Morphemes

How might prosody and morphological typology affect the acquisition of grammatical morphemes? Because of the multi-dimensionality of this problem we will not be able to cover it exhaustively. Rather, we will consider a set of generalizations gleaned by looking through the descriptive chapters in these volumes with the assumption that learners are able to draw on two major strategies for acquiring morphosyntax. The first of these is the more widely recognized SYNTACTIC strategy, in which early multi-unit constructions are formed through

---

[27]Newport (1990) and Goldowsky and Newport (1993) argue that it is precisely the fact that children are limited in their processing capacity that makes them effective language learners.

[28]Pye (1983) was one of the first to notice this.

the juxtaposition of members of major syntactic categories, which tend to be open-class items (either free morphemes or uninflected stems). The second strategy is a more MORPHOLOGICAL one, in which the basis for early multi-unit constructions is provided by fixed frames with slots for single open-class items.[29] The degree to which a given child utilizes each of these strategies varies, depending both on the language being learned and on the individual learner. We would do well to note that the analytic nature of English seems to favor a syntactic strategy, while its stress-timing may favor a more morphological strategy. Because so much language acquisition research has been done by English-speaking syntactians, who are predisposed to pay attention to the emergence of word order, only the former strategy has received much attention. Bottari, Cipriani, and Chilosi (1991) and Demuth (1992b, 1994) are the first researchers that I am aware of who have tried to address the question of how a morphological strategy of producing filler syllables could be tied to the evolution of major syntactic categories. In Bottari et al.'s analysis of the acquisition of free morphology in Italian, as soon as children produce them, (proto)morphemes in front of nouns are considered to occupy the syntactic slot of "generic determinant."[30]

4.2.1. One-Unit Utterances: Stems or Amalgams?

When nouns and verbs have an uninflected form (i.e., a bare stem, usually vocative or nominative for nouns and imperative for verbs), these forms are often the first ones produced (e.g., in German).

Amalgams are more likely to be produced when word-internal morphemes are difficult to segment. This can be true for a number of reasons, such as: when the invariance, frequency, and intonational pattern of a formulaic phrase make it hard to perceive its separate constituents; when it is difficult to segment morphemes within a word (Hebrew, K'iche'); when a fixed stress position (especially word-initial stress) causes whole words to be the most easily segmentable units, whether morphologically complex or not (Finnish, Hungarian); when a word-initial stress pattern is violated by a few prefixes that are adjoined without any juncture (Hungarian definite articles; MacWhinney, 1985, p. 1113).

Hebrew provides a particularly clear example of a situation in which segmentation is difficult, because many derivational morphemes are discontinuous strings of vowels interdigitated into tri-consonantal roots (Berman, 1985). (These are very like the vowel alternations found in the English verbs *sing, swing*, and *ring*; see Example 16.) Children learning Hebrew can only produce amalgamated stems

---

[29]I have not been able to draw conclusions about some languages because those chapters lack sufficiently detailed descriptions of prosodic characteristics and their possible effects upon learners.

[30]In the terms of Abney (1986) and Fukui and Speas (1985), these phonologically underdetermined fillers define Determiner Phrases by serving as their heads.

until they have collected enough instances of a vowel pattern to be able to extract it.

It would be interesting to know whether the kinds of infixes found in languages like Tagalog also pose interesting segmentation problems. Example 32 shows how topic-marking -VC- infixes are inserted after the initial consonant of a verb stem that begins with a consonant. Here the stem is *sipa* 'kick'; the infixed focus-marker for Agent (AF) is *-um-*, while that for GOAL (GF) is *-in-*. The respective infixed forms are *sumipa (s-um-ipa)* and *sinipa (s-in-ipa)*. (Tagalog requires that focus-markers appear in both the verb and associated noun phrases; *ang* marks the focus-link to the verb. The analysis presented here is based on that in Siewierska, 1991, p. 91.)

(32) *Sumipa ng   aso ang   tao.*
     kick-AF GOAL dog ACTOR person
                     +focus
     'The person kicks a dog.'

     Sinipa ng   tao   ang   aso.
     kick-GF ACTOR person GOAL dog
                     +focus
     'The dog is kicked by a person.'

At the very least, these infixes disrupt the syllabic coherence of the verb stem. Whether they have demonstrable effects on segmentation is not yet known.

4.2.2. *Two-Unit Utterances: Morphemes or Words?*

In most of the languages which have been reported on in these volumes, the earliest two-unit utterances are likely to be productive combinations of (parts of) two words. This is true in languages which are highly analytic (e.g., Mandarin, English, German, Swedish), in those which are fusional (e.g., Polish), and in many of those which are agglutinative (Finnish, ASL). It may be important that in these languages sentences containing verbs require a separate word for each argument. This is not true for Sesotho which marks verbs for object as well as subject; nor is it strictly true for Japanese and Korean which allow ellipsis of both subject and object if they are old information even though these are not marked on the verb. In these latter languages sentences can consist of nothing but an inflected verb.

In contrast, combinations of two morphemes precede combinations of two words in some agglutinative or polysynthetic languages (e.g., Turkish and Eskimo). In these languages it is possible for a full sentence to consist of a single word, usually a (highly) inflected verb. It is also important that it is not difficult to segment the morphemes that appear in these combinations—morphemes that tend to occur at the beginnings and the ends of words (see below).

We should bear in mind that, depending on the preferences of the individual learner, morphologically based frame-constructions can in fact be among the first productive combinations in quite a number of languages.[31] Clancy (1985, p. 482) notes the presence of different strategies among learners of Japanese, with some learners producing early constructions that seem to be of a "pivot" type (i.e., frames with slots). She suggests that "some children may be sensitive to specific local morphological markers, whereas others rely more heavily upon word order in processing sentences," and that "some children focus upon more global . . . aspects of linguistic input, such as relative word order, whereas others rely more upon local cues" (Clancy, 1985, p. 486). Among the three Kaluli children she observed, Schieffelin (1985, pp. 559–600) notes interesting individual variation in emergence of the ability to produce appropriate casemarking on three-constituent utterances. One child, Abi, seemed to avoid such constructions until he could produce them correctly at 27.2 months. A second child, Wanu, seems to have preferred what I have been calling JUXTAPOSITION of open-class items: until 30.3 months his three-constituent utterances included no casemarkers at all, after which they were correctly produced. Finally, while Mɛli correctly produced some ergative casemarkers from 26 months, she was still omitting them some of the time at 32.2. Because her errors were correlated with particular verbs, one wonders if she did not take a more "morphological" approach than Abi or Wanu. I expect that, as larger samples of children are studied longitudinally, we will find early "morphological" combinations in a wider range of languages.

4.2.3. When Are Morphemes Easy to Acquire?

Grammatical morphemes are relatively easy to acquire when they are frequent, easy to segment, have a fixed position relative to an open-class stem, have a clear function, and have an easily recognizable form (i.e., when allomorphy is regular and phonologically rather than morphologically conditioned). It may also help when the rhythm of the language makes morphemes prosodically locatable.

As suggested by Slobin as long ago as 1973, final position seems to play an especially important role. Sentence-final particles, which are both easy to segment and occupy a salient position, are produced early in both Japanese (Clancy, 1985) and Mandarin (Erbaugh, 1992; Tardif, 1993), although Mandarin's homophonous sentence-final particles, both pronounced *le*, require further sorting out (Erbaugh, 1992). Even though sentence-final particles may be added on after them, clause-final morphemes also have a kind of final salience. In Japanese, an SOV language, verb inflections are both clause-final and, except for easily segmentable sentence-final particles, sentence-final; they appear very early (Clancy, 1985, p. 381). Because of the pervasive ellipsis in Japanese, the verb may in fact be the only major constituent in the clause. In Hebrew, even selectively language- impaired

---

[31]These are constructions formed by inserting open-class items into slots defined by closed-class items; e.g., some equivalent of *this* + NOUN or VERB + *it*.

children have little trouble with inflections that are both clause-final and stressed or lengthened (Dromi, Leonard, & Shteiman, 1993).

In Section 2.2.1, we noted that evidence from Sesotho and Swedish suggests that salient tonal patterns can also draw a learner's attention to particular grammatical morphemes at quite an early stage.

4.2.4. When Are Morphemes Hard to Acquire? Evidence From Omissions

Grammatical morphemes are vulnerable to omission for a number of reasons, which may hold simultaneously in some languages. One cause is that the phonological form of a particular morpheme is difficult to perceive because it is located in the inner recesses of a word. Evidence for this is that, within words, morphemes tend to be acquired from outside in, with inner slots initially being left empty and later, perhaps, being filled with protomorphemes. For instance, in West Greenlandic Eskimo, the first combinations are of stems (which are word-initial) and inflections (which are word-final); word-internal derivational markers do not appear until later (Fortescue & Lennert Olsen, 1992). Aksu-Koç and Slobin (1985, pp. 847–848) report that an early stage Turkish learners sometimes employ "meaningless syllables" to approximate the passive and causative particles which occur in the middle of multi-morphemic verb forms.

There are three other properties which seem to make grammatical morphemes vulnerable to omission: fusion of several meanings within a single form (portmanteau morphemes), "bleaching" of semantic function (contrast English *of* with *in* or *on*), and confusability of distinct meanings because of homophony. All three of these interfere with the discovery of the function of a particle. Probably the hardest morphemes of all are those that are unstressed, are word-internal, straddle syllable boundaries, and have opaque functions.

Let us briefly consider several examples from languages where these properties exert their influence in various combinations. In German, even though rudimentary articles appear fairly early, the construction of the gender- and casemarking paradigm is achieved relatively late (Mills, 1985, pp. 172–175), evidently because of both semantic fusion (case, number, and gender are incorporated into single, unsegmentable morphemes) and homophony (e.g., the following definite articles all have the identical form *der*: nominative-masculine-singular, genitive-feminine-singular, dative-feminine-singular, genitive-plural). In both Polish and Russian, inflections are mostly suffixes, but because of fusion of case, gender, and number, the precise functions and paradigmatic organization of these inflections are not immediately obvious. In both languages children tend to omit inflections for the first three months of two-unit constructions (Smoczyńska 1985, p. 618). Because of the homophony caused by vowel reduction in Russian, paradigm construction is later in this language than in Polish (see discussion of "inflectional imperialism," below). In Japanese, Clancy (1985, pp. 402–403) reports that children at first omit the affix -ku- which is required when negating adjectives.[32] Not only is this an "inner" morpheme which must be sandwiched between the adjectival root and the negative morpheme -na-, it is both semantically opaque and ho- mophonous with a morpheme which converts adjectives to adverbs. In Sesotho, verb-internal object markers are produced later than verb-initial subject markers (Demuth, 1992a). In English, the functor *of* has little in the way of identifiable function and it tends to be much reduced; it, too, is likely to be omitted (and later to be confused with the homophonous auxiliary *(ha)ve* as in *I would of gone*). The English plural marker -*s/-z/-əz* suffers both from lack of syllabicity in its more frequent allomorphs and from homophony with several other markers: possessive, third-singular-present, contracted auxiliary *is (she's playing)*, contracted copula *is (she's here)*, and contracted auxiliary *has (she's done it)*. Peters and Menn (1993) have shown how this homophony of the -*s/-z/-əz* suffixes led at least one child initially to assume that their presence was phonologi-cally rather than morphologically conditioned.

Georgian looks as though it might be particularly interesting from the point of view of acquisition of verbal affixes. In this language, verbs and nouns have fixed slots; in verbs, the root is in the middle of the word, with three slots preceding it and five following it. Moreover, it is possible for a verbal affix to consist of only a single segment (consonant or vowel). This, coupled with the fact that Georgian can have extremely complex consonant clusters, means that a single syllable can contain two or three morphemes (Imedadze & Tuite, 1992, p. 44). It is also possible for morphemes to straddle syllables as in K'iche'.

(33) morphemes   syllables   verb roots are underlined

    g-cer   = /gcer/

    v-s-cer   = /vscer/

    m-si-a   = /mši/a/

    gw-nax-e-t   = /gwna/Xet/

    e-xmar-eb-od-a = /eX/ma/re/bo/da/

    ga-m-i-ket-eb-s = /ga/mi/ke/tebs/

    (Imedadze & Tuite, 1992, p. 44)

Word stress is unhelpful because syllables are accented quite evenly, with the first syllable of a word usually being the one that receives such stress as there is (Alice Harris, personal communication). This suggests that the root of a verb often does not receive even this small amount of contrast. Because I have not been able to infer as much as I would like about the acquisition of bound morphemes in Georgian, I will suggest some questions for which it would be

---

[32]I would like to thank Masako Izutani for bringing this example to my attention (Izutani, 1991).

interesting to have answers. How do children segment single-segment morphemes? Are they first produced as parts of amalgams? What role does syllabicity
play? Does the position of a morpheme relative to the root play a role in
acquisition? Do Georgian children start with the root and work out to the edges?
Are prefixes any easier than suffixes?

4.2.5. *Protomorphemes*

We have already noted that some children learning some languages produce
phonologically underdefined protomorphemes in positions where particular target
morphemes are required. That these forms are not produced in full may be an
indication of some measure of difficulty in their acquisition. Whether morphemes
are omitted or approximated by protomorphemes seems to depend partly on the
language and partly on the individual learner. One generalization that we can
propose is that a particular grammatical morpheme is likely to be approximated
by a filler syllable when its adult target is a full syllable which does not carry
stress (or tone, as with the neutral-toned syllables of Mandarin), when the kind
of information it carries tends to have a fixed position (or slot) but is not
particularly salient semantically. Clancy (1985, p. 483) reports that one Japanese
child first produced NOUN *no* NOUN constructions by either omitting the *no* or
inserting "a vague sound" between the two nouns. The likelihood of a filler is
even greater when the slot is defined rhythmically as well. Besides the examples
given in Section 2.2.2, we have an example of this in the "meaningless syllables"
produced by Turkish-learning children in place of passive and causative markers
(Aksu-Koç & Slobin, 1985, pp. 847–848).

It is possible that the phenomenon of "inflectional imperialism," which has
been reported for Russian (Slobin, 1966; Smoczyńska, 1985) is also a manifes-
tation of a somewhat more advanced kind of protomorpheme. Russian has both
vowel reduction, which neutralizes many word-final inflections to schwa or schwa
plus a consonant, and stress shifts, which cause many inflections to have alternative full and reduced forms (Johnston, 1991). When children first start producing inflections on nouns they seem to choose a single, maximally distinctive
form to serve as a marker for each grammatical case, such as a proto-instrumental
or a proto-dative.[33] Here they seem to have sorted out at least some of the function
but not yet grasped the full range of phonological forms that serves each function.
It is interesting that in Polish, in which vowels are not reduced in final unstressed
syllables, children use the appropriate forms as soon as they begin to produce
them (Smoczyńska, 1985, p. 645).

When morphemes straddle syllable boundaries, they will not be approximated
by full syllables; rather, those parts of morphemes will first be produced that are

---

[33]I would like to thank Patricia Donegan for suggesting this formulation.

contained in stressed syllables, as we saw in K'iche' and Mohawk (Examples 16 and 17).

When morphemes are smaller than a syllable (e.g., English plural or past tense), their acquisition path will vary, depending on the child's awareness of and ability to deal with the complexities of syllable structure. The diary data for Shem Slobin (see discussion in Peters & Menn, 1993) suggest that segmental protomorphemes are a possibility, although the evidence for these is still sparse because we lack sufficient phonetic information. It is possible that Georgian could provide interesting evidence about these tiny morphemes.

5. CONCLUSIONS

In this chapter we have considered how the acquisition of grammatical morphemes is influenced by prosodic and phonological characteristics of the language being learned as well as by its morphological typology. Although we have raised a number of interesting issues and considered some suggestive evidence, there are still many unanswered questions about this area of language acquisition. Therefore, in conclusion I will present a list of such questions, suggest an approach to comparative research in language acquisition, and raise some methodological points.

5.1. Some Unanswered Questions

- Is it generally easier for learners to discover the morphemes of languages that are more analytic (i.e., that have fewer morphemes per word) than it is to discover the morphemes of languages that are agglutinative or polysynthetic? Under what circumstances is this not the case?

- What phonetic and/or morphological characteristics of a language contribute to words or morphemes tending either to cling together into complex units or naturally to fall apart at the seams (either within words or within phrases)?

- What makes it possible to segment the morphemes of those agglutinative languages in which boundaries are not so easy to find as in Turkish?

- Do (subsets of) the grammatical morphemes in some languages have distinctive phonological characteristics that might help learners to perceive them as a separate class? For instance, English functors tend to have weak stress, a reduced set of (lax) vowels, and a somewhat distinctive set of consonants (especially /w,n,ð,t,z/).

- What generalizations are possible about the relationship of syllabicity to segmentability of morphemes? Especially interesting in this regard are morphemes that split across syllables and those that are smaller than a syllable.

- Under what circumstances are children likely to produce protomorphemes? What are the characteristics of the adult targets? Are there any languages in which children never produce protomorphemes?

- Are there formulaic learners in all languages? How does the course of their language development differ from that of non-formulaic children?[34]

- How does starting with bigger or smaller units (monomorphemes vs. amalgams) affect a child's progress toward the adult morphological system, both within a language and across languages?

- How does starting with combinations of two morphemes vs. two words affect a child's progress toward the adult morphological system, both within a language and across languages?

- What, if anything, serves the same function as stress and rhythm in languages with little stress (such as Finnish, Georgian, Japanese, Turkish, West Greenlandic Eskimo)?

- Do children learning syllable-timed languages ever impose their own stress-timing? Allen and Hawkins' (1978) data suggest that the reverse can be true; they report that as late as 3 years old, children's productions of English sound syllable-timed because the children do not fully control vowel reduction.

- Under what circumstances do tone/pitch patterns contribute useful segmentation handles, especially in languages without strong stress?

- How does the acquisition of suffixes differ from that of prefixes, both in languages that have both (Georgian, Hebrew, Sesotho), and in languages that are strongly prefixing (Navajo) or strongly suffixing (Turkish, West Greenlandic)?

We still know too little about the psycholinguistic differences between these kinds of affixes, both in acquisition and in adult processing. Hankamer (1989) proposes a parsing model of word-recognition for Turkish, a language which is both highly agglutinative and totally suffixing. He makes a good case for a left-to-right parsing process which starts with the open-class stem and uses morphotactic constraints to identify successive suffixes, each of which belongs to a small, closed set. This restricts to a minimum the amount of lexical look-up that has to take place. But how does word-recognition proceed for adult speakers of a totally prefixing language like Navajo, where the open-class root does not appear until the very end of a morphologically complex word? And how do children go about acquiring the prefix classes in such a language? One might guess that they would start with the salient final stem and proceed from the end to the beginning of the word, as seems

---

[34]We have already mentioned reports of formulaic learners of Danish (Plunkett & Strömqvist, 1992), German (Mills, 1985, p. 238; Stern & Stern, 1965), Italian (Bottari, Cipriani, & Chilosi, 1991), Japanese (Clancy, 1985), Kaluli (Schieffelin, 1985), Norwegian (Simonsen, 1991), and Portuguese (Scarpa, 1990), as well as English.

to be the case in Mohawk (Mithun, 1989). Prefixing languages would seem to be interesting ones on which to focus language acquisition research.

5.2. Directions for Future Research

One way to begin to address questions such as these is to compare the acquisition of grammatical morphemes in "minimal pair" sets of languages, that is, languages that are closely related (e.g., in their morphological systems), but which differ in interesting ways (e.g., prosodically).[35] For example, we have already noted that, while Polish and Russian are morphologically very similar, they differ prosodically, with Polish having fixed stress and no vowel reduction and Russian having movable stress and considerable vowel reduction. Here is an excellent testing ground for investigating the role of these phonological properties in the acquisition of morphology. Another interesting pair of morphologically similar languages is Spanish and (Brazilian) Portuguese, where the former is more syllable-timed with no vowel reduction, while the latter has three degrees of stress which engender considerable changes in vowel quality (Major, 1985). French, a third Romance language with a closely related system of grammatical morphemes, has roughly even syllable lengths except for marked word-final lengthening (Gårding, 1981), thus setting up a minimal triad with Spanish and Portuguese. In the interests of stimulating further research along these lines I will next suggest some questions for which such comparisons could furnish answers. I will then present a list of interesting comparisons waiting to be done.

5.2.1. Minimal-Pair Studies

5.2.1.1. Phonological Comparison. How do the languages in question compare with respect to phonological and prosodic characteristics such as: stress patterns (fixed vs. movable); timing (stress vs. syllable); rhythmicity (kinds of metrical feet, if any); the presence of clitics that interact with stress; syllable structure (is there a heavy/light contrast?); (re)syllabification across word or morpheme boundaries; elision; liaison; vowel quantity (long/short contrasts?; full/reduced contrasts?); pitch phenomena that might interact with morphology?

5.2.1.2. Morphological Comparison. How do these languages compare with respect to their morphological structure (isolating/polysynthetic; agglutinating/fusional; degree of semantic fusion). To what degree is the order of semantic units fixed (slotted) versus free?

5.2.1.3. Predicted Phonological Consequences for Acquisition of Grammatical Morphemes. SEGMENTABILITY (ease of finding boundaries): how reliable is the match between syllable and word/morpheme boundaries? Are there any

---

[35]This idea has also been suggested by Plunkett and Strömqvist (1992, p. 540).

reliable cues to wordhood, such as fixed stress position or word-internal vowel harmony? Are there processes through which boundary information can be obscured or lost, such as elision or liaison? ALLOMORPHY: are there processes that obscure the recognizability of allomorphs? Either phonologically conditioned ones such as assimilation or vowel reduction, or morphologically conditioned ones such as consonant gradation or ablaut? FOCUSERS: are there prosodic phenomena that might serve to focus the learner's attention on specific morphemes, such as marked tone, stress, or conspicuously shifting stress?

5.2.1.4. Acquisition Facts.   What do learners' first productions tend to be like in each language? Are they syllables, feet, stems, amalgams? How might these be affected by the prosodic characteristics of the input? Do the first productive combinations consist of two words or two morphemes? Which grammatical morphemes are produced first, and which ones seem to be hardest in each language? Are there any prosodic explanations for these orders? How is the acquisition picture similar and how does it differ across these languages? Is there any evidence for language-specific prosodic strategies? Is there any evidence for prosodic focus points? Within each language is there evidence for prosodically driven individual differences in acquisition patterns? Are there SYLLABLE-SEG-MENT children and TUNE children?

5.2.2. Questions to Investigate Through Comparison Studies

• What are the roles of pitch and articulatory characteristics?
A comparison of Norwegian and Danish could be revealing because these two languages are morphologically very close, but Norwegian is articulated toward the front of the mouth and has tonal word accents while Danish is articulated more toward the back of the mouth and has no tonal accents.
• What role is played by vowel reduction?
Compare Russian and Polish, or Portuguese and Spanish (see above).
• What role is played by fixed stress?
Compare Polish and Russian, or French and Spanish (see above).
• What is the role of stress-prominence?
Compare Portuguese and Spanish (see above). A comparison of Korean and Japanese might also be interesting in this regard.
• What difference is made by the presence vs. absence of tones?
Swedish and Finnish–Swedish are morphologically almost identical, but the latter does not have the tonal word accents of standard Swedish.
• Does neutral tone play an identifiable role?
Besides full tones, Mandarin also has a lower and shorter "neutral" tone (a sort

of "tonal schwa") which occurs on many particles, unstressed syllables, and the second syllables of many disyllabic words. Tseng (1991) suggests that neutral tone may be a prosodic property that children could use in identifying grammatical morphemes. Because there are many fewer neutral tones in southern (e.g., Taiwanese) than in northern (e.g., Beijing) Mandarin (ibid.), one could compare acquisition of these two dialects, looking for the influence of neutral tone.

• What are the effects of differing amounts of consonant gradation?

According to Toivainen (personal communication), Vepsian, a Finnic language which is morphologically similar to Finnish, lacks the consonant gradation prevalent in the latter. Comparison of acquisition in these two languages may shed light on the role of morphophonemic processes in the perception of morpheme boundaries and identities. From the information I have about consonant changes in Korean, I suspect that it might also be interesting to compare this language with Japanese, even though these two are not so closely related as most of the pairs suggested so far.

• What role is played by the positioning of a particular kind of functional information?

Several studies could be done on this question. We have already seen in Example 14 that in the mainland Scandinavian languages (Danish, Norwegian, Swedish), indefinite articles precede their nouns (as in English), while definite articles follow them (when there is no adjective). Does having a separate position for definite and indefinite make articles easier for Scandinavian children to acquire?[36] In a second possible project one could look at the interaction of position with stress in Danish, Norwegian, and Swedish, which present a three-way contrast in stress and location of verbal particles (Plunkett & Strömqvist, 1992, pp. 468–469). A third investigation concerns the location of classifiers relative to their nouns in Thai and Mandarin. In Thai the classifiers are in the more salient final position (Noun-Numeral-Classifier), whereas in Mandarin they are prenominal (Numeral-Classifier-Noun) (Tseng, 1991).

• What is the effect of homophony among grammatical morphemes? Does it cause confusion and delay acquisition of a particular morpheme relative to that in a similar language with no homophony? Is it easier if the morphemes in question apply to different categories (nouns vs. verbs)?

In English, three different morphemes (plural, possessive, third singular present) have an identical set of allomorphs, /z,s,əz/, which is also a subset of the allomorphs of the auxiliaries *is* and *has*. (See Peters & Menn, 1993, for discussion.) In contrast, this homophony is not present in closely-related German. Norwegian, too, has two sets of nearly homophonous morphemes; one of the

---

[36]It certainly makes it easier for adult observers to tell which kind of article a child is trying to produce!

form -er (present tense, plural indefinite, agentive, 'is'), the other of the form -e (infinitive, imperative, infinitive).[37]

• Does the marking of person, number, or gender agreement prove a facilitator or a hindrance to acquisition of these markers? Under what conditions?
The comparison technique could also be useful in the investigation of areas of morphology that are less phonologically influenced. By looking for maximally similar pairs of languages that do and do not employ agreement we might be able to tease out answers to such questions.

• Within a language, how do the proportions of regular and irregular forms of a grammatical morpheme affect the course of acquisition?
Plunkett and Marchman (1991) point out the importance of both type and token frequencies among the allomorphs.[38] They ran a series of computational experiments to model the learning of past tense verb forms in English, varying characteristics of the verb population in each experiment. Their results suggest that the existing relative proportions of regular and irregular verb classes that actually occur in English are among the easier to learn.[39] They also found that phonological similarities within morphological subclasses seem to contribute to ease of learning (see also Bybee & Slobin, 1982).

• In general, then, how do populations of e.g., past tense forms vary across languages in proportions of regulars vs. irregulars and in relative sizes of the irregular classes? How do these configurations affect acquisition? Which classes do learners focus on first? How does acquisition vary in languages that are differently configured? For instance, German has more and larger strong verb classes than English does. How big do classes have to be not to be termed irregular? How does learning differ in English and German?
The Scandinavian languages (including Icelandic) make another interesting set within which to look at acquisition of verb morphology. They are currently being investigated by Hanne Gram Simonsen (Norwegian), and Hrafnhildur Ragnarsdóttir (Icelandic).

5.2.3. Methodological Implications

If, as has been the thesis of this chapter, languages afford different paths for acquiring grammatical morphemes, and if this process is indeed influenced by

---

[37]In Eastern Norwegian, word-final /r/ is only weakly articulated, making these sets nearly homonymous. The acquisition of these morphemes is currently being investigated by Hanne Gram Simonsen.

[38]The general tendency is for irregular allomorphs to have low type frequencies but high token frequencies, while the opposite is true for regular allomorphs.

[39]These proportions were: very few completely irregular verbs of very high frequency, relatively few relatively high-frequency verbs in two irregular classes (vowel change and no change), and very many low-frequency regular verbs.

phonetic and prosodic factors such as those presented here, important methodological considerations are entailed. The possibility of different paths highlights the need to understand the range of and limitations on individual differences and how they are influenced by the typology of the language being learned, which in turn points up the need eventually to study sufficient samples of children in each language. For grammatical morphemes we would like to know the extent to which children seem to utilize the two strategies we have identified—the SYNTACTIC one whereby open-class stems or words are juxtaposed, and the MORPHOLOGICAL one which utilizes closed-class frames with slots for open-class items.

The study of the evolution of protomorphemes into full ones allows us to look at an earlier stage of the acquisition of these forms than has heretofore been possible. The data, however, must be of a more phonetic nature than has generally been deemed important by researchers who study syntax. The finding that, in languages such as Eskimo and Georgian, the first productive combinations are of two morphemes, rather than of two words, should alert researchers that morphology may either precede syntax or be nearly simultaneous with it. For this reason, in order to understand the full course of the acquisition of grammatical morphemes it is important to do several things. First, we need to start collecting data before the first productive combinations appear, so we can see if their elements are words or morphemes (bearing in mind that pivot constructions are inherently "morphological"). We also need to consider phonetic and prosodic characteristics of both the child's speech and the input. Collaborations between researchers interested in phonology and those interested in morphosyntax are to be encouraged in this regard, because those interested in the one are all too rarely experts in the other. Further exploration of some of the newer phonological frameworks, such as autosegmental phonology and metrical phonology may prove particularly fruitful.

We need more information about the interaction of phonology and morphology in the input speech in our corpora, both to get a more exact idea of the learner's immediate target, and to see what kinds of focusing devices might be being provided.

In the interest of amassing as many different kinds of evidence as possible, it will be important to follow the lead of researchers such as Gerken in investigating the interaction between perception and production. I have also found that, despite the criticisms of this mode of investigation, interesting insights regarding possible learning mechanisms can arise from sophisticated attempts at computer modeling of the acquisition of grammatical morphemes (e.g., Plunkett, Marchman, & Knudson, 1991).

It is my hope that the issues presented in this chapter will stimulate interest and further research on the influence of phonology and prosody on the acquisition of grammatical morphemes.

REFERENCES

Abney, S. P. (1987). *The English noun phrase in its sentential aspect.* Unpublished doctoral dissertation, MIT.

Aksu-Koç, A. A., & Slobin, D. I. (1985). The acquisition of Turkish. In D. I. Slobin (Ed.), *The crosslinguistic study of language acquisition: Vol. 1. The data* (pp. 839–878). Hillsdale, NJ: Lawrence Erlbaum Associates.

Allen, G. D., & Hawkins, S. (1978). The development of phonological rhythm. In A. Bell & J. Bybee Hooper (Eds.), *Syllables and segments* (pp. 173–185). New York: North Holland Publishing Company.

Berman, R. A. (1985). The acquisition of Hebrew. In D. I. Slobin (Ed.), *The crosslinguistic study of language acquisition: Vol. 1. The data* (pp. 255–371). Hillsdale, NJ: Lawrence Erlbaum Associates.

Bernstein-Ratner, N. (1984). Patterns of vowel modification in mother-child speech. *Journal of Child Language, 11,* 557–578.

Bernstein-Ratner, N. (1986). Durational cues which mark clause boundaries in mother-child speech. *Journal of Phonetics, 14,* 303–309.

Bloom, L. (1970). *Language development: Form and function in emerging grammars.* Cambridge, MA: MIT Press.

Bolinger, D. L. (1965). Author's preface. In I. Abe & T. Kanekiyo (Eds.), *Forms of English: Accent, morpheme, order* (pp. vii–viii). Cambridge, MA: Harvard University Press.

Bottari, P., Cipriani, P., & Chilosi, A. M. (1991). *Pre-syntactic devices in the acquisition of Italian free morphology.* Unpublished manuscript, Institute of Child Neuropsychiatry, University of Pisa.

Branigan, G. (1979). Some reasons why successive single word utterances are not. *Journal of Child Language, 6,* 411–421.

Brown, R. (1973). *A first language: The early stages.* Cambridge, MA: Harvard University Press.

Bybee, J. L., & Slobin, D. I. (1982). Rules and schemas in the development and use of English past tense. *Language, 58,* 265–289.

Cipriani, P., Chilosi, A. M., Bottari, P., & Poli, P. (1990, July). *Some data on transitional phenomena in the acquisition of Italian.* Paper presented at the 5th International Congress for the Study of Child Language, Budapest.

Clancy, P. M. (1985). The acquisition of Japanese. In D. I. Slobin (Ed.), *The crosslinguistic study of language acquisition: Vol. 1. The data* (pp. 373–524). Hillsdale, NJ: Lawrence Erlbaum Associates.

Comrie, B. (1981). *Language universals and linguistic typology.* Oxford, England: Blackwell.

Connelly, M. J. (1984). *Basotho children's acquisition of noun morphology.* Unpublished doctoral dissertation, University of Essex.

Cutler, A. (1990). Exploiting prosodic probabilities in speech segmentation. In G. T. M. Altmann (Ed.), *Computational and psychological approaches to language processes* (pp. 105–121). Cambridge, MA: MIT Press.

Cutler, A., & Butterfield, S. (1992). Rhythmic cues to speech segmentation: Evidence from juncture misperception. *Journal of Memory and Language, 31,* 218–236.

Cutler, A., & Carter, D. M. (1987). The predominance of strong initial syllables in the English vocabulary. *Computer Speech and Language, 2,* 133–142.

Demuth, K. (1992a). The Acquisition of Sesotho. In D. I. Slobin (Ed.), *The crosslinguistic study of language acquisition: Vol. 3* (pp. 557–638). Hillsdale, NJ: Lawrence Erlbaum Associates.

Demuth, K. (1992b). Accessing functional categories in Sesotho: Interactions at the morpho-syntax interface. In J. Meisel (Ed.), *The acquisition of verb placement: Functional categories and V2 phenomena in language development* (pp. 83–107). Dordrecht, The Netherlands: Kluwer Academic Publishers.

Demuth, K. (1993). Issues in the acquisition of the Sesotho tonal system. *Journal of Child Language, 20*, 275–301.

Demuth, K. (1994). On the 'underspecification' of functional categories in early grammars. In B. Lust, M. Suñer, & J. Whitman (Eds.), *Syntactic theory and first language acquisition: Crosslinguistic perspectives.* Hillsdale, NJ: Lawrence Erlbaum Associates.

Department of Linguistics, Ohio State University. (1991). *Language files* (5th ed.). Columbus: Ohio State University Press.

Dromi, E., Leonard, L. B., & Shteiman, M. (1993). The grammatical morphology of Hebrew-speaking children with specific language impairment: Some competing hypotheses. *Journal of Speech and Hearing Research, 36*, 760–771.

Echols, C. H. (1993). A perceptually-based model of children's earliest productions. *Cognition, 46*, 245–296.

Echols, C. H., & Newport, E. L. (1992). The role of stress and position in determining first words. *Language Acquisition, 2*, 189–220.

Engstrand, O., Strömqvist, S., & Williams, K. (1991). Acquisition of the Swedish tonal word accent contrast. *Actes du XIIème Congres International des Science Phonétiques* (pp. 324–327). Publications de l'Université de Provence.

Erbaugh, M. (1992). The acquisition of Mandarin. In D. I. Slobin (Ed.), *The crosslinguistic study of language acquisition: Vol. 3* (pp. 373–455). Hillsdale, NJ: Lawrence Erlbaum Associates.

Eriksson, A. (1991). Aspects of Swedish Speech Rhythm. *Gothenburg Monographs in Linguistics, 9.* Gothenburg, Sweden: Department of Linguistics.

Fernald, A. (1991). Prosody in speech to children: Prelinguistic and linguistic functions. In R. Vasta (Ed.), *Annals of Child Development* (Vol. 8, pp. 43–80). London: Jessica Kingsley Publishers.

Fernald, A., & McRoberts, G. (1996). Prosodic bootstrapping: A critical analysis of the argument and the evidence. In J. L. Morgan & K. Demuth (Eds.), *Signal to syntax: Bootstrapping from speech to grammar in early acquisition* (pp. 365–388). Hillsdale, NJ: Lawrence Erlbaum Associates.

Fisher, C., & Tokura, H. (1993). Acoustic cues to clause boundaries in speech to infants. Unpublished manuscript, University of Illinois at Champaign.

Fisher, C., & Tokura, H. (1996). Prosody in speech to infants: Direct and indirect acoustic cues to syntactic structure. In J. L. Morgan & K. Demuth (Eds.), *Signal to syntax: Bootstrapping from speech to grammar in early language acquisition.*

Fortescue, M. (1992). Morphophonemic complexity and typological stability in a polysynthetic language family. *International Journal of American Linguistics, 58*, 242–247.

Fortescue, M., & Lennert Olsen, L. (1992). The Acquisition of West Greenlandic. In D. I. Slobin (Ed.), *The crosslinguistic study of language acquisition: Vol. 3* (pp. 111–219). Hillsdale, NJ: Lawrence Erlbaum Associates.

Fukui, N., & Speas, M. (1985). Specifiers and projections. *MIT Working Papers in Linguistics, 8.*

Gårding, E. (1981). Contrastive prosody: A model and its application. *Studia Linguistica, 35*, 146–165.

Gerken, L. (1991). The metrical basis for children's subjectless sentences. *Journal of Memory and Language, 30*, 431–451.

Gerken, L., Landau, B., & Remez, R. E. (1990). Function morphemes in young children's speech perception and production. *Developmental Psychology, 26*, 204–216.

Gerken, L., & McIntosh, B. J. (1993). The interplay of function morphemes and prosody in early language. *Developmental Psychology, 29*, 448–457.

Gleitman, L. R., & Wanner, E. (1982). Language acquisition: The state of the state of the art. In E. Wanner & L. R. Gleitman (Eds.), *Language acquisition: The state of the art* (pp. 3–48). New York: Cambridge University Press.

Gleitman, L. R., Gleitman, H., Landau, B., & Wanner, E. (1988). Where learning begins: Initial representations for language learning. In F. J. Newmeyer (Ed.), *Linguistics: The Cambridge survey: Vol. 3* (pp. 150–193). New York: Cambridge University Press.

Goldowsky, B., & Newport, E. (1993). Modeling the effects of processing limitations on the acquisition of morphology: The less is more hypothesis. In E. V. Clark (Ed.), *The Proceedings of the 24th annual Child Language Research Forum* (pp. 124–138). Stanford: Center for the Study of Language and Information.

Goldsmith, J. A. (1989). *Autosegmental and metrical phonology*. Oxford, England: Blackwell.

Grégoire, A. (1971). L'Apprentissage du langage. In A. Bar-Adon & W. F. Leopold (Eds.), *Child language: A book of readings* (pp. 91–95). Englewood Cliffs, NJ: Prentice-Hall. (Original work published 1948)

Halle, M., & Vergnaud, J.-R. (1988). *An essay on stress*. Cambridge, MA: MIT Press.

Hallé, P., de Boysson-Bardies, B., & Vihman, M. (1991). Beginnings of prosodic organization: Intonation and duration patterns of disyllables produced by Japanese and French infants. *Language and Speech, 34*, 299–318.

Hankamer, J. (1989). Morphological parsing and the lexicon. In W. Marslen-Wilson (Ed.), *Lexical representation and process*. Cambridge, MA: MIT Press.

Harris, J. W. (1983). *Syllable structure and stress in Spanish*. Linguistic Inquiry Monograph Eight. Cambridge, MA: MIT Press.

Haugen, E., & Joos, M. (1972). Tone and intonation in East Norwegian. In D. Bolinger (Ed.), *Intonation* (pp. 414–436). Harmondsworth, England: Penguin Books.

Hayes, B. (1984). The phonology of rhythm in English. *Linguistic Inquiry, 15*, 33–74.

Hayes, B. (1985). Iambic and trochaic rhythm in stress rules. *Proceedings of the Berkeley Linguistic Society, 11*, 429–446.

Hirsh-Pasek, K., Kemler Nelson, D. G., Jusczyk, P. W., Wright Cassidy, K., Druss, B., & Kennedy, L. (1987). Clauses are perceptual units for young infants. *Cognition, 26*, 269–286.

Hogg, R., & McCully, C. B. (1986). *Metrical phonology: A coursebook*. New York: Cambridge University Press.

Imedadze, N., & Tuite, K. (1992). The acquisition of Georgian. In D. I. Slobin (Ed.), *The crosslinguistic study of language acquisition: Vol. 3* (pp. 39–109). Hillsdale, NJ: Lawrence Erlbaum Associates.

Izutani, M. (1991). *Acquisition of grammatical morphemes: Japanese and Korean*. Unpublished manuscript, University of Hawaii.

Johnston, B. (1991). *The acquisition of morphology in Polish and Russian: A comparative study*. Unpublished manuscript, University of Hawaii.

Jusczyk, P. W. (1992). Developing phonological categories from the speech signal. In C. A. Ferguson, L. Menn, & C. Stoel-Gammon (Eds.), *Phonological development: Models, research, implications* (pp. 17–64). Timonium, MD: York Press.

Jusczyk, P. W., Cutler, A., & Redanz, N. J. (1993). Preference for the predominant stress patterns of English words. *Child Development, 64*, 675–687.

Jusczyk, P. W., Friederici, A., Wessels, J., Svenkerud, V. Y., & Jusczyk, A. M. (1993). Infants' sensitivity to the sound patterns of native language words. *Journal of Memory and Language, 32*, 402–420.

Jusczyk, P. W., Kemler Nelson, D. G., Hirsh-Pasek, K., Kennedy, L., Woodward, A., & Piwoz, J. (1992). Perception of acoustic correlates of major phrasal units by young infants. *Cognitive Psychology, 24*, 252–293.

Kaiser, G., & Meisel, J. (1990). Subjekte und Null-Subjekte in Französischen. In G. Fanselow & S. Olsen (Eds.), *Det, Comp und Infl*. Tübingen, Germany: Niemeyer.

Klein, H. B. (1978). *The relationship between perceptual strategies and production strategies in learning the phonology of early lexical items*. Bloomington: Indiana University Linguistics Club.

Klein, H. B. (1981). Early perceptual strategies for the replication of consonants from polysyllabic lexical models. *Journal of Speech and Hearing Research, 24*, 535–551.

Kunene, E. (1979). *The acquisition of Siswati as a first language*. Unpublished doctoral dissertation, University of California at Los Angeles.

Lederer, A., & Kelly, M. (1993). Prosodic information for syntactic structure in parental speech. Under review.

Leonard, L., Bortolini, U., Caselli, M. C., McGregor, K. K., & Sabbadini, L. (1992). Morphological deficits in children with specific language impairment. *Language Acquisition, 2*, 151–179.

Lieven, E. (1989). The linguistic implications of early and systematic variation in child language development. *Proceedings of the Berkeley Linguistic Society, 15*, 203–214.

Macken, M. A. (1979). Developmental reorganization of phonology: A hierarchy of basic units of acquisition. *Lingua, 49*, 11–49.

MacWhinney, B. (1985). Hungarian language acquisition as an exemplification of a general model of language development. In D. I. Slobin (Ed.), *The crosslinguistic study of language acquisition: Vol. 2. Theoretical issues* (pp. 1069–1155). Hillsdale, NJ: Lawrence Erlbaum Associates.

MacWhinney, B. (1991). *The CHILDES project: Tools for analyzing talk.* Hillsdale, NJ: Lawrence Erlbaum Associates.

Major, R. C. (1985). Stress and rhythm in Brazilian Portuguese. *Language, 61*, 259–282.

Mehler, J., Dupoux, E., & Segui, J. (1990). Constraining models of lexical access: The onset of word recognition. In G. T. M. Altmann (Ed.), *Cognitive models of speech processing* (pp. 236–262). Cambridge, MA: MIT Press.

Menn, L. (1971). Phonotactic rules in beginning speech. *Lingua, 26*, 225–251.

Menn, L. (1973). On the origin and growth of phonological and syntactic rules. *Chicago Linguistic Society, 9*, 378–385.

Mills, A. E. (1985). The acquisition of German. In D. I. Slobin (Ed.), *The crosslinguistic study of language acquisition: Vol. 1. The data* (pp. 141–254). Hillsdale, NJ: Lawrence Erlbaum Associates.

Mithun, M. (1989). The acquisition of polysynthesis. *Journal of Child Language, 16*, 285–312.

Morgan, J. L., & Demuth, K. (Eds.). (1996). *Signal to syntax: Bootstrapping from speech to grammar in early acquisition.* Mahwah, NJ: Lawrence Erlbaum Associates.

Morgan, J. L., Meier, R. P., & Newport, E. L. (1987). Structural packaging in the input to language learning: Contributions of prosodic and morphological marking of phrases to the acquisition of language. *Cognitive Psychology, 19*, 498–550.

Nagano-Madsen, Y. (1992). Mora and prosodic coordination: A phonetic study of Japanese, Eskimo and Yoruba. *Travaux de L'Institut de Linguistique de Lund 27.* Lund, Sweden: Lund University Press.

Nelfelt, K. (1990). *Acquisition of definite form singular in Swedish.* Unpublished manuscript, University of Gothenburg.

Newport, E. L. (1990). Maturational constraints on language learning. *Cognitive Science, 14*, 11–28.

Newport, E. L. (1993, February). *Prosodic bootstrapping and the problem of induction.* Paper presented at Signal to Syntax: Bootstrapping From Speech to Grammar in Early Acquisition, Brown University.

Ohsiek, D. (1978). Heavy syllables and stress. In A. Bell & J. Bybee Hooper (Eds.), *Syllables and segments* (pp. 35–43). New York: North Holland Publishing Co.

Peters, A. M. (1977). Language learning strategies: Does the whole equal the sum of the parts? *Language, 53*, 560–573.

Peters, A. M. (1983). *The units of language acquisition.* (Monographs in Applied Psycholinguistics.) New York: Cambridge University Press.

Peters, A. M. (1985). Language segmentation: Operating principles for the analysis and perception of language. In D. I. Slobin (Ed.), *The crosslinguistic study of language acquisition: Vol. 2. Theoretical issues* (pp. 1029–1067). Hillsdale, NJ: Lawrence Erlbaum Associates.

Peters, A. M., & Menn, L. (1993). False starts and filler syllables: Ways to learn grammatical morphemes. *Language, 69*, 742–777.

Peters, A. M., & Strömqvist, S. (1996). The role of prosody in the acquisition of grammatical morphemes. In J. L. Morgan & K. Demuth (Eds.), *Signal to syntax: Bootstrapping from speech to grammar in early acquisition* (pp. 215–232). Hillsdale, NJ: Lawrence Erlbaum Associates.

Pizzuto, E., & Caselli, M. C. (1992). The acquisition of Italian morphology: Implications for models of language development. *Journal of Child Language, 19*, 491–557.

Plunkett, K. (1990). Identifying formulaic expressions in early language acquisition. *Center for research in language newsletter* (Vol. 4). University of California, San Diego.

Plunkett, K. (1993). Lexical segmentation and vocabulary growth in early language acquisition. *Journal of Child Language, 20*, 43–60.

Plunkett, K., & Marchman, V. (1991). U-Shaped learning and frequency effects in a multi-layered perceptron: Implications for child language acquisition. *Cognition, 38*, 43–102.

Plunkett, K., Marchman, V., & Knudsen, S. L. (1991). From rote learning to system building: Acquiring verb morphology in children and connectionist nets. In D. S. Touretzky, J. L. Elman, T. N. Sejnowsky, & G. E. Hinton (Eds.), *Proceedings of the 1990 Connectionist Models Summer School*. San Mateo, CA: Morgan Kaufman.

Plunkett, K., & Strömqvist, S. (1992). The acquisition of Scandinavian languages. In D. I. Slobin (Ed.), *The crosslinguistic study of language acquisition: Vol. 3* (pp. 457–558). Hillsdale, NJ: Lawrence Erlbaum Associates.

Pulleyblank, D. (1986). *Tone in lexical phonology*. Dordrecht, The Netherlands: D. Reidel.

Pye, C. (1983). Mayan telegraphese: Intonational determinants of inflectional development in Quiché Mayan. *Language, 59*, 583–604.

Pye, C. (1992). The acquisition of K'iche' Mayan. In D. I. Slobin (Ed.), *The crosslinguistic study of language acquisition: Vol. 3* (pp. 221–308). Hillsdale, NJ: Lawrence Erlbaum Associates.

Scarpa, E. (1990). *Prosodic strategies for the construction of long utterances*. Unpublished manuscript, University of Campinas, Brazil.

Schieffelin, B. B. (1985). The acquisition of Kaluli. In D. I. Slobin (Ed.), *The crosslinguistic study of language acquisition: Vol. 1. The data* (pp. 525–593). Hillsdale, NJ: Lawrence Erlbaum Associates.

Scollon, R. (1976). *Conversations with a one year old*. Honolulu: University Press of Hawaii.

Selkirk, E. O. (1981). *The phrase phonology of English and French*. Bloomington: Indiana University Linguistics Club.

Siewierska, A. (1991). *Functional grammar*. New York: Routledge.

Simonsen, H. G. (1990). *Barns fonologi: System og variasjon hos tre norske og et samoisk barn* [Child phonology: System and variation in three Norwegian children and one Samoan child]. Doctoral dissertation, Department of Linguistics and Philosophy, University of Oslo.

Slobin, D. I. (1966). The acquisition of Russian as a native language. In F. Smith & G. A. Miller (Eds.), *The genesis of language* (pp. 129–148). Cambridge, MA: MIT Press.

Slobin, D. I. (1973). Cognitive prerequisites for the development of grammar. In C. A. Ferguson & D. I. Slobin (Eds.), *Studies of child language development* (pp. 175–208). New York: Holt, Rinehart & Winston.

Slobin, D. I. (1985). Crosslinguistic evidence for the language-making capacity. In D. I. Slobin (Ed.), *The crosslinguistic study of language acquisition: Vol. 2. Theoretical issues* (pp. 1157–1256). Hillsdale, NJ: Lawrence Erlbaum Associates.

Slobin, D. I. (Ed.). (1985). *The crosslinguistic study of language acquisition: Vol. 1. The data*. Hillsdale, NJ: Lawrence Erlbaum Associates.

Slobin, D. I. (Ed.). (1992). *The crosslinguistic study of language acquisition: Vol. 3*. Hillsdale, NJ: Lawrence Erlbaum Associates.

Smoczyńska, M. (1985). The acquisition of Polish. In D. I. Slobin (Ed.), *The crosslinguistic study of language acquisition: Vol. 1. The data* (pp. 595–686). Hillsdale, NJ: Lawrence Erlbaum Associates.

Stern, C., & Stern, W. (1965). *Die Kindersprache*. Leipzig, Germany: Barth. Darmstadt, Germany: Wissenschaftliche Buchgesellschaft. (Original work published 1928)

Tardif, T. Z. (1993). *Adult-to-child speech and language acquisition in Mandarin Chinese*. Unpublished doctoral dissertation, Yale University.

Toivainen, J. (1990). *Acquisition of Finnish as a first language: General and particular themes.* Publications of the Department of Finnish and General Linguistics of the University of Turku, No. 35.

Toivainen, J. (1997). Acquisition of Finnish. In D. I. Slobin (Ed.), *The crosslinguistic study of language acquisition: Vol. 4.* Mahwah, NJ: Lawrence Erlbaum Associates.

Topping, D. M. (1973). *Chamorro reference grammar.* Honolulu: University Press of Hawaii.

Tseng, C. (1991). *Some notes on the acquisition of prosodic features and the acquisition of segmentation: A comparative study between Mandarin and Cantonese.* Unpublished manuscript, University of Hawaii.

Vassière, J. (1983). Language-independent prosodic features. In A. Cutler & D. R. Ladd (Eds.), *Prosody: Models and measurements* (pp. 53–66). New York: Springer-Verlag.

Waterson, N. (1976). Perception and production in the acquisition of phonology. In W. von Raffler Engel & Y. Lebrun (Eds.), *Baby talk and infant speech* (pp. 294–320). Amsterdam: Swets & Zeitlinger.

Waterson, N. (1978). Growth of complexity in phonological development. In N. Waterson & C. Snow (Eds.), *The development of communication* (pp. 415–442). New York: Wiley.

4 Variation in a Crosslinguistic Context

Elena V. M. Lieven
University of Manchester, UK

1. INTRODUCTION

The thrust of these volumes has been that studying language development in the context of differences between languages provides valuable information on how children work out the ways in which their particular language partitions the world semantically, what devices it uses to present and order information, and the relative salience to children of these devices. But, of course, children do not start by knowing any of this; they arrive at language learning with whatever cognitive, social, linguistic and processing skills they were born with and have developed over the first year of life, and learn to talk in the particular context in which they are growing up. The present chapter is an attempt to demonstrate that variation between children learning the SAME language often bears on these questions in very similar ways to the study of crosslinguistic variation.

Why should a group of children learning the same language all approach it in the same way? Much of the literature makes this assumption but it is worth reflecting on the implications. Firstly it implies that the major structural differences between languages are transparent to children. For instance that children can tell whether, in the language they are hearing, grammatical relations are largely effected through word order or inflections; or that tone is a central structuring device. But it could be the case that these differences are more apparent to linguists than initially, to children. In many languages more than one of these devices may be used for the expression of a particular syntactic or semantic relation. If a language uses more than one device, such as both inflections and lexemes to express location, there may be no reason to assume that all children must start with one or the other. The question of whether they do or not bears directly on issues of the salience of particular form-function relationships that have been so central to many of the crosslinguistic analyses in these volumes.

Secondly, if it turns out that there is a clear and limited number of dimensions on which children vary both within and across languages, this would suggest that these are the dimensions on which psychologists and linguists interested in generating psychologically realistic theories should concentrate. Thus there is a potentially direct connection between the study of variation and the construction of theory.

Even a theory based on the idea that "all children have to do" to arrive at adult grammar is to set a small set of parameters might allow that a particular parameter might be set differently by individual children in the initial stages. Do children "invent" formal devices not offered by their language? There is no necessary contradiction between studying variation and postulating that a large part of the learning of grammar is driven by innate, language-specific mechanisms. Variation informs us about the range of hypotheses that children can entertain given the evidence with which they are presented. All biological mechanisms are buffered for a range of environmental variation and some produce more strongly canalized outcomes than others. There is an assumption in our work that language learning is strongly canalized. This may be truer for some parts of the language system than others and only the study of variation can sort this out.

Finally, there is the vexed issue of the relation between input and language learning. How directly can one explain differences between children as the result of differences in the input? Are these differences always of a surface, frequency matching kind or do they result from a more complex interaction between the children's systems and that of their environments? Do differences that can be identified as the result of differences in input have any effects on how children move forward in their learning of the language? Here again it is evident that the study of variation might make an important contribution to issues of major theoretical concern.

Of course every child differs from every other child for a vast range of reasons most of which we could never hope to know. My intention in this chapter is to take a two-pronged approach to ask which aspects of variation might be significant for the theoretical questions raised in these volumes. The first step is to look at any reports of systematic variation between children learning to talk for which there is reasonably clear evidence and see whether this variation can be used to reflect on the process of language learning. The second approach is to look at the major organizing systems for structuring language and suggest where we might expect to find systematic variation between children learning the same language. Thus, the chapter is intended to be both data-driven and theory-driven. This approach results from both necessity and principle. There are very few data on variation between children for any language other than English, and even in English, as we shall see, the data are pretty sparse and often difficult to interpret. Convincing future researchers to remedy this situation and getting them to collect data with the question in mind of how variation between children might inform us about the problems that a particular language presents to language learners depends on a theoretically principled approach to what the data might look like and what the interesting questions might be.

In this chapter, I stick closely to the linguistic implications of variation between children rather than considering individual differences in a broader psychological context, though Section 3 does examine these briefly. I should say at the outset that I am not directly interested in the question of differences in RATE of development between children nor in what causes such differences unless there is evidence that rate of learning interacts with differences in the learning of language structure. There is considerable evidence to suggest that children who are talked to more learn language, or at least vocabulary, faster and that this may well have educational consequences for their success at language work in school and, therefore, their educational attainment. These are important findings that require serious theoretical and methodological analysis for their implications, but they are not the issue in the present chapter. Section 2 covers the major areas in which we know something about variation between children in their development of particular structures or systems. Section 3 outlines some proposed, non-language-based causes of individual variation in language learning. In Section 4, I look at methodological issues raised by the study of variation and make suggestions about procedures which could be included in the longitudinal study of acquisition to yield data on variation which would be of relevance to theory. Section 5 considers the implications of the data and arguments presented in this chapter for theories of language development. In Section 6, I present some guidelines for researchers interested in including the study of variation in their work.

2. DIFFERENCES IN THE LEARNING OF STRUCTURE AND THE LEXICON

In this central section of the chapter I summarize what is known about variation between children learning language for a number of different aspects of structural and lexical development and reflect on the implications of these findings for language learning more generally. I have not been able to include work on individual differences in phonological development but the reader is referred to Vihman and Greenlee (1987) for work on individual differences in English phonological development, and to Vihman, Kay, de Boysson-Bardies, Durand, and Sundberg (1994) for a crosslinguistic analysis of some aspects of phonological development.

2.1. Early Lexical and Prosodic Development

There are two major pieces of research relevant to differences between children in their early language development to which reference will be made at various points throughout Section 2.1: the work of Elizabeth Bates and her colleagues (Bates, Bretherton, & Snyder, 1988; Bates et al., 1994) and the work of Ann Peters (Peters, 1985, 1997; Peters & Menn, 1993).

The study by Bates, Bretherton, and Snyder (1988) is of 27 children studied longitudinally at 10, 13, 20, and 28 months. The more recent study (Bates et al.,

1994) is of 1,800 children in all, studied in groups of at least 60 at monthly age points between 8 and 30 months. Data were collected using the *MacArthur Communicative Developmental Inventory*, which is filled in by the child's parents. To provide longitudinal data, two different groups of 500 children were tested twice, the first group at 6 weeks apart and the second group at 6 months apart. The great advantage of both these studies lies in the sizes of the groups studied, which allow us to feel extremely confident about the reliability of the results where variation shows up. Though the earlier study has the greater potential for longitudinal analyses, it has the disadvantage that vocabulary size and vocabulary composition are confounded (see Section 2.1.3 below). The more recent study does allow the analyses to be controlled by vocabulary size as well as age, using percentile-based measures of vocabulary composition, but is essentially cross-sectional. Since direct evidence for the learning of units larger than words cannot be collected using the MacArthur checklist, there are a number of major issues in early variation which the study can only contribute to indirectly. One of the most significant findings in both of these studies is of a stable dissociation for some children between comprehension and production in both words and early sentences (as measured by the checklist). These are children who understand a great deal but say little. We shall return to the significance of this finding in Section 4.6.

Ann Peters' work concentrates on the relationship between prosody, segmentation, and morphology. The first two subsections below are very closely related to her chapter in this volume and the reader is referred to this for greater detail of how phonetic and prosodic factors might be involved in the extraction of morphology. Peters directly addresses the issue of individual differences with a range of relevant material and questions. I summarize this material below from the point of view of our theoretical interest in how the study of variation might illuminate the language learning process and I add to the large number of questions on this topic that she poses in her chapter.

2.1.1. *Prosody and "Sound Babies"*

PROSODY consists of the interplay between pitch, intensity, and duration, which can act separately or together and which operate at a number of different levels ranging from the phonological (e.g., stressed syllables) through to the pragmatic force of utterances (e.g., interrogative prosody). There are a number of studies of English acquisition, which suggest that children may differ from very early on in the extent to which they pick up the major tunes of the language, while other children tend to produce shorter and more clearly articulated utterances, which are often single words (Dore, 1975; Ramer, 1976; Peters, 1977). This makes sense because both utterance tune and segmentation into words are relatively accessible aspects of English. The pragmatics associated with the prosodic contours of questions, attentional utterances, naming utterances, and imperatives must be very salient aspects of children's interactions with adults and indeed are often highly exaggerated in adults' speech to children. Furthermore, utterance contour in English is relatively straightforwardly tied to these pragmatic differences while in other languages the child may have to contend with tone, not only at the level of the overall utterance contour, but also through tonal sandhi rules and lexical tone. On the other hand, individual words can also be very salient in an isolating language such as English where there is relatively little inflectional morphology and words tend to "stay the same," particularly because English is a stress-timed language in which stress tends to land on content words and again this is exaggerated in adult speech to children. As Peters points out in her chapter, children who tend to concentrate on extracting individual units of the language will be likely to extract words in some languages but stems or syllables in others—we return to this below in Section 2.1.2.

What might be the causes of children differing in the size and prosodic shape of their initial units? Suggestions have ranged from something inherent in the child to environmental explanations. It is sometimes suggested that individuals might be differentially sensitive to language tune, a sensitivity which might be manifested in differences between second language learners as well (Wong Fillmore, 1979; Vihman, 1982). Perhaps this sensitivity is underpinned by differences between the relative amount of language processing taking place in the right or left hemispheres of different individuals. Environmental explanations have suggested that children concentrate on a word-by-word approach when they spend a lot of time in one-to-one communication with adults, whereas children who are more immersed in a sound world containing other adults and children might be more likely to pick up the tunes associated with pragmatic differences between utterances. For instance Bates (in Bates et al., 1988) reports that her daughter Julia took a classically word-by-word approach to her learning English, which mainly occurred in dyadic contexts, but that she used much longer, intonationally contoured, sound patterns when learning Italian in the context of large family gatherings.

For this chapter the issue is whether these differences are to be found among language learners learning other languages than English and to ask what the implications of this might be for languages which differ typologically from English. There are reports from many languages of individual children who start with what Berman (1979) calls "speech without words" (e.g., Hebrew: Berman, 1985; Hungarian: MacWhinney, 1985; French: Clark, 1985; Danish: Plunkett, 1986). It is fairly clear from these reports that there are other children learning the same language who do NOT show the same behavior. This then signals a separation of these two aspects of how meaning can be conveyed: the tune of an utterance and its constituent units. It would be interesting to know whether there are languages in which this behavior does not occur, but the empirical data are hard to interpret. Authors very frequently start their account of language development with the first words and/or inflections. If they do not mention "sound babies," this may be because they do not occur, not enough children have yet been studied, the research started after this point in development, or the author did not think the issue relevant. However, we can ask from a theoretical point of view whether, on the grounds of typology, we would expect some languages to make "sound babies" less likely. Are languages in which tone is operating at a number of complex and interacting levels (for instance, Sesotho) less likely to provide the child with a relatively clear set of prosodic distinctions at the utterance level that she or he can reproduce? Are there languages where the tonal contour of utterances is relatively unambiguous and tied to meanings that are accessible to the child while the analytic structure of the language is particularly hard to crack? Highly agglutinating languages such as Warlpiri or Georgian might be examples, though it is unfortunately not possible to tell how accessible tonal prosody might be in these languages from the chapters in Volume 3 (Slobin, 1992: Bavin, 1992; Imedadze & Tuite, 1992). We know that, later on, where a particular structure (e.g., *yes/no* questions in English, German, and Japanese) have a special intonation contour, some children learn them earlier, and that in Japanese, where *yes/no* questions can be done both with morphology and intonation, the latter comes first at least for some children. But the records are not sufficient to tell us whether there are differences between children in these developments. What they do indicate is that intonation differences can signal important linguistic information, and it is interesting that some, but not all, children reflect this in their early production.

This strategy of concentrating on prosodic contour can become very important for some children as they start to work out the internal structure of the sentence because it can provide them with information about the placement and ordering of items. Individual differences in the extent to which children use filler syllables, schwas, and sentence frames are well attested for English and some other languages and provide a rich field of data for the questions raised in this chapter.

2.1.2. *Prosodic "Place Holders"*

Some children learning English use schwas, fillers, and reduplication to achieve a meaningful prosodic pattern while others do this much less or not at all, starting with relatively clearly enunciated single words and moving on to juxtapose words in the telegraphic style which has been the subject of so much analysis. This phenomenon was first given serious attention by Peters (1977), Lieven (1978, 1980), Bloom (1970), and Bloom, Lightbown, and Hood (1975), all of whom had children in their samples who did not fit the classic one-word-at-a-time pattern. It is probably related to the existence of children learning English who use a large number of positionally based pivotal patterns by contrast with others of the more telegraphic, juxtapositional style. We deal with this in Section 2.1.3, while here we concentrate on the relation of this prosodic strategy to the emergence of morphology.

In this volume, Peters characterizes these two approaches as those of "tune" and "syllable-and-segment." She suggests the latter type of child attempts to reproduce individual syllables, perhaps the most salient or most stressed, aiming at their skeletal shapes (e.g., CVC) while "tune" children pay attention to all three tiers of syllable, stress, and skeletal structure. This results in the production of syllabic fillers or vowel-like schwas which fill out the prosodic envelope and reproduce a relatively adult-like utterance contour.

As Peters discusses, these prosodic place holders can act as a stepping stone to working out the structure and placement of morphemes. While syllables, feet, and accent may be "naturally" extractable units, children have to move to morphological units and they do so early. A close analysis of the development of these prosodic slots can help us see how some of them do so. This has been done for the emergence of the determiner slot in English (Peters & Menn, 1993) and the definite article in Italian (Bottari, Cipriani, & Chilosi, 1991). At a less detailed level, Aksu-Koç and Slobin (1985) in their chapter on Turkish acquisition report that early in development children sometimes attempt to retain the rhythmic picture of a complex verb by inserting morphemes which sound like passive or causative particles but which are, in fact, meaningless. They point out that this "unmotivated analysis of words into combinable syllables (is) an obvious pre-requisite to the discovery of productive morphology" (p. 848). By "unmotivated," I take Aksu-Koç and Slobin to mean that the child's production of these slots is not meaning-driven but prosody driven. Thus the meaning is "enabled" by the prior prosodic identification of the slots.

The Turkish example is one of a number from languages other than English. Sometimes variation between children is mentioned in these examples; in others, data from an individual child who uses filler syllables or pseudomorphemes are mentioned without reference to whether this is common to all children or only a characteristic of some. Peters (1997) lists Danish, Finnish, German, and Nor-wegian as languages for which both "tune" and "word" children have been found, while "tune" children are reported in both Italian and Portuguese. Other studies in Italian (Camaioni & Longobardi, 1993) and Portuguese (Simonetti, 1980) suggest that children learning these languages can also start with a strategy based on the production of one, word-like, syllable or segment at a time. In her chapter, Peters presents a detailed analysis of how prosody (in terms of foot and accent), syllabic structure, and morphology might interact to aid or hinder the language learner. She raises a number of important questions about how language typology and rhythmic structure might interact in development and whether one could predict which languages might be inaccessible to children following a more syllable-based or more tone-based approach. She, however, concludes that there are not enough data, particularly not enough transcribed at a sufficiently detailed phonetic and prosodic level, to draw any firm conclusions. She points out that the maintenance of rhythmic structure is not always related to the production of pseudomorphemes and draws attention to a Norwegian and a Danish child who appear simply to be trying to maintain the rhythmic structure of their utterances. Thus while it may be that for all languages, some children will try to preserve the overall rhythmic structure, this may interact more or less fruitfully with the morphological level. Mora-timed languages, such as Japanese, might make the detection of inflectional morphology through prosody particularly difficult, whereas syllable-timed, highly agglutinative languages, such as Turkish, might be particularly accessible to a prosodically based strategy. Equally, whether a prosodic strategy helps or hinders the detection of infixes will depend on whether the stress patterns of the spoken language regularly fall on, or in some other way "isolate," those infixes. These matters cannot be decided because the data are not available, but the crucial issue for the present chapter is that they have been raised in the context of variation between children. Once enough reports of "tune-type" children have come in and enough researchers have tried to work out what it is that the children are doing, it might become possible to see how this strategy could be involved in language development rather than just something external and irrelevant to the process. This would then enable us to look with a sharper focus at places in later development where a child's attempt to reflect his or her emerging knowledge prosodically can be a guide to what that knowledge is and how it is developing.

Thus, later in development, Sesotho-learning children are reported to use shadow vowel and nasal prefixes before they develop the full, and phonologically appropriate, set of noun class prefixes by the age of 3;0 (Demuth, 1992). Mills (1985) reports the use by one child learning German of a meaningless syllable inserted in the place of the relative pronoun; again until about the age of 3;0. Smoczyńska (1985) reports on the use by both her twin sons of a reduplication strategy to "replace" syllabic prepositions and, later, syllabic verbal prefixes "indicating perfectivity and/or modulation of verb meaning" (p. 632). Imedadze and Tuite (1992) report the use by one child of a word-initial vowel which corresponded to any of several preverbs, while other children were more successful in producing these initial segments of the verb (p. 36, Section 4.1.4). These examples certainly suggest that "tune" can be an important indicator of the leading-edge of development as both Demuth (1992) and Bottari, Cipriani, and Chilosi (1991) indicate. The tendency to see all children developing in a word-juxtapositional way and to ignore other phonetic material has resulted in a very incomplete story in the crosslinguistic study of morphological acquisition.

Peters also characterizes "tune" children as perceiving sentences as frames with slots in them to be filled, where the frames are functors, protofunctors, and pivots, and the slots are open-class words. Syllable children, on the other hand, are characterized as paying less attention to the frames and focusing on the slots which they juxtapose in their early utterances. This distinction between children who are more dependent on pivots and those who concentrate on the juxtaposition of words is of very long standing and much research has referred to it, albeit, in ways that are often more confusing than clarifying. The distinction forms the subject of Section 2.2.1, but we first examine the research that initially gave rise to it, namely the contrast between referential and phrasal children.

2.1.3. *Early Vocabulary Referential vs. Expressive*

The referential/expressive dimension is the most widely used in the study of stylistic differences between children learning English. The original distinction was made by Nelson (1973) on the basis of the first 50 words learned by each child in her sample. She divided the sample into two groups and defined as "referential" any child whose first 50 words contained more than 50% of words for objects. The remaining children were defined as "social-expressive," on the grounds that they had significantly more "personal-social" words and significantly more function words which tended to be embedded in "stereotyped phrases and expressions useful for dealing with people" (Nelson, 1973, p. 24).

A central problem in Nelson's study rests on her attempt to define FUNCTIONAL categories for the children's early lexicons, despite the fact that the data were collected by maternal diary and that there was no guarantee that children used a particular word with always the same function. Thus words for objects can be used for highly sociable purposes such as attracting attention, demanding, and showing, and this makes the functional distinction between referentiality and social-expressiveness extremely difficult to draw. The second central difficulty with Nelson's study was the way in which social-expressiveness was purely negatively defined, that is, children who did NOT have more than 50% object words in their 50-word lexicons. Defining children by what they are not doing (learning object words) greatly diminishes the utility of the category. However, Nelson's observation that many of these function words and personal-social words were embedded in larger, unanalyzed phrases was noted by many researchers and related to the frequent observation, already discussed in the sections above, that some children appear to learn a relatively higher proportion of phrasal segments by contrast with individual words: these children were often called "holistic" learners and this style was explicitly related to social-expressive style in many studies (Peters, 1983; Bates et al., 1988).

In 1992, we published a paper in which we tried to clarify these issues using a sample of 12 children learning English (Lieven, Pine, & Dresner-Barnes, 1992). Arguing that the use of diaries to collect the lexicons made it impossible to define the categories functionally, we defined them formally: common nouns, proper nouns, and so forth. We also explicitly defined a category of frozen phrases. We showed that there was a significant inverse correlation between the proportions of common nouns and frozen phrases that children had in their 50-word lexicons and that there was significant continuity of these styles between the acquisition of the first and the second 50 words. To our satisfaction, at least, we had provided evidence of early stylistic difference between English-learning children based on the relative proportions of common nouns and frozen phrases in their vocabularies.

A final and important finding in our study was that, as Nelson also reported, there was no rate effect for these different styles. That is, it was not that children with relatively higher numbers of frozen phrases were learning their first 50 and

100 words more slowly than the more referential children—that is, we were not dealing with slow, but with different children. This is important because it conflicted with other findings in the literature that had often led researchers to conclude that children learning larger numbers of frozen phrases might be the slower children who had failed to crack the combinatorial properties of language (e.g., Bates et al., 1988). However, as Pine and Lieven (1990) have shown, this was due to a confound between the different proportions of nouns in children's lexicons at a particular level of vocabulary, and the fact that the relative proportion of nouns increases in all children's lexicons as vocabulary size increases. That there is a confound is confirmed in a study of 1,800 children by Bates and her colleagues (1994), who found no differences in age as a function of the numbers of object words in children's vocabularies for a particular vocabulary size. The implication of this is that the study of early differences in style must be done by controlling for the size of the lexicon rather than cross sectionally by age.

We now consider two issues: first what are the implications of these early stylistic differences for the question of how children develop into the next stages of their language learning, and second, how do these stylistic differences which have been found for English relate to the learning of languages other than English.

2.2. Breaking Into Structure

2.2.1. *Open-Class Combinations and Phrases*

There is an important issue of continuity in these early stylistic differences. As we have seen, variation can illuminate the process of acquisition, however, it becomes even more interesting if it can be shown that it affects how children move on to the next phase of their development. The current state of the literature does not make it easy to sort this out. There is, for instance, an assumption that "tune" children become social-expressive/phrasal children. This requires further research on a reasonably sized sample. Other suggestions have been that highly referential children are more likely to look telegraphic in their two-word utterances while the early learning of frozen phrases might be related to a greater tendency to produce pivot-type utterance structure in the early multiword stage (Nelson, 1981; Bloom, Lightbown, & Hood, 1975; Peters, 1997; Lieven, 1980; Starr, 1975). Bates and her colleagues (Bates et al., 1994) also attempt to look at the issue of continuity between referential style and telegraphic speech and conclude that because there is no correlation, either positive or negative, between referential style and closed-class vocabulary or grammatical complexity six months later, this continuity does not exist. However, it is not at all clear how telegraphic speech might be reflected in these measures, one of which depends on the identification by parents of closed class items on the MacArthur checklist and the other on parents picking the sentence most similar to what their child is saying from a pair in which one sentence is more grammatical than the other. As we shall see, my suggestion is that both stylistic approaches aid in the development of grammar, but perhaps somewhat differently (see Braunwald, 1995) and a consideration of languages other than English may help us to see how.

There is some evidence of continuity between the phrasal style and the use of pivotal types of structure. In both Lieven et al. (1992) and Pine and Lieven (1993), we found a significant correlation between the numbers of frozen phrases in children's 100-word lexicons and the numbers of productive utterances that the child produced, where productivity was defined in terms of positional consistency (i.e., pivots). The Pine and Lieven study also found that the number of frozen phrases at 100 words predicted the degree to which productive utterances later in development are derived from initially frozen utterances. This supports the idea that there can indeed be continuity between frozen phrase learning and a form of productivity based on frames with slots in them. Agreeing with Braine (1976), we suggest that children pick up the positional regularities between a set of patterns with a repeated item such as *its a ball, its a cow, its a car* and develop a low-scope structure for generating novel utterances of the form: *itsa + X*. These slots can then become a diagnostic for grammatical development. Some children fill them from the beginning with words from the correct grammatical category (e.g., nouns in the *itsa + X* example) while others may start off much more eclectically (*itsa running round, itsa roll the barrel*). The slots also expand as children move from filling them with single words to using phrases (e.g., from *want juice* to *want more juice* in *want + X* or from *find it* to *me find it* in *X + it*). The defining characteristic of a phrasal style is, then, the regular positioning of a frequently repeated set of words with little evidence from the remainder of the corpus of wider grammatical categories. Thus in the examples above, the determiner *a* might only appear in the pattern *itsa + X*; *want* might be the only verb which takes a direct object; and verbs occurring with *it* might not occur with any other direct object.

The question is what are juxtaposers doing? Peters (this volume) makes the suggestion that phrasal (or formulaic) children treat functors as frames with fillable slots while, for juxtaposers, functors act as segmentation cues thus segmenting out the open-class items. But how are they organizing them once they are separated out? Until recently this would have been answered in terms of semantic relations; children were generating utterances on the basis of underlying rules for combining semantic categories, and this may well be part of the answer. This is reflected in Peters' description of these children as "syntactic" (i.e., juxtaposing using rules) whereas formulaic children are described as "morphological." An example would be that many of these children seem to have a POSSESSOR + POSSESSED pattern where the possessor is named from very early on. However, there has been increasing difficulty with the idea of semantic categories as providing anything like a complete explanation for the telegraphic style of speech. Using data from her daughters' language development, Bowerman (1990) shows that preverbal nouns can be patients and instruments, and are not initially confined to actors or agents as would be predicted if this were the underlying semantic category from which children develop the more abstract and grammaticized category of Subject (cf., Schlesinger, 1982). It may be that what these children are doing is not dissimilar to the pivotal children in that, having extracted these content words, they are working out what can be placed on either side of them. In other words, they too may be working on positional regularities but for items which, unlike pronouns, copulas, demonstratives, and auxiliaries, are of low frequency. It is these latter items which show up as pivots in the more phrasal child's speech whereas the units that the telegraphic child is working with are shorter, of lower frequency, and are unlikely to be functors. It is ironic that, as Peters notes, for many years it was the formulaic/phrasal children's style that was neglected in terms of what it could tell us about language development, whereas that of telegraphic speech was thought of as the "royal road" to grammar. It is now, in principle at least, clear how phrasal children can build up both categories (paradigms) and templates (syntagms) from their slot-and-frame formulae. It is less clear what the developmental pattern is for a child who shows few of these formulae and juxtaposes large numbers of open class words, almost always in either canonical and/or most frequently heard word order. Many of these may in fact be partial and/or delayed imitations, and they may indeed be driving these children toward an earlier focus on thematic roles and linking rules than is the case for the more phrasal children, though I would argue that the semantics is emergent rather than structuring. This would be supported by the earlier emergence of productive inflections on open class words. An example is the early appearance of the possessive *'s* in some children's speech and these may well be those children who mark the relation of possession by using consistent word order. We also know from Slobin (1985) and many others that, where semantics is marked overtly and clearly, children can acquire productive morphology very quickly. This may well be the developmental path for juxtaposers. Clearly the spotlight needs to be turned back on these children to see if these hypotheses can be confirmed.

Both these examples of potential continuity make it clear that it is important to have a theory of how a development at one stage might lead to subsequent developments. The same measure (e.g., numbers of nouns) is not likely to reflect the same aspects of language development at different points. Thus Nelson (1975) shows that the individual differences between the children in terms of relative numbers of nouns and pronouns had disappeared by MLU = 2.5. All children have in the end to learn the major features of their native tongue. Therefore, as we track the acquisition of a particular feature, there will be no difference between children once that feature is acquired, despite the fact that they may acquire it in a somewhat different order or way. But the route that they take in acquiring the feature may well inform us as to the separability of different aspects of language in the learning process. Equally, the fact that children may take a different route to a particular acquisition does not necessarily advantage or disadvantage them. Thus while we (Pine & Lieven, 1993) found continuity between the numbers of frozen phrases and the proportion of productive patterns which had derived from frozen utterances, this does not mean that children with larger numbers of frozen phrases will produce productive speech any earlier, but that they may do so via a different route. Bates et al. (1988, 1994) discuss this issue in terms of heterotypic and homotypic continuity. By heterotypic continuity they mean a continuity of strategy which is reflected by different measures at different points in development (e.g., the hypothesized relation between a highly referential vocabulary and the development of grammatical categories) whereas homotypic continuity reflects a continuity in the same measure (e.g., relative vocabulary size). They suggest that the former is of much the greater significance and argue, as I have done here, that while significant correlations between different measures at different stages can be obtained, it requires a theoretical framework to know how such findings should be interpreted.

This rather detailed look at two, well-attested developmental styles for children learning English has, I hope, demonstrated the utility of paying attention to differences between children. It has helped us to isolate three different tasks: syntagmatic learning (frames), paradigmatic learning (slots), and learning the relationship between thematic roles and syntactic arguments. Many children will be relatively evenly balanced between these aspects of language learning and all children over the course of development will have to deal with all three, but paying attention to those children who seem to emphasize one task over another early in development, has helped us to clarify the nature of the tasks themselves and to begin to ask more concentrated questions about how they might be accomplished.

The question of why children might differ in these strategies has been addressed by a number of researchers. Pine (1994) shows that mothers who use relatively more descriptives, and, more specifically, descriptives with nouns in them, have more referential children. I have suggested that children, who are being brought up in polyadic contexts where they spend a far greater proportion of their time with groups of adults and children (e.g., Brice Heath, 1983; Schieffelin, 1985; Ochs, 1985) than do most of the children so far studied, will have to learn more by observation and overhearing the talk of others and may therefore be more likely to pick up phrases (Lieven, 1994). Pine's study of the lexical development of siblings could also be seen as supporting this idea (Pine, 1995). But the particular language being learned may also push children towards or away from these strategies. Peters points out that English might well encourage both tendencies: it is strongly word-order based, allowing a juxtapositional strategy, and it is also stress-timed, allowing a pivotal strategy. Japanese might be thought of as adding to the difficulty of either strategy. As Clancy notes (1985, p. 375) there is a great deal of NP-ellipsis, which makes the identification of "telegraphic speech" difficult, and Peters suggests that the mora-timing of Japanese prosody might make phrasal segmentation more difficult. Yet Clancy's observation that the most frequent contrastive verbal inflections in the input are produced by some children before the onset of two-word utterances and by some after, suggests that the two strategies may be at work. It is clear that Hebrew-learning children produce both pivotal and telegraphic utterances (Berman, 1985, pp. 269–270) though it is not clear whether there are individual differences between children in the extent to which they emphasize one or the other strategy. Hayashi (1994), in a study of two children growing up bilingual in Danish and Japanese, has shown individual differences in the use of formulae but also that both children show more formulaic use in Danish than in Japanese. She suggests that this may be due to the greater use of pronouns in Danish which can act in a pivot-like way in subsequent frames. If the pivotal strategy is continuous with a prosodically-based approach at an earlier stage, then since we noted above that there are reports of "tune" children learning Hebrew, we would also expect some highly pivotal, Hebrew-speaking children. Schieffelin makes the same point as Clancy about the naturalness of deletion and ellipsis in the adult language and the consequent difficulty of deciding whether the child's utterance is in fact missing anything. She also notes errors of oversegmentation made by the Kaluli children in her study (1985, p. 538), which might reflect as yet unsegmented phrasal learning (similar to *find it the book*, where *find it* is learned as a whole). Clark (1985, p. 755) cites Lightbown's observation that one of the children in her study of French language learning was pronominal at the two-word stage and the other, more nominal (similar to Nelson's 1975 findings). We (Pine & Lieven, 1993) have argued that pronominal children are better thought of as reflecting the phrasal strategy. Turkish children's early speech tends not to have the telegraphic look that we see for children learning some other languages since Turkish is highly agglutinative with stressed suffixes as inflections, and children learn contrastive nominal and verbal inflections very early. Nevertheless it would be most interesting to know whether there are children who arrive at this competence through the production of small isolated units and others who do it, as we know they can later on, by the reproduction of the rhythmic patterns produced by the agglutinated morphemes. The size of the extracted unit presumably affects both subsequent extraction and the further registering of regularities, and this may have important consequences for what the child tackles next in the course of development.

As the above brief survey of languages other than English shows, the data are pretty sparse and very hard to interpret. Clearly children learning languages that have a great deal of deletion and ellipsis will tend not to look telegraphic, and it is much harder for the researcher to be sure whether aspects of morphology and syntax have not yet been acquired. A further problem is that very few researchers have looked at acquisition in terms of the potential productivity of a phrasal/pivotal strategy for any language other than English and even for English, methods of collecting data (e.g., the use of vocabulary checklists) have made the detailed study of this approach extremely difficult (though see the next section). Yet the evidence is suggestive that, in languages for which the basic characteristics allow it, there is scope for children initially to exploit to differing extents the information represented in the ordering of categories of words and that represented in the provision of frames within which to place words.

2.2.2. *Nouns and Verbs*

There are suggestions in the literature that both between languages, and between children learning the same language, there may be different emphases on the early learning of nouns and verbs. This is in sharp contrast to a position which suggests that noun learning is primary and acts to bootstrap children into other categories. Gentner (1982), for instance, has argued that the object category is perceptually based and that this explains the early learning of relatively large numbers of nouns, while Markman (1989) has suggested that the learning of object words is aided by a series of constraints on how the child will interpret the relationship between a word and what it is intended to refer to. The assumptions behind these approaches are (a) that object words form the single most frequent category of early words across all languages and that (b) this cannot be explained by input frequency. The effect of this has been to place a strong emphasis on the centrality of noun learning and ostension to children's progress in language development and largely to ignore the learning of other types of words and the issues that such learning might raise. It has led to the idea that the central basis of children's early word learning rests on the learning of mapping between words and concrete, unitary referents in the world. We deal first with two methodological issues before moving onto the challenge to this approach which derives from work in individual differences and crosslinguistic research.

The first issue is that while, for many of the languages studied, it IS the case that nouns form the single largest category of words in children's early lexicons, it is not at all clear that these nouns are always objects and could, therefore, be learned under the constraints that have been proposed. So, for instance, in some studies words which form part of rote-learned phrases are included in the list of nouns (e.g., *God* and *birthday* in Nelson's 1973 study); in all studies mass nouns like *milk, juice,* and *rain* and collectivities like *toes* and *cars* can be among the earliest learned. Secondly, there is suggestive evidence for frequency matching between specific words in the input and those same words in the child's lexicon for English (Huttenlocher, Haight, Bryk, Setzer, & Lyons, 1991). This frequency matching also appears to extend to the lexical categories of noun and verb—in other words, in some languages at least, children produce most instances of the class that they hear the most (English: Gillis, 1990; Hart, 1991; Korean: Choi, 1997; and Mandarin: Tardif, 1994). This conflict with Gentner's findings could be accounted for by the fact that she used the Kucera and Francis (1967) norms derived from written English rather than a count based on what the child was actually hearing. Frequency matching does not, of course, mean that nouns are unimportant, just that their numerical significance cannot be taken as an argument for their importance or otherwise.

If, in fact, we look at data from individual children it is the differences in relative numbers of nouns that is so immediately striking. Thus in studies of English language learning, Nelson (1973) found a range of 34–76% in the proportions of general nominals in children's 50-word lexicons; Lieven et al. (1992) found a range of 14–48% in the proportion of common nouns at 50 words and of 23–55% in the proportion at 100 words; Bates et al. (1994) found a range of 12–100% nouns in children with vocabularies from 20–50 words. Clearly while some children are indeed learning a very great number of nouns, others are learning many fewer for the same size of vocabulary. As discussed above, Nelson (1981) suggested that some children are learning a relatively higher proportion of frozen phrases and the Lieven et al. study confirms this finding. At the very least, this work on variation in children's early lexicons makes it difficult to argue for the total preeminence of nouns as a tool in early language learning. All children learn quite a few words which are not the names of objects, and some children learn very large numbers of these words. This learning has to be explained, and this cannot be done by an account based either on the perceptual status of objects nor on any inherent constraints that children might have on object reference. As Tomasello (1995) has argued, many of these words either cannot be learned in ostensive contexts or are not in fact learned in such contexts. This suggests that lexical acquisition is not simply or even largely referential and that we need to attend with much greater care to the pragmatics, as well as the semantics, of contexts in which words are learned. Precisely the same arguments apply if we now look at the crosslinguistic data on this issue.

Thus Choi and Gopnik (1993) in a study of Korean-speaking children show that, as a group, they are considerably less referential than a comparable group of English-speaking children. They suggest that this is because verbs carry much more information in Korean than they do in English, with nouns often being ellipted in grammatically correct adult speech. Tanouye (1979, cited by Clancy, 1985, p. 482) found Japanese children to be verb-dominant by comparison with American children and, given the degree of deletion and ellipsis in spoken Japanese, this may well be for the same reason. And Tardif (1996) finds that the nine Mandarin-speaking children in her study with total lexicons of over 70 different words all produced significantly more verb types than noun types. It is important to note that we are talking about the RELATIVE emphasis on nouns between language-learning communities or individual children; with the possible exception of West Greenlandic, all the studies in these volumes suggest that nouns form a significant part of early vocabulary learning. This becomes very clear if we consider another study of Japanese language-learning cited by Clancy (Okubo, 1980) of two siblings, an older boy and his younger sister. Nouns were the most frequent part of speech for both children, but the boy was noun-dominant compared to his sister, while the girl used a far greater proportion of verbs. What is extremely interesting about this study is that these differences had implications for other aspects of the children's language development: The girl had a greater variety of verbal inflections and was more advanced in the use of sentence-final particles, which typically follow the verb in Japanese. The boy had more complex nominal arguments including modifiers. Both children used pivotal constructions in their two-word utterances but they differed along predictable lines; the girl's pivots tended to be *kore* 'this' and people's names, which she combined with a range of predicates and sentence-final particles, whereas the boy's pivots were a few simple predicates (e.g., *nai* 'does not exist' and *akai* 'red') and he used these with a wide range of nouns. Interestingly, Okubo suggests that the noun–dominance of the boy might be the result of the style of interaction with his mother, which was more dyadic than that of his younger sibling and less concerned with reporting the activities and speech of others than was his sister's.

It may be that English-speaking children who concentrate less on nouns and produce large numbers of subjectless predicates are those whose interactional style is more similar to that of the younger Japanese child in Okubo's study. Alternatively they may be listening to speech in which nouns are relatively deemphasized, since although pronominalization is the major way of de-emphasizing nouns in English, deletion and ellipsis of nouns is actually a feature of informal spoken English as well. This would be an alternative explanation for the large numbers of subjectless predicates produced by some children learning English to one that suggests that they have not set their "prodrop-parameter" correctly.

Bates et al. (1994) suggest that language learning proceeds from an early emphasis on nouns (elements with a stand-alone function or meaning) through the learning of verbs and adjectives (which depend on a relationship with at least one noun or primary word) to function words (most of which depend on a further order of complexity). Thus it is argued that during the period in which their vocabulary size moves from 0–600 words (up to 30 months), children move from learning about reference to learning about predication and then finally to grammar. While in some sense this latter point has to be true, the above discussion suggests that it may be unwise to read it through the relative numerical presence in children's lexicons of particular classes of words. Some languages, some environments, and some methods of segmentation may lead to an initially greater emphasis on words other than nouns. It would take a painstakingly detailed study to see if the use of these words could be pinned down to the developmental hierarchy proposed by Bates et al. (1994) but the knowledge that Turkish children can use some inflections productively before the age of 2 and quite probably with lexicons of less than 400 words casts some doubt on the suggestion.

The overemphasis on nouns in discussions of children's early lexical development has resulted in part from a narrow focus on a particular conception of reference but also from a concentration on a rather small and unrepresentative set of children learning to talk largely in dyadic contexts in which adults use a great deal of ostension and object description. Consideration of a wider range of children and of a wider range of languages has served to refocus attention on the contexts in which children have to work out what words to use to get what task done.

2.2.3. Word Order, Inflections, and Case

In comparing across languages, we know that when verb arguments are relatively unambiguously indicated by either word order or case inflections on nouns, children have little difficulty in learning to express them early and without error. But what about languages in which the method of indicating verb argument structure is either mixed and/or relatively opaque? Is there any evidence that within such languages children vary in the strategies they initially utilize to indicate verb argument structure? And how do verb agreement patterns fit into this picture?

A central task in early language development is working out how the language marks the major arguments of verbs. In two- and three-constituent utterances, how does the child learn to indicate whether a particular noun is the subject or the object of the verb? The three options utilized by languages are word order, case inflections on nouns, and agreement markers on the main verb. Some languages are almost exclusively dependent on one of these (e.g., Turkish case inflections, English word order—with the exception of casemarking on some pronouns), while others use more than one. And these systems may be more or less transparent; ranging, for instance, from the Turkish case system of agglutinative markers, each form corresponding to one function, to a system with many portmanteau morphemes and a high degree of homophony, such as Warlpiri. In addition, the syntax, casemarking, and agreement marking may be fully in accord, that is, either both may be nominative–accusative or both may be ergative, or they may differ, as in split-ergative languages. When children are presented with more than one way of indicating case relations or with an extremely opaque method of doing so, do they show variation in how they initially try to deal with the problem? Any evidence of this would bear on the issue of how accessible each of these systems is as well as on the question of the initial preparedness state of the child.

There are a number of reports of differences between children learning the same language in the learning of verb argument structure and in the types of errors that they make. It is, however, extremely difficult to arrive at a clear account of the implications of these differences for both theoretical and methodological reasons. Theoretically, there are problems in analyzing the pragmatic functions of different word orders in languages that do not depend heavily on word order for basic syntax—this makes it difficult to know precisely what functions, if any, are being fulfilled by word order patterns. Methodologically, the problem is that informal speech between children and adults tends to have rather few utterances which contain the three classic constituents of subject, verb, and object, upon which to base hypotheses about argument role marking. The existence of languages which allow huge amounts of ellipsis only makes this worse. It is this problem that has led researchers to the experimental testing of children's understanding of syntactic relations. I shall return briefly to this experimental work after reviewing the evidence from naturalistic studies.

An early account of individual differences between children in the marking of argument structure came from Argoff's (1976) dissertation on the acquisition of Finnish by two children, Kai and Tuomas. Canonical word order in Finnish is SVO but there is some flexibility in the adult language. Objects are marked using either an accusative or partitive inflection, depending on whether the verb is resultative or not (see Dasinger, 1997). Argoff reports that while Kai's word order was more rigid than that of the adults around him, Tuomas' was considerably more flexible than that of his input. On the other hand, Tuomas had earlier productive control of object marking than Kai though his production of the object marker in obligatory contexts took a considerable length of time to reach 100%. Only after Tuomas approached full provision of object markers in obligatory contexts, did his word-order patterns approach those of his input, that is, they became less flexible. Precisely the opposite appeared to be the case for Kai, whose word order became more flexible once he had gained productive use of object-marking inflections. However it is important to note that Tuomas was not directly using inflections "instead of" word order since there was a complex interaction between his inflectional marking of objects and whether or not he preposed them to the verb. Argoff suggests that Tuomas' language learning system was picking up and partially correlating both inflectional and word-order regularities in relation to the marking of objects but Kai's production system was initially selectively dependent on word order for expressing argument roles. While Bowerman (1973) in her study of Finnish acquisition found a closer correlation between the word order of the input and that of the child than did Argoff, she also found variation in the dependence on word order and the provision of inflectional marking. These findings suggest that Finnish is sufficiently opaque to allow children to take a number of different routes into this aspect of the language.

This possible relationship between dependence on particular word-order strategies and the accessibility of the inflectional system has been discussed as an issue of comparison between languages. For instance Radulović (1975) claims that children learning Serbo-Croatian rely much more heavily on rigid word-order strategies than do their parents, who use the inflectional system to vary the order of elements, and suggests that this is because Serbo-Croatian casemarking is highly opaque and difficult to acquire. Within languages, we have reports of variability between children in word-order patterns from Korean (Kim, 1997), Japanese (Clancy, 1985), Samoan (Ochs, 1985), Kaluli (Schieffelin, 1985), Romance (Clark, 1985), Hungarian (MacWhinney, 1985), German (Mills, 1985), Polish (Smoczyńska, 1985), and West Greenlandic (Fortescue & Olsen, 1992). However, while all these languages have at least some casemarking for major arguments of the verb, it seems that only in some of them is variability in reliance

on word order related to the development of productive control of the relevant
parts of the inflectional system.

Clancy reports a study of Japanese acquisition by Miyahara (Clancy, 1985,
p. 460) in which one child, at 1;11, uses rigid word order until the direct object
marker appears and only then does she start using the postpositional, as well as
preverbal, word orders that other children have been using flexibly from the start.
Kim (1997) suggests that Korean-speaking children are more rigid in their use
of word-order patterns than Japanese-speaking children and this may be related
to the fact that productive and contrastive nominative-accusative casemarking
seems to take a considerable time to develop. However she does report that one
of the children in a study by Cho (1981) used less rigid word orders and that
her word-order patterns were less highly correlated with her mother's use of
word order. It would have been interesting to look at this particular child's
development of productive casemarking to see if it was advanced by comparison
to the other children in the study.

The Kaluli case is more complex. While subject agreement on the verb is
nominative-accusative, casemarking on nouns follows two systems: neutral and
ergative-absolutive. The semantics of nouns in relation to animacy and agency
are marked by an interaction of word order and case inflections. Kaluli is
verb-final and the position before the verb is reserved for the informational
highlight of the sentence, that is, the NP placed here is in focus. The unmarked
order is AgentOV when both nouns receive neutral casemarking unless both are
proper nouns in which case the Agent carries the ergative marker. If the order
is OAV, then the agent is in focus and obligatorily receives ergative casemarking.
Schieffelin (1985) found individual differences in the relation between the correct
provision of ergative casemarking and the placing of the agent in AV and OAV
utterances. One child provided the ergative marker correctly as soon as he
produced any agent-focused utterances at all. The second went through a period
of producing agent-focused utterances, but without the correct casemarking for
the Agent. The third child sometimes did and sometimes did not provide the
ergative marker in agent-focused utterances and Schieffelin suggests that this
child's errors may be related to particular verbs. All this needs to be seen against
a background in which, according to Schieffelin, Kaluli children never make the
error of overextending the ergative marker to the actors of intransitive verbs. The
children seem to be sensitive to this basic semantic-syntactic distinction in their
language but two of the children have picked up selectively on one part of how
it is marked in the language while the third may be operating more in terms of
"verb islands" (Tomasello, 1992).

There are a number of reports of variation between children in the use of
different word-order patterns but without this being correlated with differences
in reliance on casemarking. As with all work on variation, a considerable amount
of caution in interpreting these reports is needed because the number of children
is usually tiny and the authors are rarely addressing directly the question of

variation between children and, still less often, considering the causes of it. For Polish, in which word-order variation fulfills pragmatic purposes, work by Smoczyńska and Weist (Smoczyńska, 1985, p. 669) illustrates these problems. Smoczyńska reports a large degree of variation in the degree to which children adhere to a rigid word order. However Weist argues that this is not because word order is acting as a remedial strategy for some children, and presents evidence from verb-noun combinations in the indicative for two children (*op. cit.*, pp. 671–672) as well as some experimental evidence. The data from these two children show that the number of utterances in which the nominative- and accusative-marked nouns come before or after the verb is roughly equal. But the children are of sequential age (1;7–2;0 and 2;2–2;8) rather than of comparable age, and there is some evidence from the older child of a more rigid word-order strategy towards the end of the period (at 2;8) with nominative-marked nouns predominantly placed before the verb and accusative-marked nouns predominantly following it. While Weist is clearly right to argue that there is no reliance on rigid word order before casemarking develops, these data relate only to utterances containing one noun rather than two, and we would need more detail before we could work out precisely any later interactions between word order and case in Polish children's development.

If we can accept Weist's conclusion that word order is not acting remedially for Polish children while they acquire casemarking, this suggests that even in a system with as much opacity in terms of fused inflections as there is in Polish, pragmatic variations in word order or, at least, variations as complex as those in Polish, block word order from being used to express basic semantic or syntactic relations between constituents. The question of why Polish children vary so greatly in their adherence to rigid word orders must, as Smoczyńska says, await further work on the relations between word order and pragmatics in adult Polish as well as how these relations manifest themselves in caretaker speech.

It is not clear what it would mean to think about this situation in reverse, that is, where children might be over-reliant on case- or agreement-marking until they had worked out the word order. The only possible example I can think of is the phenomenon first noticed by Brown (1973) concerning the way in which Adam initially filled the postverbal direct object slot with *it*. Given that the next stage was for Adam to postpose the direct object NP, one could think of *it* as a putative agreement marker on the verb. Lieven, Pine, and Baldwin (1997) find something very similar in a number of children in their study of English acquisition. Although there is not enough evidence to know whether children vary in their relative emphasis on agreement markers on verbs, they can be very important in languages where the degree of ellipsis means that the agreement marker may be the only clue, and it is clear that children can recover nominal referents for them in the absence of other information (Sesotho: Demuth, 1992; Greek: Stephany, 1997).

Individual differences in the reliance on either more or less rigid word-order patterns or different word orders are also reported in languages for which casemarking may not be very central to working out which NP is the subject because casemarking occurs only on a subgroup of words (e.g., pronouns in Romance and determiners in German) or its use is infrequent in caretaker speech (e.g., the ergative marker in Samoan). For instance, in German acquisition, some children retain a verb-final order for much longer than others who, as soon as they start to produce utterances with more than two words, immediately observe the verb-second rule of adult German (but see Jordens, 1990). A number of explanations for this have been offered by different authors ranging from that of Mills (1985), which is in terms of the high predominance of verb-final word-order patterns in the input, to that of Roeper (1973), who suggests that German is SOV in its deep structure and that some children may be reflecting this (see Mills, 1985, p. 238 for a discussion).

For Romance languages, Clark (1985) makes a number of useful cautions before reporting a considerable range of variation in word-order patterns by children learning French (1985, pp. 709–712). The most important of these is that intonational evidence must be taken into account before deciding whether a sequence of words in a child's utterance constitutes one or two utterances, because of the level of pre- and postposing of elements in the input. She cites Guillaume's (1927) example of the "incorrect" *fermée fenêtre* (shut window = window shut) being based on the adult utterance of *Elle est fermée, la fenêtre* (or, indeed, *Fermée la fenêtre!* or *Quelqu'un a fermée la fenêtre*). However it is clear that children vary in the extent to which they depend on the canonical SV (intransitive) and SVO (transitive) word orders as opposed to VS and VOS word orders. Here it may be that some children are picking up on the pragmatic aspects of word order, while others are operating more with syntactic word-order patterns. Of course in the adult system, these two aspects of word order will interact closely and in a complex fashion, but if different children concentrate on one or the other of these aspects, this accords with the central thrust of this chapter—namely, that while development is taking place, it is possible to see the splitting of processes that are more closely related in the adult system.

Ochs makes another important methodological point in relation to Samoan (1985), namely that word-order preferences may vary as a function of the social register. Thus she reports that VOS is more preferred in domestic contexts while VSO is preferred in more formal contexts. This is reflected in her finding that most of the children in her study followed the adults around them in preferring either Agent-Verb-Patient order or Verb-Patient-Agent word order. Despite the fact that the ergative marker is often dropped in informal speech, Ochs argues that both the adults and children are marking ergativity syntactically by preserving the position following the verb for the major arguments of intransitive verbs and for patients, that is, for absolutive constituents, and by excluding agents (i.e., ergative constituents) from this position. But what then of the one child in her study who, as Ochs reports, shows some evidence of a preference for placing the agent directly after the verb (1985, p. 822)? It is not clear from the data how to interpret this, especially since the total number of utterances is very small, but the child is certainly not using freer word order because she is already using the ergative case marker. In fact, what we see is not really a preference but more variability in word-order placement—something that has been noted as a difference between children learning other languages.

Differences in the way children use word order are reported in very many languages. We have seen that these may sometimes be related to their specific input; in other cases, children may be relying differentially on the systems available to them to mark the major constituents in the utterance; in still others, they seem to be picking up on differences between word order used for pragmatic and word order used for syntactic purposes. It should be clear from this variation that individual differences in word-order patterns ought to be of considerable theoretical significance to researchers working in very different traditions. Obvious examples are the question of whether we can talk about a "deep structure word order" in contrast to a "surface structure word order" and the complex relationship of pragmatic and syntactic word orders in different languages.

We come, finally, to the question of individual differences in the development of the casemarking of major constituents. Again, in languages where this is relatively straightforward, children learn it quickly, without difficulty and with little reported variation. But if a language provides children with cross-cutting principles, we may well expect to find variation as one child's language appears to reflect one principle and another child's language a different principle. An example is provided by Georgian acquisition in relation to the complex pattern of case assignment for verbs in the aorist series (Imedadze & Tuite, 1992, p. 92). Imedadze and Tuite argue that children formulate one of two semantic hypotheses to deal with this: one centers on the aspect of the verb, the other on the agentivity of the subject, and this results in different patterns of case assignment errors for different children. Both of these patterns observe the split intransitive nature of the language but solve the question of how to mark it in different ways.

Japanese also provides an example of difficulties in the casemarking of major constituents, which involves the subject marker *ga*. As well as marking subjects (transitive and intransitive) *ga* also marks the objects of stative predicates and of verbs in the potential or desiderative, which makes it difficult for children to work out any underlyingly unified semantic function for it. Clancy reports one child in her study as marking both the agent of transitive verbs but also, and incorrectly, the patients of transitive verbs where this is the only argument expressed (Clancy, 1985, p. 389). She suggests that the child has developed a syntactic or positional hypothesis which places *ga* after the first nominal argument in a sentence. She also cites Fujiwara as reporting a refinement of this hypothesis by a child who did this ONLY if the first nominal argument was ALSO ANIMATE (p. 391).

Summarizing this section, we have found that variation between children can reflect the following distinctions: word order and casemarking; syntactic and pragmatic uses of word order; aspect and agentivity; positional and semantic uses of casemarking; and, if this distinction is thought to be theoretically viable, the difference between deep and surface canonical word-order patterns. These are some of the major distinctions between the ways in which languages are organized, and this then lends support to the idea of a parallel between variation within and between languages.

There have been many experimental studies of children's relative dependence on word order and case in the comprehension of utterances with two nominal constituents, especially when these are both animate and there are no semantic cues. Most of these experiments have tended to confirm that when the system in a language is both predominant and clear, children largely depend on the information provided by it. However, because of the difficulties of testing young children, these studies are typically carried out with children whose productive systems may be too advanced to be characterized by reliance on a clear preference for one device allowed in their language over another.

2.2.4. *Morphology*

I cannot hope to do more than sketch in what I think are the theoretically and empirically interesting issues in terms of variation between children in the development of morphology. This is partly because it is such a vast area—one has only to think of the 400 derivational affixes and 300 inflectional endings in just one language, West Greenlandic—and also because the data on variation that are available to us simply cannot bear the weight of much detailed interpretation. When authors report that children show differences in the patterns of development of particular morphological systems, they rarely give enough detail to be clear how significant this behavior might be in terms of (a) the relative numbers of children showing the pattern; (b) its consistency for the individual child; (c) clarity about alternative patterns of marking for different children; and (d) the longevity of the particular behavior and how it changed.

Let us start with issues concerning the order of emergence of particular morphemes or morphological systems. We know from the work of Peters (1985) and Slobin (1973, 1985) that perceptual salience and semantic/syntactic complexity are important factors in determining differences in order of emergence between children learning different languages. As far as children learning the same language are concerned, the classic study by Brown, Cazden, and Bellugi (1969) indicated that frequency of modeling in the input was correlated with order of emergence of particular morphemes, and more recent and detailed work by Farrar (1990) also indicates that the frequency of particular types of constructions in the input is correlated with the emergence of particular inflections (e.g., the past tense, plural, and present progressive inflections). But of itself, this finding is not very significant except for those who would wish to deny any direct role at all for input. However, order of emergence within a language becomes much more significant when it is tied theoretically to the issues of system-wide as opposed to more local learning.

Thus, claims for the stage-like development of the INFL-system as a result of maturation (Radford, 1990) are made problematic by major lags between the development of inflectional morphology in one part of the system as opposed to another. This is particularly the case if these lags do not go in the same way for different children. Thus Imedadze and Tuite (1992, p. 87) report that, for some children, case assignment clearly preceded person-marking on the verb, while for others this was not the situation. Similarly, evidence that children differ in the relative levels of development in their noun and verb morphology (Clancy, 1985; also see Section 2.2.2 above) is a problem for this theory. On the other hand, this evidence also bears on the issue of whether lexical categories develop at different rates. Tomasello (1992) suggests that, in English acquisition, the verb category develops later than the noun category because verbs involve second-order relations while nouns do not. On these grounds, we might expect productive inflectional marking on verbs to appear later than on nouns. The evidence on variation between children from Farrar (1990, for English) and Clancy (for Japanese, 1985) suggests that the issue is rather more complex both within and across languages. This complexity may have to do with the considerable theoretical tension between thinking of morphological acquisition as merely the passive registration of distributional dependencies on the one hand and seeing it as connected to syntax and form-function relationships on the other.

We know that children can pick up a great deal of the morphology in their language before the age of 2;0, where that morphology is regular, agglutinative, and transparent as to the relations between form and function. More impressive still is clear evidence that children are capable of relatively unproblematic acquisition of morphological distinctions which have little or no semantic base (e.g., grammatical gender in many languages) or where semantics is clearly not driving the system (e.g., marking nouns, verbs, and adjectives correctly even when they do not conform to any clear semantic core of the category [Levy, 1988; Maratsos, 1988]). This suggests that children possess a particularly powerful distributional analyzer, the output of which is reflected in the types of operating principles that Slobin (1985), MacWhinney (1985), and Peters (1985) have delineated. The precise power that we need to hypothesize for such an analyzer will depend on how we formulate what else the child has to bring to the task of learning grammatical structure and morphology. Thus a position based on universal grammar says that the child ALSO brings a universal and necessarily highly abstract grammar to the task of interpreting the output of the analyzer. As we shall see, variation between and within languages in what provides resistance to early, error-free morphology, bears importantly on this debate.

Smoczyńska (1985, p. 618) reports that, while the level of syntactic development for the two children in her 1978 study was the same, four months after word combinations started coming in, their morphological development was not, with Jaś producing many inflectional contrasts not produced by Tenia. Smoczyńska suggests that this could be due to phonological difficulties that Tenia may have had, but this leaves open the question of whether Tenia "knew" the inflectional distinctions but could not produce them—a position that would be supported by a UG perspective, or whether her problems with production could have affected her ability to analyze out the inflections. This latter suggestion would be supported by a view that children may initially work on their own productions in building up their knowledge of early structure (Elbers, 1995). One way of sorting this out would be to know whether, when Tenia started to use inflections productively, she showed rapid and across-the-board provision, or whether she seemed to go through the same stages of morphological development as children who had been developing them earlier. It is clear from the literature that there are differences between children learning many different languages in the provision of productive morphology for the same level of language development as measured in a variety of ways (MLU, syntactic complexity). For instance, Bates and Rankin (1979) in a study of the acquisition of adjectives and inflections by two children learning Italian, found that one child acquired both the adjectival and inflectional expressions for reference to size at the same time while the second child used lexical adjectives for size for a number of months before acquiring the relevant inflection. Similarly Savić and Mikeš (1974) find differences between children learning Serbo-Croatian in whether they first express the possessive relation by word order (placement of possessive attribute in prenoun phrase position) or inflectionally, by adding suffixes that denote the possessive relation to the noun.

This difference among children learning the same language in when they "take off" into inflectional structure could, in fact, be used to argue that some children's I-system develops before that of others so that some children continue to develop their language structure based on lexical categories while, for others, the I-system matures earlier and the children therefore show a more advanced grip of the inflection system. However, the fact that this difference among children learning the same language is, in a sense, mirrored by differences between children learning different languages goes against such a position. We have already referred to Turkish, for which Aksu-Koç and Slobin report productive inflections before the period of two-word combinations while children learning Georgian show evidence of using word order contrastively for pragmatic effect well before they use any contrastive inflections (Imedadze & Tuite, 1992, p. 85). According to these authors there is a period of between several months to a year after the production of multiword combinations during which children only use nouns in the "base" nominative form. It is not clear that a theory based on a Universal Grammar to which all children have maturational access can accommodate these widespread differences in the development of productive morphology between children learning different languages. In addition, the evidence for initially local as opposed to system learning, and for the importance to some children, at least, of syntagmatic as opposed to paradigmatic learning, tends to go against the UG proposals (Pine & Lieven, 1997).

Thus, Fortescue and Olsen (1992) report that for children learning West Greenlandic "acquiring a morpheme may not be an all-or-nothing matter, but rather one of increasing flexibility of word-internal combination possibilities" (p. 113). They show that for the youngest child in their sample (2;2) there is productivity for a limited number of nominal and verbal inflections, but that this productivity is limited to a very small number of stems in the case of each inflection. While the second child in their sample, who was nearly a year older (3;1), showed development on all fronts, he was still limited to one affix per stem and to acquiring new affixes in familiar contexts before trying them out in new ones (p. 161). In other words, there is a long period of partial productivity. This may be the route that all children learning West Greenlandic must follow when faced with such a range of morphology and with potentially infinite possibilities for inflecting stems, particularly when we consider that considerable stem-change also takes place. But, as yet, it is not possible to be sure of the extent of variation, since Fortescue and Olsen's study is designed with a lagged cross-sectional methodology. However, one striking feature of their study is how closely the process they describe for the development of productive morphology matches the role that semi-formulaic utterances are hypothesized to play in the development of those children whose language development shows a high preponderance of them. Fortescue and Olsen's concerns about how to measure genuine productivity, and that MLU is an inappropriate measure for this type of language, are very similar to those outlined in Pine and Lieven (1993) and Lieven, Pine, and Baldwin (1997) for these types of children.

MacWhinney calls these sorts of low-scope patterns "item-based patterns" (1985, p. 1122) and points out that in some cases they are the only appropriate way of dealing with linguistic phenomena. For instance, in Hungarian (and English for that matter), the governance rules of particular verbs can be very idiosyncratic and will often have to be learned on a verb-by-verb basis. In other words, the child has to discover which parts of the language she or he is learning are accessible to more broadly applicable rules and which are not. Thus, in some cases children may have to "cut back" to more local solutions after having experimented with more general ones. It may be that there is variation in the extent to which children attempt to provide general rules and this accounts for the variation in the extent to which children experiment with and overgeneralize case frames for verbs in different languages (Pinker, 1989).

A child who shows evidence of overmarking, inflectional imperialism, double marking, or affix checking is showing signs that her or his system is developing beyond these low-scope, local patterns. But there are individual differences reported in many languages for the extent to which children show evidence of these processes (e.g., West Greenlandic: Fortescue & Olsen, 1992, p. 162) and this then raises methodological and theoretical problems for interpreting the development of children who are less experimental and do not show these "errors."

One explanation is that some children and adults are genuinely conservative learners when it comes to morphology and never go beyond the direct evidence provided by the language. Evidence from experimental studies by Indefrey (1993) suggests that this may indeed be the case. Indefrey's study was concerned with the learning of weak noun declension for novel forms in German. He contrasts this with the provision of plurals for novel forms, and looked at five groups of children (mean age: 5, 6, 7, 8, and 9 years respectively) and two of adults: teenagers going on to nonuniversity education and university students. He drew two important conclusions from his findings. First, that frequency cannot be the only factor in how children learn the correct marking for forms—nouns in the weak noun declension are highly infrequent compared to other nouns which, unlike weak declension nouns, take no marking for genitive, dative, and accusative. Second, and more importantly for this discussion, he shows that while there is a major developmental shift in the number of subjects providing the correct marking for novel forms, there are individual differences at each age group from 5-year-olds to adults. Even among the 5-year-olds, there are some children who seem already to have grasped the rule for weak declension, while among both groups of adults there is a small number who appear to be operating on the basis of item-by-item rote learning; that is, they will not extend the marking of masculine nouns with weak declension to novel forms. In the case of these adults, they did however pluralize novel forms, so this was not just to do with the unfamiliarity of the novel words.

Indefrey's study highlights several important issues for the present section of this chapter. The first is that we have to take seriously the possibility that, for some speakers, and perhaps, for some parts of the system, low-scope, semi-formulaic learning may be more prevalent than has sometimes been thought. This in turn suggests that we must look extremely carefully for tests of genuine productivity. It would of course be possible to argue that low-scope learners are at the uninteresting end of the spectrum of development compared to those who appear to be generating more powerful rules with wider scope. However, the tenability of this position depends on a careful analysis of the precise strategy that speakers are using and the proportions of speakers using each strategy. If it turns out that there is indeed very wide variation, this has important implications for theories of adult language processing and language change.

However, it is also clearly the case that some learners may show overgeneralization in one part of the system and not in others. An example is Smoczyńska's (1985, pp. 627–628) discussion of some children's overgeneralization of the -ów genitive plural ending for masculine nouns to feminine and neuter nouns, which actually take a null ending. According to Smoczyńska, most children make this error for differing lengths of time, and she provides five explanations, which together account well for the data. However, as she points out, they do not explain those children who do NOT make the error. These three children fall into two groups: two children whose use of -ów and the null ending was correct from the beginning and one child who did not make errors but avoided contrastive use over a long period. Smoczyńska explains the non-occurring error for the first two children in terms of the zero form being highly salient and learned early, whereas the children who overgeneralized had developed a system in which there was compulsory provision of inflections, zero inflections being unusual in Polish. This explanation is interesting in that it suggests that children may differ in the "feel" they develop for the kind of inflectional language with which they are dealing. Perhaps most Polish children develop, through distributional analysis, some kind of slot after nouns, which has to be filled, whereas a few are either driven to notice the zero form by features of their environment or by early rote-learning of particular words. The third strategy of avoiding difficulties is the most problematic to account for because it appears to involve some kind of "gating" mechanism which prevents the child using words she does not know how to inflect. Thus according to Smoczyńska, this child initially avoided all use of forms not taking -ów; she then started to produce nouns with the zero ending but only those that also involved vowel insertion in the stem so that there was some change. Finally, ten months later she started to use forms with zero endings and no vowel change. It remains an open question as to whether we should be positing some block on production late on in the process, which sounds inherently rather unlikely, or alternatively some very low-scope and conservative learning. There are reports of the avoidance of difficulties for children learning other languages, which make this an issue that would repay more investigation and thought in terms of information processing in the development of speech production.

Overmarking, a strategy shown by some children learning highly inflectional languages, is interesting in that it cannot be the result of the automatic registration of distributional regularities, since endings appear on words that do not take them. Thus Smoczyńska reports the way in which Jaś marked not only the conditional particle -by for person (correctly) but also the past participle (incorrectly). In Polish this seems to be a transient and infrequent phenomenon but it would be correct in some other languages, such as Warlpiri, where any word with the same referent in the clause will carry the same casemarking (Bavin, 1992, p. 316). Again we see that, for a brief moment, a pattern of marking produced by a child learning one language can reflect a much more generally applicable pattern in a different language. Another example which makes the same point is Erbaugh's claim (1992, p. 442) that some children learning Mandarin are attempting to provide more inflectional structure than is actually present in the language through analytic and redundant double-marking.

The overwhelming impression gained from studying the acquisition of morphology crosslinguistically is how relatively unproblematic it is. Children seem to acquire systems which to the Anglocentric eye look exceedingly complicated with little difficulty and without much variation between them. One reason for this impression of ease is that, in contrast to a grammatical analysis of morphology in terms of paradigms and the marking of syntactic relations, morphological development seems largely to take place through the automatic registration of morphophonological regularities. However, as we have seen, where there is difficulty, there is often variation; and while this variation among children can usually be explained in terms of the specific difficulties they are encountering, the solutions they attempt would often be recognizable to the student of a different language. An important question then arises as to when this registration of regularity becomes connected to meaning on the one hand or to the sense of a paradigm on the other. While the evidence of local and low-scope learning tends to argue against an overly general theory such as those proposed by UG, there is a great deal of work which remains to be done on tracking the development of wider productivity and more global patterns of application. The study of variation between children and adults should, I maintain, be a central source of evidence in trying to track such development.

2.3. Later Development

Much less work has been done on variations among children in their later language development for all but a very few languages. A partial exception to this is experimental work on the comprehension and production of passives, dative alternation, and various kinds of conjoined clauses, including relative clauses. However, relating the results of these experiments to naturalistic accounts of language development has proved problematic for reasons which largely have to do with the very unnatural sentences that children are required to imitate or act out in experimental tasks designed to untangle their syntactic capacities. Additional problems for the investigation of variation are that such experimental work tends to present group data which makes the identification of individual strategies impossible and that even when strategies are identified (e.g., Bridges, 1980) it is difficult to relate them to evidence for variation among children taken from naturalistic studies. In this section, I take up areas for which there is some evidence from naturalistic data of variation among children learning the same language and where these data bear on interesting theoretical issues raised by comparing acquisition across languages. We look first at the clause-internal operations of negation and interrogation before turning briefly to complex sentences and, in particular, to relative clauses.

2.3.1. *Negation*

Of course some form of negation is among the earliest meanings that all children learn to express, usually early on in the "one-word stage" and often long before they express *yes* or its equivalent! Yet even here there are reports of individual differences in the order in which the expression of different negative meanings comes in. Thus Bloom (1970) and Pea (1979) claim that the order of emergence follows the level of cognitive difficulty in expressing each meaning and argue that this order is non-existence, rejection, and finally denial. Berman (1985, p. 320) for Hebrew and Kim for Korean (1997) found the same order of emergence. But Ramer (1976) reports individual differences between children in this order as do Plunkett and Strömqvist for Scandinavian acquisition (1992, p. 544). The Korean data also indicate that some children used different mappings of forms to functions than did others (Kim, 1997), which provides a good example of how crucial attention to variation can be in trying to elucidate the underlying reasons for orders of emergence. In fact, it seems that differences in the order of emergence of these notions between languages may, in part, be accounted for by whether each negative meaning is expressed with a different morpheme or lexeme (as is the case in both Scandinavian and Hebrew), while some of the explanation for differences between children learning the same language is, according to de Villiers and de Villiers, due to differences in the input (1985, p. 83). In either case, it is clear that level of cognitive difficulty cannot be the only explanation; we shall return to this question in Section 4 below.

A second issue of major importance in the development of negation is the question of placement of the negative operator or operators. This can be quite complex, as in English, where negation involves changing the form of the main verb and the use of auxiliaries, or in French, where this is also the case and, in addition, there are two operators, at least in the formal language (*ne . . . pas*). This becomes even more complex where there are multiple auxiliaries in the verb phrase. Maratsos and Kuczaj (1976) have shown that children differ in whether they initially place the negator correctly after the first auxiliary (as in *the boy should not have been eating Jello*) or whether they place the *not* immediately before the main verb, incorrectly (as in *she could have been not sleeping*). The authors point out that both are plausible analyses of input data based on the presence of a single auxiliary.

In an early and path-breaking analysis of the development of negation in English, Bellugi (1967) found that there were two major types of errors made by the children. One was the incorrect use of double negatives. All the children did this sometimes and so it was not a matter of individual variation, but it is of interest because although this is incorrect for the standard English dialect, it is not, of course, incorrect for some other languages (e.g., Spanish) or other dialects of English (e.g., Black English Vernacular: Labov, 1976). However, the other type of error which seemed to characterize the speech of some children and not others was sentence-initial placement of the negative particle rather than its correct placement in the auxiliary complex. Slobin (1985, p. 1239) suggests that the children who do this are following a preference for placing the negative operator in a position which would reflect the fact that its scope is the entire proposition and not just the element that it is placed closest to. He supports this argument by referring to similar data from other languages (Polish, Turkish, Japanese, and ASL). Given that, for Japanese and Turkish, the negative operator is placed in sentence-final position in accordance with the basic configurational structure of the languages, Slobin rejects the argument that the English data could be accounted for by the researchers mistaking anaphoric negation for syntactic negation. In Greek it is choice of negator rather than its position that indicates whether constituent negation or sentence negation is taking place and here, too, there appear to be individual differences in that two of the children in Stephany's study overextended the constituent negator to negate a clause while the third child did not (Stephany, 1997).

However, two factors make the story more complex. First there are languages in which children seem to handle the internal syntactic placement of negative operator without error from the start (German, Scandinavian, K'iche' Maya). This may well reflect a more transparent and accessible method of negating in these languages, which allows for the child to learn rapidly how to correctly place the negative operator. Thus for mainland Scandinavian, Plunkett and Strömqvist (1992) report that while syntactic negation is delayed compared to discourse negation, when it does appear, it is sudden and without error. They point out that discourse and syntactic negation are coded by different lexemes, which is not the case for English, and also that the placement of the negative is determined by the finiteness of the verb. Both these factors, they suggest, may help the child. Secondly, and of most significance to this chapter, it is clear that there is considerable variation between children learning the same language in the extent to which they show sentence-external negation. It may be that children learning languages which present some difficulties in the learning of negation initially develop different analyses for how to do it. Van Valin (1991) discusses this in detail with an explanation which derives from Role and Reference Grammar and its postulation of a layered structure to the clause. He suggests that "some children start off by taking the clause as the reference point for the clausal operators . . . whereas some choose the nucleus as the reference point for all operators from the beginning and will therefore not produce any displaced negatives" (p. 26). Here we have a theoretical explanation that potentially accounts for the differences found within languages as to what children take as the scope of the negative operator. An obvious issue is whether it can also account for what appears to be the ABSENCE of variation in other languages.

2.3.2. Interrogatives

Interrogatives are somewhat similar to negatives in that their scope can vary from the whole clause to the individual lexeme and that their operation in some languages is considerably more transparent than in others both as to form-function relations and whether or not syntactic alternations are required. This is a situation where, for those languages in which the marking of interrogatives is not entirely straightforward, and for which we have enough data, we should expect variation among children. This is indeed what we find.

Most languages appear to use a simple intonational contrast for interrogatives; sometimes this is optionally combined with an interrogative particle. In addition, all languages appear to have a range of question morphemes and these may be placed in utterance-initial or final position or in the position of the word being questioned. And, finally, some languages, most notably the Indo-European ones, involve a syntactic alternation for interrogative constructions. The evidence is that children appear to have no difficulty with intonational contrast for the interrogative but they can have difficulties with (a) the placement of the inter-rogative lexeme, particle, or affix and (b) any required syntactic alternations.

De Villiers and de Villiers (1985, p. 88) report for English a wide range of individual variation between children in whether they produce correct subject-auxiliary inversion at the same time for *yes/no* and *wh*-questions and which *wh*-questions they succeed in inverting earliest. The authors discuss both cognitive and linguistic explanations for these different orders of development but, as they point out, until we can sort out the relationship between individual variation on the one hand and an analysis based on both form and function on the other, it is difficult to draw any over-arching conclusions. Mills (1985), too, reports that one German-speaking child failed to invert after the question word *wo*, though it was not possible to tell, in this case, whether this was a failure in interrogative syntax or in placing the verb in final position in the main clause. In Hebrew, information questions require sentence-initial question words to replace the miss-ing information but no subject-auxiliary inversion or *do*-support. Berman notes that there are some reports of very young children not fronting the question word but leaving it in the "correct" place for declarative syntax (1985, p. 320). This is how questions are formed in Japanese (Clancy, 1985, p. 416), with the question word in the position of the questioned constituent. Interestingly there are no individual differences reported for Japanese because, as Clancy remarks, it is very difficult to make a mistake.

There is some evidence of individual differences between children when they are attempting to deal with the scope of interrogative particles. Thus MacWhinney (1974, p. 464) reports for Hungarian that while the interrogative particle -*e* is attached to the main verb or predicate, it has the scope of the whole proposition. One child tried to mark this by attaching it to the initial element in the sentence while another attached it to the final element. Between them therefore these children made clear that they were attempting to mark the whole proposition AND reflected the two canonical word orders of Hungarian! (cf. Dasinger, 1997). Some Kaluli children also have difficulties with interrogative suffixes (Schieffe-lin, 1985). They acquire the equivalent of *wh*-words and an interrogative suffix used exclusively for items with nominal morphology without error by 25 months. However, although one child showed no errors in acquiring the other interrogative suffixes, one child went through a period of overmarking which probably reflected non-segmentation of certain phrases, and the third child showed sustained diffi-culty in sorting out the correct placing of the suffix -ɛlɛ, which can be applied across all word types and to verbs after the 1st or 3rd person tense inflections. Instead he applied it directly to verb stems. This had the effect of always making it utterance-final. It may be that this child is mistakenly treating the suffix as if its scope is the whole proposition.

It is difficult to draw very wide-ranging or firm conclusions from these data but it is clear that two areas would repay a detailed study of differences within and between languages. These are: (1) the separation and nonseparation by some children in some languages of propositional and lexical interrogatives, and (2) the separation by some children of two stages in the formation of interrogatives: (a) *wh*-fronting and (b) subject-auxiliary inversion. Close attention to such data as there are suggests that children may be reflecting some of these wider issues when they start trying to work out the specific details of how to mark interrogatives in their particular language.

2.3.3. *Complex Sentences*

This is an area which is in critical need of detailed naturalistic work. There are scattered reports of individual differences in the literature which raise important issues but with which it is difficult to do much at the moment. So for instance, it is clear that some two-verb utterances come in very early in many languages (e.g., Korean, Kim, 1997; English, de Villiers & de Villiers, 1985; the serial verb structures of Mandarin, Erbaugh, 1992) and may, in fact, derive from early semi-formulaic expressions, such as in English: *want to* + *x, going to* + *x, have to* + *x* (Bloom, Takeff, & Lahey, 1984; Lieven, Pine, & Baldwin, 1997). But when, if at all, do the children who use these structures reanalyze them to make them part of a wider syntactic representation? How might this be related to differences in which semi-formulaic expressions are learned first and their potential as building bricks for a wider-scope and more formal system? These questions are difficult to answer partly because the naturalistic longitudinal data are not available but also because how one thinks about them is so dependent on how the relationships between different kinds of complex sentence structures—for instance verbal complementation, coordination and subordination—are described theoretically. This in turn makes the scattered reports of individual differences in the development of these structures hard to interpret. Thus Demuth (1992) reports that one Sesotho-speaking child analyzed infinitival complements as if they were conjoined main clauses: so, incorrectly, 'I refuse I sit down' for 'I refuse to sit down'; but without more system-wide data, it is not clear how to assess the significance of this behavior.

Another example of these problems is provided by the development of children's abilities in phrasal and clausal coordination, where there is much theoretical argument about which forms of conjunction should be easier, together with some evidence of variation in the order of emergence of: (1) backward and forward phrasal conjunction (Tager-Flusberg, de Villiers, & Hakuta, 1982) and

(2) phrasal and sentential conjunction (Bloom, Lahey, Hood, Lifter, & Fiess, 1980). However, much of the experimental work is designed within particular linguistic frameworks and uses highly peculiar sentences. The naturalistic data tend to indicate that the order of emergence of particular conjunctions depends first on pragmatic factors and second on the frequency of their provision in the input, but beyond this it is difficult to arrive at any clear conclusions or hypotheses about variation.

When we come to subordination, Smoczyńska (1985) reports that some Polish children use simple juxtaposition of clauses for a considerable time (as does Stephany, 1997, for Greek) while others use conjunctions from the beginning. Clearly the cognitive capacity is in place but, according to Smoczyńska, these telegraphic children were systematic in providing fewer functors in their speech and this extended beyond the early stages. This contrasts with a strategy on the part of many language learners to make form-function relations explicit, exemplified by the findings on the development of relative clauses.

Thus children acquiring relative clauses in Scandinavian often supply the unambiguous relative marker *som*, where adults would omit it (Plunkett & Strömqvist, 1992). Stern's son, learning German, seems to have gone through three stages in learning to mark relative clauses (Mills, 1985). He first simply juxtaposed the clauses, but subsequently started to insert a meaningless syllable as a relative marker and only finally produced the correct case-inflected forms of the relative pronoun. However, there is not enough information to know if this strategy is a general one for children learning German or characterizes some individuals and not others. For Polish, Smoczyńska reports that only one child produces the relative pronoun, which requires declension and agreement, the others initially depending on -*co* which does not, though it DOES require that the children repeat the whole antecedent clause, which they duly do. Kim (Korean, 1997) reports simple juxtaposition as the first step, with some children then following an intermediate step of using the semantically indeterminate head noun *kes* 'thing, one' as the only relativized noun. These data lead the author into a discussion of two opposing theoretical explanations to which we shall return below in Section 5.1.1 on the theory of Universal Grammar. For the moment, however, while it is clear that in some languages at least, children can move straight into the correct formation of relatives, many children actually take a more or less piecemeal approach to the problem with a number of intermediate steps on the way (cf. Berman, 1990). Thus while initial juxtaposition can be followed by immediately correct relativization, many children produce a single unambiguous marker for the relative, even where there are either other more correct or flexible options or where the marker has to agree with other constituents. Aksu-Koç and Slobin (1985) report the acquisition of relative clauses to be very late in Turkish because of the difficulty involved in nominalizing the subordinate clause. Indeed, some Turkish children attempt strategies akin to those used for the formation of relatives in other languages, for instance the provision of an obligatory relative marker without any changes in the syntax or morphology of the relative clause (Slobin, 1986).

Other issues concerning the development of relative clauses await detailed naturalistic and crosslinguistic study, for instance the question raised by experimental approaches as to which kinds of relativization are easiest for children and why. De Villiers and de Villiers note that, in comprehension, "some children make subject coreference errors as if they treated the relative clause as a flat coordinate structure rather than embedding" (1985, p. 117). They also note that this is not true of all children in these experiments. Perhaps in treating this aspect of English syntax as flat, these children are exploring a possible linguistic option unacknowledged by the UG grammar approach. A highly speculative and dangerous suggestion!

In summary, most studies, experimental or naturalistic, suggest that there is considerable variation between children in the phases they go through as they develop more complex constructions in their language. There appears to be variation in the order in which different semantics is expressed, in the extent of piecemeal, as opposed to more wide-scope learning and in the degree to which children depend on intermediate forms as they attempt to express more complex ideas with more abstract forms within one sentential contour. A clear sense of how prevalent and systematic such variation is and how it might reflect on current theoretical debates in comparative linguistics and developmental psycholinguistics must await both better, naturalistic data and better frameworks for understanding how these constructions are actually used by speakers.

3. CAUSES OF VARIATION

I have suggested in the course of this chapter that many differences among children could be caused by an interaction between the characteristics of the language being learned (both its structure and how it is presented in the child's environment) and various starting mechanisms or assumptions that children bring to the language learning task. Clearly these starting mechanisms or assumptions might be innate or learned, more or less universal, and more or less tied specifically to language. Hardy-Brown (1983), in a useful theoretical article, points out that these do not all necessarily go together. For instance, there might be a genetic underpinning to individual differences in language learning without this bearing on the issues of whether it depends on the presence of an innate, and/or specifically linguistic module. Equally, correlations between aspects of the speech of biological mothers to their children and those children's language development could be due to correlated genotypes rather than the direct effect of the mother on the child. However, this requires a much more sophisticated theoretical approach in studying the role of genetic, biological, environmental, and developmental factors in generating individual differences than has usually characterized the field. The best example of such an approach is provided by the work of Plomin and DeFries (1985) on adopted infants and the relatedness of various measures of their communicative and language development to characteristics of their adoptive and biological parents. It is impossible to do justice to this extremely detailed study in a few sentences. But briefly, it suggests a significant genetic effect of the IQ measures, though not of the language measures, of biological parents on communicative development measures at 12 months; an increased influence of environmental variables on language development between 12 and 24 months; and a specific effect of the environment on lexical development between 12 and 24 months.

Of course, there remains the question of how such genetic, biological, and environmental differences are manifested behaviorally in the process of development and whether we can find correlates for them at other levels of description and explanation. There have been attempts to account for variation between children in language learning at the neuropsychological, temperamental, cognitive, and input level (cf. Shore, 1995 for a summary of these approaches), though it is important to point out that these are also not necessarily distinct, that is, neuropsychological differences might give rise to both temperamental and cognitive differences which might in turn, either through the child's language behavior, or more directly, affect how others respond. On the whole, however, with the important exception of Bates and her co-workers (Bates et al., 1988) researchers have tended to deal with each of these potential sources of variation separately.

3.1. Neuropsychological Explanations

To the non-expert, this is a minefield of conflicting claims about whether and what aspects of language are localized, where in the brain, and the degree to which this modularization is already present at birth or develops. Issues of how to conceptualize the potentially separable aspects of language in order to hypothesize their separate locations in the brain interact in complex ways with the little hard evidence that exists. Until recently the availability of such evidence depended on very abnormal subjects, damaged early in development, and often on post-mortem examination of their brains. Bates et al. (1988) provide an excellent account of this field written from the point of view of non-modularity and brain plasticity (updated by Bates, 1993). Image-scanning techniques are rapidly changing the methods available and making it possible to study aspects of localization of function *in vivo*. However, they are in their methodological infancy, and relating the complexities of language processing to different parts of the brain remains an extremely contentious and novel art at the present time. Ultimately, though, we would expect systematic variation between individuals to involve either differences in neural architecture and/or in the precise processing relationships involved in production and comprehension, and there have been a number of suggestions in the literature as to what these might be.

Bates et al. (1988) raise two possibilities. One is that those children who are more dependent on prosody and on the use of formulae might make relatively greater use of the right hemisphere in processing language whereas those using a more "analytic" approach may depend more on the left (Bates et al., 1988, pp. 63–64). Locke (1995) has a variant on this, suggesting that early vocabulary development is subsumed by the right hemisphere in normally right-handed people but that syntactic development is subsumed by the left. He postulates that it is the inability of the normal rote-memorization capacity of the right hemisphere to process the volume of novel items being learned that "kicks in" the left hemisphere's syntax module, and he suggests that there might be variation between individuals in when this happens relative to vocabulary size. These ideas are not dissimilar to those of Karmiloff-Smith (1992) who sees language development as a process of "redescription," in which the earliest stages could be accounted for by inputs to and outputs from (a) connectionist net(s), but the outputs become subject to rules which are developed through internal re-analysis of the output from these nets in a constant process of bootstrapping to higher levels of representation. This, too, could lead to predictions about variation between individuals, related to the point at which such redescription takes place and the relative balance, for different individuals, between relying on more local regularities or more broad-scope, abstract processes.

The second suggestion by Bates et al. is that the mechanisms subserved by Wernicke's and Broca's areas in the left hemispheres of most right-handed people might develop in slight asynchrony with those children for whom Wernicke's area is "leading" having a heavier dependence on function words and formulaic phrases, while those for whom Broca's area is "leading" would tend to be more telegraphic. Akhutina (1993) also suggests that developmental asynchrony in the skills that children recruit to language development may be responsible for systematic variation between children in aspects of language learning. Although it is difficult to compare her results to other work in the field, partly because the children in her study are so much older (7;0) and partly because she takes a resolutely general cognitive approach to the problem of learning to talk, these suggestions that maturational asynchronies could play a part in generating variation between normally developing individuals are interesting and could, potentially, be a very fruitful avenue of further research. This even applies to researchers from a highly nativist tradition. For instance, those who see the maturational development of α-neurons as responsible for the emergence of linking rules (e.g., Borer & Wexler, 1987) should be able to develop empirical hypotheses about the variation between children for whom this maturation is early as opposed to those for whom it is late.

My feeling is that if these ideas are to get beyond being interesting speculation there are three requirements: first, we need very much better theories of how the brain is involved in adult language processing; second, that we have an adequate account of how children's language processing skills develop; and, last but by no means least, we need an accurate account of systematic variation between children within and across languages that can be brought to bear on the first two areas. Without a coherent account of variation, we are likely to find continuing confusion in which dichotomies are picked as being relevant to issues of brain structure and processing—to say nothing of the added complexity that we are not really discussing DICHOTOMIES into which individuals fall but DIMENSIONS on which they vary (as Bates et al., 1988, point out forcefully, p. 66).

3.2. Cognitive Explanations

Two types of cognitive explanations have been offered as causes or at least correlates of variation in language learning. The one derives from the idea that asynchronies in parts of the developing cognitive system might underpin these differences and the other that variation might derive from differences in cognitive style among children.

The work of Gopnik and her colleagues (Gopnik, 1988; Gopnik & Meltzoff, 1987; Gopnik & Choi, 1995) suggests that there may be relationships between specific aspects of cognitive development at the end of the sensorimotor period and specific aspects of language development. For children learning English, French, and Korean, they find correlations between: (1) the achievement of means-end coordination and the emergence of words for success/failure, (2) the naming explosion and a measure of categorization skills, and (3) the achievement of Stage 6 object permanence and the emergence of words for appearance and disappearance. The suggestion is that these early stages of language development may reflect developments in underlying symbolic functioning which are also reflected in the cognitive achievements. Gopnik is not saying that cognitive development causes language development, since the work on Korean suggests that a cognitive skill might be delayed by aspects of the language spoken to the child—both its structure and the way that caretakers use it. Gopnik and Choi (1995) claim that Korean input is more heavily dependent on verbs for conveying meaning relevant to the child and that there is a de-emphasis on nouns (see, also, Choi, 1997). The authors use this to explain the later emergence of BOTH the naming explosion and categorization skills in their Korean sample by comparison with the English- and French-speaking samples. Since we know that one of the most robust dimensions on which children vary is the proportions of nouns in their early vocabularies, it would be interesting to see if those children who show a relatively late rapid increase in nouns also show a relatively late increase in categorization skills. In fact, Gopnik and Meltzoff (1993) suggest that this is the case. Work by McCune-Nicolich (1981) on the relationship between stages in symbolic play and stages in the development of multiword utterances might also repay investigation from the perspective of variation among children.

The second approach is to suggest that differences between children in language development might be related to the extent of their field-dependence or field-independence. One problem here is trying to map this onto what we actually know of variation. The suggestion is usually made in terms of referential children developing telegraphic multiword utterances and having a more analytic, abstract, and rule-governed approach to language, while prosodic children become expressive-phrasal, are more holistic, and are more concerned with reproducing what they hear (see Bates et al., 1988, pp. 64–65 for some details). While this suggestion has some plausibility, there is no evidence of a direct correlation between measures of field dependence and these measures of early language development. A further conceptual problem lies in the question of consistency across the developmental span. Cognitive style is supposed to characterize an individual; while it may be the case that individuals are consistently more towards the gestalt or analytic ends of the scale in their language development, this has not yet been shown except perhaps for the earliest stages. When we add the crosslinguistic dimension and see that children can be equally dependent on, say, a phrasal style, but one can be concentrating on noun-phrase structure and another on verb-phrase structure, the dimension of cognitive style may be rather too crude to be of much help.

A final and intriguing thought, consistent with the approach that has been taken in this chapter, derives from consideration of the work of Choi and Bowerman (1991) on the relation between the semantics of the language the child is learning and their cognitive development. Choi and Bowerman have argued that children reflect, from extremely early on, the major semantic distinctions made in their language and that these distinctions can vary quite considerably from one language to another. One wonders if a microanalysis of the ways in which different children use their early words might not yield a range of semantic distinctions, some of which are closer to those in other languages than in the particular language that the child happens to be learning, particularly if the child is not receiving very tailored input. A recent paper by Pye, Frome, Loeb, and Pao (1995) comparing the acquisition of "paper-manipulation" verbs in English-, Chinese-, and K'iche'-speaking children provides the type of data needed to investigate this idea, although analysis in terms of the strategies of individual children, and how these might relate to the semantics of the different languages involved, has yet to take place.

3.3. Temperamental/Affective Explanations

An initial idea in this field, first tentatively hypothesized by Nelson (1973), was that the referential and social-expressive language styles might derive from the former group of children being more interested in objects while the latter might be more people-oriented. But although this suggestion aroused a great deal of interest and was repeated frequently in the literature, it has been shown to be deeply problematic. Both Lieven (1980) and Goldfield (1985/86) have described highly sociable referential children, whilst Bretherton, McNew, Snyder, and Bates

(1983), Olson, Bayles, and Bates (1986), and Lloyd (1987) have all failed to find significant associations between social–expressiveness (i.e., nonreferentiality defined in Nelson's terms) and temperamental measures of sociability in larger scale samples.

A more promising line, for which there is scattered support from children learning English and other languages, is that children differ in the degree to which they "take risks" in language learning. The suggestion that this might be related to temperamental differences along a dimension of impulsivity/reflectivity was made by Kuczaj and Maratsos (1983) for Kuczaj's sons Abe and Ben. One style, which characterized Ben and which the authors call "risk-taking," involved the child using utterances and structures as soon as he had any control over them, thus making a relatively high number of errors. Abe, by contrast, tended to consolidate small bits of the system and be more cautious in expressing them until they were fully mastered. Kuczaj suggests that each child maintained his style across the acquisition of a number of different syntactic forms, namely, auxiliaries, negatives, and modals. This sort of stylistic difference has been noticed a number of times. For English, we have Ramer's (1976) observation of differences in the error rate in very early language development, while Eisenberg and Renner (1981) found something similar at a much later stage for the emergence of complex sentence structures. These latter authors report that some children expressed a wide range of semantic relations in their complex sentences but also made a large number of errors; a second group of children made fewer errors but were more limited in the semantic range expressed. Fortescue and Olsen (1992, p. 162) report that one of the children in their study of the acquisition of West Greenlandic was "more experimental" than the other. In general, where there are reports of individual differences, one often finds that some children develop, at least in a particular system, without overt error, while others make a number of errors. Thus Smoczyńska reports for Polish that one child, Jaś, was much more adventurous with morphology than the other two children (1985, pp. 618–619); for Korean too, in a study of the relation between word order in the speech of mothers and their children by Cho (1981), one child is reported as being less rigid than the other two. However, the interpretation of these results is rather problematic. At the moment it is impossible to tell whether what we have here is a general temperamental characteristic of the child which extends across his or her approach to all aspects of language development and derives from a general temperamental style—as suggested by Kuczaj and possibly also by Smoczyńska—or whether, rather, children can differ across systems as to whether they take a more cautious, data-driven approach which generates few errors but rather narrower scope, or a more wide-scope approach which is likely to generate a greater number of errors. This is an issue that, with the right methodology for measuring rate of error and for controlling for stage of language development and the language structure being learned, might yield an answer quite quickly.

3.4. Environmental Influences

In this section I deal with relationships between input variables and stylistic variations. In Section 4 below, I consider the methodological implications of this work for the study of variation. The literature is full of literally hundreds of statistically significant correlations between aspects of children's input (almost always maternal) and aspects of children's development, particularly rate but also style. However, it should also be noted that there are also many or more FAILURES to find significant correlations and that replicating the significant findings of previous studies is frequently unsuccessful. There has been a tendency to correlate raw frequencies in many of these studies and a related failure to theorize the complex relationships that must exist among specific aspects of input, expected outcomes, and variability between children. Thus working out what the significant findings might mean and how important they are is a more difficult task than finding them, and here I cannot hope to do more than sketch the important issues. For much more detailed reviews and an attempt to provide a theoretical framework, the reader is referred to my own article on the study of input in a crosscultural context (Lieven, 1994) and to that of my colleague Julian Pine (1994), who deals with the vast range of data for children learning English.

It seems fairly incontrovertible that a primary source of the referential style in early vocabulary development lies in the ways in which the caretakers of these children talk to them. Many studies have found significant correlations between the provision of nouns in caretakers' speech and the proportion of nouns in children's early lexicons (e.g., Klein, 1980; Furrow & Nelson, 1984; Goldfield, 1987, 1990; Hampson, 1989) although it is important to note that early differences between children may contribute to the ways in which caretakers speak to them (Pine, Lieven, & Rowland, 1997). This seems particularly tied to labeling routines and is very typical of the rather selective group of middle-class mothers from highly industrialized societies whose children have tended to form the focus of much child language research. However, it also seems to be the case that there may be crosscultural differences not only in the extent to which mothers use object labels in their speech to children but also in what they use them for. Thus Fernald and Morikawa (1993) compared how mothers talk to infants about objects in English and Japanese and found that American mothers used more object labels than did Japanese mothers, but they also discovered that when Japanese mothers used object words they used them less for labeling and more in social routines than the American mothers did. In my 1994 article, I suggested that children who were not being so frequently engaged in labeling routines might rely on other strategies for starting to use language and that these strategies might, in turn, be supported by their environment. Most children in the world grow up in contexts characterized more by polyadic than by dyadic interaction, and this of course includes children who are not first-borns. This may make the initial isolation of utterance–meaning pairs more problematic for these children and lead them to segment larger chunks of what they are hearing. For instance Pine, Lieven, & Rowland (1997) show that where mothers' speech is less 'segmentable,' children are significantly more likely to be phrasal. Another good example of this is Brice Heath's (1983) observation that children in the social group she named Trackton start by imitating the ends of adults' utterances in conversations not addressed to them and then subsequently start to use these imitations creatively by substituting and adding words. Snow (1983) also provides excellent examples of this kind of behavior in contexts of delayed imitation. These sorts of observations fit well with what we know of prosodic-phrasal children's development and, more importantly, in the context of the present discussion, they fit well with data from other cultures and social groups which suggest that caretakers' strategies for interacting with children in these societies may be supportive of this kind of style. An example is Schieffelin's (1985, pp. 531–533) discussion of the *elema* strategy used by Kaluli caretakers when encouraging children to talk. This involves getting the child to repeat exactly what the caretaker has just said on the child's behalf and is thus explicit training in the relation between utterance and meaning.

Pine (1995) provides an interesting example of the interaction between familial influences and birth order effects on stylistic development. In his study of nine pairs of siblings, he finds a significant difference in the proportion of phrases in the early lexicons of first- and second-borns, with the first-borns being less phrasal. This suggests that there was some difference in how the first- and second-borns were segmenting their input and may well reflect the sorts of differences in that input suggested above. However there was, additionally, an extremely high correlation between siblings in rate of development as measured by age at which the children acquired their 50 and 100 word lexicons, suggesting a strong direct or indirect familial influence on BOTH children. This highlights the point that it is a mistake to think of the environment as having a unitary influence on the one hand or independently of how individual children are interacting with it on the other. This point is also reinforced by Gillis and Verhoeven (1992) in their study of MLU development in two sets of triplets. Despite the fact that all six children were quite similar in their development of both utterance length and the provision of morphemes, there were significant differences within each set of triplets which could have been due either to constitutional factors and/or to differences in the microstructure of the types of interaction each child had with those around her/him. Similarly, Räisänen (1975, reported in Dasinger, 1997) finds that only one of his sons produced anomalous forms for marking the partitive and illative in Finnish despite, presumably, both of them being exposed to very similar input. Thus although, as noted above, there is suggestive evidence of tendencies for somewhat different styles of language development by different cultural and social groups, most studies which find variation between children have samples drawn from the same social group or even, in the case of the studies cited above, from the same family.

There is a great deal of evidence both within and across languages for a very high degree of matching between characteristics of the input and related aspects of language development. Thus differences in word-order patterns and patterns of ellipsis between children can often be accounted for by differences in their relative frequency in the caretaker's speech to the child (Mandarin: Erbaugh, 1992; Korean: Kim, 1997; Finnish: Argoff, 1976). And this can also be true for the order of emergence of functor words and morphemes. The earliest example in the literature is probably Brown's 1973 study of the order of emergence of grammatical morphemes, which shows that rate of provision of a particular morpheme in the mother's speech to the child is significantly correlated with the order of emergence of that morpheme in the child's speech, as measured by its provision in obligatory contexts (p. 356). Much more recently, Farrar (1990) has shown that this may be mediated through the different ways in which mothers provide feedback to the child's utterances. Farrar's study shows that, for a sample of children learning English, the emergence of present progressive and plural marking was correlated with the mothers' use of recasts in responding to their children, but that this relationship did not hold for other markers. This suggests that the relationship between the provision of grammatical features in the input, the discourse frame in which they are provided, and the child's developing grasp of them may be highly specific and require a much more detailed focus than is provided by studies which correlate global aspects of caretaker speech with rather general measures of language development. Here too we have a kind of matching in that the child is learning something that is provided very frequently by the mother but in a context that is to some extent controlled by the child. In other words, one cannot look at the provision of the form without examining the functional context within which it is provided since this will critically affect the child's attention to, and therefore intake of, the utterances concerned. We have already seen that the provision of nouns in labeling contexts is positively correlated with the early acquisition of relatively high proportions of nouns. It may be possible to find functional correlates in caretaker speech to a relatively higher proportion of verbs in the child's speech which might explain the correlations that have sometimes been found between directives and a less referential style (Della-Corte, Benedict, & Klein, 1983).

Common sense suggests that much variation between children can be accounted for by differences in the ways in which they are spoken to and, as we have seen, there is much support for this in the literature. The question of how significant this is for important developmental issues depends on the nature of the variation induced and its role in how the child moves on to develop the next stage in language structure. Earlier sections of this chapter have established that early differences between phrasal and referential children may be important in how they begin to construct multiword utterances and that differences between children in their relative concentration on the learning of nouns or verbs may affect their initial development of noun-phrase and verb-phrase morphology. The order of emergence of morphemes may affect the generalizations that children are able to make and, therefore, the scope of their system at any one time—and this may be more crucial in languages with rich morphological systems, particularly if these are both complex and irregular.

A final interesting issue here is to consider the implication of cases where particular children are NOT matching the characteristics of their input. Are these the children who are particularly inclined to risk-taking? Are they interacting with a wider range of interlocutors with a variety of styles than are those children whose production matches that of their mothers very closely? Or are these children following some universal developmental course which is relatively more independent of the input? Are they for instance, the more rapid developers? These are questions which cannot be answered at the moment since there has been rather little attempt to think about the relationship between characteristics of the input and characteristics of the child's language developmentally as opposed to cross-sectionally. They are important questions both in their own right and because they provide a potential method of controlling for input—a point taken up immediately in Section 4 below.

4. METHODOLOGICAL ISSUES

In this section, we consider the methodological problems involved in studying variation as well as methodological issues which the study of variation raises. I have organized the section in terms of the common framework that Slobin suggested to the authors of the specific language chapters in these volumes (Slobin, 1985, pp. 19–20) but have added the question of pragmatic pacesetting to the range of topics he suggested. The topic headings under which Slobin organized the framework for the chapters in these volumes provide a convenient method of raising important methodological points about variation and relating them to crosslinguistic study.

4.1. Grammatical Sketch of the Language Being Studied

Many of the chapters in these volumes make it clear that there can be substantial differences between the grammar of a language as described by linguists and the actual language that the child hears. An example of this is given by Ochs (1985) in her chapter on Samoan acquisition in which she points out that the ergative marker, which is important in linguistic descriptions of the language, very rarely occurs in domestic contexts and is largely confined to formal and public contexts. Clearly then, its absence in children's speech is easily explained. Children often omit verb agreement in the development of ASL, but Newport and Meier (1985) suggest that this may well be because the mothers also do this. A similar point applies to the study of variation. Just as it is important to look at input rather than some theoretical grammar of language, we must look at ACTUAL input to child. This is important not just because dialectal differences might result in variation between children but also because of consequences for intake of different styles of interaction and input which were discussed in Section 3.4 above. Where differences between children are noted, the first and most obvious explanation must be in terms of what they are hearing.

And this, in turn, raises interesting questions about the implications for theories of development of instances where matching does occur and where it does not, as for example, in Pye's study of K'iche' Maya where frequency of maternal use of particular morphemes does NOT determine order of acquisition (1986, 1992). In a crosslinguistic context too, the absence of variation in children in the face of variation between the adults they are interacting with, could provide an example of canalization in development; while a crosslinguistic comparison of the types of structures for which one gets matching between adults and children and those for which one does not would be of major interest.

4.2. Summary of Basic Sources of Evidence

Evidence on differences between children is extremely thin in languages other than English and this is particularly true if one wishes to study variation systematically rather than just noticing that all children differ from each other in a number of ways. For understandable reasons, longitudinal studies, particularly in languages other than English, tend to be of one, or at best, a very small number of children. This makes it either impossible or very difficult to discuss variation. Large-scale studies are extremely rare and, again for understandable reasons, either use age to control across children (which confounds rate and style) or have to use measures of language (e.g., vocabulary size) which are difficult to relate to theoretical issues in the study of language development. While this is true to some extent of the studies by Bates and her colleagues of English (Bates et al., 1988), Camaioni and Longobardi (1993) of Italian, and Serra, Solé, and Torrens (1990) for Spanish, all three discuss variation between children in detail and present interesting results which relate to the issues raised in this chapter. One of the aims of the present chapter is to pull together some theoretically motivated dimensions of variation which would repay longitudinal study in a crosslinguistic context. Three examples are the size of children's initial units, the relative proportions of nouns and verbs learned by different children within and between languages, and possible differences between children in the ways in which they mark basic sentential relations. It seems clear to me that without some motivated theorization, the study of variation will not fulfill the potential it has to illuminate these and other basic issues in the study of language development.

4.3. Summary of Overall Course of Linguistic Development

It would be extremely useful if researchers providing such a brief summary were sensitive to the areas in which, for the language they are studying, there are signs of systematic variation. Obviously this interacts with the provision of suggestions as to where one would expect such variation—and each focus of study would start to inform the other. Language development research has now arrived at the point where it should start to be possible to mark, in a summary of development, major foci of variation.

4.4. Typical Errors and Error-Free Acquisition

The most fundamental importance of individual differences research is as a check on what constitutes the typical. How many children do we need to study to decide that a particular phenomenon is typical or learned without errors? And how do we decide between errors that we can treat as processing or production errors as opposed to errors which bear on the child's competence and thus on how to theorize development? When does variation matter and when not? This question cannot be answered independently of quantitative data on the extent of variation between different children. But it is also not separate from theory. Any theory that claims that certain errors, constructions, or behaviors should not occur is clearly vulnerable if some children turn out to show them. A potentially telling example here is the explanation given for island constraints in various versions of Chomskian theory. There are now linguistic accounts which suggest that these constraints may well not exist for some languages (e.g., Van Valin, 1991) and that some children learning English may violate them (Wilson & Peters, 1988).

4.5. Timing of Acquisition

Differences in order of emergence are crucial to any predictions based on a theory as to what an order of emergence should be. For instance, any theory that makes strong claims about order of emergence can, other things being equal, be falsified by evidence of variation either between language development in different languages or between different children. An example might be Radford's claim that the INFL-, DET-, and COMP-systems come in together and after the lexical category system (Radford, 1990). This is called into question by the evidence which suggests that Turkish children provide productive morphology before they use more than one lexical item in their utterances (Aksu-Koç & Slobin, 1985). But it is equally called into question by any account of language development which suggests that it takes place in a "piecemeal" fashion with children developing quite sophisticated local productivity around particular lexemes or groups of lexemes without necessarily generalizing this across the whole grammatical system. An example is Tomasello's (1992) study of his daughter, which suggests that her development of verb argument structure is indeed piecemeal and dependent on learning the argument structure of each verb independently. This does not support the idea of an early, underlying, and across-the-board knowledge of adjunct, specifier, and complement lexical relations as posited by Radford. Our work on the development of the determiner (Pine & Lieven, 1997) suggests that particular children can know a great deal about the distributional relationships of a particular determiner in (a) particular context(s) without necessarily having a fully fledged determiner category. Some of the variation between children in learning the correct contexts for *det* and *den* in Scandinavian (Plunkett & Strömqvist, 1992, p. 548) may possibly be explained by these sorts of processes. Fortescue and Olsen (1992) for West Greenlandic and MacWhinney for Hungarian (1985) make similar points about the development of correct and productive morphology. Thus timing of acquisition is crucially tied up with the methodological issues involved in defining "acquisition." Serious attention to issues of productivity and the specificities of individual children's language development tends to suggest that acquisition is often a much more drawn out and jigsaw-like process than has been argued for in some accounts.

A further, and potentially extremely important, complicating factor is the evidence that there are some children whose level of language development is much more accurately reflected in their comprehension than in their production (Bates et al., 1988; Braunwald, 1995). Virtually all the research reviewed in this chapter, and indeed in all four volumes of this series, depends on production data, for the obvious reason that it is much easier to study; however, we know that children can learn to comprehend language fully without any overt production (Bishop, 1993). An extreme approach to this issue would be to claim that comprehension provides the true guide to what the child knows about language and that production data are so confounded with performance problems that it is difficult to draw firm conclusions from them. This might be a position taken up by those who posit the maturational unfolding of a Universal Grammar. But we also know from Bates et al. (1988) that for many children, production data are highly correlated with comprehension data and therefore produce an accurate reflection of the child's level of language development; in other words, there is systematic variation between children in the extent to which their production and comprehension are correlated. The existence of children whose comprehension is well ahead of production is not well attested in any language other than English and would certainly repay further study.

4.6. Cognitive Pacesetting

Early attempts to establish that children had to reach a certain stage of cognitive development before a related linguistic development could occur were made problematic by findings that repeatedly showed variation between children in the order of emergence of cognitive stage and linguistic milestone (Corrigan, 1978, 1979). One of the major methodological problems in this research has been the nature of the language measures used. Thus the existence of children who start with units larger than a word and of children who use productive inflections before starting to put words together makes simple measures such as the emergence of the first word or first multiword combinations highly problematic. In addition, until the nature of the child's language use is studied in context, it is not easy to tell whether a child who is taking part in a labeling game has really grasped the nature of referring, or a child who uses verbs in low-scope phrasal formulae has really grasped predication. Gopnik's (1988) study avoids this problem to some extent by much more narrowly defining the language measures used, however even here the measure of vocabulary explosion is problematic in that (a) there is much dispute over how to define it and (b) not all children appear to show a sharp change in the rate of vocabulary expansion—some simply show a gradual increase in the slope of the curve (van Geert, 1991; Bates & Carnevale, 1993). At later stages of language development there are similar problems in that children may use expressions without really understanding fully what they mean, having picked up roughly correct contextual cues for their use and some productivity based on a distributional analysis of the input (Lieven & Pine, 1991; Pine & Lieven, 1993).

One of the original motivations for comparing acquisition across languages was that cognitive development could be assumed to be equivalent; therefore, differences in the emergence of the related linguistic form between languages told us something about the difficulty involved in the way the concept was encoded linguistically (see Slobin, 1973, and a critique by Johnston, 1985). Clearly this methodology can be matched by looking at either cognitive or linguistic variation between children speaking the same language and checking for the related linguistic/cognitive development. Hypothesizing the relevant relation between cognition and language and defining the cognitive measures independently of language remains a major theoretical and methodological challenge. It is also essential to do this sort of work in naturalistic or semi-naturalistic situations as well as in experiments since the ambiguities introduced by the experimental need for control often obscure rather than clarify the issue under consideration. Nevertheless, if two groups of children could be identified, one group already showing the cognitive skills in question and the other not, it ought to be possible to check for the presence of the linguistic form. Equally the finding of linguistic differences between children, despite the presence of the hypothesized prerequisite cognitive skill, would call the nature of the relation into question.

The difficulties in theorizing the relation between cognitive and linguistic development mean that I can only produce the most tentative list of a few examples of reported differences between children learning the same language which one might be able to relate to differences in aspects of cognitive development. These are: the order of emergence of coordinate and complex sentences in English (Clancy, Jacobsen, & Silva, 1976; and Ramer, 1976) differences in whether children learning Georgian link the case patterns of interactive verbs to the semantic concept of aspect or agentivity (Imedadze & Tuite, 1992); orders of emergence of negative concepts in English, Hebrew, and other languages (cf. de Villiers & de Villiers, 1985) and the relative emphasis by children on tense, aspect, and aktionsart in their use of different verbs (Wiest, Wysocka, Witkowska-Stadnik, Buczowska, & Konieczna, 1984; Bloom, Lifter, & Hafitz, 1980).

4.7. Pragmatic Pacesetting

A great deal of evidence suggests that children are especially sensitive to the coding of pragmatic distinctions. We know that where pragmatic distinctions are coded structurally they are acquired easily and early by contrast with constructions which are more purely syntactic (e.g., Berman, 1985, p. 275). Another example comes from the coding of sentence-final particles in Japanese, which children also acquire very early. (Choi, 1997, reports similar findings for Korean.) Clancy suggests that this is partly because they are both highly salient and frequently used by adults, but also because correct usage has a pragmatic and emotional basis. She points out that correct usage also requires "some ability to deal with presuppositions about shared and unshared information" (Clancy, 1985, pp. 435, 511). This raises the possibility that an investigation of the use of these particles by young children might be relevant to issues of cognitive pacesetting raised in the section above, since the question of children's understanding of shared information is relevant to their understanding of other minds as discussed in research on children's theory of mind (Wimmer & Perner, 1983). Clancy also suggests (1985, p. 512) that there may be individual differences in the strategies which individual children might follow in acquiring sentence-final particles, which one can well imagine if they are so closely tied to interaction, emotion, and cognition. As well as children's interests or emotional tone possibly affecting how they acquire particular constructions, it is also possible that some children may entertain pragmatic hypotheses about the meaning of a particular construction while others concentrate on more directly semantic or distributional relations. Plunkett and Strömqvist (1993) report early acquisition of feedback morphemes for children learning Scandinavian languages but also differences in these acqui-sitional patterns across the languages and between children learning the same language. As the authors say, this whole area of the sociocognitive determinants in the use of feedback morphemes would repay study as "an important window on our understanding of children's early pragmatic and discourse skills" (p. 546). And finally, Smoczyńska provides a particularly good example of the interaction of pragmatics and syntax in an example from her son, Wawrzont's, development. In the context of a particular interactional situation, he developed a productive causative construction based on the verb *karmić* 'to feed', which involved adding an infinitival complement to the accusative object normally governed by the verb. This construction does not exist in Polish though it does, of course, in other languages (1985, p. 635).

A second consequence of the centrality of pragmatics is that some differences between children may be accounted for fairly directly by differences in the input which derive from pragmatic factors. Thus Kim (1997) reports individual differ-ences in the acquisition of the subject honorific marker -*s* and the politeness marker -*yo*, probably because it depends on how the family uses them and how explicitly they are taught.

4.8. Linguistic Pacesetting

Differences between children in how they start to break into aspects of the language they are learning may well constrain how they move to the next stage. We have seen some evidence for this in the probable continuity between an early prosodic style and the development of relatively large number of low-scope phrasal formulae. Clancy suggests that differences between children learning Japanese in whether they start with relatively more nouns or verbs may lead on to differences in their relative elaboration of the noun or verb phrase. This may be more widely the case, so that being pushed toward referential vocabulary might then, depending on the language, draw the child toward elaborating the noun phrase first rather than the verb phrase. The implication of these findings is that where systematic variation between children in how they acquire or use a particular linguistic form has been identified, it is important to ask whether this might affect how the child moves onto the next stage. Whether these differences between children in what they are tackling in their language development has consequences for their cognitive development depends on the precise relationship envisaged between cognition and language. My feeling is that variation between children should be an important factor in attempting to refine the issues involved in attempting to answer this question.

4.9. Input and Adult–Child Interaction

Methodologically, one needs always to check the input as a potential source of variation between children before looking for other factors. An example is Budwig and Wiley's (1991) study of the development of personal pronouns for a sample of English-speaking children in which they find that there is a far higher degree of matching between the frequency of provision of these pronouns in the adults' speech and the patterns of emergence found in children than had been realized in previous studies which attempted to produce cognitive or linguistic accounts of the development of personal pronouns. But even when the input has been identified as the source of a variation, it is important to go on to consider the consequences for development as discussed in Section 3.4 and at the beginning of Section 4 above. The input acts as the backdrop against which to assess the range of variation and its limits and it is from this backdrop that we have to try to assess the effects of affect, pragmatics, cognition, and structural complexity on intake, that is, the child's current system plus what is being attending to. As Dasinger points out when discussing morphophonemic development in Hungarian (1997), there are complex relationships between grammatical complexity and input frequency which have to be sorted out for an adequate account. It is extremely important, therefore, to use this "input backdrop" to identify genuine evidence of error-free acquisition and of typical errors either for a large enough group of children learning the language or for individual children. Children who appear less closely tied to the forms in their input will be particularly interesting in that they potentially provide a window onto the way in which language development can bootstrap into broader and more abstract representations.

5. THE RELEVANCE OF VARIATION
TO DIFFERENT THEORETICAL POSITIONS

In this section we consider the way in which variation between children might bear on different theoretical positions. This should not be seen in an entirely negative light. There is often a tendency to think that differences between children are only relevant to showing that a particular general statement is wrong because, at the limit, one child does not fit it. However, variation could be used to test hypotheses about the separateness of particular developmental phenomena, about orders of development, and about the relationship between particular environmental factors and particular aspects of language development. In other words, the study of variation could greatly enrich our theoretical frameworks to say nothing of our descriptive adequacy.

5.1. Grammars

5.1.1. *Universal Grammar*

While UG approaches could in principle deal with some aspects of variation and, indeed, some people have attempted it (Hyams, 1986; Torrens, 1992), most approaches see all variation as noise in the system, the result of performance problems and certainly irrelevant to the core grammar. However, despite the tendency of those following the nativist linguistic paradigm to dismiss variation between children as irrelevant, certain differences between children are, in fact, broadly compatible with any position on the nativist-environmentalist theoretical continuum and, if used properly, could actually be used to dissociate and test certain nativist positions. The idea that because something is biologically innate, there are no differences between individuals in its pattern of emergence derives from a view of biological innateness that insists on the invariable unfolding of a single blueprint. In fact there is nothing about a nativist account that makes differences impossible. Quite the reverse; a biologist would expect there to be differences which would allow the system to use environmental variation in a way that buffered against too much variation in outcome. So, even in their own terms, nativist theorists should be interested in differences between children and how these might interact with the various theoretical postulates associated with different versions of nativist language acquisition theory.

An example of an attempt to accommodate individual differences within parameter-setting theory is provided by Torrens (1992) for Spanish and Catalan acquisition. Torrens chose two highly referential and two highly expressive children for his study and showed that though there were no differences in the specifier parameter for inflection phrases (sentences), there were differences in the learning of the head-first/head-last parameter for VPs. He interprets this as indicating that IPs and VPs are in horizontally modular parts of the system. We might produce alternative accounts of these differences, based on the idea of the learning of low-scope formulae or verb islands, but the attempt to incorporate individual differences into UG theory is interesting. Clearly any idea of modular systems allows for the possibility that each system could develop on a slightly different timescale in different children, leading to different orders of development. Equally any hypothesis about orders of development such as Radford's (1990) or Borer and Wexler's (1987) must have an account which can cope with any variation between children in the order in which the systems postulated in these theories develop.

The chapter on Korean by Kim (1997) provides an extremely elegant account of the way in which variation between children can challenge certain supposed claims to universality in some theories of language development. The first example concerns the incorrect use of the semantically indeterminate head noun *kes* in the formation of relative clauses. Kim argues that erroneous *kes* insertion (referred to in Section 2.3.3 above) should be analyzed as the provision of a syntactic head nominal and challenges the hypothesis put forward by Whitman, Lee, and Lust (1991) that *kes* insertion occurs under the command of Universal Grammar. The discussion is long and detailed but the relevant point for this chapter is that, as Kim argues, it is difficult to see how the error can be under the command of Universal Grammar since only two out of the five children in Kim's study and 22% of the subjects in the sample studied by Whitman, Lee, and Lust make the error (Kim, 1997).

While I think that, even in their own terms, UG theorists of language acquisition could use variation to test theories, I have to admit to finding UG approaches to language learning so essentially anti-developmental that differences between children which are often suggestive of more local and piecemeal development are ignored in favor of theories that rapidly lose any purchase on the reality of what children are saying or doing.

5.1.2. *Functionalist Theories of Grammar*

Just as nativist theories are not inherently incapable of including variation, so functionalist theories are not necessarily sympathetic to issues in variation. Thus the postulation of universal aspects of communication or cognition which languages are thought to represent does not necessarily allow any room for variation among children. However, in practice these theories do address issues of language change and linguistic variation more successfully than more nativist theories. Almost all functionalist approaches produce descriptions of grammar in which relatively independent features of form interact with aspects of semantics and pragmatics (Croft, 1995). This allows for the possibility that children might vary in their emphasis on one or other. Givón (1985) raised this in general terms when he suggested that some children may be more sensitive to the formal distributional regularities of the system they are learning whereas others may be picking up aspects of the organization of information structure earlier. Ultimately of course, both have to be integrated, but children may start off being more productive with one of the other.

A more detailed example comes from Role and Reference Grammar (Foley & Van Valin, 1984), which describes the structure of the clause as being organized by two major components: the first is the representation of predicates, arguments, and clausal modifiers and the second is the representation of operators such as tense, aspect, and modality. Van Valin (1991) suggests that children may differ in how they apply the rules for operator ordering (which are based on cognitive universals) to the structure of the clause and that this may lead to the kind of variation we have seen in whether children start with sentence-external or sentence-internal negation (Section 2.3.1). Thus we may get a separation between different aspects of the system which in the end have to be interconnected. In principle, clear evidence of initial separation could be used to validate hypotheses about what these different systems are and how they might interact in the development of more abstract structure.

5.2. Connectionist Theories of Grammatical Learning

At the level of theory, connectionism can cope well with variation since small differences in the structure of the input can have major effects on the patterning of the output. An early and non-implemented version of connectionist theory was the competition model of Bates and MacWhinney (1987). Here variation was accounted for by competing strengths of association and cost, based on cue frequency, accessibility, and non-ambiguity. The difficulty here is predicting the precise forms of variation that are found and, more importantly, dealing with the absence of variation if and where there is such an absence. My feeling is that in order to make connectionist theories interesting to the developmental psycholinguist we shall have to work back from a systematic description of the major kinds of variation found, to an attempt to model them in terms of variations in the structure of the net and the structure and relative frequencies in the input. Otherwise we are faced with a situation in which a connectionist account can explain everything *post-hoc* but is not able to predict the expected outcomes from a description of the input—especially when we move from morphology to problems of word-order and distance dependencies (cf. Bates & Elman, 1993).

5.3. Variation and Theory

This has been a very brief and selective survey of the ways in which the study of variation might be relevant to each of the three major theoretical schools now operating in the study of language development. Children differ one from the other—and I hope that this chapter has demonstrated that they do so in ways which are of significance to any account of how they learn to talk. Variation can inform us as to the possible ways in which the language system can be split up during acquisition. It can throw light on whether a number of different linguistic phenomena can be accounted for by a uniform analysis or whether separate analyses may be necessary. It may provide information on the ways in which language variants or language contact are changing the underlying structure of the languages children are learning. Theories which cannot account for variation either in general, or in the specific ways in which it is manifest, may be interesting as challenges to our ways of thinking about language development, but they cannot hope for even descriptive adequacy let alone explanatory adequacy.

6. GUIDELINES TO THE RESEARCHER

Building up a comprehensive and systematic account of variation in children's language development depends on researchers being sensitive to differences between the children they are studying which may be important and interesting. But if such an account depended on every difference between children being noted and discussed, this would obviously be a hopeless task—researchers must have some idea of what to attend to and what to ignore. The guidelines will vary depending on whether the task at hand is largely descriptive—an account of language development in a language not yet studied, for instance—or is based on questions or predictions derived from theoretical concerns.

In the case of description, it is important to build on the major dimensions of difference identified in this chapter, as well as on those suggested by Peters at the end of her chapter in this volume:

1. Is there evidence that some children are taking a more prosodic route into early utterances while others segment between units more clearly? Do some children use prosodic placeholders? If so, for what, if any, grammatical units are they holding a place? And how does this relate to the prosodic, lexical, and morphological structure of the language being learned?

2. Are there differences in the types of lexical items that children concentrate on? Whole phrases? Nouns? Verbs? If such differences can be identified, how are these differences involved in the way the child moves into the next stage of language?

3. Are differences in children's positionally based formulae responsible for major differences in the way their language appears to be structured? If so, how do these formulae develop as children converge on the "adult system"?

4. Does the language the child is learning have a variety of ways of expressing the major arguments of the verb (e.g., word order and casemarking)? If so, is there any evidence that some children concentrate on one method while others concentrate on another?

5. Are there rules of sentence and clause formation in which information structure and syntactic structure interact? If so, is there any evidence that different

children concentrate on one or the other initially? For instance, do children differ in the positioning of operators either externally to the sentence or internally?

6. Are some children consistently more error-prone than others? If so, is this correlated with more linguistically advanced systems or not?

7. Are there children whose comprehension appears to be well in advance of their production? If so, does this appear to be across the board or only on certain parts of the language?

8. Can the patterns of variation shown by children learning the language be related to its typological characteristics?

9. How close is the match between the adult language and the child's language? In cases where the child's language seems relatively independent of the adult input, how can this be accounted for?

In the case of more theoretically motivated studies, the importance of thinking about the implications of variation from the start cannot be overestimated. What kinds of differences between children can the theory tolerate and what not? This amounts to saying that theoreticians should start to make the attempt to predict variation from their postulates. This chapter ought to have made it clear that it is not possible to relegate all instances of differences between children to on–line production errors or noise in the system, though clearly these sorts of explanations will account for some of the variation found. However, a theory which claims to be psychologically realistic must be able to account for the major dimensions of difference that have been found. I am looking forward to the time when theories will be able to predict what kinds of systematic variation we would expect from that particular theory rather than the situation at the moment where even the most realistic theory can hardly begin to account for those differences already identified.

7. CONCLUSION

Where there is uniformity in the process of language development it is difficult, if not impossible, to separate the relative contribution of predisposition, language structure, cognition, and input. Variation between children gives us one of the few investigative handles we have for starting to discuss explanations of language learning. As Slobin argued eloquently in 1973, and as the chapters in these volumes show, crosslinguistic variation is another. The problem with research on individual differences is that researchers get interested in the differences for their own sake rather than seeing them as a tool for the investigation and testing of developmental, and in the case of language development, linguistic theory. It is my hope that this chapter will make a contribution to changing this.

ACKNOWLEDGMENTS

My thanks to Dan Slobin, who has waited patiently for this work to reach completion and given a great deal of support on the way; to Julian Pine for his careful reading of an earlier draft; to Catherine Snow, who read a final draft; and to Gill Baldwin for her hard work in helping to put the final version together. All errors are entirely my own. Research of my own, reported in this chapter, was partially supported by the University of Manchester Research Support Fund, and partially by the Economic and Social Science Research Council of the UK (Grants R000234221 and R000221285).

REFERENCES

Akhutina, T. V. (1993, July). *Individual differences and dissociable mechanisms of language development: A neuropsychological approach.* Paper presented at the Sixth International Congress for the Study of Child Language, Trieste.

Aksu-Koc, A. A., & Slobin, D. I. (1985). The acquisition of Turkish. In D. I. Slobin (Ed.), *The crosslinguistic study of language acquisition: Vol. 1. The data* (pp. 839–880). Hillsdale, NJ: Lawrence Erlbaum Associates.

Argoff, H. D. (1976). *The acquisition of Finnish inflectional morphology.* Unpublished doctoral dissertation, University of California, Berkeley.

Bates, E. (1993). *Modularity, domain specificity and the development of language.* (Tech. Rep. No. 9305). San Diego: University of California, Center for Research in Language.

Bates, E., Bretherton, I., & Snyder, L. (1988). *From first words to grammar: Individual differences and dissociable mechanisms.* New York: Academic Press.

Bates, E., & Carnevale, G. F. (1993). New directions in research on language development. *Developmental Review, 13,* 436–470.

Bates, E. A., & Elman, J. L. (1993). Connectionism and the study of change. In M. H. Johnson (Ed.), *Brain development and cognition: A reader* (pp. 623-642). Oxford: Blackwell.

Bates, E., & MacWhinney, B. (1987). Competition, variation and language learning. In B. MacWhinney (Ed.), *Mechanisms of language acquisition* (pp. 157–193). Hillsdale, NJ: Lawrence Erlbaum Associates.

Bates, E., Marchman, V., Thal, D., Fenson, L., Dale, P., Reznick, J. S., Reilly, J., & Hartung, J. (1994). Developmental and stylistic variation in the composition of early vocabulary. *Journal of Child Language, 21,* 85–123.

Bates, E., & Rankin, J. (1979). Morphological development in Italian: Connotation and denotation. *Journal of Child Language, 6,* 29–52.

Bavin, E. L. (1992). The acquisition of Warlpiri. In D. I. Slobin (Ed.), *The crosslinguistic study of language acquisition: Vol. 3* (pp. 309–372). Hillsdale, NJ: Lawrence Erlbaum Associates.

Bellugi, U. (1967). *The acquisition of negation.* Unpublished doctoral dissertation, Harvard University.

Berman, R. (1979). The (re)emergence of a bilingual: Case study of a Hebrew-English speaking child. *Working papers on Bilingualism, 19,* 157–179.

Berman, R. A. (1985). The acquisition of Hebrew. In D. I Slobin (Ed.), *The crosslinguistic study of language acquisition: Vol. 1. The data* (pp. 255–371). Hillsdale, NJ: Lawrence Erlbaum Associates.

Berman, R. A. (1990, July). *Subordination as a developmental yardstick.* Paper presented at the Fifth International Congress for the Study of Child Language, Budapest, Hungary.

Bishop, D. (1993). Language development in children with abnormal structure and function of the speech apparatus. In D. Bishop & K. Mogford (Eds.), *Language development in exceptional circumstances* (pp. 220–238). Hillsdale, NJ: Lawrence Erlbaum Associates.

Bloom, L. (1970). *Language Development: Form and function in emerging grammars*. Cambridge, MA: MIT Press.

Bloom, L., Lahey, M., Hood, L., Lifter, K., & Fiess, K. (1980). Complex sentences: Acquisition of syntactic connections and the semantic relations they encode. *Journal of Child Language, 7*, 235–261.

Bloom, L., Lifter, K., & Hafitz, J. (1980). Semantics of verbs and the development of verb inflections in child language. *Language, 56*, 386–412.

Bloom, L., Lightbown, P., & Hood, L. (1975). Structure and variation in child language. *Monographs of the Society for Research in Child Development, 40*, (2), Serial No. 160.

Bloom, L. M., Takeff, J., & Lahey, M. (1984). Learning to in complement constructions. *Journal of Child Language, 11*, 391–406.

Borer, H., & Wexler, K. (1987). The maturation of syntax. In T. Roeper & E. Williams (Eds.), *Parameter setting*. Dordrecht: D. Reidel.

Bottari, P., Cipriani, P., & Chilosi, A. M. (1991). Presyntactic devices in the acquisition of Italian free morphology. Unpublished manuscript, Institute of Child Neuropsychiatry, University of Pisa.

Bowerman, M. (1973). *Early syntactic development: A crosslinguistic study with special reference to Finnish*. London: Cambridge University Press.

Bowerman, M. (1990). Mapping thematic roles onto syntactic functions: Are children helped by innate linking rules? *Linguistics, 28*, 1253–1289.

Braine, M. D. (1976). Children's first word combinations. *Monographs of the Society for Research in Child Development, 41*, (1), Serial No. 164.

Braunwald, S. (1995). Differences in the acquisition of early verbs: Evidence from diary data from sisters. In M. Tomasello & E. Merriman (Eds.), *Beyond names for things* (pp. 81–111). Hillsdale, NJ: Lawrence Erlbaum Associates.

Bretherton, I., McNew, S., Snyder, L., & Bates, E. (1983). Individual differences at 20 months: Analytic and holistic strategies in language acquisition. *Journal of Child Language, 10*, 293–320.

Brice Heath, S. (1983). *Ways with words*. Cambridge, MA: Cambridge University Press.

Bridges, A. (1980). SVO comprehension strategies reconsidered: The evidence of individual patterns of response. *Journal of Child Language, 7*, 89–104.

Brown, R. (1973). *A first language: The early stages*. Cambridge MA: Harvard University Press.

Brown, R., Cazden, C., & Bellugi-Klima, U. (1969). The child's grammar from I to III. In J. P. Hill (Ed.), *Minnesota symposia on child psychology, Vol. 2* (pp. 28–73). Minneapolis: University of Minnesota Press.

Budwig, N., & Wiley, A. (1991, March). *The contribution of caregivers' input to children's talk about agency and pragmatic control*. Paper presented at the Child Language Seminar, Manchester.

Camaioni, L., & Longobardi, E. (1993, July). *Nature and stability of individual differences in early lexical development*. Paper presented at the Sixth International Congress for the Study of Child Language, Trieste.

Cho, S. W. (1981). *The acquisition of word order in Korean*. Unpublished master's thesis, University of Calgary.

Choi, S. (1997). Language-specific input and early semantic development: Evidence from children learning Korean. In D. I. Slobin (Ed.), *The crosslinguistic study of language acquisition: Vol. 5. Expanding the contexts* (pp. 41–133). Mahwah, NJ: Lawrence Erlbaum Associates.

Choi, S., & Bowerman, M. (1991). Learning to express motion events in English and Korean. *Cognition, 41*, 18–121.

Choi, S., & Gopnik, A. (1993, April). *Nouns are not always learned before verbs: An early verb explosion in Korean*. Paper presented at the Stanford Child Language Research Forum, Stanford, CA.

Clancy, P. M. (1985). The acquisition of Japanese. In D. I. Slobin (Ed.), *The crosslinguistic study of language acquisition: Vol. 1. The data* (pp. 373–524). Hillsdale, NJ: Lawrence Erlbaum Associates.

Clancy, P. M., Jacobsen, T., & Silva, M., (1976). The acquisition of conjunction: A crosslinguistic study. *Papers and reports on child language development* (Department of Linguistics, Stanford University), *12*, 71–80.

Clark, E. V. (1985). The acquisition of Romance, with special reference to French. In D. I. Slobin (Ed.), *The crosslinguistic study of language acquisition: Vol. 1. The data* (pp. 687–782). Hillsdale, NJ: Lawrence Erlbaum Associates.

Corrigan, R. (1978). Language development as related to stage 6 object permanence development. *Journal of Child Language, 5,* 173–189.

Corrigan, R. (1979). Cognitive correlates of language: Differential criteria yield differential results. *Child Development, 50,* 617–631.

Croft, W. (1995). Autonomy and functionalist linguistics. *Language, 71,* 490–532.

Dasinger, L. (1997). Issues in the acquisition of Estonian, Finnish, and Hungarian: A crosslinguistic comparison. In D. I. Slobin (Ed.), *The crosslinguistic study of language acquisition, Vol. 4.* Mahwah, NJ: Lawrence Erlbaum Associates.

Della-Corte, M., Benedict, H., & Klein, D. (1983). The relationship of pragmatic dimensions of mothers' speech to the referential-expressive distinction. *Journal of Child Language, 10,* 35–43.

Demuth, K. (1992). The acquisition of Sesotho. In D. I. Slobin (Ed.), *The crosslinguistic study of language acquisition: Vol. 3* (pp. 557–638). Hillsdale, NJ: Lawrence Erlbaum Associates.

Dore, J. (1975). Holophrases, speech acts and language universals. *Journal of Child Language, 2,* 21–40.

Eisenberg, A. R., & Renner, T. (1981). *Acquisition of complex sentences in English: Similarity and variation across children.* Unpublished paper, University of California, Berkeley.

Elbers, L. (1995). Production as a source of input for analysis: Evidence from the developmental course of word-blend. *Journal of Child Language, 22,* 47–71.

Erbaugh, M. S. (1992). The acquisition of Mandarin. In D. I. Slobin (Ed.), *The crosslinguistic study of language acquisition: Vol. 3* (pp. 373–455). Hillsdale, NJ: Lawrence Erlbaum Associates.

Farrar, M. (1990). Discourse and the acquisition of grammatical morphemes. *Journal of Child Language, 17,* 607–624.

Fernald, A., & Morikawa, H. (1993). Common themes and cultural variations in Japanese and American's speech to infants. *Child Development, 64,* 637–656.

Foley, W. A., & Van Valin, R. D., Jr. (1984). *Functional syntax and universal grammar.* Cambridge: Cambridge University Press.

Fortescue, M., & Olsen, L. L. (1992). The Acquisition of West Greenlandic. In D. I. Slobin (Ed.), *The crosslinguistic study of language acquisition: Vol. 3* (pp. 111–220). Hillsdale, NJ: Lawrence Erlbaum Associates.

Furrow, D., & Nelson, K. (1984). Environmental correlates of individual differences in language acquisition. *Journal of Child Language, 11,* 523–534.

Gentner, D. (1982). Why are nouns learned before verbs: Linguistic relativity versus natural partitioning. In S. A. Kuczaj (Ed.), *Language thought and culture. Language development* (Vol. 2, pp. 301–334). Hillsdale, NJ: Lawrence Erlbaum Associates.

Gillis, S. (1990, July). *Why nouns before verbs? Cognitive structure and use provide an answer.* Paper presented to International Child Language Conference, Budapest.

Gillis, S., & Verhoeven, J. (1992). Developmental aspects of syntactic complexity in two triplets. *Antwerp Papers in Linguistics, 70.*

Givón, T. (1985). Function, structure, and language acquisition. In D. I. Slobin (Ed.), *The crosslinguistic study of language acquisition: Vol. 2. Theoretical issues* (pp. 1005–1028). Hillsdale, NJ: Lawrence Erlbaum Associates.

Goldfield, B. A. (1985–1986). Referential and expressive language: A study of two mother-child dyads. *First Language, 6,* 119–131.

Goldfield, B. A. (1987). The contributions of child and caretaker to referential and expressive language. *Applied Psycholinguistics, 8,* 267–268.

Goldfield, B. A. (1990). Pointing, naming, and talk about objects: referential behavior in children and mothers. *First Language, 10*, 231–242.

Gopnik, A. (1988). Three types of early word. *First Language, 8*, 49–70.

Gopnik, A., & Choi, S. (1990). Do linguistic differences lead to cognitive differences? A crosslinguistic study of semantic and cognitive development. *First Language, 10*, 199–215.

Gopnik, A., & Choi, S. (1995). Names, relational words, and cognitive development in English and Korean speakers: Nouns are not always learned before verbs. In M. Tomasello & W. Merriman (Eds.), *Beyond names for things: Young children's acquisition of verbs* (pp. 63–80). Hillsdale, NJ: Lawrence Erlbaum Associates.

Gopnik, A., & Meltzoff, A. (1987). Early semantic developments and their relationship to object permanence, means-end understanding, and categorization. In K. E. Nelson & A. van Kleeck (Eds.), *Children's language* (Vol. 6, pp. 191–212). Hillsdale, NJ: Lawrence Erlbaum Associates.

Gopnik, A., & Meltzoff, A. (1993). Words and thoughts in infancy: The specificity hypothesis and the development of categorization and naming. In C. Rovee-Collier & L. Lipsett (Eds.), *Advances in infancy research* (pp. 223–255). Norwood, NJ: Ablex.

Guillaume, P. (1927). Les débuts de la phrase dans le langage de l'enfant. *Journal de Psychologie, 24*, 1–25 (Trans. in C. A. Ferguson & D. I. Slobin (Eds.), *Studies of child language development* (pp. 522–540). New York: Rinehart, & Winston, 1973).

Hampson, J. (1989). *Elements of style: Maternal and child contributions to referential and expressive styles of language acquisition.* Unpublished doctoral dissertation, City University of New York.

Hardy-Brown, K. (1983). Universals and individual differences: Disentangling two approaches to the study of language acquisition. *Developmental Psychology, 19*, 610–624.

Hart, E. (1991). Input frequency and order of children's first words. *First Language, 11*, 289–300.

Hayashi, M. (1994). *A longitudinal investigation in bilingual children.* Unpublished doctoral dissertation, University of Aarhus.

Huttenlocher, J., Haight, W., Bryk, A., Seltzer, M., & Lyons, T. (1991). Early vocabulary growth: Relation to language input and gender. *Developmental Psychology, 17*, 236–248.

Hyams, N. (1986). *Language acquisition and the theory of parameters.* Dordrecht: Reidel.

Imedadze, N., & Tuite, K. (1992). The acquisition of Georgian. In D. I. Slobin (Ed.), *The crosslinguistic study of language acquisition: Vol. 3* (pp. 39–109). Hillsdale, NJ: Lawrence Erlbaum Associates.

Indefrey, P. (1993, July). The acquisition of weak noun declension in German. Paper presented at the Sixth International Congress for the Study of Child Language, Trieste, Italy.

Johnston, J. R. (1985). Cognitive prerequisites: The evidence from children learning English. In D. I. Slobin (Ed.), *The crosslinguistic study of language acquisition: Vol. 2. Theoretical issues* (pp. 961–1004). Hillsdale, NJ: Lawrence Erlbaum Associates.

Jordens, P. (1990). The acquisition of verb placement in Dutch and German. *Linguistics, 28*, 1407–1448.

Karmiloff-Smith, A. (1992). *Beyond modularity: A developmental perspective on cognitive science.* Cambridge, MA: MIT Press.

Kim, Y. (1997). The acquisition of Korean. In D. I. Slobin (Ed.), *The crosslinguistic study of language acquisition: Vol. 4.* Mahwah, NJ: Lawrence Erlbaum Associates.

Klein, D. (1980). *Expressive and referential communication in children's early language development: The relationship to mothers' communicative styles.* Unpublished Doctoral dissertation, Michigan State University.

Kucera, H., & Francis, W. (1967). *Computational analysis of present-day American English.* Providence: Brown University Press.

Kuczaj, S. A., & Maratsos, M. P. (1983). The initial verbs of yes-no questions: A different kind of general grammatical category. *Developmental Psychology, 19*, 440–443.

Labov, W. (1976). Is the black English vernacular a separate system? In W. Labov, *Language in the inner city* (pp. 36–64). Philadelphia: University of Pennsylvania Press.

Levy, Y. (1988). The nature of early language: Evidence from the development of Hebrew morphology. In Y. Levy, I. Schlesinger, & M. D. S. Braine (Eds.), *Categories and processes in language acquisition* (pp. 73–98). Hillsdale, NJ: Lawrence Erlbaum Associates.

Lieven, E. V. M. (1978). Conversations between mothers and their young children: Individual differences and their possible implications for the study of language learning. In C. E. Snow & N. Waterson (Eds.), *The development of communication: social and pragmatic factors in language acquisition* (pp. 173–187). Chichester: Wiley.

Lieven, E. V. M. (1980). Different routes to multiple-word combinations? *Papers and Reports on Child Language Development, 19*, 34–44.

Lieven, E. V. M. (1994). Crosslinguistic and crosscultural aspects of language addressed to children. In C. Gallaway & B. J. Richards (Eds.), *Input and interaction in language acquisition* (pp. 56–73). Cambridge: Cambridge University Press.

Lieven, E. V. M., & Pine, J. M. (1991, July). *Breaking down and building up—The role of distributional frequency in early multiword utterances*. Paper presented at Workshop on Mechanisms of Cognitive and Linguistic Change, University of Barcelona.

Lieven, E. V. M., Pine, J. M., & Barnes, H. D. (1992). Individual differences in early vocabulary development: Redefining the referential-expressive distinction. *Journal of Child Language, 19*, 287–310.

Lieven, E. V. M., Pine, J. M., & Baldwin, G. (1997). Distributional learning and the development of grammar in early multi-word speech. *Journal of Child Language, 24*.

Lloyd, E. (1987, March). *Child characteristics and the referential-expressive distinction in early language*. Paper presented at the Child Language Seminar, York, UK.

Locke, J. L. (1995). Development of the capacity for spoken language. In P. Fletcher, & B. MacWhinney (Eds.), *The handbook of child language* (pp. 278–302). Oxford: Blackwell.

McCune-Nicolich, L. (1981). Toward symbolic functioning: Structure of early pretend games and potential parallels with language. *Child Development, 52*, 785–797.

MacWhinney, B. (1974). *How Hungarian children learn to speak*. Unpublished doctoral dissertation, University of California, Berkeley.

MacWhinney, B. (1985). Hungarian language acquisition as an exemplification of a general model of grammatical development. In D. I. Slobin (Ed.), *The crosslinguistic study of language acquisition: Vol. 2. Theoretical issues* (pp. 1069–1156). Hillsdale NJ: Lawrence Erlbaum Associates.

Maratsos, M. (1988). The acquisition of formal word classes. In Y. Levy, I. M. Schlesinger, & M. Braine (Eds.), *Categories and processes in language acquisition* (pp. 31–44). Hillsdale, NJ: Lawrence Erlbaum Associates.

Maratsos, M., & Kuczaj, S. (1976). Preschool children's use of not and n't: Not is not (isn't n't). *Papers and Reports on Child Language Development, 12*, 157–168.

Markman, E. (1989). *Categorization and naming in children*. Cambridge, MA: MIT Press.

Mills, A. E. (1985). The acquisition of German. In D. I. Slobin (Ed.), *The crosslinguistic study of language acquisition: Vol. 1. The data* (pp. 141–254). Hillsdale, NJ: Lawrence Erlbaum Associates.

Nelson, K. (1973). Structure and strategy in learning to talk. *Monographs of the Society for Research in Child Development, 38*(1–2, Serial No. 149), 1–135.

Nelson, K. (1975). The nominal shift in semantic-syntactic development. *Cognitive Psychology, 7*, 461–479.

Nelson, K. (1981). Individual differences in language development: Implications for development and language. *Developmental Psychology, 17*, 170–187.

Newport, E. L., & Meier, R. P. (1985). The acquisition of American sign language. In D. I. Slobin (Ed.), *The crosslinguistic study of language acquisition: Vol. 1. The data* (pp. 881–938). Hillsdale, NJ: Lawrence Erlbaum Associates.

Ochs, E. (1985). Variation and error: A sociolinguistic approach to language acquisition in Samoa. In D. I. Slobin (Ed.), *The crosslinguistic study of language acquisition: Vol. 1. The data* (pp. 783–838). Hillsdale, NJ: Lawrence Erlbaum Associates.

Okubo, A. (1980). Gengo shuutoku no kojinsa-kyoomai ni arawareta chigai. *Yoonen Jidai, 10*, 22–31.

Olson, S. L., Bayles, K., & Bates, E. (1986). Mother child interaction and children's speech progress: A longitudinal study of the first two years. *Merrill Palmer Quarterly, 32*, 1–20.

Pea, R. D. (1979). The development of negation in early child language. In D. R. Olson (Ed.), *The social foundations of language and thought: Essays in honour of Jerome S. Bruner* (pp. 156–186). New York: W. W. Norton.

Peters, A. M. (1977). Language learning strategies: Does the whole equal the sum of the parts? *Language, 53*, 560–573.

Peters, A. M. (1983). *The units of language acquisition.* Cambridge: Cambridge University Press.

Peters, A. M. (1985). Language segmentation: Operating principles for the perception and analysis of language. In D. I. Slobin (Ed.), *The crosslinguistic study of language acquisition: Vol. 2. Theoretical issues* (pp. 1029–1068). Hillsdale, NJ: Lawrence Erlbaum Associates.

Peters, A. M., & Menn, L. (1993). False starts and filler syllables: Ways to learn grammatical morphemes. *Language, 69*, 742–777.

Peters, A. (1997). Language typology, individual differences and the acquisition of grammatical morphemes. In D. I. Slobin (Ed.), *The crosslinguistic study of language acquisition: Vol. 5. Expanding the contexts.* Hillsdale, NJ: Lawrence Erlbaum Associates.

Pine, J. M. (1994). The language of primary caregivers. In C. Gallaway & B. J. Richards (Eds.), *Input and interaction in language acquisition* (pp. 15–37). Cambridge: Cambridge University Press.

Pine, J. M. (1995). Variation in vocabulary development as a function of birth order. *Child Development, 66*, 272–281.

Pine, J. M., & Lieven, E. V. (1990). Referential style at thirteen months: Why age-defined cross-sectional measures are inappropriate for the study of strategy differences in early language development. *Journal of Child Language, 17*, 625–631.

Pine, J. M., & Lieven, E. V. (1993). Reanalysing rote-learned phrases: Individual differences in the transition to multi-word speech. *Journal of Child Language, 20*, 551–571.

Pine, J. M., & Lieven, E. V. (1997). Slot and frame patterns and the development of the determiner category. *Applied Psycholinguistics.*

Pine, J. M., Lieven, E. V., & Rowland, C. (1997). Stylistic variation at the 'single-word' stage: Relations between maternal speech characteristics and children's vocabulary composition and usage. *Child Development.*

Pinker, S. (1989). *Learnability and cognition.* Cambridge MA: MIT Press.

Plomin, R., & DeFries, J. C. (1985). *Origins of individual differences in infancy.* Orlando, FL: Academic Press.

Plunkett, K. (1986). Learning strategies in two Danish children's language development. *Scandinavian Journal of Psychology, 27*, 64–73.

Plunkett, K., & Strömqvist, S. (1992). The acquisition of Scandinavian languages. In D. I. Slobin (Ed.), *The crosslinguistic study of language acquisition: Vol. 3* (pp. 457–556). Hillsdale, NJ: Lawrence Erlbaum Associates.

Pye, C. (1986). Quiché Mayan speech to children. *Journal of Child Language, 13*, 85–100.

Pye, C. (1992). The acquisition of K'iche' Maya. In D. I. Slobin (Ed.), *The crosslinguistic study of language acquisition: Vol. 3* (pp. 557–638). Hillsdale, NJ: Lawrence Erlbaum Associates.

Pye, C., Frome Loeb, D., & Pao, Y. (1995, April). *The acquisition of breaking and cutting.* Paper presented at the Stanford Child Language Research Forum, Stanford University.

Radford, A. (1990). *Syntactic theory and the acquisition of English syntax.* Oxford: Basil Blackwell.

Radulović, L. (1975). *Acquisition of language: Studies of Dubrovnik children.* Unpublished doctoral dissertation, University of California, Berkeley.

Räisänen, A. (1975). Havaintoja lastenkielestä [English summary: Observations on child language]. *Virittäjä, 79*, 251–266.

Ramer, A. (1976). Syntactic styles in emerging language *Journal of Child Language, 3*, 49–62.

Roeper, T. W. (1973). Theoretical implications of word order, topicalization, and inflections in German language acquisition. In C. A. Ferguson & D. I. Slobin (Eds.), *Studies of child language development* (pp. 541–554). New York: Holt, Reinhart & Winston.

Savić, S., & Mikeš, M. (1974). Noun Phrase expansion in child language. *Journal of Child Language, 1*, 107–110.

Schieffelin, B. B. (1985). The acquisition of Kaluli. In D. I. Slobin (Ed.), *The crosslinguistic study of language acquisition: Vol. 1. The data* (pp. 525–594). Hillsdale, NJ: Lawrence Erlbaum Associates.

Schlesinger, I. (1982). *Steps to language: toward a theory of native language acquisition.* Hillsdale, NJ: Lawrence Erlbaum Associates.

Serra Raventos, M., Torrens Garcia, V., & Sole Planas, R. M. (1990). *The role of individual differences in early syntax.* Unpublished manuscript, University of Barcelona, Spain.

Shore, C. M. (1995). *Individual differences in language development.* Thousand Oaks, CA: Sage.

Simonetti, M. Z. (1980, August). *The emergence of determiners in Portuguese: A case study.* Paper presented at the Summer Meeting, Linguistic Society of America, University of New Mexico, Albuquerque.

Slobin, D. I. (1973). Cognitive prerequisites for the development of grammar. In C. A. Ferguson & D. I. Slobin (Eds.), *Studies of child language development* (pp. 175–208). New York: Holt, Rinehart & Winston.

Slobin, D. I. (1985). Crosslinguistic evidence for the Language-Making Capacity. In D. I. Slobin (Ed.), *The crosslinguistic study of language acquisition: Vol. 2. Theoretical issues* (pp. 1157–1256). Hillsdale, NJ: Lawrence Erlbaum Associates.

Slobin, D. I. (1986). The acquisition and use of relative clauses in Turkish and Indo-European languages. In D. I. Slobin & K. Zimmer (Eds.), *Studies in Turkish linguistics* (pp. 273–294). Amsterdam: John Benjamins.

Smoczyńska, M. (1985). The acquisition of Polish. In D. I. Slobin (Ed.), *The crosslinguistic study of language acquisition, Vol. 1: The data* (pp. 595–686). Hillsdale, NJ: Lawrence Erlbaum Associates.

Snow, C. E. (1983). Saying it again: The role of expanded and deferred imitations in language acquisition. In K. E. Nelson (Ed.), *Children's language* (Vol. 4, pp. 29–58). Hillsdale, NJ: Lawrence Erlbaum Associates.

Starr, S. (1975). The relationship of single words to two-word sentences. *Child Development, 46*, 701–708.

Stephany, U. (1997). The acquisition of Greek. In D. I. Slobin (Ed.), *The crosslinguistic study of language acquisition: Vol. 4.* Mahwah, NJ: Lawrence Erlbaum Associates.

Tager-Flusberg, H., de Villiers, J. S., & Hakuta, K. (1982). The development of sentence coordination. In S. A. Kuczaj (Ed.), *Language development: Syntax and semantics* (Vol. 1, pp. 201–244). Hillsdale, NJ: Lawrence Erlbaum Associates.

Tanouye, E. K. (1979). The acquisition of verbs in Japanese children. *Papers and Reports on Child Language Development, 17*, 49–56.

Tardif, T. Z. (1994). *Adult-to-child speech and language acquisition in Mandarin Chinese.* Unpublished doctoral dissertation, Yale University, New Haven.

Tardif, T. Z. (1996). Nouns are not always learned before verbs: Evidence from Mandarin speakers' early vocabulary. *Developmental Psychology, 32*(3), 492–504.

Tomasello, M. (1992). *First verbs: A case study of early grammatical development.* Cambridge: Cambridge University Press.

Tomasello, M. (1995). Pragmatic contexts for early verb learning. In M. Tomasello & W. E. Merriman (Eds.), *Beyond names for things: Young children's acquisition of verbs* (pp. 115–146). Hillsdale, NJ: Lawrence Erlbaum Associates.

Torrens, V. (1992). *Individual differences in the learning of categorial rules.* Paper presented at the Fifth European Conference on Developmental Psychology, Seville, Spain.

van Geert, P. (1991). A dynamic systems model of cognitive and language growth. *Psychological Review, 98*, 3–53.

Van Valin, R. (1991). Functionalist linguistic theory and language acquisition. *First Language, 31*, 7–40.

Vihman, M. M. (1982). The acquisition of morphology by a bilingual child: A whole word approach. *Applied Psycholinguistics, 3*, 141–160.

Vihman, M. M. (1982). Formulas in first and second language acquisition. In L. Obfer & L. Menn (Eds.), *Exceptional language and linguistics* (pp. 261–284). New York: Academic Press.

Vihman, M. M., & Greenlee, M. (1987). Individual differences in phonological development: ages one and three years. *Journal of Speech and Hearing Research, 30*, 503–521.

Vihman, M. M., Kay, E., de Boysson-Bardies, B., Durand, C., & Sundberg, U. (1994). External sources of individual differences? A crosslinguistic analysis of the phonetics of mothers' speech to 1-year-old children. *Developmental Psychology, 30*, 651–662.

de Villiers, J. G., & de Villiers, P. A. (1985). The acquisition of English. In D. I. Slobin (Ed.), *The crosslinguistic study of language acquisition: Vol. 1. The data* (pp. 27–140). Hillsdale, NJ: Lawrence Erlbaum Associates.

Wiest, R. M., Wysocka, H., Witkowska-Stadnik, K., Buczowska, E., & Konieczna, E. (1984). The defective tense hypothesis: on the emergence of tense and aspect in child Polish. *Journal of Child Language, 11*, 347–374.

Whitman, J., Lee, K.-O., & Lust, B. (1991). Continuity of the principles of Universal Grammar in first language acquisition. *NELS (North Eastern Linguistics Society), 21*.

Wilson, B., & Peters, A. M. (1988). What are you cooking on a hot? Movement constraints in the speech of a three year old blind child. *Language, 64*, 249–273.

Wimmer, H., & Perner, J. (1983). Beliefs about beliefs: Representation and constraining function of wrong beliefs in young children's understanding of deception. *Cognition, 13*, 103–128.

Wong Fillmore, L. (1979). Individual differences in second language acquisition. In C. J. Fillmore, D. Kempler, & W. Wang (Eds.), *Individual differences in language ability and language behavior* (pp. 203–228). New York: Academic Press.

5 The Origins of Grammaticizable Notions: Beyond the Individual Mind

Dan I. Slobin
University of California at Berkeley

Human languages, broadly speaking, provide two kinds of meaningful elements, using both to create grammatical constructions. On the one hand, there are morphemes that make reference to the objects and events of experience, and on the other, there are morphemes that relate these bits of experience to each other and to the discourse perspectives of the speaker. Linguistic theories of all stripes honor this duality, using such distinctions as "material content" versus "relation" (Sapir, 1921/1958), "lexical item" versus "grammatical item" (Lyons, 1968), or, most commonly, "content word" versus "function word" (or, to include both free and bound morphemes, "functor"). Typically, the first class includes nouns and verbs, and usually also adjectives; the second class includes free morphemes such as conjunctions and prepositions, and bound morphemes such as affixes marking categories of number, case, tense, and so forth.

Two important characteristics of the latter class have stimulated a large amount of theoretical innovation and debate: (1) functors express a limited and universal set of meanings ("grammaticizable notions"), and (2) functor classes are small and closed, while content word classes are large and open. The first has led to proposals that the set of meanings is, in some sense, "prespecified" for language; the second has led to proposals that this collection of morphemes plays a critical role in both the acquisition and processing of language. Furthermore, many attempts have been made to relate these two "design features" of language:

- Theorists with a nativist bent—including both generative and cognitive linguists—equip the mind/brain with predispositions to relate particular types of meaning to grammatical elements and syntactic constructions. Such predispositions make it possible for the child to crack the code and for expert language-users to successfully parse sentences. (This position, for example, can be found in Bickerton, 1981; Pinker, 1984; Slobin, 1985.) On such accounts, the relations between the two design features—limited sets of meanings and limited sets of functors—are facts about the language module or language-making capacity, perhaps in relation to other modules or capacities, but not in need of developmental explanation.

- Theorists more concerned with language USE—functionalists—point to recurrent diachronic processes that inevitably result in small, closed classes of grammatical morphemes with their characteristic meanings across languages. On these accounts, this design feature of language cannot be attributed to the mental structure of the individual alone.

- And further, arching above both of these attempts to pin down the origins of grammatical meanings, Whorfians make their case on the basis of striking diversity in the array of notions that receive grammaticized expression across languages.

Regardless of the theoretical implications of these phenomena, everyone agrees that grammaticizable notions are "special." Here I want to examine the consequences for acquisition theory that flow from taking grammaticizable notions as special in one way or another. If it is supposed that the mental lexicon consists of two classes of items, with two distinct kinds of meanings, then there are two separate semantic tasks for the learner. Further, if one class draws on prespecified meanings, its acquisition consists of procedures of lookup and elimination, while the acquisition of meanings in the other class requires some kind of more general learning abilities. I will propose, however, that such theorists—including myself—have erred in attributing the origins of structure to the mind of the child, rather than to the interpersonal communicative and cognitive processes that everywhere and always shape language in its peculiar expression of content and relation. As Sapir put it: "language struggles towards two poles of linguistic expression—material content and relation"; but he went on to add: "these poles tend to be connected by a long series of transitional concepts" (1921/1949, p. 109). I will argue that the cline between the two poles, when properly understood, makes it unlikely that the child comes to the task of language acquisition prepared with the relevant categories—either semantic or syntactic—thereby challenging my own previous assumptions and those of both generative and cognitive linguists. But first, some necessary preliminaries.

1. GRAMMATICALLY SPECIFIED NOTIONS

Again, we can turn to Sapir for a lucid exposition of the range of grammatically specified notions. His classic presentation of crosslinguistic variation is worth quoting in full (Sapir, 1924/1958, pp. 157ff). This is not only one of the clearest statements of linguistic relativity, but it also sounds the *Leitmotif* of this chapter—namely, that there is no direct and universal mapping between the ways in which human beings experience events and express them in language.

> The natural or, at any rate, the naïve thing is to assume that when we wish to communicate a certain idea or impression, we make something like a rough and rapid inventory of the objective elements and relations involved in it, that such an inventory or analysis is quite inevitable, and that our linguistic task consists merely of the finding of the particular words and groupings of words that correspond to the terms of the objective analysis. Thus, when we observe an object of the type that we call a "stone" moving through space towards the earth, we involuntarily analyze the phenomenon into two concrete notions, that of a stone and that of an act of falling, and, relating these two notions to each other by certain formal methods proper to English, we declare that "the stone falls." We assume, naïvely enough, that this is about the only analysis that can properly be made. And yet, if we look into the way that other languages take to express this very simple kind of impression, we soon realize how much may be added to, subtracted from, or rearranged in our own form of expression without materially altering our report of the physical fact.

In German and in French we are compelled to assign "stone" to a gender category—perhaps the Freudians can tell us why this object is masculine in the one language, feminine in the other; in Chippewa we cannot express ourselves without bringing in the apparently irrelevant fact that a stone is an inanimate object. If we find gender beside the point, the Russians may wonder why we consider it necessary to specify in every case whether a stone, or any other object for that matter, is conceived in a definite or an indefinite manner, why the difference between "the stone" and "a stone" matters. "Stone falls" is good enough for Lenin, as it was good enough for Cicero. And if we find barbarous the neglect of the distinction as to definiteness, the Kwakiutl Indian of British Columbia may sympathize with us but wonder why we do not go a step further and indicate in some way whether the stone is visible or invisible to the speaker at the moment of speaking and whether it is nearest to the speaker, the person addressed, or some third party. "That would no doubt sound fine in Kwakiutl, but we are too busy!" And yet we insist on expressing the singularity of the falling object, where the Kwakiutl Indian, differing from the Chippewa, can generalize and make a statement which would apply equally well to one or several stones. Moreover, he need not specify the time of the fall. The Chinese get on with a minimum of explicit formal statement and content themselves with a frugal "stone fall."

These differences of analysis, one may object, are merely formal; they do not invalidate the necessity of the fundamental concrete analysis of the situation into "stone" and what the stone does, which in this case is "fall." But this necessity, which we feel so strongly, is an illusion. In the Nootka language the combined impression of a stone falling is quite differently analyzed. The stone need not be specifically referred to, but a single word, a verb form, may be used which is in practice not essentially more ambiguous than our English sentence. This verb form consists of two main elements, the first indicating general movement or position of a stone or stonelike object, while the second refers to downward direction. We can get some hint of the feeling of the Nootka word if we assume the existence of an intransitive verb "to stone," referring to the position or movement of a stonelike object. Then our sentence, "The stone falls," may be reassembled into something like "It stones down." In this type of expression the thing-quality of the stone is implied in the generalized verbal element "to stone," while the specific kind of motion which is given us in experience when a stone falls is conceived as separable into a generalized notion of the movement of a class of objects and a more specific one of direction. In other words, while Nootka has no difficulty whatever in describing the fall of a stone, it has no verb that truly corresponds to our "fall." (Reprinted with permission)

Sapir's little exercise reveals that components of a situation can be differentially allocated to nouns and verbs, and that particular general notions cluster around each of these parts of speech. In his examples, nouns can be grammatically marked for various types of class membership (gender, animacy), number, and discourse perspective (definiteness); verbs can be grammatically marked for tense, grounds of evidence, relations of discourse participants, direction of movement, and type of moving figure. These are the types of notions that are at issue. It turns out that they constitute a peculiarly limited and apparently universal set of possible semantic distinctions.

1.1. Conceptual Restrictions on Grammaticizable Notions

This problem has been explored in depth by Leonard Talmy (1978, 1983, 1985, 1988). He has been struck by the finding that many notions seem to be excluded from grammatical expression. Thus no known language has grammatical morphemes indicating the color of an object referred to by a noun; nor are there verb inflections indicating whether an event occurred in the light or the dark, or on a hot or a cold day. In his most extensive study, Talmy (1985) lists conceptual domains which are typically realized as verb inflections or particles, and contrasts this list with a collection of domains which are apparently not amenable to grammaticization.[2] The two domains are listed in (1a) and (1b) (extracted from Talmy, 1985, pp. 126–138).

(1a) *Grammaticizable Domains (Marked on Verbs)*[3]
    tense (temporal relation to speech event)
    aspect and phase (temporal distribution of an event)
    causativity
    valence/voice (e.g., active, passive)
    mood (e.g., indicative, subjunctive, optative)
    speech act type (e.g., declarative, interrogative, imperative)
    personation (action on self vs. other)
    person (1st, 2nd, etc.)
    number of event participants (e.g., singular, dual plural)
    gender of participant
    social/interpersonal status of interlocutors (e.g., intimate, formal)
    speaker's evidence for making claim (e.g., direct experience, hearsay)
    positive/negative status of an event's existence

    manner of action (e.g., run, float, fly)
    purpose ("in order to")

---

[2]At present there are two roughly synonymous terms in the literature: "grammaticization" and "grammaticalization." I prefer the former, shorter form, but nothing hangs on the difference. Theorists working within the same overall theoretical framework have not agreed. It seems that American researchers prefer "grammaticization" (e.g., Wallace Chafe, Marianne Mithun, Joan Bybee and her associates), while those of European origin prefer "grammaticalization" (e.g., Elizabeth Traugott, Paul Hopper, Bernd Heine and his associates).

[3]The first group, above the line in (1a), can be expressed as either inflections or verb particles ("satellites"); the second group only by satellites to the verb. This suggests that the domains in the first group are more highly grammaticized. I will refer to all of the domains in (1a) as "grammaticizable." Note, also, that Talmy's analysis applies mainly to verb morphology, and within that syntactic domain, primarily to semantic categories that are expressed by affixes in inflecting and agglutinating language types.

result
figure participating in event (e.g., person, liquid)
path of movement (e.g., entering, crossing)
ground of movement (source/goal of motion event)
combination of path and ground (e.g., into an areal enclosure, down onto the ground)
direction (e.g., toward/away from speaker)
distribution of a participant (e.g., separately, together)
speaker's attitude (e.g., approval, disapproval)

(1b) *Conceptual Domains* NOT *Amenable to Grammaticization*[4]
color of an event participant (?)
symmetry of an event participant
spatial setting (e.g., indoors, outside)
speaker's state of mind (e.g., bored, interested)
relation to comparable events (e.g., 'only', 'even', 'instead') (?)
rate (e.g., slowly, quickly) (?)
degree of realization (e.g., 'almost', 'just barely') (?)
temporal setting (e.g., in the morning) (?)

We are faced here with the first major question about grammaticizable notions: Why are some conceptual domains apparently excluded from grammatical expression? Talmy goes on to raise a second major issue: Within grammaticizable domains, there are striking restrictions in the number and type of distinctions that are grammatically marked. He has explored this question most fully with regard to restrictions on the notions that can be CONFLATED in a single grammatical morpheme. The most widely cited examples concern locative terms, and these will figure in some of the acquisition issues discussed later. For example, an English preposition like *through* indicates motion that proceeds in some medium (*through the grass/water/crowd*), but does not indicate the shape or contour of the path (e.g., zigzag, direct, circling), the nature of the medium, or the precise extent of the path. Another type of restriction suggests that grammar is concerned with RELATIVE, rather than quantified distinctions. For example, the deictic demonstratives *this* and *that* are neutral with regard to magnitude. One can just as well compare "*this* leaf and *that* leaf" as "*this* galaxy and *that* galaxy." Talmy (1988, p. 171) summarizes across numerous examples to conclude that

---

[4]The items in (1b) followed by a parenthetical question mark are in dispute. Elizabeth Traugott and David Wilkins have pointed out to me that these domains do receive grammatical expression in some languages. In addition, Balthasar Bickel (personal communication, 1996) notes that in Belhare there are two forms of the specific article, one reserved for color terms (e.g., 'the:COLOR red house' vs. 'the:NON-COLOR big house'). Note, however, that this is not a grammaticization of particular color distinctions, but simply COLOR versus NON-COLOR. It should also be noted that Talmy's list in (1b) is based on the grammaticization of conceptual domains as marked on VERBS (inflections or satellites), while the counterexamples seemed to be based most often on other sorts of grammatical expression. In any event, Talmy's list of non-grammaticizable domains is not the last word.

the notions excluded from grammatical expression "involve Euclidean–geometric concepts—for example, fixed distance, size, contour, and angle—as well as quantified measure, and various particularities of a quantity: in sum, characteristics that are absolute or fixed." By contrast, grammaticizable notions are "topological, topology-like, or relativistic." He offers the following two lists. (For details, see the cited references.) I will call them QUALITIES to distinguish them from the DOMAINS listed in(1a/b).

(2a) *Topological/Topology-Like and Grammaticizable Qualities.* point, linear extent, locatedness, within, region, side, partition, singularity, plurality, same, different, "adjacency" of points, one-to-one correspondence, pattern of distribution

(2b) *Non-Topological and Non-Grammaticizable Qualities.* material, motion, medium, precise or quantified space or time

Finally, Talmy (1988) notes a series of restrictions that impose a limited schematization of semantic content for any grammatically specified notion. These restrictions apply to both nouns and verbs. For example, Talmy introduces the term "plexity" to characterize the distinction of number. Thus a "uniplex" noun becomes "multiplex" by pluralization (e.g., *bird/birds*) and a uniplex verb can become multiplex by verbal inflection and/or auxiliary (e.g., *sigh/keep sighing*). Talmy calls these CATEGORIES OF GRAMMATICALLY SPECIFIED NOTIONS. In the course of a lengthy analysis (Talmy, 1988, pp. 173–192), he lists the following types of distinction:

(3) *Categories of Grammatically Specified Notions*
dimension (continuous/discrete)
plexity (uniplex/multiplex)
boundedness (unbounded/bounded)
dividedness (particulate/continuous)
disposition (combinations of the above)
extension (point, bounded extent, unbounded extent)
distribution (one-way non-resettable, one-way resettable, full-cycle, multiplex, steady-state, gradient)
axiality (relation to border)
perspectival mode (long-range/close-up; moving/static)
level of synthesis (Gestalt/componential)
level of exemplarity (full complement/single exemplar)

Putting together the various parts of Talmy's analysis—DOMAINS, QUALITIES, and CATEGORIES of grammaticizable notions—we can more precisely characterize the meanings of grammatical morphemes such as those enumerated by Sapir. To take just one example, consider the sentence *The boy-s were runn-ing in-to the house*. The grammatical elements in boldface point to particular domains and categories within those domains, while the lexical items *boy*, *run*, and *house* provide the items of content that are related by the grammatical frame. The article *the*, together with the plural *-s*, categorizes DISPOSITION of the actors as MULTI-PLEX and PARTICULATE (as opposed to *Boys were running*, where the absence of the article categorizes the actors as MULTIPLEX and CONTINUOUS). The plural past-tense *were* categorizes the reported event in the domains of TENSE(PAST) and NUMBER(PLURAL), while the progressive *-ing* categorizes ASPECT (PROGRES-SIVE). The form *in-to* schematizes PATH and GROUND OF MOVEMENT as directed across a border into an enclosed, bounded extent. The quality of the path is topological: simply movement across a partition to within a region. (The two uses of *the* also situate the sentence in a discourse context of presupposed information—that is, the speaker assumes that the listener has specific referents in mind for *boys* and *house*. Talmy's analysis does not include the pragmatic functions of grammatical morphemes. The interpersonal domain must also figure heavily in any account of the origins and functions of these items.)

To return to the guiding question: Why should precisely THESE types of notions receive grammatical expression across the languages of the world? Talmy offers two kinds of accounts. One is presented in cognitive terms: "The grammatical specifications in a sentence . . . provide a conceptual framework or, imagistically, a skeletal structure or scaffolding, for the conceptual material that is lexically specified" (1988, p. 166). That is, the grammatical elements—functors and syntactic construction types—provide a schematization of experience. The cognitive argument is that this particular schematization is a consequence of schematization at a nonlinguistic conceptual level. For example, Talmy (1978, 1983, 1988) proposes parallels between structuring in visual perception and in language. Landau and Jackendoff (1993) make a similar proposal, tying the limited set of locative prepositions across languages to a "sub-module" of the brain specialized for object location: "Our hypothesis is that there are so few prepositions because the class of spatial relations available to be expressed in language—the notions prepositions can mean—is extremely limited" (p. 224).

1.2. The Nativist Proposal

Such parallels between cognitive domains, however, do not explain the linguistic division of labor between content words and functors, nor do they explain all of the peculiarities of grammaticizable notions. For Talmy, and other linguists, the division of labor is apparently taken as given, as is the set of grammaticizable notions. The second type of account is thus nativistic (Talmy, 1988):

> A fundamental design feature of language is that it has two subsystems which can be designated as the grammatical and the lexical. . . . [A]cross the spectrum of languages, the grammatical elements that are encountered, taken together, specify a crucial set of concepts. (p. 165)

While each language has to some extent a different set of grammatical specifications, there is great commonality across languages, so one can posit that each set is drawn from an innate inventory of concepts available for serving a structuring function in language. (p. 197)

The same position is taken by Bickerton, in his proposal of an innate bioprogram for language, although based on a different sort of semantic and syntactic analysis (1981, p. 205):

But when we consider that the same semantic factors are marked grammatically over and over again across the range of human languages, that in effect languages select out of a very short list of semantic primes the ones that they are going to mark ... it becomes more reasonable to assume that the child has advance knowledge of the contents of the category "grammatically-markable semantic feature."

Such "advance knowledge," of course, would facilitate the acquisition task. I made such a proposal in 1979 (Slobin, 1979, p. 16):

The "topology-like and relativistic notions" that Talmy is beginning to discover look like notions that might be salient to a child at the end of the stage of sensorimotor cognition. This match between grammar and cognition may aid the child in delimiting the range of possible functions of grammatical elements in the language he or she hears. Indeed, such an approach to grammatical universals may cast light on what Chomsky (1965, p. 27) has called "the initial assumptions concerning the nature of language that the child brings to language learning"—i.e., that language encodes in its grammar certain types of notions and not others.

In later work on "operating principles" for acquisition, I suggested "that such notions must constitute a privileged set for the child, and that they are embodied in the child's conceptions of 'prototypical events' that are mapped onto the first grammatical forms universally" (Slobin, 1985, pp. 1173f). The proposal was that the division between the two classes of grammatical morphemes reflected a cognitive division between concrete and relational concepts, and that the relational concepts were, to some extent, already in place at the beginning of grammatical acquisition (whether on the basis of an "innate list" or arising from prior cognitive development).

A similar position was taken by Pinker (1984) in his proposal that "the child can extract ... the potentially grammatically relevant semantic features of the sentence participants (their number, person, sex, etc.) and of the proposition as a whole (tense, aspect, modality, etc.)" (p. 30). He, too, was agnostic about the prelinguistic origins of such features: "the theory is, of course, mute as to whether these cognitive distinctions are themselves innate or learned, as long as the child is capable of making them" (p. 363). The position continues in *Learnability and cognition* (Pinker, 1989, pp. 254f):

Consider the target in the learning of an inflection, namely, a list of features ...
The features are drawn from a finite universal set of possible grammaticizable
features. Each one has a conceptual or perceptual correlate: the child can determine,
for example, whether the referent of a noun in a particular context is singular or
plural, human or nonhuman. When attempting to learn a given inflection from its
use in a given utterance, the child samples a subset of features with their currently
true values from the universal pool.

1.3. Accessibility Hierarchies

The purpose of these proposals was to clear the way for "operating principles"
or "procedures" to work out inflectional paradigms and other form-function
mappings. However, such procedures also run into the problems that the set of
grammaticizable features, although limited, is still large and many of the features
are not relevant to the particular language being acquired. The solution here was
to appeal to a pre-established ranking of notions with regard to their applicability
to grammar. Again, the idea comes from Talmy (1988, p. 197):

> It can be observed that grammatically specified concepts range cross-linguistically
> from ones that are of extremely widespread (perhaps universal) occurrence and of
> broad application within a language, down to ones appearing in a scant few
> languages with minimal application. Thus the innate inventory of available
> structuring notions that is posited here seems to be GRADUATED as to significance
> for the language faculty (cf. the tabular listing of grammatical notions in Talmy
> [1985, pp. 126ff] [=(1a) "*Grammaticizable Domains*" above]).

This observation finds its way into learning theories in the form of an accessibility
hierarchy. For example (Pinker, 1984, pp. 170f):

> [I]n determining which notions are encoded in a language's morphology, the child
> is faced with a formidable search problem.... [B]y imposing a weighting on the
> child's hypotheses, one could account for the large disparities in the prevalence of
> various grammatical encodings in the world's languages, and in the speed of
> acquisition of various encodings by children.

Bowerman has made an explicit prediction about the relation between crosslinguistic frequency and ease of acquisition (1985, p. 1306):

> One intriguing possibility is that the relative accessibility for children of alternative
> schemes for partitioning meaning in a given conceptual domain is correlated with
> the FREQUENCY WITH WHICH THESE SCHEMES ARE INSTANTIATED IN THE LANGUAGES
> OF THE WORLD. ... It is plausible that relative frequency is correlated with "ease"
> or "naturalness" for the human mind ... (emphasis in original)

This is, indeed, intriguing and plausible—but we lack the necessary data and theory to evaluate it adequately. There are three kinds of problems: (1) The linguistic analysis that leads to the postulation of an accessibility or naturalness hierarchy is grounded only in the statistics of frequency of occurrence of grammaticized notions across languages. (2) There is no independent cognitive or psycholinguistic theory of what is "easy" or "natural." (3) It is a mystery that "difficult" or "unnatural" form-function relations are learned and used.

First, considering the available data, we have adequate descriptions of perhaps no more than ten percent of the five or six thousand languages currently spoken in the world, with limited information about a few dead languages. (Furthermore, semantic analysis of grammatical forms has not been fully developed in the available grammars of these languages.) Systematic samples are even smaller—for example, Hawkins' (1983) 350 languages or the Bybee, Perkins, and Pagliuca (1994) sample of 76 languages. However, in order to make a claim about the relative frequency of occurrence of a form across human languages, one would need a theoretically motivated sample of ALL of the languages that have ever been spoken, because there is no reason to believe that the contemporary set of languages is a set that has arisen from LINGUISTICALLY motivated causes. It is, for example, an accident of history that the Indo-European languages experienced the spread that they did, obliterating or marginalizing other languages in their path. (Where are all the sisters of Basque, for example?) If the discovery of agriculture had occurred at a different time or place in history, we would not have the present distribution of languages on the planet. Or if the European discovery of America had occurred after the spread and consolidation of one or more Amerindian empires, the pattern of linguistic diversity might have been quite different. We cannot assume that particular speech communities disappeared because of a psycholinguistic problem. If one were to use distributional facts in this fashion with regard to other cultural domains, one might argue, for example, for the naturalness of eating with fork and knife versus chopsticks; or, in the twenty-second century, to argue for the unnaturalness of languages without writing.

One can attempt to overcome this problem—but only in part—by motivated sampling of the surviving languages. This field is in its infancy, and it is premature to make any generalizations on the basis of available data. In any event, there is something psycholinguistically dissatisfying to claim that a particular linguistic form (or, in some instances, an entire type of language) is "dispreferred" or "relatively inaccessible," even though it is acquired by children and used by a viable speech community. (Do such speakers all carry out a remarkable feat in the face of great odds?) The only way to substantiate claims of relative accessibility and utility of linguistic forms is to measure aspects of their actual acquisition and use. The relevant measures must be based on such factors as difficulty or lateness of acquisition, processing load in adult speech or comprehension, relative infrequency of use of a form within the language, historical modification of the form, etc. Mere frequency of occurrence in a sample of existing languages (*pace*

Jakobson, Talmy, and many others) is, in my opinion, of no cognitive or psycholinguistic interest in itself.[5]

Nevertheless, I am convinced that there ARE accessibility hierarchies of grammatical forms and constructions—even if they cannot be discovered by statistical sampling of languages. Their basis must be sought in terms of cognitive and processing variables. That is, notions that receive grammatical expression earlier in the child's development must be more salient—but on NON-linguistic grounds, rather than built into a grammar module. My solution was to attempt to ground the accessibility hierarchy in the child's cognitive development. On this account, the first notions to receive grammatical marking in a child's speech are those that correspond to the child's conceptions of "prototypical events." For example, with regard to the order of development of locative adpositions, I proposed a match between Talmy's hierarchy and a developmental hierarchy (Slobin, 1985, pp. 1180f):

> Semantic Space provides a basic set of locative relations arranged in an accessibility hierarchy determined by cognitive development. All crosslinguistic acquisition data point to an initial salience of topological notions of containment, support, and contiguity, with later development of projective and Euclidean notions of spatial orientation to particular features of objects or angles of regard ... [The child], then, will map locative functors onto prototypical examples of Figure-Ground relations, beginning with the most accessible relations.

Attempts such as these, along with work by Bowerman (1993, 1994, 1996a, 1996b; Choi & Bowerman, 1991), Clark (in press; Clark & Carpenter, 1989a, 1989b), and others, seek to place the conceptual origins of grammaticizable notions in domains of cognitive development, but tempered by the semantic organization inherent in the exposure language. These are empirical issues, and much more research is needed before we can make claims about universal "starting points" for the meanings of grammatical morphemes. It is important, though, to distinguish between the course of development of grammaticizable notions in the child and explanations for their existence as linguistic phenomena. On closer inspection, crosslinguistic diversity in patterns of grammaticization points to adult communicative practices as the most plausible source of form-function mappings in human languages, rather than prototypical events in infant cognition. The following sections of the chapter explore the roles of grammaticizable notions in ontogeny and diachrony, drawing on recent findings in cognitive linguistics and grammatic(al)ization theory.

---

[5]This is not an argument against the use of crosslinguistic samples to determine implicational universals—that is, patterns of cooccurrence of features. The work of Bybee (1985; Bybee, Pagliuca, & Perkins, 1994), Greenberg (1963), Hawkins (1983, 1988, 1995), and others has demonstrated the value of looking for such patterns.

2. THE LEARNING TASK

This historical and theoretical introduction sets the stage for defining the task that the child faces in determining the meanings of grammatical morphemes. The task assumes the following linguistic conditions to be true:

Condition 1. There is a distinct and identifiable collection of grammatical morphemes, arranged in small, closed classes.

Condition 2. These morphemes map onto a universal, limited set of semantic entities (grammaticizable notions).

Condition 3. Grammaticizable notions are arranged in a universal accessibility hierarchy.

According to standard accounts, acquisition occurs on the basis of assumptions about biology and cognition:

Assumption 1. Conditions 1, 2, and 3 exist because of the structure of the mind/brain (in modules for aspects of language, perhaps in conjunction with other modules).

Assumption 2. The role of linguistic input is to allow the relevant mental capacities to organize themselves in terms of the exposure language.

Assumption 3. The child learns the meaning of a grammatical form by isolating and identifying a particular stretch of speech as instantiating a grammatical form and attempting to map it onto a relevant grammaticizable notion.

I propose that Conditions 1, 2, and 3 are only partly true, and that therefore Assumption 1 must be seriously modified or abandoned. Assumption 2 remains, but with a shift of emphasis to structures inhering in the exposure language. Assumption 3 must be seriously modified, posing challenges to our learning theories.

3. SYNCHRONIC EVIDENCE FOR MODIFYING THE LINGUISTIC CONDITIONS ON LEARNABILITY

3.1. What Is a Grammatical Morpheme?

Prototypical grammatical morphemes are affixed to content words, are general in meaning, phonologically reduced, and not etymologically transparent. Familiar examples are elements like plural markers on nouns and tense/aspect inflections on verbs. Another obvious type of grammatical morpheme is represented by "little words" like prepositions and auxiliaries, which consist of small sets of items occurring in syntactically fixed positions. But there are also items that are not so obvious. Consider several examples that demonstrate the lack of clear boundaries of syntactic categories defined as "functors," "grammatical morphemes," or "closed-class elements."

3.1.1. *English Modals and Equivalents*

English has a grammatical class of modal auxiliaries that fit in the frame, SUBJECT *MODAL* VERB, such as *You **should/must/can/might** ... go*. This is a prototypical small, closed class: *can, could, shall, should, will, would, may, might, must*. The forms do not function as normal verbs; rather, they have a number of grammatical peculiarities—for example, they don't have normal past tenses (**you shoulded go*) or person inflections (**he shoulds go*); they can take a contracted negative clitic (*shouldn't*); and they "move" under certain syntactic conditions (e.g., *Should you go?*). However, there are other items that can occur in the same slot, such as *You **hafta/needa** ... go*. These function as normal verbs—e.g., PAST: *You **had** to go*; PERSON: *you **hafta**, he **hasta***; QUESTION: ***Do** you **hafta** go?*; NEGATIVE *You **don't hafta** go*. Nevertheless, they, too, are part of a small, closed, and specialized set, with phonological reduction in some contexts. Therefore, some linguists refer to them as "quasi-modals." Non-verbs can also fall in the specialized slot of modals and quasi-models, but with other syntactic constraints. Consider *You **better** go*, which (in American English) has no obvious past tense or question form. It is negated like an auxiliary, but only in the uncontracted form; compare *you should not go / you better not go* with *you shouldn't go / you *bettern't go*. Looking across contexts of use, *better* is another sort of specialized "modal-like" element in American English. If you are a child learning this dialect, you can identify a set of full auxiliaries on syntactic grounds, and find that it maps onto a restricted set of grammaticized meanings in the domain of modality. However, when you are concerned with speech PRODUCTION, and access the set of modal notions from your mental set of grammaticizable notions in this domain, you find that there is, indeed, a small, closed set—but that it does not have a clear or unitary syntactic definition. The slot in declarative sentences that is reserved for expressing categories within the grammaticizable domain of modality can be filled with a heterogeneous collection of modal auxiliaries, semi-modals, and an adjective/adverb *better* that does not act like a normal adjective or adverb in this function. The semantic and syntactic tasks do not seem to run in parallel as neatly as in the textbook cases, which take only well-defined grammatical morphemes into account in their expositions. In addition, there is a mismatch between comprehension and production. That is, the closed class of true modals fall together in terms of the processing strategies needed to identify them when listening to speech; but when you begin with an intention to express a particular modality, you encounter a somewhat larger and heterogeneous set of items with regard to their syntactic expression.

This is, in fact, a widespread problem in acquisition—only coming to light when we consider production, rather than comprehension. Consider several more examples of the fuzziness of the category "grammatical morpheme" or "closed-class element."

3.2.1. *Spanish Modal Verbs and Auxiliaries*

In Spanish the equivalents of English modal verbs do not have syntactic peculiarities. That is, they function just like normal, full verbs, using the standard paradigms for person/number and tense/aspect, and behaving like other verbs in negative and interrogative constructions. Yet they, too, are a small, closed set, performing similar functions. The set, however, can only be defined on semantic grounds, listing those verbs—such as *poder* 'can', *deber* 'should', and the like—that perform a modal function. For example, *puedo ir* 'I.can go' and *debo ir* 'I.should go' have the same morphosyntactic characteristics as constructions with non-modal verbs (e.g., *recordé ir* 'I.remembered to.go'). Lacking the peculiar morphosyntactic definition of English modals, however, the corresponding Spanish verbs are a small, closed set WITHIN THE "OPEN CLASS." (I will argue that, in fact, the "open class" of verbs is better conceived of as a collection of closed classes.) There is also a small class of about 24 "semi-auxiliaries" (Green, 1982) which have restricted meanings in particular semantic/syntactic contexts. These are verbs that can function both as main verbs and semi-auxiliaries—again, making it difficult to draw a clear boundary around "grammatical morphemes." In their grammatical function, such verbs have restricted meanings in comparison to their uses as fully lexical verbs. For example, the verb *llevar* 'carry', in construction with a participle, takes on an auxiliary aspectual meaning: *Juan lleva entendido que X* 'Juan **carries** understood that X' predicates an established state of understanding in Juan that X; *la diferencia viene motivada por X* 'the difference **comes** motivated by X' means that the difference can be accounted for by X. Green notes that some of the 24 semi-auxiliaries are more specialized and limited in their functions than others.

A critical feature is the "fullness" versus "abstractness" of lexical meaning of an item. This is not a criterion that a child could use to identify an item as belonging to either the lexical class or the grammatical class. Green notes that his analysis "strongly favours a gradient analysis ... At one extreme of the gradience would be verbs like *haber* [have] which have lost virtually all trace of lexical meaning, and at the other, verbs like *mostrarse* [show.self] and *notarse* [note] which have lost virtually none of theirs" (p. 127). Looked at in diachronic perspective, some are more "grammaticized" than others (as I will discuss later in more detail). Some may remain on the borderline between lexical and grammatical items for centuries, and may never become fully grammaticized.

The Spanish "modal" and "semi-auxiliary" verbs attract our interest because their semantic and discourse functions parallel the more highly grammaticized auxiliaries of English. This leads one to wonder whether Spanish-speaking children are using their prespecified "grammatical acquisition device" or their more general "lexical acquisition device" in learning such forms.

Note also that the "semi-grammaticized" uses of such verbs occur in specified syntactic constructions, such as the VERB + PARTICIPLE construction of *lleva entendido* 'carries understood'. The task of mapping grammaticizable notions cannot be understood without also treating syntactic constructions as part of the meaning-bearing system of grammar (cf. Goldberg, 1995).

Many more examples could be adduced, underlining the point that there is no clear dividing line between "content words" and "functors." Rather, there is a continuum with clearly lexical items on one end (nouns like *computer, couch, zebra*, verbs like *tackle, broil, sneeze*) and grammatical inflections on the other (such as English PROGRESSIVE *-ing*, Turkish ACCUSATIVE *-I*, Warlpiri ERGATIVE *-ngku*). In between, there are lexical items that play more or less specialized roles, sometimes on their way to becoming grammatical morphemes over time. What, then, is a grammatical morpheme? It depends on the purposes of the analysis. In any event, it would be difficult to preprogram the child with an adequate definition. And even if children were to begin learning with a binary distinction between "grammatical" and "lexical," they would soon need to cope with the many forms that cannot be accommodated within this dichotomy.

3.2. What Is a Closed-Class Item?

One way of getting the child started in the task of grammatical form-function mapping has been to equip the language acquisition device with a special detector for members of the "closed class." The terminology is deceptive here, however. Obviously, the child cannot define a class as "closed" before having acquired all of its members and finding that there are no more to acquire. Therefore this can't be part of early acquisition. Lila Gleitman and her associates have proposed an acoustic, rather than a semantic or syntactic cue to closed-class membership (Gleitman & Wanner, 1982; L. R. Gleitman, H. Gleitman, Landau, & Wanner, 1988; Landau & Gleitman, 1985). On this model, the child eventually comes to pay attention to elements in the speech stream that are unstressed or otherwise perceptually non-salient. They propose that "the distinction between open and closed class may play a role in the child's discovery of linguistic structure. This is because, though this distinction may be discovered through a physical property (i.e., stress), it is well correlated with syntactic analyses the child will have to recognize to recover the structure of sentences" (Gleitman & Wanner, 1982, p. 23). However, this analysis obliterates both the syntactic and semantic characteristics of closed classes as well as their statistical distribution. An acoustic definition of the class leads Gleitman and her associates to define stressed grammatical inflections, paradoxically, as open class. For example, when discussing the fact that grammatical morphemes are acquired earlier in Turkish than in many other languages, they argue: "According to Slobin, the relevant inflectional items in Turkish . . . are a full syllable long, are stressed, do not deform the surrounding words phonetically, and do not cliticize. Thus these items are OPEN CLASS, not CLOSED CLASS, under phonological definitions of this partitioning of the morphological stock" (Gleitman et al., 1988, p. 158). On this account, agglutinating languages like Turkish and Japanese have no closed-class morphemes, thus exempting children acquiring such languages from the learning task defined in Section 2. This solution clearly throws out the baby with the bath water.

In other formulations, Gleitman and her associates rely on the traditional definition of the two classes. Landau and Gleitman (1985, pp. 44ff) define the closed class on distributional grounds alone, including such items as auxiliaries, prepositions, and determiners, which are full syllables and can receive stress. On this model, the child must have some means of identifying members of these grammatical categories. The only possible cues are meaning, syntactic position, and statistical distribution—the traditional cues used in all models of language acquisition. Thus, there is no evident definition of "closed-class morpheme" that can give the child a solution to the learning task. At best, some kind of "prosodic bootstrapping" can help children learning particular types of languages to identify particular types of grammatical morphemes. But this leaves open the question of how grammatical morphemes in general are mapped onto linguistically relevant notions.[6]

There is also a long tradition in aphasiology that has sought to find a neurological basis for grammatical morphology in syndromes of telegraphic speech. The classical claim has been that closed class items are lost, thus proving that they reside in a distinct module. However, by now there is ample evidence against the view that agrammatism is simply an impairment of linguistic structure. Crosslinguistic studies of aphasia show differential loss of grammatical morphemes, depending on both their "functional load" in the language and their acoustic salience. Bates, Friederici, and Wulfeck (1987) have found additional evidence for Arnold Pick's (1913) old observation that omission of function words and inflections is much less frequent in patients who speak richly inflecting languages such as German and Czech. They have found greater preservation of inflected articles in Italian and German, in comparison with English, and note that articles in Italian indicate number and gender, and in German indicate these categories and case as well. That is, the relative retention of grammatical mor-

---

[6]Paul Bloom has suggested that open and closed classes can be detected by a statistical counter that is structurally sensitive (personal communication, 1996): "It is possible that children notice that some syntactic and morphological positions are occupied by classes containing a few members, each of which is frequently used, while others are occupied by classes containing many members, each of which is rarely used. This would suggest to the child (though it would not deductively entail) that some classes are open and others are closed." Such a procedure is certainly plausible, and is built into systems of operating principles (Peters, 1985; Slobin, 1985). But this only gives the child sets of classes of VARYING sizes, and not the ontological distinction between "open" and "closed."

phemes is sensitive to their grammatical functions in the language. Acoustic/ articulatory factors also play a key role. For example, I have found full preservation of inflectional morphology in Turkish Broca's aphasics (Slobin, 1991a), no doubt due to the characteristics of Turkish morphology singled out by Wanner and Gleitman. In addition, a number of studies have shown that judgments of grammaticality are not impaired in "agrammatic" patients, and that grammatical morphemes can sometimes be accessed in tasks that remove time pressure from processing. All of these findings remove any basis for a neurological definition of the closed class as a linguistic subsystem. What remains is a congeries of factors which lie outside of the various attempts to distinguish the two classes on linguistic grounds. David Caplan (1992), in a recent review of research on agrammatism, lists a number of such factors (p. 340): "the sonorance hierarchy, the status of an affix with respect to derivational and inflectional morphology, the lexical status of a root or stem, the salience of a lexical item, attentional and control processes."

Bates and Wulfeck (1989), in a review of crosslinguistic studies of aphasia, fail to find any support for a "dual-lexicon hypothesis" which postulates that open- and closed-class items are mediated by different mechanisms and/or stored separately. Their conclusion is far-reaching, pointing to processing factors alone as distinguishing the two classes, and proposing a single-lexicon approach (pp. 351f):

> [W]e think it is appropriate to treat bound and free items in a similar way. In fact, we think it is useful to handle ALL lexical items (closed- and open-class, bound and free) within a single lexicon; the dissociations observed between different kinds of items will derive from differences in the perceptual/motor and cognitive/semantic processing mechanisms that are involved in retrieving items from the lexicon.

One conclusion of the present chapter is that the same reasoning applies to acquisition and unimpaired language use.

3.3. What Makes a Notion Grammaticizable?

The other side of the coin is to equip the child with grammaticizable notions that can be mapped onto the specialized morphemes of the "closed class," however defined. When we look across languages, though, we find that the same notions are often also used to delimit the meanings of content words—members of the open class—depending on the language and the type of analysis chosen. Simply identifying a notion as grammaticizable does not allow the child to determine WHETHER it is actually grammaticized in the exposure language or HOW it is grammaticized. (That is, crosslinguistic diversity precludes a preestablished table of correspondences between grammatical forms and semantic meanings, as in Pinker (1984, p. 40). That table contains pairings of grammar and semantics such as "Accusative or Absolutive" ~ "Patient of transitive action" and "Aspect" ~ "Durativity.") Again, there are many possible examples. I will consider three types of problem: (1) morphemes that are called closed class, or grammatical, in one language, compared with similar morphemes that are called open class or lexical in another; (2) languages in which variants of the very same lexical item can function as either closed or open class; and (3) pairs of languages in which the same type of conceptual material is lexicalized in one and grammaticized in the other. The dichotomy between two types of learning mechanisms becomes questionable in the light of all three phenomena.

3.3.1. Mandarin and English Classifiers

First, it is useful to consider one language from the point of view of grammaticized categories in other types of languages. For example, a Mandarin perspective on English brings our covert CLASSIFIER system into focus. In Mandarin, as in many languages (cf. Craig, 1986), when objects are counted or otherwise pointed to linguistically it is necessary to use a classifier morpheme along with the noun that makes object reference. Classifiers are considered grammatical morphemes in Mandarin because they constitute a small set with categorial meanings and are obligatory in certain contexts. One says, for example, *yi* **qún** *yáng* 'one **flock** sheep', *nèi* **duī** *lāx* 'that **pile** garbage', *zhèng* **chuàn** *zhūzi* 'whole **string** pearl'. Li and Thompson (1981, p. 105) say that Mandarin has "several dozen classifiers" and Erbaugh (1986, p. 406) reports that adults tend to almost always use the single general classifier *gè* rather than one of the special classifiers. It is apparent that there is a syntactic slot for a classifier, but that it is rarely occupied by a form that has specific meaning. Is this really any different from English, with regard to grammaticizable notions? In most cases, it is sufficient in English to use a numeral or demonstrative, without indicating class membership, and to use a plural morpheme for numbers greater than one; in Mandarin, in most cases, it is sufficient to use a numeral or demonstrative, with an empty classifier, and no noun marking for number. When it IS necessary to classify in addition to counting or demonstrating, English has a set of classifiers quite analogous to Mandarin, as is evident in the translations above: *flock, pile, string*. In fact, there is no other way to refer to such collections or pluralities in English. The English-speaking child must learn words like these—and *grain, piece, sheet, slice, stack, cup, bowl, drop*, etc.—just as the Mandarin-speaking child must learn classifiers that translate as 'slice', 'animal', 'row', 'sheet', 'pot', 'grain', and so on. Yet Chinese classifiers, by tradition, strike us as "grammatical" in a way that English measure terms do not. From the point of view of learning theory, though, it is not evident that the Chinese child is faced with a grammatical task, played off in a prespecified component of the language module, while the American child has to learn a very similar system using a quite different set of linguistic and cognitive resources.

3.3.2. *Mayan Motion Verbs and Directionals*

Mayan languages typically have a small, closed class of directional suffixes that can be used on verbs, stative predicates, and nonverbal predicates of various types, such as adjectives. For example, in Jakaltek (Craig, 1993) there are ten directional suffixes, such as *-(a)y* 'down' and *-toj* 'away from'. Consider an example in which these two forms are affixed to a caused motion verb (p. 23):

(4) *sirnih-**ay-toj** sb'a naj sat pahaw b'et wichen*
     A3.E3.threw-**DIR-DIR** E.3.REFL NCL/he E3.in.front cliff into gully[7]
     '. . . he threw himself down over the cliff into the gully'

The first word, *sirnih-ay-toj*, affixes two directionals to a verb meaning 'throw', similar to English verb particles. The directionals have all of the defining features of closed-class morphemes: there is a small, phonologically reduced set of bound morphemes, with schematic and generalized meanings. However, each of these suffixes corresponds to a full verb of motion, and such verbs are clearly open class by standard definitions. Craig presents the following parallels (p. 23):

MOTION VERBS		DIRECTIONALS	
toyi	'to go'	*-toj*	'away from'
tita	'come!'	*-tij*	'toward'
ahi	'to ascend'	*-(a)h*	'up'
ayi	'to descend'	*-(a)y*	'down'
oki	'enter'	*-(o/e/i)k*	'in'
eli	'to exit'	*-(e/i)l*	'out'
ek'i	'to pass'	*-(e/i)k'*	'passing through'
paxi	'to return'	*-pax*	'back, again'
hani	'to remain, to stay'	*-kan*	'remaining, still'
kanh	'to rise, to burst'	*-kanh*	'up, suddenly'

It would be strange to postulate two different learning mechanisms for these two sets of obviously related items. In fact, both sets are small and closed, and both have the familiar semantic characteristics of grammaticizable notions. Clearly, the directionals are grammaticized forms of the verbs. And just as clearly—within the "open class"—these ten motion verbs constitute a small, closed class. Indeed, as I will argue later, the verb class seems to consist of a number of small, closed sets, thus blurring further the distinction between "open" and "closed" classes.

---

[7]Abbreviations: A = Absolutive, DIR = Directional, E = Ergative, NCL = Nominal classifier, REFL = Reflexive.

3.3.3. *Motion in English and Korean*

Soonja Choi and Melissa Bowerman, in an important paper (1991), compare how children learn to express motion events in English and Korean. The two languages lexicalize the semantic components of motion events differently, as can be seen in terms of Talmy's (1985) analysis. Following Talmy, there are four basic components to such events:

MOTION: the fact of motion itself
FIGURE: the object that is in motion
GROUND: the object(s) with respect to which the figure moves
PATH: the course followed by the figure with respect to the ground

In addition, there are "external" or "supporting events":

MANNER: the particular motor pattern used in achieving motion
CAUSE: the event that is responsible for motion
DEIXIS: motion with respect to viewpoint (added by Choi and Bowerman)

To simplify the presentation, consider only events of self-movement in a particular manner. In English the components are typically arrayed as follows:

(5a) [*John*] [*ran*] [*into*] [*the room*].
       [FIGURE] [MOTION+MANNER] [PATH] [GROUND].

The fact of motion, conflated with manner, is expressed by the verb; the path is grammaticized; and there is no grammaticization of deixis. German, a closely related language, has the same pattern, with the addition of a grammatical expression of deixis:

(5b) [*John*] [*lief*] [*ins*] [*Zimmer*] [*hinein*].
       [FIGURE] [MOTION+MANNER] [PATH] [GROUND] [DEIXIS].
       'John ran into the room thither.inwards.'

The expression of the same components is arrayed quite differently in Korean:

(5c) [*John-i*] [*pang-ey*] [*ttwui-e*] [*tul-e*] [*o-ass-ta*].
       [John-SUBJ] [room-LOC] [run-CONN] [enter-CONN] [come-PAST-DECL].[8]
       [FIGURE] [GROUND] [MANNER] [PATH] [MOTION+DEIXIS].
       'John came into the room running.'

---

[8]Abbreviations: CONN = connecting suffix, DECL = declarative ending, LOC = locative marker, SUBJ = subject marker.

In languages of this type (including, for example, Japanese, and the Turkic, Semitic, and Romance languages), path is not grammaticized, but rather is expressed by verbs—"open-class" words.

Choi and Bowerman examine children's acquisition of path expressions in English verb particles and Korean path verbs. Note, however, that this is a comparison of closed-class (English) and open-class (Korean) elements. Yet, a common developmental story can be told. This crosslinguistic comparison presents the same pattern as the intralinguistic pattern in the Mayan languages—namely, the expression of comparative locative notions in small, closed sets, as either "content words" or "functor morphemes." Compare the set of Korean path verbs with the set of English particles:

KOREAN	ENGLISH
olla 'ascend'	*up*
nayle 'descend'	*down*
tule 'enter'	*in*
na 'exit'	*out*
cina 'pass'	*past, by*
ttala 'move.along'	*along*
thonghay 'move.through'	*through*
kalocille 'cross'	*across*
tulle 'move.via'	*along, through*

This is a quite "standard" set of path verbs, found repeatedly in language after language of this type. For example, the Romance languages typically have the following set:

advance, approach, arrive—recede, depart
ascend, climb—descend, fall
enter—exit
pass, cross
come, return

It is not evident that the task of learning a small, closed set of path VERBS is qualitatively different from the task of learning a small, closed set of verb PARTICLES expressing path—though these two tasks would be assigned to two different modules or types of acquisition mechanisms on the standard account.

More broadly, Talmy's (1985) analysis shows that every component of a motion event, except perhaps the fact of motion itself, can be marked by a grammatical element in one type of language or another. For example, there are Germanic particles and affixes for PATH and DEIXIS, Turkic CAUSE affixes, Atsugewi GROUND affixes (e.g., *-ict* 'into liquid'), Caddo FIGURE particles (e.g., *dá'n-* 'powder'), and Nez Perce MANNER prefixes (e.g., *wilé-* running). Thus, while it may be possible to equip the child with the global components of motion events, it is not possible to specify which ones are likely to receive grammatical expression or what kinds of morphemes are to be expected for any particular component. Four of the grammaticizable components—PATH, DEIXIS, CAUSE, and MANNER—are amenable to expression by independent verbs as well as by grammatical elements. When this is the case, however, the set of verbs tends to be small and closed, with definable semantics. The more noun-like components, FIGURE and GROUND, are more amenable to expression by nouns, in which case the set of available nouns is, indeed, large and open. When MANNER is expressed by verbs, there seem to be two types of options. If the language is of the type in which MOTION and MANNER are conflated, as in the Germanic and Slavic languages, there is a large set of such verbs. But in languages in which MOTION and PATH are conflated, and MANNER is expressed as a secondary verb in a path description, there seems to be a small and limited set of manner verbs. It seems, then, that the size of a class is more important than its grammatical status, and that the sizes of various classes are influenced by the typology of the language. (This issue is discussed in more detail in Section 3.4.4.)

3.4. How Are Grammaticizable Notions Organized?

Up to this point I have treated grammaticizable notions as a universally specified collection, applicable across languages. However, it has become more and more evident in research over the past decade or so that there is considerable crosslinguistic variation in the meanings of closed-class categories, including both functors and small, closed verb classes. Melissa Bowerman has been a pioneer in pointing out this issue and providing relevant data. Ten years ago she argued (1985, p. 1313):

> In spite of the general interest in meaning shown by our field in recent years, variation among languages in the makeup and scope of grammatically-relevant semantic categories has been persistently neglected in crosslinguistic studies of grammatical development. In general, the way in which languages organize meaning has not been regarded as an integral part of their structure, equivalent in status to syntactic or morphological structure and comparable to these in its potential to influence rate of acquisition, likelihood of errors, and so on.

Her work has done much to correct this situation (Bowerman, 1994, 1996a, 1996b; Bowerman, de León, & Choi, 1995; Choi & Bowerman, 1991) and to stimulate others to do likewise (e.g., Berman & Slobin, 1994; Choi, this volume; de León, 1994; Slobin, 1991b, 1996a). Crosslinguistic variation in types of "conceptual packaging" in a semantic domain poses another serious challenge to learning models, because there is no unique set of prelinguistic categories that can be directly mapped onto the meanings of linguistic elements. (See Bowerman, 1996a, for a recent and cogent exposition of this problem in the domain of spatial concepts and language.) Four types of problems must be faced by learning theories: (1) Languages differ in how finely they divide up a conceptual continuum and in where they place cuts for grammatical purposes. (2) Languages differ in the combinations of semantic components that are packaged into grammatical morphemes in common conceptual domains. (3) Languages differ in the overall division of a semantic domain into linguistically relevant categories. (4) The array of concepts relevant to a particular domain is distributed across several types of linguistic elements in any given language, and the patterns of distribution also vary across languages. I will give examples of each of these four problem types.

3.4.1. *Dividing a Continuum into Linguistically Relevant Categories*

Izchak Schlesinger has long argued for a distinction between cognitive and semantic levels of categorization (1979, 1982, 1988, 1995). In a broad crosslinguistic study (1979), he offers evidence for the proposal that "conceptually, the instrumental and comitative are really only two extreme points on what is a conceptual continuum" (p. 308). This continuum is marked by a single preposition in English—*with*—as shown in the following ten sentences that Schlesinger used in his study:

1. The pantomimist gave a show with the clown.
2. The engineer built the machine with an assistant.
3. The general captured the hill with a squad of paratroopers.
4. The acrobat performed an act with an elephant.
5. The blind man crossed the street with his dog.
6. The officer caught the smuggler with a police dog.
7. The prisoner won the appeal with a highly paid lawyer.
8. The Nobel Prize winner found the solution with a computer.
9. The sportsman hunted deer with a rifle.
10. The hoodlum broke the window with a stone.

English speakers were asked to rank these sentences on a continuum from the meaning of "together" (as in "He went to the movie with his friend") to the meaning of "by means of" (as in "He cut the meat with a knife"). The respondents agreed, at a high level of statistical significance, on the ranking given above. Schlesinger then presented these sentences to speakers of languages that use distinct grammatical forms for parts of this continuum. Speakers of twelve different languages divided the continuum at different points and agreed in treating it as a continuum.[9]

---

[9]The languages were Slovak, Serbo-Croatian, Iraqi Arabic, Polish, Luo, Akan, Alur, Finnish, Swahili, Japanese, Korean, and Tamil. This ordering of languages reflects the division point on the continuum, from mainly comitative to mainly instrumental. For example, Slovak uses a distinct instrumental only for sentence 10 ("with a stone"), whereas Tamil uses a special comitative form only for sentences 1 and 2 ("with the clown," "with an assistant").

In general, wherever they may have made a division they did not violate the ranking. For example, sentences 1–8 received the same form in Iraqi Arabic, while 9–10 received a different form; Swahili, by contrast, required a separate form for 7–10. Schlesinger concludes that "the finding that languages differ widely in their cut off points runs counter to the hypothesis that the instrumental and comitative are two disparate categories in our cognitive structures. . . . [Rather], there seems to be a continuum in our cognitive system, which each language segments in its own way" (p. 313). (Schlesinger, 1995, presents studies revealing clines in other domains as well.)

Bowerman and Pederson (1992) report a similar pattern in the spatial domain. They found that it was possible to rank pictured situations of locative relations between two objects along a continuum from CONTAINMENT to SUPPORT, with differences between languages in their division of the continuum. Thus, even if the child were equipped with predefined conceptual continua, it would not be evident how many linguistically relevant cuts to make on a continuum, or even whether it is divisible at all, since some languages use a single term for an entire continuum such as COMITATIVE-INSTRUMENTAL (e.g., English *with*) or CONTAINMENT SUPPORT (e.g., Spanish *en*).

3.4.2. *Packaging Components into Linguistically Relevant Categories*

Languages differ in terms of the "granularity" of their division of conceptual material into linguistically relevant categories. For example, one language may have a simple CONTINUATIVE aspect for any temporally unbounded situation, while others may subdivide this aspect to distinguish between HABITUAL and ITERATIVE events, or between PROGRESSIVE events and STATES. Further, events can be cross-classified on different dimensions: one language may mark such distinctions only in the past, for example, while another might mark them in other tenses as well. It is the hope of cognitive linguists such as Jackendoff (1983, 1987, 1990) that there is a universal set of conceptual components underlying crosslinguistic diversity in the semantics of lexical items. I share this hope—but even if the child had a definitive set of such components, the task would remain of packaging them into the linguistically relevant categories of the particular exposure language.

In some learning theories such packages are given in advance, as in Pinker's (1984, p. 41) table of correspondences between grammatical and conceptual categories. On closer inspection, however, considerable diversity remains to be accounted for. As one example, consider the grammatical category ACCUSATIVE, which appears in various languages in the form of case affixes or particles associated with nouns, or as verb affixes, or as special construction types. In Pinker's table, "Accusative" is linked with "Patient of transitive action." However, in many languages this semantic category is subdivided—and in different ways. That is, it is not a unitary notion, nor does it lie on a one-dimensional continuum with other case categories, because the subdivisions cut across different types of categories. Here are just a few examples of the many possibilities:

> **Some factors influencing choice of grammatical marking of patient:** definite patient only (Turkish case inflection)
> masculine animate versus other, whole versus partial patient, singular versus plural patient, affirmative versus negative clause (Russian case inflections)
> whole versus partial patient, completed versus non-completed action (Finnish case inflections)
> direct physical action on patient only (Mandarin particle)
> patient marking (direct and indirect conflated) in present tense only (Georgian)
> one marker for patient, goal, recipient, beneficiary (English personal pronouns)

This is just a very brief and simplified list, but it makes it clear that the notion of "patient" or "direct object" conflates with various other notions from language to language, including such categories as tense, aspect, definiteness, nature of effect, and so forth. (A similar problem arises with regard to Pinker's alignment of "Aspect" with "Durativity," given the range of aspectual categories briefly noted above.)

It may well be that some packagings are more accessible to the child than others, and that children across languages begin with similar notions of patient (e.g., the prototypical event of direct physical manipulation proposed in my "Manipulative Activity Scene" [Slobin, 1985]). This is, of course, an empirical question. But however children may break into the mapping of such grammaticizable notions, our learning theories will have to account for the selective fine-tuning required for arriving at language-specific patterns of grammaticization. That is, regardless of a child's starting point in grammaticizing a particular notion, a DEVELOPMENTAL account is needed because the endpoints vary so much across languages.

3.4.3. *Carving Up a Conceptual Domain into Grammaticized Categories*

The work of Melissa Bowerman and Soonja Choi is perhaps the clearest example of how languages not only place cuts at different points on a continuum or conflate different categories in particular grammatical forms—but, more broadly, differ in structuring entire conceptual domains. This work has been presented in detail in a number of places (see references to Bowerman and to Choi in Section 3.4 and Choi's chapter in this volume). The domain in question is spatial location and movement of various types. We can return here to the comparisons of Korean and English, this time taking as given that it is reasonable to compare the semantics of "open-class" items (Korean verbs) and "closed-class" items (English prepositions and particles). Consider the domain of locative placement—that is, caused movement of an object from or to a location. It is evident that each of the two languages has a different overall conceptual organization of what is important to mark linguistically in this domain. For example, English is concerned with relations of containment and support—whether one object is *in* or *on* another, whether an object is taken *off* or *out* in relation to another. Korean, by contrast, is concerned with the type of surface contact between two objects—tight or loose containment, contact or attachment with a surface. Thus, where English uses the same term for putting an apple *in* a bowl or a tape cassette *in* its case, Korean uses two terms, indicating loose vs. tight fit. On the other hand, where English uses two terms to differentiate between putting a cassette *in* a case and a lid *on* a jar, Korean uses one, because these are both instances of tight fit. It is apparent that one unique conceptual starting point will not equip children for learning these two different types of semantic organization. Working across entire semantic domains in several languages, Bowerman finds distinctly different arrays and combinations of conceptual features employed in the overall structuring of a domain for purposes of linguistic expression. In a recent paper, she concludes (1996a, p. 425):

> I have argued that the existence of crosslinguistic variation in the semantic packaging of spatial notions creates a complex learning problem for the child. Even if learners begin by mapping spatial morphemes directly onto precompiled concepts of space—which is not at all obvious—they cannot get far in this way; instead, they must work out the meanings of the forms by observing how they are distributed across contexts in fluent speech.

3.4.4. *Distributing a Concept Across Linguistic Elements*

The child not only has to keep track of the distribution of forms across contexts, but also the distribution of concepts across forms. Up to this point we have primarily considered individual forms such as verbs, affixes, prepositions, and particles. But, in fact, most linguistic elements are only interpretable in relation to other cooccurring elements. To take a trivial example, an English personal pronoun, taken out of context, only indicates the global thematic relations of subject or object, and the object forms—*me, us, him, her, them*—do not distinguish such roles as patient, recipient, or goal. However, the forms are not ambiguous in context. The *me* of *she loves me* is not the same *me*, conceptually, as the *me* of *she sent me a letter* or *she approached me*. In English, these concepts are distinguishable in combination with verb semantics and construction type. In any given utterance, the meaning of the closed-class element, *me*, does not reside in that element alone.

Chris Sinha and Tania Kuteva (1995) have explored this issue in detail with regard to the semantics of locative particles in several types of languages, introducing the useful term, DISTRIBUTED SPATIAL SEMANTICS. To begin with, spatial relational meaning is expressed in English by a variety of word types, both lexical and grammatical: prepositions (*in*), adverbs (*inwards*), verbs (*enter*), nouns (*inside*), adjectives (*inner*). Sinha and Kuteva also point out that construction types can distinguish aspects of spatial meaning, as in the following Dutch example, where the meaning of a locative particle, *in*, varies with its position in construction with verbs of motion:

(6a) *Mieke loopt in het bos.*
   'Mieke walks **in** the woods.'
(6b) *Mieke loopt het bos in.*
   'Mieke walks **into** the woods.'

Thus spatial relational meaning is DISTRIBUTED over different form classes and constructions, and within any given utterance, meaning is COMPOSITIONAL. For the language learner, grammatical morphemes come to be organized into systems. We have already seen this in examples such as the distribution of modal notions over several form classes in English (Section 3.1.1), the pairs of Mayan verbs and directional particles (Section 3.3.2), and in the comparison of expressions for motion events in English, German, and Korean (Section 3.3.3).

Further, as pointed out at the beginning of this section, patterns of distribution vary across languages. Motion verbs provide a useful example (Slobin, 1991b, 1996a, b; Slobin & Hoiting, 1994). English and Korean represent two distinct types of lexicalization patterns in this domain. In English, the main verb indicates only the fact of MOTION, with possible conflation of MANNER (*go, move, walk, run* . . .), and associated particles indicate PATH (*in, up, down, through* . . .). In Talmy's analysis, PATH is the core meaning of a motion event. Because it is expressed by "satellites" to the verb in English, he characterizes such languages as "satellite-framed" (Talmy, 1991). The Germanic and Slavic languages are of this type. In Korean, PATH is expressed by the verb, as listed in Section 3.3.3. Talmy calls such languages "verb-framed." As indicated in Section 3.3.3, the Romance languages are also verb-framed; other languages of this type are the Semitic and Turkic languages and Japanese.

These typological patterns of distributed semantics have consequences for both acquisition and language use (Berman & Slobin, 1994; Slobin, 1991, 1996a, 1996b, this volume). We have already noted that the child has to identify where PATH is expressed, and that the task involves learning a small, closed set of either path particles (in satellite-framed languages) or path verbs (in verb-framed languages). In addition, the child has to learn (1) how to encode the other elements of a motion situation—FIGURE, GROUND, MANNER, CAUSE, and DEIXIS, and (2) whether their expression is obligatory. For example, in languages where MANNER is an optional adjunct to a main path verb, it is typically expressed in a nonfinite verb form, syntactically linked with certain types of path verbs. (For details, see Slobin & Hoiting, 1994). We have seen this in the Korean example in (5c). A similar construction in Spanish expresses MANNER by means of a gerund:

(7) *Juan entró corriendo a la casa.*
   'John entered running to the house.' (= John ran into the house)

In many languages of this type there is a small set of manner verbs, by comparison with the very large sets in the Germanic and Slavic languages (e.g., *crawl, limp, hobble, creep, slither, wriggle* . . .) where the manner verb tends to be the main verb in the clause, along with a path satellite (e.g., *crawl in, wriggle out*). As a consequence, the acquisition of manner verbs in English looks like a classical task of vocabulary learning in the open class, whereas in Spanish it looks more like learning a small, closed class. (I estimate that there are about 30 such verbs in Spanish in comparison with hundreds in English.)

Distributed spatial semantics can also have consequences for learning the meanings of the core, closed-class elements, depending on their overall functional load in the grammar. English has a relatively large set of differentiated locative prepositions (at least 40), probably due to its satellite-framed typology. These forms can often distinguish between paths and figure-ground relationships on their own, with no further information provided by the verb. For example, using a neutral non-path verb such as *put*, English can differentiate PLACEMENT from INSERTION by choice of particle: *put the book **on/in** the box*. In a language like Spanish, where path is expressed by means of verb selection, there is a small collection of prepositions, each with a wider and more general range of meanings, such as *en* 'in, on', *a* 'at, to,' *de* 'from, of', *por* 'through, via, along, by means of'. Distinctions such as PLACEMENT versus INSERTION must therefore be carried by the verb and by associated noun properties: ***poner** el libro **en** la mesa* '**place** the book **en** (= on) the table', ***meter** el libro **en** la caja* '**insert** the book **en** (= in) the box'. In both types of languages, sentences such as these require understanding of the meanings of all of the lexical items in order to build up the appropriate mental image of the event. However, because parts of the overall semantic content are differentially distributed across linguistic elements, the acquisition tasks differ. Although English and Spanish prepositions appear to be syntactically comparable closed-class items, they play distinctly different roles in the overall structure and use of the language.

Similarly, although English and Spanish motion verbs are "open class," they are distinctly different kinds of "open-class sets," in that Spanish presents a small, closed class of path verbs (listed for Romance languages in general in Section 3.3.3) which play a central role in describing motion events. Therefore, I disagree with Landau and Jackendoff's proposal that spatial verbs are qualitatively different from spatial prepositions (1993, p. 238):

> An important methodological question is how one decides which elements in a language to consider. We have restricted our discussion to prepositions—closed-class elements—and have essentially left untouched spatial verbs, which are open class and seem to have much more latitude in what kinds of geometric and nongeometric elements they can represent. We agree with Talmy (1983) that crosslinguistic investigation should focus on closed-class elements (whether verb markers, prepositions, postpositions, etc.) that express spatial relationships.

This claim must be relativized to the overall typology of the language under consideration. One cannot "leave spatial verbs untouched" if one wishes to understand the patterning and acquisition of grammaticizable notions in a verb-framed language.

3.5. Summary

Let us briefly summarize the answers to the questions posed in the preceding four subsections before moving on to the diachronic evidence.

3.5.1. *What Is a Grammatical Morpheme?*

There is a cline of linguistic elements from fully lexical content words to fully specialized grammatical morphemes, but there is no obvious place to draw a line between lexical and grammatical items.[10] This point has been underlined by Hopper and Traugott (1993, p. 7):

> Synchronically a cline can be thought of as a "continuum": an arrangement of forms along an imaginary line at one end of which is a fuller form of some kind, perhaps "lexical," and at the opposite end a compacted and reduced form, perhaps "grammatical." . . . Linguists may not agree . . . on whether a particular form is to be placed . . . in the lexical area or the grammatical area of the cline.

3.5.2. *What Is a Closed-Class Item?*

The lexicon is made up of a number of classes, ranging from almost entirely open (prototypically nouns) to almost entirely closed (prototypically grammatical morphemes such as clitics and inflections). This is, by definition, a diachronic factor. The issue is whether speakers are likely to encounter new members of a class during their lifetimes. Languages are most free in adding new nouns over time, as new artifacts are created and new phenomena are categorized and labeled. It is my impression that verbs are hardly ever invented "out of whole cloth," as nouns are; rather, they tend to be derived from nouns or adjectives by morphological or phrasal means—for example, *to xerox, to skateboard, to privatize, to finalize, to test drive, to do a number.*

The verb lexicon of a language can be subdivided into many limited, fairly closed classes that provide the language's analysis and categorization of a given conceptual domain. We have seen this with regard to path verbs in verb-framed languages. Other examples are easy to come by. Consider, for example, the set of English verbs of manner of talking (*shout, scream, whisper, mumble, mutter* . . .), posture (*sit, stand, lie, crouch* . . .), or cooking (*bake, fry, roast, boil* . . .). Within such a subclass it is possible to find systematic sets of semantic compo-

---

[10]Note that the existence of clines wreaks havoc with parameter-setting theories, which rely on discrete categories and principles that are applicable throughout a language.

nents in quite the same fashion as componential analyses of grammatical mor-phemes. A good example is the domain of object destruction, which is quite elaborated in the English verb lexicon. We make distinctions of the nature of the object to be destroyed (e.g., *break, tear, smash*), force dynamics (e.g., *tear* vs. *rip*), the degree of destruction or deformation (e.g., *cut* vs. *shred*), the texture or constituency of the object (e.g., *crumple, crumble, shatter*), and so forth. In learning this "closed-class set" of verbs, the English-speaking child has acquired a language-specific set of linguistically relevant notions, and will not go on learning more and more such verbs throughout life. This process is, in principle, no different than the acquisition of the set of English spatial prepositions.

The reader might object that one can continue to acquire specialized terms in adulthood. An experienced cook, for example, must acquire verbs such as *sauté* and *braise*. However, an experienced academic must acquire grammatical forms such as *notwithstanding* and *nevertheless*, and an experienced author might find the need for complex prepositions such as *in the midst of* and *alongside*. One might also object that there are no formal criteria for classes such as "verbs of cooking" or "verbs of speaking." However, from the point of view of the speaker, if one wants to convey the fact that someone delivered a message in a certain manner, one must choose from the set of available verbs of speaking in the language—not the entire "open class" of verbs, but the small collection of verbs in this conceptual domain. Formal criteria are not the only grounds for organizing a mental lexicon.

Recent research suggests, however, that there may also be formal criteria for some semantic subclasses of verbs. As Beth Levin (1993) has documented in detail in her recent book, *English Verb Classes and Alternations*, "verbs in English and other languages fall into classes on the basis of shared components of meaning" (p. 11), and the members of a class "have common syntactic as well as semantic properties" (p. 7). This pioneering attempt to characterize the "open class" of verbs as a collection of grammatically definable subclasses poses another type of challenge to theories that postulate a special psycholinguistic module devoted to the acquisition and processing of the "closed class."

3.5.3. *What Makes a Notion Grammaticizable?*

At present there is no useful answer to this question beyond an empirically based list of the notions that receive grammatical expression in the languages of the world. The same notions are found repeatedly in the analysis of both lexical and grammatical items. This fact has been noted by linguists working in various traditions. Lyons provides a useful textbook discussion (1968, p. 438):

> The main point that must be made here is that there seems to be no essential difference between the 'kind of meaning' associated with lexical items and the 'kind of meaning' associated with grammatical items ... If there is any generalization that can be made about the meaning of grammatical elements ... ,

it would seem to be that grammatical 'choices' have to do with the general notions of spatial and temporal reference, causation, process, individuation, etc....
However, we cannot assume in advance that such notions, even if they are clearly identifiable, will necessarily be 'grammaticalized', rather than 'lexicalized', in the structure of any particular language.

A modern statement of this position can be found in Pinker's (1989) analysis of the acquisition of argument structure. He suggests that a single "Grammatically Relevant Subsystem" of concepts (derived from Jackendoff and Talmy) provides the "privileged semantic machinery" (p. 166) needed BOTH to specify the meanings of closed-class morphemes AND to organize verbs into subclasses that are sensitive to various types of lexical rules and patterns of syntactic alternation.

3.5.4. *How Are Grammaticizable Notions Organized?*

There is great diversity across languages in the level of granularity, the number and positions of cuts on semantic continua, the types of semantic components employed, and the balance between different parts of the linguistic system in expressing grammaticizable notions. This diversity has not yet been sufficiently systematized to make claims about its conceptual or developmental underpinnings. At the present state of our knowledge, it is premature to attribute a particular organization of grammaticizable notions to the child at the beginning of language acquisition (*pace* Slobin, 1985). It would seem more plausible to endow the child with sufficient flexibility to discern and master the particular organization of the exposure language. As Bowerman has put it (1994, p. 44):

> There is, then, no initial stage in which children's grammars rely exclusively on meanings provided by non-linguistic cognition. From the very beginning, form and meaning are analysed together, and learners are sensitive not only to the formal linguistic devices their language uses to encode meanings, but also to the way the meanings themselves are structured for linguistic expression. We as yet know little about how this subtle, linguistically driven kind of semantic learning takes place ... The first step toward coming to understand the process is simply to recognize that it does take place, and this awareness is only recently beginning to dawn.

4. DIACHRONIC EVIDENCE FOR MODIFYING THE LINGUISTIC CONDITIONS ON LEARNABILITY

All of the dominant accounts of learnability attempt to relate the structure of the mind with the structure of language, as if these were the only two factors to consider. When the social factor IS considered, it is only as a source of data: the "input" language, perhaps with some attention to the interactive speech contexts in which the "input" is situated. Accordingly, when there is not enough information in the input to account for the structure of language, it must be sought in the individual mind. The end result is always some kind of nativism, whether of syntactic form, semantic content, or some interaction between form and content, perhaps with various cognitive prerequisites added in. This argument has been re-stated thousands of times since Chomsky first proposed it some three decades ago. Of the many formulations, the following representative summary by Jackendoff (1987, p. 87) is useful in clearly revealing the limited options that flow from this conception of the problem:

> The claim, then, is that some aspects of our language capacity are not a result of learning from environmental evidence. Aside from divine intervention, the only other way we know of to get them into the mind is biologically: genetic information determining brain architecture, which in turn determines the form of possible computations. In other words, certain aspects of the structure of language are INHERITED.
>
> This conclusion, which I will call the INNATENESS HYPOTHESIS, provides a potential solution to the paradox of language acquisition by appealing to evolution. The child alone does not have enough time to acquire all the aspects of language that linguists are struggling to discover. But evolution has had more time at its disposal to develop this structure than linguists will ever have . . .

Note a jump in the argument: It begins by discussing "some aspects of our language CAPACITY," but ends up with the claim that "certain aspects of the STRUCTURE of language are inherited." There can be no disagreement that aspects of the capacity to acquire and use language are inherited: this is a general truth about species-specific behavior. But the STRUCTURE of language arises in TWO diachronic processes: biological evolution and the ever-changing processes of communicative interaction. The structure of language could not have arisen in the genetically determined brain architecture of an individual ancestor alone, because language arises only in communication between individuals. That is, after all, what language is for. As soon as we free ourselves of this confusion of levels of analysis—the individual and the social—many of the puzzles of language structure appear to have solutions beyond divine intervention or genetic determinism. The traditional attempt to account for linguistic structure is rather like trying to locate the law of supply and demand in the minds of the individual producer and consumer, or the shape of a honeycomb in the genetic structure of the individual bee.[11]

---

[11]Bates (1979, p. 18) has used this example to argue persuasively for a view of language development in which structure emerges from the interaction of a number of processes. Drawing on D'Arcy Thompson's (1917) classic *On growth and form*, she argues: "No individual bee need embody the hexagonal 'blueprint' of his hive. Instead, all the individual bee needs is a relatively simple 'local' principle: to pack wax by burrowing his little hemispheric head in it. If enough bees with round heads do enough packing from a variety of directions, a hexagonal three-dimensional structure will emerge at the interface."

In the past 20 years or so there has been a rapidly growing interest in the HISTORICAL, rather than the evolutionary processes that shape language—particularly with regard to the ways in which languages acquire and modify grammatical elements and constructions. A field calling itself "grammaticization" or "grammaticalization" (see footnote 2) has revived long-standing interest in language change, using a wealth of new typological, historical, and psycholinguistic data and theory.[12] As I have suggested, this field helps to explain the nature and origins of grammaticizable notions.

A central phenomenon of language change was already identified at the beginning of the century by the French linguist Antoine Meillet. In 1912, in a paper titled "L'évolution des formes grammaticales," he introduced the term *grammaticalisation* to designate the process by which a word develops into a grammatical morpheme ("le passage d'un mot autonome au rôle d'élément grammatical"). This process provides an explanation of why it is impossible to draw a line between lexical and grammatical items, as well as why grammatical morphemes have their peculiarly restricted and universal semantics. In Section 3.5.1 we encountered Hopper and Traugott's synchronic definition of a cline of linguistic elements from a "lexical area" to a "grammatical area." They present the following "cline of grammaticality":

content item > grammatical word > clitic > inflectional affix

Their discussion continues on the diachronic plane (Hopper & Traugott, 1993, p. 7):

> Each item to the right is more clearly grammatical and less lexical than its partner to the left. Presented with such a cline, linguists would tend to agree that generally the points (labels) on the cline could not be arranged in a different order. . . . It is often difficult to establish firm boundaries between the categories represented on clines, and indeed the study of grammaticalization has emerged in part out of a recognition of the general fluidity of so-called categories. It has also emerged out of recognition that a given form typically moves from a point on the left of the cline to a point further on the right . . .

---

[12]Two overviews, both with the title *Grammaticalization*, have been provided by Heine, Claudi, and Hünnemeyer (1991) and Hopper and Traugott (1993). An early and insightful approach was developed by Bybee (1985), elaborated in successive papers with various collaborators, and most recently presented as *The evolution of grammar* (Bybee, Perkins, & Pagliuca, 1994). Two volumes of conference papers, *Approaches to grammaticalization*, have been edited by Traugott and Heine (1991) and published in the John Benjamins Series, "Typological Studies in Language," which includes many books dealing with diachronic linguistic issues. The journal *Language Variation and Change* is a forum for diachronic research using statistical methods. The closely-related field of "typology and universals" places diachronic issues in a synchronic framework; see textbooks by Comrie (1981) and Croft (1990), and *Linguistic Typology*, the new journal of the recently established Association for Linguistic Typology.

The literature is full of examples of the lexical origins of grammatical items. Familiar English examples are the development of the verb *go* from a full verb of motion to a reduced future marker *gonna*, and the development of modals from verbs of cognition and ability—e.g., *can* originally meant 'know how to', *may* and *might* developed from a verb meaning 'have the (physical) power to'. The English contracted negative, *n't*, began in Old English as an emphatic form, *ne-a-wiht* 'not-ever-anything', used to reinforce another negative form, *ne*. By the time of Middle English it had contracted to *nat* and eventually replaced the nonemphatic *ne*, becoming the new nonemphatic negative and finally contracting (Traugott, 1972, pp. 146f). This is the typical progress along the cline—from full, stressed form with a more specific meaning, to reduced, unstressed form with a more general meaning. When such processes are traced out in full, the nature of grammatical morphemes—unstressed and general in meaning—is no longer mysterious. Here I will explore only one set of diachronic patterns in some detail, because it is relevant to several of the basic synchronic problems discussed in the previous section.

4.1. Origins and Extensions of Accusative Markers

In the long history of Mandarin Chinese it is possible to see the entire developmental path from a lexical item to a grammatical morpheme (Lord, 1982, with examples from Li & Thompson, 1974, 1976). In the fifth century B.C. the verb *bǎ* was a full lexical verb meaning 'take hold of'. Much later, in the time of the Tang Dynasty (seventh–ninth centuries A.D.), it appears in serial-verb constructions, opening the way to reanalysis and eventual grammaticization. For example, the following sentence is open to two different interpretations:

(8) *Zuì bǎ zhū-gēn-zì xì kàn*
    drunk *bǎ* dogwood careful look

In the expected serial-verb interpretation the sentence means:

(a) 'While drunk, (I) *took* the dogwood and carefully looked at it.'

However, a verb meaning 'take' can also be interpreted, in this context, as simply reinforcing the act of examining something that has been taken or held:

(b) 'While drunk, (I) carefully looked at the dogwood.'

On this interpretation, *bǎ* has become a sort of object marker. Such possibilities of alternate interpretations open the way to the reanalyses that result in grammaticization. Sentence (8) "invites" a hearer to consider a single act—looking carefully, rather than two acts—taking and then looking carefully. This kind of "conversational implicature" (Grice, 1975) or "pragmatic inferencing" (Hopper & Traugott, 1993) can set a full verb like *bǎ* off on the course toward a grammatical marker. And, indeed, that is what has happened in this case. In modern Mandarin, *bǎ* no longer has all of the syntactic properties of a full verb: it can't take an aspect marker and can no longer occur as the predicate of a simple sentence meaning 'take' (Li & Thompson, 1981, pp. 464ff). Now it functions as an objective casemarker in the frame, SUBJECT *bǎ* DIRECT.OBJECT VERB, as in:

(9) *nǐ bǎ jiǔ* màn-màn-de hē
     you *bǎ* wine slowly drink
     'You drink the wine slowly!'

However, the *bǎ*-construction is still not a full objective or ACCUSATIVE case-marker. The process of grammaticization is long, and traces of the original meaning of a lexical item linger on to influence or restrict its grammatical function. The construction can only be appropriately used with a DEFINITE direct object, that is, to indicate a referent that the speaker believes the hearer knows about. And, most interestingly, it is further restricted to situations in which something happens to the object—in Li and Thompsons' terms (1981, p. 468), "how an entity is handled or dealt with." It cannot mark objects of verbs of emotion, like 'love' and 'miss', or verbs of cognition, like 'understand' or 'see', because these verbs do not imply manipulation or handling of the object. It may come to mark such objects at some future time, like accusative casemarkers in languages like German and Russian, but at present it still retains traces of its semantic origin.

Lord (1982) describes almost identical grammaticization processes in several West African languages of the Benue-Kwa group. In Akan and Ga, a verb that meant 'take, hold, possess, use' no longer occurs as a verb in simple sentences and does not inflect for tense/aspect. It is now an invariant, noninflecting morpheme that functions as a casemarking preposition—but only when referring to physical manipulation and only in affirmative sentences (that is, manipulation that is actually realized). However, in a related language, Idoma, the corresponding morpheme has become a prefix and, although still restricted to affirmative clauses, can also mark the objects of experience, such as 'she PREFIX-tree saw'. Lord cites a parallel development in the Native American language, Chickasaw, which seems to be at an earlier stage in the process of using a verb meaning 'take' to mark instruments and objects that are moved by an agent.

This is a brief summary of a long and interesting story, which also includes the development of transitive casemarking in ergative languages (e.g., Chung, 1977). But this is sufficient to raise several important points about learnability and nativism. It should now be evident why it is not possible to draw a line between lexical and grammatical items (Sections 3.1, 3.5.1). These continua do not have natural cutting points between the two syntactic categories because of the successive types of change that go on, in language use, over time. The Idoma prefix is "more grammaticized" than the Akan and Ga prepositions in that it is phonologically reduced and has a wider semantic range of application. The Chickasaw prefix is "less grammaticized" than any of the West African examples in that its semantic range is narrower, but it is "more grammaticized" than Akan and Ga prepositions, in that it is a prefix. All of these, including modern Mandarin *bǎ* are "less grammaticized" than German and Russian casemarkers, in that they don't mark the direct objects of all possible transitive verbs. Turkish is like Mandarin in that the accusative inflection is restricted to definite direct objects, but it is like German and Russian and Idoma in that it is not restricted to objects of manipulation. Russian, however, is like Mandarin in that its accusative inflection is limited to affirmative clauses.

It is unlikely that one of these language-specific variants of the "accusative" or "direct object" or "patient" category corresponds to children's initial assumptions about the "grammaticizable notion" underlying the object marker. Clearly, the child must be guided by the patterns of the exposure language. To be sure, all of these examples are consistent with a COLLECTION of "grammatically relevant notions"—definiteness, negation, manipulability, agent vs. experiencer—but there are too many different packagings of such semantic and pragmatic characteristics to build in all of the possible packages in advance or rank them in terms of "naturalness" or "accessibility."

At the same time, there is something intriguing about the fact that a verb like 'take' can repeatedly develop into an object marker in languages that have nothing in common geographically or typologically. In earlier work (Slobin, 1981, 1985) I suggested that children might begin to relate accusative or ergative casemarkers to a general notion of "prototypical direct manipulation," that is, "the experiential gestalt of a basic causal event in which an agent carries out a physical and perceptible change of state in a patient by means of direct body contact or with an instrument under the agent's control" (1985, p. 1175). Verbs like 'take' clearly fit this definition. Can we conclude, then, that this is a privileged grammaticizable notion (Sections 3.3, 3.5.3)? It is important here to distinguish between what is salient to the cognition and life experience of a 2-year-old and the processes that drive grammaticization in the discourse of adult speakers of a language. The "manipulative activity scene" is central to a 2-year-old's interaction with the world, and grammatical markers that regularly occur in conjunction with such events may well come to be associated with the notion of manipulation or direct effect on an object. But adult speakers of Tang dynasty Chinese, Akan, Ga, or Chickasaw do not set out to grammaticize manipulation or effect. Rather, they use a verb like 'take' in constructions that allow it to be interpreted as a marker of manipulation, and, over time, such verbs follow the familiar cline described by Hopper and Traugott. The processes, then, are quite different, though superficially similar.[13] In order to fill out the picture, it is necessary to understand the psycholinguistic forces that move a linguistic element along that cline. Before turning to those forces, though, let us consider one more diachronic example, which reveals a different type of grammaticization path for accusative markers.

Quite another history of an accusative marker can be found in Persian (Hopper & Traugott, 1993, pp. 158ff, based on Bossong, 1985). Here the origin is a noun, *rādiy*, meaning 'goal' or 'purpose'. Given the semantics of this starting point, the path does not begin with manipulation. As a result, much of the path is different, yet there are similarities to the examples we have just reviewed. In Old Persian (*c.* 600 B.C.) this noun is used as a postposition. By Middle Persian it is reduced to a suffix, *-rað*, used as a casemarker for dative-benefactive objects. In New Persian (beginning in the ninth century A.D.) it is reduced further, to the suffix *-râ*, and its use includes direct objects—but only if definite. At this point, then, its meaning is partly similar to the grammaticization paths reviewed above, but, because of its origin, the Persian suffix also marks dative-benefactive objects. In Classical Persian (twelfth–fourteenth centuries A.D.) the dative-benefactive uses expand to include marking of possessors and experiencers. At the same time, the accusative uses expand from marking individual human objects that are affected by an action to include inanimates and, eventually, indefinites. Note that these extensions are as much pragmatic as semantic. Hopper and Traugott point out that this follows a cline of discourse topicality, from animate, human participants to inanimate objects, and from referential to indefinite topics. In Modern Persian the suffix has become restricted to direct objects only, losing all of its capacity to mark dative-like indirect objects. It has thus become a "standard" sort of general accusative marker.

These several paths of accusative development raise critical questions for the Conditions and Assumptions of Section 2. In Persian, as in the earlier examples, each step in the long evolution can be motivated by semantic and discourse factors—but at which point does the form mark a "true grammaticizable notion," and at which point is it a "true grammatical morpheme"? Which of the many "accusatives" in all of these language histories is the one to put on Pinker's innate chart of form-function correspondences? Which of these many historically attested grammatical morphemes corresponds to "core notions" like manipulation or purpose or goal? And, to return to the issue of language sampling, if the earlier versions of Persian were lost from the written record, would we be able to accurately assess the frequency of conflations of certain types of accusative with certain types of dative-benefactive casemarking? Or if the restricted Mandarin and West African object markers evolve into a Persian-type accusative by the twenty-second century, thereby reducing the number of such object markers in the sample of the world's languages, should linguists propose at that point in history that such object markers are "less accessible" to children?

---

[13]For a similar argument against equating processes of ontogeny and grammaticization, see my discussion of the development of the English PERFECT (Slobin, 1994).

4.2. Psycholinguistic Forces Responsible for Restrictions on Grammaticizable Notions

Grammaticization paths such as those just sketched out take place, to begin with, in the processes of communication. Therefore they are shaped by the online demands on the speaker to be maximally clear within pragmatic constraints and maximally efficient within economy constraints, and by online capacities of the listener to segment, analyze, and interpret the message. Experimental and theoretical psycholinguists have learned much about these processes, in a literature far too large to cite or review here. It is clear that pressures of expressivity, economy, and clarity are always in competition, keeping language always changing in shifting states of balancing equilibrium (e.g., Slobin, 1977; Bates & MacWhinney, 1987; Bybee, 1985; Hawkins, 1983, 1995; MacWhinney & Bates, 1989). This is not the place for a detailed exposition of the psycholinguistic bases of language change. What I want to do is point to some psycholinguistic processes that seem to account for the peculiar semantic limitations on grammaticizable notions that Talmy and others have discussed.

4.2.1. *Frequency of Use and Generality of Meaning*

Bybee (1985; Bybee, Perkins, & Pagliuca, 1994) has explained much of grammaticization in terms of the fact that lexical items that are used with high frequency also have general meanings. For example, motion verbs such as *crawl, limp, hobble, creep, slither, wriggle* are applicable to describing a small number of situations and are, accordingly, not very frequent. By contrast, generalized motion verbs like *come* and *go* do not have such restrictions; they are applicable to a wide range of contexts and are used frequently. Generality of meaning and frequency of use go hand in hand—both in the "open" and "closed" classes. For example, compare highly frequent English prepositions like *in* and *on* with less frequent and more specialized propositions such as *alongside, underneath, in back of, throughout*. The latter require more detailed attention to the geometry of the objects involved, and are therefore applicable to more limited contexts.

4.2.2. *Frequency of Use and Reduction of Form*

It is also a commonplace that any motor program that is called upon frequently is reduced and automatized. Zipf (1935) demonstrated the strong tendency for the length of a word to be negatively correlated with its frequency. Note that the more specialized prepositions just listed are also much longer than *in* and *on*. They are also more etymologically transparent—that is, they still have recognizable lexical components, including nouns (*side, back*) and more frequent prepositions (*in, of,* etc.). It is no mystery that as lexical items move along the grammaticization cline they become phonologically reduced and bound to associated content words.

4.2.3. *Frequency of Use and Decidability*

In order for a speaker to express any notion in language, it is necessary to make a rapid decision with regard to the appropriate means of expression of that notion. Elements that are highly frequent and general—both content words and grammatical forms—must be easily accessible to online processing for both speaker and listener. Again, the same processing demands apply to content words and grammatical forms alike. Eve Clark (1978) has observed that early in English child language development the most frequent verbs are *go, put, get, do*, and *make*. She reports similar findings for Finnish, French, Japanese, and Korean. This pattern probably reflects the high frequency of such verbs in adult speech, but the fact of their early frequency also bears on the issue of decidability. In Clark's examples, when a child says *Do it!* it might apply to unrolling some tape, taking out a toy, or building a tower. *Make* + NOUN can mean *write, draw, move, cut out*, and so forth. *Do* and *make* place low demands on decidability. In order to say *write* or *draw* or *cut out* the speaker must decide what kind of act of construction is involved, and determine the distinctions that are lexicalized in the language (for example, in some languages a single verb means both 'write' and 'draw').

These same sorts of "light" verbs appear as the sources of grammatical morphemes, as the examples of 'go' and 'take' discussed earlier. Hopper and Traugott (1993, p. 87) present this as a general fact of grammaticization:

> As we have noted in previous chapters, the lexical meanings subject to grammaticali-zation are usually quite general. For example, verbs which grammaticalize, whether to case markers or to complementizers, tend to be superordinate terms (also known as "hyponyms") in lexical fields, for example, *say, move, go*. They are typically not selected from more specialized terms such as *whisper, chortle, assert, squirm, writhe*. Likewise, if a nominal from a taxonomic field grammaticalizes into a numeral classifier, it is likely to be selected from the following taxonomic levels: beginner (e.g., *creature, plant*), life form (e.g., *mammal, bush*), and generic (e.g., *dog, rose*), but not from specific (e.g., *spaniel, hybrid tea*), or varietal (e.g., *Cocker, Peace*) (Adams & Conklin, 1973). In other words, the lexical items that grammaticalize are typically what are known as "basic words."

Again, it is an illusion that child language development and grammaticization are due to the same sorts of processes. Children use basic verbs early on because they are easy to learn: They do not place high demands on decidability; they are frequent; they are used across a wide range of situations; they are short. But basic verbs appear at the beginnings of grammaticization clines because, when they are used in a conversational context, they contrast with the more specific verbs that COULD be used in that context, thereby allowing the hearer to infer that a more specific meaning may not have been intended. This opens the way for the kinds of pragmatic inferencing and reanalysis that lie at the heart of grammaticization.

Given these facts, it is evident that the special character of grammaticizable notions has its origin, in part, in the lexical items from which grammatical markers are prone to develop. That is, the "open class" is already organized into general and specialized terms—and this division can be accounted for by quite ordinary psycholinguistic and communicative processes. There is no need to postulate a special "grammar module" as responsible for these facts about the meanings of frequent lexical items. Why are such words prone to grammaticize? Because of their generality they are both highly frequent and likely to be used in situations in which the speaker either does not intend a more specialized meaning or assumes that such a meaning can be reliably inferred by the listener as background information in context. If I say, for example, "While drunk, I GRASPED the dogwood" or "SEIZED the dogwood," the choice of a specialized verb of taking or holding suggests to the hearer that I wish to focus on the manner of taking or holding. This is simply an application of Grice's second maxim of Quantity: "Do not make your contribution more informative than is required" (Grice, 1975). The hearer may well assume that I used a specialized verb because I intended to draw attention to the manner of acting. If, however, I use a more general verb like 'take', the hearer is likely to assume that I have followed the first maxim of Quantity, "Make your contribution as informative as is required (for the current purposes of the exchange)," and will not attend to the manner of taking the dogwood. In fact, following this maxim, the hearer might arrive at the interpretation given earlier in example (8b)—that is, backgrounding the fact of taking entirely and focusing on the act of looking, which is, after all, what may be relevant in this communicative situation. In such situations, the way has been opened for the grammaticization of 'take' as an object marker.

4.2.4. Frequency of Use and Schematicization of a Domain

If a small set of linguistic items ends up being used frequently to reference divisions within a semantic domain, pressures toward easy decidability will inevitably move the system toward a schematic representation of that domain, selecting a set of parameters or features for sorting instances. The most familiar example of schematicization is an inflectional paradigm, in which slots are filled in for such features as person and number, or case and gender, and so forth. But schematicization is also evident in linguistic systems which might appear to be more lexical than grammatical. A good example is Levinson's (1994) analysis of the Tzeltal use of body-part terminology to locate an object in relation to a ground. In English we have suggestions of such a system in grammaticized expressions such as *in back of the house* and lexicalized descriptions such as *the foot of the mountain*. In Tzeltal, as in many Mesoamerican languages, body-part terms are used systematically to specify the grounds involved in locative relations. One says, for example, that an object is at the 'ear' (= corner) of a table or at the 'butt' (= bottom) of a bottle (P. Brown, 1994, p. 750). Levinson (1994) shows that choice of body-part term is based on a precise geometric schematicization of objects. For example, the base of an arc defines the 'butt' of an object, including the large end of a pear, the bottom of a bowl, and the point where a stem is attached to a leaf. If an object has two surfaces, the flatter, less-featured surface will be labeled 'back' and the opposing surface will be 'belly' if concave or convex and 'face' if flat. In order to use the system, in Levinson's analysis, the speaker must carry out a series of algorithms, such as finding the orthogonal axis, finding the direction of the subsidiary arc, and finding junctures between surfaces. He proposes that by applying such calculations of the intrinsic shape of an object, speakers know how to use the body-part terms with regard to any particular object. Thus, Tzeltal words like 'butt', 'ear', 'belly', and 'neck' are as fully grammaticized as English prepositions. They constitute a small, closed set, with schematized representations of those features of their spatial characteristics that are used in the language to specify locative relations of particular types. Because body-part terms must be used to designate parts of any object in the world—doors, tables, computers, chile beans—speakers must be able to decide easily which term to apply to which part or surface of an object. Such a system cannot simply leave the speaker to pick a body-part term and search for a possible metaphorical extension; nor can it leave the speaker to use all possible body parts. Out of several hundred such terms, the language uses about 20 to label parts of inanimate objects. In order to apply this small set to all possible objects, there is no choice but to develop a way of schematizing their meanings within a structured semantic domain. Again, the system is a compromise between possible conceptual differentiation and the demands of online production and comprehension. The results of compromises of this sort cannot be built into the language module, but arise in processes of language use.[14]

4.3. A Functionalist Account of the Classes of Grammaticizable and Non-Grammaticizable Notions

If a domain is to be divided up such that each of the subcategories can be rapidly accessed online, by speaker and hearer, there cannot be too many divisions in the domain, nor can the deciding factors be infrequent or idiosyncratic. Typically, as forms become highly grammaticized, they divide up a domain exhaustively into a very small number of options: SINGULAR VS. PLURAL (with possible additions of DUAL), PERFECTIVE VS. IMPERFECTIVE, the six cases and three genders of Russian. Markers such as these are obligatory, which means they must be accessed in almost every utterance. There can be no ambiguities of online decidability. The notions that evolve into such very small and obligatory sets must (1) unambiguously divide

---

[14]Levinson proposes that the schematicization is given by the visual system, thus raising a problem for modularity theories: "According to modularity arguments, linguistic processes should have no access to strictly visual processes. Although the present facts are not decisive, together with other observations they favor models where there is shared linguistic and visual access to the underlying processes of volumetric shape analysis" (1994, p. 791).

the domain, and must (2) use criteria that are generally relevant to that domain. Thus it is no mystery that grammatical inflections do not indicate color or rate or ambient temperature: these are not generally salient aspects of experience; they are not universally decidable, applicable, or memorable with regard to all of the event types that we talk about. That is, they are not aspects that are relevant to how we interpret and store events IN GENERAL. In order, for example, to grammaticize a temperature marker or a color marker, it would be necessary, first, to have a speech community in which lexical items of temperature or color occurred frequently in discourse, and in which there were a few general terms that marked readily agreed-upon distinctions, such as *cold - cool - warm - hot*, or *black - white - red - yellow - blue/green*. Such scenarios are unlikely for several reasons. For one, these distinctions are not relevant to most of human discourse. The things that we care to communicate about, by and large, are true on cool and warm days; the things we act upon are important regardless of their color.[15] Because we don't tend to store such information in memory, such a language would place terrible burdens on decidability. For example, if I wanted to tell you a juicy bit of gossip, I would have to remember whether the reported event (or the time of my hearing about it) occurred on a warm or cool day. Or when a newscaster reports a bomb explosion in the Paris Metro, he would have to know the color of the bomb, or the Metro, or the explosion. We do not grammaticize such notions because we do not think or talk in such terms.

"Lower" on grammaticization clines there are relatively small sets that provide options. For example, as discussed in Section 3.1.1, English has a small set of modal auxiliaries, supplemented by quasi-modals and some less clearly gram- maticized terms. Most of the time modality can be simply left unmarked. The "zero option" means that it is not necessary to decide about the modality of every utterance. A similar function is provided by the general classifier *gè* in Mandarin. When a speaker does choose to mark modality in English or to classify a class in Mandarin, a small set of terms is provided, with more flexibility in their applicability. Erbaugh (1986) finds about 22 classifiers in ordinary speech in Mandarin, and she reports that the same object occurs with different classifiers in discourse; e.g., different speakers viewing the same film referred to a goat with the classifiers *yī-zhī* 'one.animal', *yì-tó* 'one.head', and *yì-tíao* 'one.long.thing'. The choices in a set like the Mandarin classifiers do not unam- biguously divide up a domain, but they are still semantically relevant to the nouns that are marked.

Relevance, however, does not have to be part of a UNIVERSAL or INNATE human "semantic space." There is nothing in the nature of our cognitive and linguistic systems that precludes grammaticization of idiosyncratic information if it assumes sufficient social or cultural relevance to be regularly communicable. For example, social structure is repeatedly grammaticized in choices of personal pronouns and

---

[15]Although, as mentioned in footnote 4, presence or absence of color may be more salient than distinguishing between colors.

verb inflections. Although a European speaker would find it hard to decide whether each person addressed is older or younger than the speaker, this is obligatory in Korean, and children learn to pay attention to this feature. English speakers in France might find it hard to decide if an interlocutor falls into the *tu* or the *vous* category, and, as Roger Brown and Albert Gilman (1960) have shown, the criteria for choosing one of the two pronoun types has changed historically and varies between European countries. The languages of the world grammaticize an array of social categories of rank, status, relative age, servitude, and the like. These are sociocultural facts, and could not possibly be part of the child's innate linguistic categories or prelinguistic sensorimotor concepts. Yet they are grammaticized in those societies where they are relevant, and are marked with a small number of forms that are frequent and decidable online. The reason why languages have no grammatical markers for quantified categories of "fixed distance, size, contour, and angle" (Talmy, 1988, p. 171) is simply because human beings do not regularly code, store, and report their experience in these terms—not because these categories are *a priori* excluded from the grammar module. I would suggest, then, that anything that is important and salient enough for people to want to refer to it routinely and automatically most of the time, and across a wide range of situations, CAN come to be grammatically marked, within the constraints of online processing briefly alluded to earlier.[16]

I believe that similar arguments could be made with regard to each of the "conceptual domains NOT accessible to grammaticization," such as those listed in (1b). These arguments would draw on the factors of across-the-board relevance

---

[16]The discussion of grammaticizable notions in the literature has focused almost entirely on "synthetic" language types ("inflecting" and "agglutinating"), and primarily on inflectional, rather than derivational categories in those languages. "Isolating" and "polysynthetic" languages pose problems for the division between "grammatical" and "lexical." In Talmy's analyses, serial verbs are treated as "satellites" in isolating languages such as Chinese, on the assumption that a "main verb" can be identified in a verb series. Similarly, grammatical morphemes in polysynthetic languages such as Atsugewi are also treated as "satellites" in relation to a central verb stem. Verbs in serial-verb constructions, and affixes in polysynthetic languages, are often more "contentful" or "lexical" in their meanings, while still having a degree of generality and abstractness that characterizes the meanings of grammatical morphemes in synthetic languages. As such, they qualify as notions that speakers can refer to routinely and automatically across a wide range of situations. For example, Marianne Mithun (personal communication, 1996; also see 1989) has commented on culturally specific notions that can be marked by affixes in Amerindian languages: In Central Pomo, the verb root *léy* 'exhaust, use up', when prefixed with *čʰ-* 'by gambling', results in *čʰéy* 'lose all in gambling'; when prefixed with *ča-* 'by sitting', the result is *čaléy*, which Mithun glosses as 'to wear a hole in the seat of your pants' or perhaps 'wear out the upholstery in the driver's seat of your car'. She also notes that Yup'ik Eskimo has a suffix that means 'have a cold NOUN', which combines with body-part noun roots such as 'nose' or 'toe' to yield 'have a cold nose', and so on. Thus, when one extends the definition of "grammatically marked," it seems that anything that is culturally significant can be expressed by grammatical morphemes associated with "content words." (The high incidence of "scare quotes" in this footnote indicates the degree to which all of the quoted terms are inadequate to the task of sorting out the relations between grammar and cognition!)

to human experience and communication, online decidability, and the availability of high-frequency and general lexical items that could start off paths of grammaticization in those domains. I leave it to the reader to try to find examples or counterexamples.

5. CHALLENGES TO LEARNING THEORY

5.1. The Conditions and Assumptions of the Learning Task

In Section 2 I listed three linguistic Conditions and three psychological Assumptions underlying standard definitions of the task of learning to use grammatical morphemes. It is time to return to that starting point.

5.1.1. *The Conditions*

Condition 1: There is a distinct and identifiable collection of grammatical morphemes, arranged in small, closed classes. It turns out that there is a cline of linguistic elements, arising naturally over time, and that the "distinct and identifiable collection of grammatical morphemes" only defines the endpoint of that cline. However, looking at an entire language, one can only rank elements on various dimensions, both formal and functional. There are, to be sure, many small, closed and semi-closed sets of items—but they are not all grammatical morphemes. Thus the language does not present itself to the learner as a neat set of little packages labeled as "grammatical" and "lexical."

Condition 2: These morphemes map onto a universal, limited set of semantic entities (grammaticizable notions). The further one moves to the right on the cline, the more true is this condition. And there are regular diachronic progressions of particular types of meanings toward the highly grammaticized pole of the cline.

Condition 3: Grammaticizable notions are arranged in a universal accessibility hierarchy. If "accessible" means either "learnable" or "more frequent in human languages," we lack the data to evaluate this condition. If "accessible" means that some notions are more likely to grammaticize than others, the claim can be filled out with more and more data, and the patterns are amenable to explanation in terms of such interacting factors as online processing, pragmatic inference, and syntactic reanalysis.

5.1.2. *The Assumptions*

Assumption 1: Conditions 1, 2, and 3 exist because of the structure of the mind/brain (in modules for aspects of language, perhaps in conjunction with other modules). There is a great deal of evidence that the Conditions exist because of conditions on the processing, social use, and learning of form-function relations. Such evidence greatly reduces the role of *a priori* specification of grammatical structures and their specialized meanings.

Assumption 2: The role of linguistic input is to allow the relevant mental capacities to organize themselves in terms of the exposure language. This, of course, remains true—but relativized to the definition of "relevant mental capacities." Linguistic diversity in the domains considered here precludes a simple selection between prespecified alignments of formal and semantic categories. The role of linguistic input is to guide the child toward discovery and construction of the form-function relations inherent in the exposure language. That is, input is not a "trigger" but a "nutrient."

Assumption 3: The child learns the meaning of a grammatical form by isolating and identifying a particular stretch of speech as instantiating a grammatical form and attempting to map it onto a relevant grammaticizable notion. This formulation is built upon *a priori* definitions of "grammatical form" and "relevant grammaticizable notion"—the very concepts that demand reanalysis. The result of that reanalysis is, of course, the challenge to learning theory.

5.2. Toward a Solution

It is not (and cannot be) the goal of this chapter to answer these challenges by presenting The Adequate Learning Theory. At best, a reorientation might serve to head us toward different kinds of solutions. Once we have established a social-historical, rather than an individual-mind source of grammaticized notions and their means of expression, we can abandon the search for an innate form-function module and follow Annette Karmiloff-Smith (1992) "beyond modularity." That is, we can take a DEVELOPMENTAL approach to the structuring of grammaticizable notions in the child. A major theme that emerges from the reanalysis is the proposal that the same learning mechanisms apply across the lexicon, including "content words" and "functors." To be sure, the child requires specialized mechanisms of perception (auditory for speech, visual for sign), storage, and analysis of linguistic material. And the ARCHITECTURE of syntax is certainly determined by quite different processes than those involved in learning the kinds of form-function mappings considered here. The reanalysis of the learning task places "grammaticizable notions" in the more general domain of concept formation.

5.2.1. *The Problem of Constraints on Hypotheses:*
What Is "Economy"?

Regardless of the revision of the task definition, the child will always be faced with a large set of possible form-function mappings. My very brief overview of a few problems of grammatical marking of semantic and pragmatic categories makes it evident that the child could be prey to many false starts and dead-end attempts. This fact alone has led to the proliferation of "constraints," "predispositions," "parameter settings," "operating principles," and the like in the theoretical literature of recent decades. But there are no obvious constraints on the constraints, because we have no plausible metric of what makes a task "too hard" for a child learner. We know that children do acquire the manifold and subtle complexities of language. And we realize that this is a hard task for conscious, problem-solving adults (even linguists). Therefore we try to make the task "easier" for children by providing bootstraps that they can use to pull themselves up with (an unclear metaphor at best). The list of grammaticizable notions was intended to provide an aid—intended to prevent the child from making too many false hypotheses. But, I would propose, we really have no way of knowing how many false hypotheses it takes to overburden the vastly complex human brain, or how quickly and efficiently they can be revised or dismissed. It is unsettling to realize how many of our theories are aimed at the simplistic criterion of "economy," when we have no rational measure of that economy.

We have been called upon, in our training, to apply Occam's Razor to our theories. This is entirely reasonable: "What can be done with fewer [terms] is done in vain with more." But remember that William of Occam was concerned with choosing between theories that are equivalent in accounting for the data and differ only with respect to their complexity as theories. This is an aesthetic criterion, and has nothing to do with the functioning of organisms or machines or planetary systems. The technology of producing and marketing goods has given us the criterion of economy or efficiency—a standard based on time, cost, and value, and not elegance of theoretical formulation. These two norms, parsimony in explanation and economy in the marketplace, have become confused in our evaluations of psychological explanations. We are not in a position to apply Occam's Razor, because we do not have learning theories which are equal in accounting for the data, differing only in formal complexity. (In fact, we are at the stage in which all of our theories are vastly underdetermined by the available data.) If we, accordingly, abandon Occam and try to establish a metric of the efficiency or economy of a complex biological system, functioning with a complex language and culture, it should be evident that we have neither ground rules nor plausible criteria, and that therefore arguments based on "economy" are illusory.

5.2.2. What Is "Reasonable"?

Having voiced these qualms about the soundness of our endeavor, I return to the attempt to give the child some guidelines for the task. Our theories are haunted by the risk that children might think that everything might be relevant to everything. Our data, however, suggest that children are more "reasonable" than that. Frank Keil's (1994) discussion of the general problem of concept formation is helpful in placing our problem in a larger framework:

People do not simply note feature frequencies and feature correlations; they have strong intuitions about which frequencies and correlations are reasonable ones to link together in larger structures and which are not. Without these intuitions, people would make no progress in learning and talking about common categories given the indefinitely large number of possible correlations and frequencies that can be tabulated from any natural scene. These intuitions seem much like intuitive theories of how things in a domain work and why they have the structure they do . . . (p. 173)

Keil summarizes results of experiments on children's understanding of word meanings (Keil, 1989), giving the following example of children's "reasonable-ness":

Even the youngest children were never simply tabulating up all salient feature frequencies and correlations. No child thinks that uncles must have glasses even if all the uncles they happen to have seen wear them. The features selected by even the earliest word learners were always constrained by some notions of reasonableness for the kind of thing in question (Keil, 1994, p. 177).

Where might such "reasonableness" come from in learning the specialized meanings of linguistic items? How does the child know the reasonable factors to consider when encountering, say, verbs of motion or locative particles or casemarkers? Recall the diachronic processes of grammaticization (and, I would add, the processes of forming small sets of specialized verbs). The only available items are those which occur again and again in talking about a great range of experiences. They occur so frequently because they are applicable so generally. Therefore it should be no surprise that children find these notions salient. For example, the factors that apply to many instances of moving and placing objects include the force-dynamic and motoric aspects of picking up an object, moving it, and placing it in another location. It is "reasonable" for grammatical items and small verb sets dealing with these actions to be sensitive to such factors as characteristics of figure and ground objects, direction of movement, and relation of the two objects at the endpoint of the action (e.g., tight fit, located near the bottom of another object, etc.).[17] The color of the objects or the amount of daylight are not RELEVANT to this type of scene, just as eyeglasses are not relevant to the social and kinship status of uncles. In part, children are reasonable because languages are reasonable. It has been assumed in the literature that it is odd that systems of grammatical meaning, and children acquiring such systems, seem to be indifferent to "non-grammaticizable" notions such as those listed by Talmy (in 1b). However, if we look carefully at the communicative contexts in which

---

[17]What was, in retrospect, not "reasonable" was my Platonic hope that all children would start with the same semantic notions—the "Basic Child Grammar" of Slobin (1985). This issue must be explored in detail, domain by domain, before we can make any claims about the range and types of particular starting points in particular domains across languages and children.

language is used—both on the diachronic and ontogenetic planes—the situation seems much less odd. I suggest that the same factors that keep certain notions from becoming grammaticized also keep children from postulating them as the meanings of grammatical forms.

There are at least two parts to this argument: frequency and relevance. For example, particular colors do not occur frequently in association with the linguistic encoding of particular event types. The child is not likely to encounter one set of object placement events that consistently occur with red objects and another with black ones. Even a simple model of statistical sampling, not to mention a connectionist network, would quickly drop color as a determining factor in choice of linguistic form—even if it is salient to the child in particular situations. Other features, however, do occur frequently. For example, every event takes place in an ambient temperature, and many events occur on hot days that do not occur on cold days. But, given the ways in which humans interact with each other and with the world, ambient temperature is not relevant to most of our behaviors. We put objects in containers, experience the visual world, maintain social status relations, and so forth, on days which are hot or cold, in daylight or at night. There is no reason to build into a language module factors that are basic to human life and action in general.

5.2.3. *Why Ontogeny Does Not Recapitulate Diachrony*

Parallels between development of language in the individual and changes in languages over time have intrigued linguists for a very long time. With regard to the phenomena under investigation in this chapter, the parallel that has attracted attention is the fact that some of the notions that are salient to small children are also salient in the process of grammaticization. But it is important to underline, yet again, an important difference between aspects of experience that are salient to the child and those that end up as grammaticized notions. Consider features of temperature—which are NOT grammaticized in the languages that we know of. Children certainly do orient to temperature—both to temperature of objects and temperature of the surrounding air. And a child may very well expect, on first hearing a new linguistic item (either lexical or grammatical), that it relates to a salient temperature experience. How else could children learn adjectives like *hot* and *cold*? However, given the nature of human culture and interaction, temperature does not occur regularly and frequently with regard to the GRAMMATICAL structuring of utterances. In the presence of a hot object, mommy might say, "Don't touch it, it's hot." The lexical item *hot* DOES cooccur repeatedly with the salient experience of temperature—but *touch, don't*, and the syntactic constructions of subject-object relations and negative imperative do not. This is because most of the time temperature is irrelevant to human speech and action. Note, however, that this is not because children think that temperature is an unimportant feature of the world. (Nor do we know whether children might, fleetingly, postulate temperature as a possible grammaticizable notion.) To repeat my theme, the child does not recapitulate the history of the language, nor is the history of the language based on what is salient to the child. Rather, the only meanings that can end up as grammaticizable notions are those that are general, applicable, decidable, and so forth, as discussed above. Speech communities are at work (very slowly) in modifying grammars. Children are at work (quite quickly) in mastering ALREADY EXISTING grammars.

5.2.4. Iconic Bootstrapping

There is a different sort of "relevance" that also plays a role in form-function mappings. It has long been noted by linguists that grammatical morphemes are placed in association with the content words with which they have the most conceptual affinity—for instance, tense is marked on verbs rather than nouns, shape classifiers are placed in relation to object nouns or verbs of handling, and so forth. A classic formulation of this principle was offered by the German linguist Behaghel (1932, p. 4): "What belongs together mentally is placed close together syntactically."[18] Bybee (1985) has refined the principle, showing not only that particular notions are relevant to verb stems, but that grammatical morphemes reflecting such notions are ordered in a reasonable way, with those meanings that are most relevant to the meaning of the stem occurring closest to the stem. The details are not important here, but Bybee's conclusion gives the child another part of a "reasonableness bootstrap" (pp. 11f):

> Verbal inflections differ with respect to the extent to which they are RELEVANT to the verb, that is, the extent to which their meanings DIRECTLY AFFECT THE LEXICAL CONTENT OF THE VERB STEM. The different degrees of relevance of verbal categories that can be inflectional is reflected diagrammatically in three ways: (1) The more relevant a category is to the verb, the more likely it is to occur in a synthetic or bound construction with the verb; (2) The more relevant a morphological category is to the verb, the closer its marker will occur with respect to the verb stem; (3) The more relevant a morphological category is to the verb, the greater will be the morpho-phonological fusion of that category with the stem.

Bybee's analysis is part of a series of discoveries of the "inconicity" of form-function mappings in language (e.g., Haiman, 1985a, 1985b). To the extent that the arrangement of linguistic items is a "diagram" or "icon" of the arrangement of mental items, the child may be aided by "iconic bootstrapping." There are many examples of iconicity in children's early grammars, across languages, summarized in Slobin (1985).

---

[18]"Das oberste Gesetz ist dieses, daß das geistig eng Zusammengehörige auch eng zusammengestellt wird."

5.2.5. *Typological Bootstrapping*

Keil's analysis of concept formation emphasizes that children are building up "explanatory systems" that are relevant to classes of phenomena (cf. Gopnik & Meltzoff, 1996, on children as "theorists"). He proposes (pp. 178f):

> There are shifts in understanding which explanatory system is most relevant to a class of phenomena. A child might realize that 'uncle' is better understood in terms of a set of biological relations that comprise kinship and not in terms of social relations that govern friendship; the social explanation is discovered to generate more serious mistakes and is abandoned.

This example comes from the learning of word meanings, but the framework is applicable to learning the meanings of grammatical morphemes and constructions as well. What is important in this approach is the child's ability to learn "which explanatory system is most relevant to a class of phenomena." I suggest that as the child develops a successful explanatory structure for part of the exposure language, other parts become more accessible—that is, a coherent theory of the language begins to emerge. This is true, in part, because the language really IS a fairly coherent system—as a result of constant balancing out of competing forces. Over time, each language acquires a typological character resulting from the particular interplay of forces in its history. (There is a small number of language types, but this is not because there is a small number of innate parameter settings; rather, there is a small number of solutions to the kinds of competing forces which shape language in use.) At the risk of overburdening the child's shoe-rack, I propose yet another kind of bootstrapping: TYPOLOGICAL BOOTSTRAPPING (for further discussion, see Slobin, this volume).

Consider verbs of motion again. As the Korean-speaking child learns more linguistic constructions describing motion events, the lexicalization patterns and grammaticized notions of the language become an established pattern. She comes to expect that paths will be lexicalized in verb stems, that caused-motion verbs attend to factors of tightness of fit, and so forth. The English-speaking child comes to expect verb particles to structure domains in terms of locative and temporal relations, and finds that certain locative and temporal notions occur again and again. That is, to some extent, the language structures itself as it is learned. Certain patterns of semantic and formal organization become more and more familiar, and, to use an old term, habits are established. This is possible because of the fact that languages naturally develop into coherent systems of various types. In the process of learning various pieces of the system, they come to interrelate because of inherent typological factors. In Karmiloff-Smith's (1992) terms, "representational redescription" occurs—in this case aided by the systematicity inherent in the language that is being learned. (I am aware that this formulation still leaves open the mechanisms that a child might use to detect such systematicity and "representationally redescribe" it. The goal of this chapter is to reformulate the question.)

An intriguing consequence of typological bootstrapping is that children come to formulate experience for linguistic expression in quite different ways, depending on the type of language they are learning. I have suggested that each type of language fosters its own modes of "thinking for speaking" (Slobin, 1991, 1996a). Because of the systematic crosslinguistic diversity in selection and patterning of grammaticizable notions, different patterns of online mental organization result. In crosslinguistic work on narrative development, Ruth Berman and I have identified a number of ways in which children come to structure discourse in terms of the typological characteristics of the particular language (Berman & Slobin, 1994). By school age, children have acquired typologically distinct ways of describing events and constructing connected texts. From this point of view, grammaticizable notions have a role in structuring language-specific mental spaces, rather than being there at the beginning, waiting for an input language to turn them on.

I am aware that this formulation still leaves open the mechanisms that a child might use to detect and "representationally redescribe" the systematicity of the exposure language. Various sorts of "operating principles" and "procedures" will be needed in order to give substance to the formulation. However, the very fact that form-function relations become systematically patterned in the course of acquiring a particular language points to an importance learning mechanism. As suggested above, in the course of development the child comes to attend to particular types of meanings and to expect them to be expressed by particular types of forms. Such a combination of thinking for speaking and typological bootstrapping seems to guarantee that language-specific form-function patterns will be established and maintained by learners.

5.2.6. *The Problem of Primitives*

The child learner must begin the task of form-function mapping with SOME semantic notions, and must continue to employ semantic hypotheses in the process of being "guided" by the language to the specific notions that are packaged into linguistic forms. In 1985, I assumed that the starting points were unanalyzed semantic configurations or prototypes, and that language-specific categories would emerge later (p. 1174):

> When functors are first acquired, they seem to map more readily onto a universal set of basic notions than onto the particular categories of the parental language. Later in development, of course, the language-specific use of particular functors will train the child to conceive of grammaticizable notions in conformity with the speech community . . . At first, however, there is considerable evidence that children discover principles of grammatical marking according to their own categories— categories that are not yet tuned to the distinctions that are grammaticized in the parental language.

It is clear from the argument of the present chapter, however, that the picture is not that simple. We have evidence both for language-specific categories from the start, and for idiosyncratic categories that do not directly reflect the exposure language. Eve Clark (in press) discusses the latter as "emergent categories." These are "categories that surface fleetingly during acquisition and then vanish again." She notes, for example, that a general notion of SOURCE appears in early child speech in various languages, such as the use of a locative preposition (English *from*, Dutch *van*, Italian *de*) to mark agents of actions, possessors, and standards-of-comparison—although this array of meanings is not a unitary category in the exposure language (for details, see Clark & Carpenter, 1989a, 1989b). The "prototypical scenes" of Slobin (1985) can also be seen as emergent categories: manipulative activity, result, and the like. They are fleeting because they are at the wrong level of granularity for the language being acquired. For example, English uses the preposition *by* to express the SOURCE of AGENCY, uses *than* to express the SOURCE of STANDARD OF COMPARISON, and so forth. If the child begins with a global notion of SOURCE, it must later be analyzed on some dimensions, using relevant semantic features or components.

Emergent categories are intriguing because they seem to reveal conceptual starting points for grammaticized notions. As Clark and Carpenter put it (1989a, p. 22): "Emergent categories offer evidence for the conceptual representations that underlie linguistic categories and that have linguistic consequences. . . . Emergent categories, we propose, reflect universals of conceptual representation." However, we do not yet know whether such patterns are truly universal, or whether there is a great range of individual variation, by child and by language.

Another approach is to equip the child with fine-grained "primitives" and let linguistic experience sort them out into the appropriate categories. This is implicit in the various discussions of "semantic packaging" reviewed above: Something has to "get packaged." For example, in Bowerman's (1996a, 1996b) studies of the language of space, children learning different languages must attend to various features of locative relations. She lists many such features: for example, "spontaneous versus caused motion," "contact with and support by an external surface," "attachment by hooking," "put elongated object to base," "juxtapose surfaces that are flat," and so forth. Using such semantic characterizations, Bowerman succeeds in delineating the differences between English, Dutch, and Korean in the meanings of spatial terms and traces out the course of acquisition of these languages. Could the child be using distinctions at these levels of granularity to arrive at the proper definition of grammaticized notions in the language? As Bowerman puts it (1996a, p. 422):

> If semantic categories are constructed, they must be constructed out of something, and an important question is what this something is. Here we come squarely up against one of the oldest and most difficult problems for theorists interested in the structure of mind: identifying the ultimate stuff of which meaning is made.

The facts of crosslinguistic diversity, and the inadequacy of current formulations, make Bowerman skeptical of accounts which attribute semantic primitives to the child; however, she DOES succeed in using various kinds of "primitives" to make her exposition comprehensible. It seems to me that our task is to find the proper level of analysis to distinguish between languages and to adequately describe children's uses of linguistic forms over the course of development. This is, indeed, "one of the oldest and most difficult problems." But it should ultimately be solvable on the basis of converging attempts at careful analysis and description of many languages and many child learners. In the end, the overlap between such descriptions should reveal psychologically plausible levels of primitives for the construction of grammaticizable notions and lexical forms in general. It may well turn out that some developmental paths go from general to specific and others from specific to general; that some domains show great uniformity in underlying organization across children and languages while others are open to considerable variation; and so forth. For now, however, I believe that these questions must remain open.

5.2.7. *In My End Is My Beginning*

Allow me to end on a retrospective note. For more than thirty years our linguistic, psychological, and philosophical disciplines have sought to replicate themselves in the mind/brain of the child. The modules that are postulated often have names that evoke suspicion: they are the names of our own academic fields (linguistics, mathematics, physics, biology) or subfields (closed-class morphemes, grammaticizable notions). Could God or evolution have anticipated the academic and intellectual organization of late twentieth-century America? At the beginning of my career I was skeptical of building academia into the child. Later I found it attractive to "help" the child by removing some problems from the learning task. Now—partly to my surprise—I find myself thinking things that I said long ago (Slobin, 1966, pp. 87ff):

> [According to Chomsky] the reason that human languages utilize such strikingly universal grammatical relations and formal devices is . . . due to the fact that these universal characteristics are themselves part of the innate structure of man. . . . I would rather think of the child as learning [a category such as the Russian animate accusative] through feedback than to have him waiting for confirmation of dozens of such categories from his mother's expansions. It seems to me more reasonable to suppose that it is language that plays a role in drawing the child's attention to the possibility of dividing nouns on the basis of animacy; or verbs on the basis of duration, or determinacy, or validity; or pronouns on the basis of social status, and the like.

I propose that it is reasonable to return to this formulation and study how children use linguistic cues to discover the collections of semantic elements that are packaged in the lexical and grammatical items of the language.

AKCNOWLEDGMENTS

The ideas developed in this chapter were presented to a conference on "Language Acquisition and Conceptual Development," Max Planck Institute for Psycholinguistics, Nijmegen, The Netherlands, Nov. 13–17, 1995. A shorter version appears under the title "Form/Function Relations: How Do Children Find Out What They Are?" in M. Bowerman and S. C. Levinson (Eds.) (in press), *Language Acquisition and Conceptual Development* (Cambridge University Press). I have benefited from many long discussions of these topics with Melissa Bowerman, and she will find her influence obvious in the revisions of my earlier position. I also owe much to Joan Bybee, Alison Gopnik, Len Talmy, David Wilkins, the many colleagues in Nijmegen who have provided stimulation and (re-)education, and the 1995 conference participants. Thanks also to Paul Bloom, Marianne Mithun, Izchak Schlesinger, Elizabeth Traugott, and Tania Kuteva for valuable correspondence on topics raised here.

REFERENCES

Adams, K. L., & Conklin, N. F. (1973). Toward a theory of natural classification. In C. Corum, T. C. Smith-Stark, & A. Weiser (Eds.), *Chicago Linguistic Society 9* (pp. 1–10).

Bates, E. (1979). On the evolution and development of symbols. In E. Bates, *The emergence of symbols: Cognition and communication in infancy* (pp. 1–32). San Francisco/London: Academic Press.

Bates, E., Frederici, A., & Wulfeck, B. (1987). Grammatical morphology in aphasia: Evidence from three languages. *Cortex, 23,* 545–574.

Bates, E., & MacWhinney, B. (1987). Competition, variation, and language learning. In B. MacWhinney (Ed.), *Mechanisms of language acquisition* (pp. 157–193). Hillsdale, NJ: Lawrence Erlbaum Associates.

Bates, E., & Wulfeck, B. (1989). Crosslinguistic studies of aphasia. In E. Bates & B. MacWhinney (Eds.), *The crosslinguistic study of sentence processing* (pp. 328–374). Cambridge: Cambridge University Press.

Behaghel, O. (1932). *Deutsche syntax: Eine geschichtliche Darstellung: Vol. 4. Wortstellung. Periodenbau.* Heidelberg: Carl Winters.

Berman, R. A., & Slobin, D. I. (1994). *Relating events in narrative: A crosslinguistic developmental study.* Hillsdale, NJ: Lawrence Erlbaum Associates.

Bickerton, D. (1981). *Roots of language.* Ann Arbor, MI: Karoma Publishers.

Bossong, G. (1985). *Empirische Universalienforschung: Differentielle Objekt-markierung in den neuiranischen Sprachen.* Tübingen: Gunter Narr.

Bowerman, M. (1985). What shapes children's grammar? In D. I. Slobin (Ed.), *The crosslinguistic study of language acquisition: Vol. 2. The data* (pp. 1257–1319). Hillsdale, NJ: Lawrence Erlbaum Associates.

Bowerman, M. (1993). Typological perspectives in language acquisition: Do crosslinguistic patterns predict development? In E. V. Clark (Ed.), *The proceedings of the Twenty-fifth Annual Child Language Research Forum* (pp. 7–15). Stanford, CA: Center for the Study of Language and Information.

Bowerman, M. (1994). From universal to language–specific in early grammatical development. *Philosophical Transactions of the Royal Society of London B, 346,* 37–45.

Bowerman, M. (1996a). Learning how to structure space for language—A crosslinguistic perspective. In P. Bloom, M. A. Peterson, L. Nadel, & M. F. Garrett (Eds.), *Language and space* (pp. 385–436). Cambridge, MA: MIT Press.

Bowerman, M. (1996b). The origins of children's spatial semantic categories: Cognitive vs. linguistic determinants. In J. J. Gumperz & S. C. Levinson (Eds.), *Rethinking linguistic relativity* (pp. 145–176). Cambridge, England: Cambridge University Press.

Bowerman, M., de León, L., & Choi, S. (1995). Verbs, particles, and spatial semantics: Learning to talk about spatial actions in typologically different languages. In E. V. Clark (Ed.), *The Proceedings of the Twenty-seventh Annual Child Language Research Forum* (pp. 101–110). Stanford, CA: CSLI.

Bowerman, M., & Pederson, E. (1992, December). *Crosslinguistic perspectives on topological spatial relationships.* Paper presented to Annual Meeting of the American Anthropological Association, San Francisco.

Brown, P. (1994). The INs and ONs of Tzeltal locative expression: The semantics of static descriptions of location. *Linguistics, 32,* 743–790.

Brown, R., & Gilman, A. (1960). The pronouns of power and solidarity. In T. Sebeok (Ed.), *Aspects of style in language* (pp. 253–277). Cambridge, MA: MIT Press.

Bybee, J. L. (1985). *Morphology: A study of the relation between meaning and form.* Amsterdam/Philadelphia: John Benjamins.

Bybee, J., Perkins, R., & Pagliuca, W. (1994). *The evolution of grammar: Tense, aspect, and modality in the languages of the world.* Chicago: Chicago University Press.

Caplan, D. (1992). *Language: Structure, processing, and disorders.* Cambridge, MA: MIT Press.

Choi, S. (this volume). Language-specific input and early semantic development: Evidence from children learning Korean. In D. I. Slobin (Ed.), *The crosslinguistic study of language acquisition: Vol. 5. Expanding the contexts.* Mahwah, NJ: Lawrence Erlbaum Associates.

Choi, S., & Bowerman, M. (1991). Learning to express motion events in English and Korean: The influence of language-specific lexicalization patterns. *Cognition, 41,* 83–121.

Chung, S. (1977). On the gradual nature of syntactic change. In C. N. Li (Ed.), *Mechanisms of syntactic change* (pp. 3–56). Austin: University of Texas Press.

Chomsky, N. (1965). *Aspects of the theory of syntax.* Cambridge, MA: MIT Press.

Clark, E. V. (1978). Discovering what words can do. In D. Farkas, W. M. Jacobsen, & K. W. Todrys (Eds.), *Papers from the parasession on the lexicon* (pp. 34–57). Chicago: Chicago Linguistic Society.

Clark, E. V. (in press). *Emergent categories in first language acquisition.* In M. Bowerman & S. Levinson (Eds.), *Language acquisition and conceptual development.* Cambridge: Cambridge University Press.

Clark, E. V., & Carpenter, K. L. (1989a). The notion of source in language acquisition. *Language, 65,* 1–30.

Clark, E. V., & Carpenter, K. L. (1989b). On children's uses of 'from', 'by', and 'with' in oblique noun phrases. *Journal of Child Language, 16,* 349–364.

Comrie, B. (1981). *Language universals and linguistic typology.* Chicago: University of Chicago Press.

Craig, C. (Ed.). (1986). *Noun classes and categorization.* Amsterdam/Philadelphia: John Benjamins.

Craig, C. G. (1993). Jakaltek directionals: Their meaning and discourse function. *Languages of the World, 7,* 23–36.

Croft, W. (1990). *Typology and universals.* Cambridge: Cambridge University Press.

Erbaugh, M. S. (1986). Taking stock: The development of Chinese noun classifiers historically and in young children. In C. Craig (Ed.), *Noun classes and categorization* (pp. 399–436). Amsterdam/Philadelphia: John Benjamins.

Gleitman, L. R., Gleitman, H., Landau, B., & Wanner, E. (1988). Where learning begins: Initial representations for language learning. In F. J. Newmeyer (Ed.), *Linguistics: The Cambridge Survey:*

Vol. III. Language: Psychological and biological aspects (pp. 150–193). Cambridge: Cambridge University Press.

Gleitman, L. R., & Wanner, E. (1982). Language acquisition: The state of the state of the art. In E. Wanner & L. R. Gleitman (Eds.), *Language acquisition: The state of the art* (pp. 3–48). Cambridge: Cambridge University Press.

Goldberg, A. E. (1995). *Constructions: A Construction Grammar approach to argument structure.* Chicago: University of Chicago Press.

Gopnik, A., & Meltzoff, A. N. (1996). *Words, thoughts, and theories.* Cambridge, MA: MIT Press.

Green, J. N. (1982). The status of the Romance auxiliaries of voice. In N. Vincent & M. Harris (Eds.), *Studies in the Romance verb* (pp. 97–138). London/Canberra: Croom Helm.

Greenberg, J. H. (1963). Some universals of grammar with particular reference to the order of meaningful elements. In J. H. Greenberg (Ed.), *Universals of language* (pp. 73–113). Cambridge, MA: MIT Press.

Grice, H. P. (1975). Logic and conversation. In P. Cole & J. L. Morgan (Eds.), *Syntax and semantics: Vol. 3. Speech acts* (pp. 41–58). New York: Academic Press.

Haiman, J. (Ed.). (1985a). *Iconicity in syntax.* Amsterdam/Philadelphia: John Benjamins.

Haiman, J. (1985b). *Natural syntax: Iconicity and erosion.* Cambridge: Cambridge University Press.

Hawkins, J. A. (1983). *Word order universals.* New York: Academic Press.

Hawkins, J. A. (1988). Explaining language universals. In J. A. Hawkins (Ed.), *Explaining language universals* (pp. 3–28). Oxford: Blackwell.

Hawkins, J. A. (1995). *A performance theory of order and constituency.* Cambridge: Cambridge University Press.

Heine, B., Claudi, U., & Hünnemeyer, F. (1991). *Grammaticalization: A conceptual framework.* Chicago: University of Chicago Press.

Hopper, P. J., & Traugott, E. C. (1993). *Grammaticalization.* Cambridge: Cambridge University Press.

Jackendoff, R. (1983). *Semantics and cognition.* Cambridge, MA: MIT Press.

Jackendoff, R. (1987). *Consciousness and the computational mind.* Cambridge, MA: MIT Press.

Jackendoff, R. (1990). *Semantic structures.* Cambridge, MA: MIT Press.

Karmiloff-Smith, A. (1992). *Beyond modularity: A developmental perspective on cognitive science.* Cambridge, MA: MIT Press.

Keil, F. C. (1989). *Concepts, kinds and cognitive development.* Cambridge, MA: Bradford Books.

Keil, F. C. (1994). Explanation, association, and the acquisition of word meaning. *Lingua, 92,* 169–196.

Landau, B., & Gleitman, L. R. (1985). *Language and experience: Evidence from the blind child.* Cambridge, MA: Harvard University Press.

Landau, B., & Jackendoff, R. (1993). "What" and "where" in spatial language and spatial cognition. *Behavioral and Brain Sciences, 16,* 217–265.

de Léon, L. (1994). Exploration in the acquisition of location and trajectory in Tzotzil. *Linguistics, 32,* 857–884.

Levin, B. (1993). *English verb classes and alternations: A preliminary investigation.* Chicago: University of Chicago Press.

Levinson, S. C. (1994). Vision, shape, and linguistic description: Tzeltal body-part terminology and object description. *Linguistics, 32,* 791–855.

Li, C., & Thompson, S. (1974). Coverbs in Mandarin Chinese: Verbs or prepositions? *Journal of Chinese Linguistics, 2,* 257–278.

Li, C., & Thompson, S. (1976). Development of the causative in Mandarin Chinese: Interaction of diachronic processes. In M. Shibatani (Ed.), *Syntax and semantics: Vol. 6. The grammar of causative constructions.* New York: Academic Press.

Li, C., & Thompson, S. (1981). *A functional reference grammar of Mandarin Chinese.* Berkeley/Los Angeles: University of California Press.

Lord, C. (1982). The development of object markers in serial verb languages. In P. J. Hopper & S. A. Thompson (Eds.), *Syntax and semantics: Vol. 15. Studies in transitivity* (pp. 277–299). New York: Academic Press.

Lyons, J. (1968). *Introduction to theoretical linguistics.* Cambridge: Cambridge University Press.

MacWhinney, B., & Bates, E. (Eds.). (1989). *The crosslinguistic study of sentence processing.* Cambridge: Cambridge University Press.

Meillet, A. (1912). L'évolution des formes grammaticales. *Scientia (Rivista di scienza), 12*(26). [Reprinted in Meillet, A. (1982). *Linguistique historique et linguistique générale* (pp. 130–148). Geneva: Slatkine/Paris: Champion.]

Mithun, M. (1989). The subtle significance of the locus of morphologization. *International Journal of American Linguistics, 55,* 265–282.

Pick, A. (1913). *Die agrammatischen Sprachstörungen.* Berlin: Springer-Verlag.

Pinker, S. (1984). *Language learnability and language development.* Cambridge, MA: Harvard University Press.

Pinker, S. (1989). *Learnability and cognition: The acquisition of argument structure.* Cambridge, MA: MIT Press.

Sapir, E. (1949). *Language: An introduction to the study of speech.* New York: Harcourt Brace. (Original work published 1921)

Sapir, E. (1958). The grammarian and his language. *American Mercury, 1,* 149–155. [Reprinted in D. G. Mandelbaum (Ed.), (1958). *Selected writings of Edward Sapir in language, culture and personality* (pp. 150–159). Berkeley/Los Angeles: University of California Press.] (Original work published 1924)

Schlesinger, I. M. (1979). Cognitive and linguistic structures: The case of the instrumental. *Journal of Linguistics, 15,* 307–324.

Schlesinger, I. M. (1982). *Steps to language: Toward a theory of language acquisition.* Hillsdale, NJ: Lawrence Erlbaum Associates.

Schlesinger, I. M. (1988). The origin of relational categories. In Y. Levy, I. M. Schlesinger, & M. D. S. Braine (Eds.), *Categories and processes in language acquisition* (pp. 121–178). Hillsdale, NJ: Lawrence Erlbaum Associates.

Schlesinger, I. M. (1995). *Cognitive space and linguistic case.* Cambridge: Cambridge University Press.

Sinha, C., & Kuteva, T. (1995). Distributed spatial semantics. *Nordic Journal of Linguistics, 18.*

Slobin, D. I. (1966). Comments on "Developmental psycholinguistics": A discussion of McNeill's presentation. In F. Smith & G. A. Miller (Eds.), *The genesis of language: A psycholinguistic approach* (pp. 85–91). Cambridge, MA: MIT Press.

Slobin, D. I. (1977). Language change in childhood and in history. In J. Macnamara (Ed.), *Language learning and thought* (pp. 185–214). New York: Academic Press.

Slobin, D. I. (1979, April). *The role of language in language acquisition.* Invited Address, Fiftieth Annual Meeting of the Eastern Psychological Association, Philadelphia.

Slobin, D. I. (1981). The origins of grammatical encoding of events. In W. Deutsch (Ed.), *The child's construction of language* (pp. 185–200). London: Academic Press.

Slobin, D. I. (1985). Crosslinguistic evidence for the Language–Making Capacity. In D. I. Slobin (Ed.), *The crosslinguistic study of language acquisition: Vol. 2. Theoretical issues* (pp. 1157–1256). Hillsdale, NJ: Lawrence Erlbaum Associates.

Slobin, D. I. (1991a). Aphasia in Turkish: Speech production in Broca's and Wernicke's patients. *Brain and Language, 41,* 149–164.

Slobin, D. I. (1991b). Learning to think for speaking: Native language, cognition, and rhetorical style. *Pragmatics, 1,* 7–26.

Slobin, D. I. (1994). Talking perfectly: Discourse origins of the present perfect. In W. Pagliuca (Ed.), *Perspectives on grammaticalization* (pp. 119–133). Amsterdam/Philadelphia: John Benjamins.

Slobin, D. I. (1996a). From 'thought and language' to 'thinking for speaking'. In J. J. Gumperz & S. C. Levinson (Eds.), *Rethinking linguistic relativity* (pp. 70–96). Cambridge: Cambridge University Press.

Slobin, D. I. (1996b). Two ways to travel: Verbs of motion in English and Spanish. In M. Shibatani & S. A. Thompson (Eds.), *Grammatical constructions: Their form and meaning* (pp. 195–219). Oxford: Clarendon Press.

Slobin, D. I. (1997). The universal, the typological, and the particular in acquisition. In D. I. Slobin (Ed.), *The crosslinguistic study of language acquisition: Vol. 5. Expanding the contexts*. Mahwah, NJ: Lawrence Erlbaum Associates.

Slobin, D. I. (in press). Form/function relations: How do children find out what they are? In M. Bowerman & S. C. Levinson (Eds.), *Language acquisition and conceptual development*. Cambridge: Cambridge University Press.

Slobin, D. I., & Hoiting, N. (1994). Reference to movement in spoken and signed languages: Typological considerations. *Proceedings of the Twentieth Annual Meeting of the Berkeley Linguistics Society, 487–505.*

Talmy, L. (1978). The relation of grammar to cognition—A synopsis. In D. Waltz (Ed.), *Proceedings of TINLAP-2 (Theoretical Issues in Language Processing)*. New York: Association for Computing Machinery.

Talmy, L. (1983). How language structures space. In H. Pick & L. Acredolo (Eds.), *Spatial orientation: Theory, research, and application*. New York: Plenum Press.

Talmy, L. (1985). Lexicalization patterns: Semantic structure in lexical forms. In T. Shopen (Ed.), *Language typology and semantic description: Vol. 3. Grammatical categories and the lexicon* (pp. 36–149). Cambridge: Cambridge University Press.

Talmy, L. (1988). The relation of grammar to cognition. In B. Rudzka-Ostyn (Ed.), *Topics in cognitive linguistics* (pp. 166–205). Amsterdam/Philadelphia: John Benjamins.

Talmy, L. (1991). Path to realization: A typology of event conflation. *Proceedings of the Seventeenth Annual Meeting of the Berkeley Linguistics Society, 480–519.*

Thompson, W. D. (1917). *On growth and form*. Cambridge: Cambridge University Press.

Traugott, E. C. (1972). *The history of English syntax*. New York: Holt, Rinehart & Winston.

Traugott, E. C., & Heine, B. (Eds.). (1991). *Approaches to grammaticalization: Vol. 1. Focus on theoretical and methodological issues: Vol. 2. Focus on types of grammatical markers*. Amsterdam/Philadelphia: John Benjamins.

Zipf, G. K. (1935). *The psycho-biology of language*. Boston: Houghton Mifflin.

Author Index

Subject Index

The abbreviations given below indicate discussion of an index category with regard to a particular language. Entries without a language code refer to a general discussion of the category in question. All references refer to discussions of acquisition or of general linguistic issues in the chapters.

ABBREVIATIONS FOR LANGUAGE CODES

Ab	Arabic	Ko	Korean
ASL	American Sign Language	Ma	Mandarin
BEn	Black English	Mo	Mohawk
Ba	Bantu	My	Mayan languages
Ca	Catalan	Na	Navaho
Ch	Chinese	No	Norwegian
Cz	Czech	Pl	Polish
Da	Danish	Pr	Portuguese
Du	Dutch	Ro	Romance languages
En	English	Rs	Russian
Ek	Eskimo	Sa	Samoan
Es	Estonian	SC	Serbo-Croatian
Fi	Finnish	Se	Semitic languages
Fr	French	Si	SiSwato
Ge	German	Sl	Slavic languages
Gn	Georgian	Sp	Spanish
Gk	Greek	Ss	Sesotho
Ha	Hawaiian	Sc	Scandinavian
He	Hebrew	Sw	Swedish
Hu	Hungarian	Ta	Tamil
Ic	Icelandic	Tg	Tagalog
IE	Indo-European languages	Tu	Turkish
It	Italian	Tz	Tzeltal
Jp	Japanese	Wa	Warlpiri
Ka	Kaluli	Zu	Zulu
Ki	K'iche'		

A

accent, **Sw** 158f, 188
accent group, 144, 163
accessibility, 166, 203
accessibility hierarchy, 274–277, 301, 309
accusative, 5, 289, 290, **Chickasaw** 300f, **Ge** 301, **Ma** 299ff, **Persian** 302, **Pl** 7, **Rs** 7, 301, **Tu** 301, **West African** 300f
acoustic salience (*see* salience, acoustic)
adjective, **It** 225

agglutinating languages, 139f, 169, 281, 308, **ASL** 180, **Fi** 180, **Gn** 205, **Ki** 157, **Ss** 169, **Tg** 170, **Tu** 169f, 180, 207, 213, **Wa** 205
agrammatism, 281f
agreement, 190, 217, **ASL** 244, **En** 220, **Gk** 220, **Si** 165, **Ss** 165, 220
Akan, 300f
allomorphy, 169–172, 188, 190, **En** 183
amalgam, 179f, 186, **He** 179f
American Sign Language (ASL), 180, 230, 244

H

Hawaiian, 146
hearsay (*see* evidentials)
Hebrew, 3, 15, 26–28, 32, 34, 45, 140, 150f,
    168–170, 174, 179, 181f, 186, 204, 213,
    230, 232, 248
historical language change (*see* diachrony, lin-
    guistic; grammaticization)
homophony, 182f, 189f, **En** 183, 189, **Ge** 182,
    Jp 183, **Ma** 181, **No** 189f, **Rs** 6, 182,
    Wa 217
honorifics (*see also* politeness), **Ko** 249
Hungarian, 3, 140, 142, 146, 168, 169, 171,
    172, 179, 204, 218, 226, 232, 246, 250

I

iconicity, 314
Icelandic, 28, 190
Idoma, 300f
IDS (*see* infant-directed speech)
imitation, 120, 211, 242, **En** 137, 177, **Jp** 115,
    Ko 115, 118
implicature, conversational, 299f
incorporating languages, 168
individual differences (*see also* style; strategy;
    variation, individual), 200–255
    causes of, 235–244
    cognitive explanations for, 238f, **En**
        238, **Fr** 238, **Ki** 239, **Ko** 238f,
        Ma 239
    guidelines for research, 254f
    input explanations for, 241–244
    methodology, 244–250
    neuropsychological explanations for,
        236ff
    in phonology, 139, 155, 159f, 162ff,
        166, 176ff, 186, 188, 191, 202,
        Da 137, **En** 137ff, 202, **Ge** 137,
        It 137, **Jp** 181, **Ka** 181, **No** 137,
        Pr 137
    pragmatic explanations for, 248f
    temperamental explanations for, 239f,
        Ek 240, **En** 240, **Ko** 240, **Pl** 240
Indo-European languages, 17, 170, 275
infant-directed speech, 136, 152ff, 191, **En**
    153f, **Jp** 153, 176, **Ma** 154, **Pl** 153
inference, pragmatic, 300, 304, 309
infinitival complement, **En** 233, **Ss** 233
infixation, 207, **Bontoc** 151f, **Chamorro** 151,
    Micronesian 170, **Palauan** 151, **Tg**
    169f, 180

inflecting languages, 281, 308, **Ek** 137, **Ge** 137,
    Tu 137
    vs. isolating, 137, 139
    vs. agglutinating 139f
inflection, **En** 136, **Fi** 136, **Fr** 169, **He** 181f, **Jp**
    181, **Pl** 6f, **Rs** 6f, 136, 184, **SC** 6, **Tu**
    136, 216
inflectional imperialism, 182–184, 226
innateness (*see also* nativism), 5, 13f, 48f, 93,
    99f, 126f, 201, 235f, 251f
input, 42–49, 214, 277, 310, 313, 318, **ASL**
    244, **En** 49, 57, 60–62, 243, **Fi** 242f, **Ka**
    242, **Ki** 245, **Ko** 56f, 60–63, 100f, 109,
    115, 118, 243, **Ma** 54, 57, 243, **Sa** 244
    and individual differences, 201, 212,
        241–244, 250, 255, **En** 241f, **Fi**
        242, **Jp** 241
    and semantic development, **Ko**
        120–128, 238
instrumental, 288f
intensity, 141, 143
interdigitation, **He** 150f, 169f, 179
interrogatives (*see* questions)
irregularity, **En** 190
isolating languages, 308, **En** 137, 204, **Fr** 137,
    Ma 137
    vs. inflecting languages 137, 139f
Italian, 28, 34, 137, 143, 170, 173, 174, 179,
    186, 206, 207, 225, 245, 281

J

Jakaltek, 284
Japanese, 3, 17, 23, 29, 65, 67, 93–95, 97, 115,
    123, 140–144, 153, 168f, 174, 176, 180f,
    186, 183f, 188f, 205, 207, 212f, 215f,
    218f, 222, 224, 230, 232, 241, 249, 281,
    286, 292, 304

K

Kaluli, 181, 186, 213, 218f, 232f, 242
K'iche´, 140, 148, 150, 154, 155–158, 162f,
    166, 168, 179, 183, 185, 231, 239, 245
knowledge, shared (*see also* expectation; newly
    acquired information; old vs. new infor-
    mation), 120, **Jp** 115, 249, **Ko** 115–118,
    120
Korean, 3, 17, 41–128, 140, 169, 180, 188f,
    214f, 218f, 230, 233, 238–240, 243,
    248f, 252, 285f, 290f, 304, 308, 315, 317
Kwakiutl, 268

L

language acquisition theories, 2, 4f, 266f

W

Z